Authorizing Readers: Resistance and
Respect in the Teaching of Literature
PETER J. RABINOWITZ and
MICHAEL W. SMITH

On the Brink: Negotiating Literature
and Life with Adolescents
SUSAN HYNDS

Life at the Margins:
Literacy, Language, and
Technology in Everyday Life
JULIET MERRIFIELD, MARY BETH
BINGMAN, DAVID HEMPHILL, and
KATHLEEN P. BENNETT DeMARRAIS

One Child, Many Worlds: Early
Learning in Multicultural Communities
EVE GREGORY, Editor

Literacy for Life:
Adult Learners, New Practices
HANNA ARLENE FINGERET and
CASSANDRA DRENNON

Children's Literature and
the Politics of Equality
PAT PINSENT

The Book Club Connection:
Literacy Learning and Classroom Talk
SUSAN I. MCMAHON and TAFFY E.
RAPHAEL, Editors, with VIRGINIA J.
GOATLEY and LAURA S. PARDO

Until We Are Strong Together:
Women Writers in the Tenderloin
CAROLINE E. HELLER

Restructuring Schools for Linguistic
Diversity: Linking Decision Making to
Effective Programs
OFELIA B. MIRAMONTES, ADEL NADEAU,
and NANCY L. COMMINS

Writing Superheroes:
Contemporary Childhood, Popular
Culture, and Classroom Literacy
ANNE HAAS DYSON

Opening Dialogue: Understanding
the Dynamics of Language and
Learning in the English Classroom
MARTIN NYSTRAND with ADAM
GAMORAN, ROBERT KACHUR, and
CATHERINE PRENDERGAST

Reading Across Cultures: Teaching
Literature in a Diverse Society
THERESA ROGERS and
ANNA O. SOTER, Editors

"You Gotta Be the Book":
Teaching Engaged and Reflective
Reading with Adolescents
JEFFREY D. WILHELM

Just Girls: Hidden Literacies and
Life in Junior High
MARGARET J. FINDERS

The First R: Every Child's Right to Read
MICHAEL F. GRAVES,
PAUL VAN DEN BROEK, and
BARBARA M. TAYLOR, Editors

Exploring Blue Highways:
Literacy Reform, School Change,
and the Creation of Learning
Communities
JOBETH ALLEN, MARILYNN CARY, and
LISA DELGADO, Coordinators

Envisioning Literature:
Literary Understanding and
Literature Instruction
JUDITH A. LANGER

(Continued)

LANGUAGE AND LITERACY SERIES (*continued*)

Teaching Writing as Reflective Practice
GEORGE HILLOCKS, JR.

Talking Their Way into Science:
Hearing Children's Questions and
Theories, Responding with Curricula
KAREN GALLAS

Whole Language Across the
Curriculum: Grades 1, 2, 3
SHIRLEY C. RAINES, Editor

The Administration and Supervision
of Reading Programs, SECOND EDITION
SHELLEY B. WEPNER, JOAN T. FEELEY, and
DOROTHY S. STRICKLAND, Editors

No Quick Fix: Rethinking
Literacy Programs in America's
Elementary Schools
RICHARD L. ALLINGTON and
SEAN A. WALMSLEY, Editors

Unequal Opportunity:
Learning to Read in the U.S.A.
JILL SUNDAY BARTOLI

Nonfiction for the Classroom:
Milton Meltzer on Writing, History,
and Social Responsibility
Edited and with an Introduction by
E. WENDY SAUL

When Children Write: Critical
Re-Visions of the Writing Workshop
TIMOTHY LENSMIRE

Dramatizing Literature in Whole
Language Classrooms, SECOND EDITION
JOHN WARREN STEWIG and
CAROL BUEGE

The Languages of Learning:
How Children Talk, Write, Dance,
Draw, and Sing Their Understanding
of the World
KAREN GALLAS

Partners in Learning: Teachers and
Children in Reading Recovery
CAROL A. LYONS, GAY SU PINNELL,
and DIANE E. DeFORD

Social Worlds of Children Learning to
Write in an Urban Primary School
ANNE HAAS DYSON

The Politics of Workplace Literacy:
A Case Study
SHERYL GREENWOOD GOWEN

Inside/Outside:
Teacher Research and Knowledge
MARILYN COCHRAN-SMITH
and SUSAN L. LYTLE

Literacy Events in a
Community of Young Writers
YETTA M. GOODMAN
and SANDRA WILDE, Editors

Whole Language Plus:
Essays on Literacy in the
United States and New Zealand
COURTNEY B. CAZDEN

Process Reading and Writing:
A Literature-Based Approach
JOAN T. FEELEY,
DOROTHY S. STRICKLAND,
and SHELLEY B. WEPNER, Editors

The Child as Critic: Teaching
Literature in Elementary and Middle
Schools, THIRD EDITION
GLENNA DAVIS SLOAN

The Triumph of Literature/
The Fate of Literacy: English in the
Secondary School Curriculum
JOHN WILLINSKY

The Child's Developing Sense of
Theme: Responses to Literature
SUSAN S. LEHR

Literacy for a Diverse Society:
Perspectives, Practices, and Policies
ELFRIEDA H. HIEBERT, Editor

The Complete Theory-to-Practice
Handbook of Adult Literacy:
Curriculum Design and
Teaching Approaches
RENA SOIFER, MARTHA IRWIN,
BARBARA CRUMRINE, EMO HONZAKI,
BLAIR SIMMONS, and DEBORAH YOUNG

On the Brink

Negotiating Literature and Life with Adolescents

Susan Hynds

Foreword by Judith A. Langer

International
Reading
Association

TEACHERS COLLEGE PRESS

Teachers College
Columbia University
New York and London

Author's Note: Every effort has been made to contact student informants in this study for permission to reprint their words and their work. I regret any oversights that may have occurred, and would be happy to rectify them in future printings of this work.

Funding for this study was provided by the Syracuse University Senate Research Fund and the National Council of Teachers of English Research Committee.

The excerpt on p. 224 is quoted from Maya Angelou's "Still I Rise" In *And Still I Rise* (pp. 41–42). New York: Random House. Copyright © 1978. Used by permission of Random House, Inc.

Published simultaneously by Teachers College Press, 1234 Amsterdam Avenue, New York, NY 10027 and the International Reading Association, 800 Barksdale Road, Newark, DE 19714

Library of Congress Cataloging-in-Publication Data

Hynds, Susan.
   On the brink : negotiating literature and life with adolescents /
Susan Hynds : foreword by Judith A. Langer.
     p. cm.—(Language and literacy series)
   Includes bibliographical references (p.) and index.
   ISBN 0-8077-3688-0 (cloth : alk. paper).—ISBN 0-8077-3687-2 (paper :
alk. paper)
   1. Reading (Middle school)—United States. 2. Literature—Study
and teaching (Middle school)—United States. 3. English language—
Composition and exercises—Study and teaching (Middle school)—
United States. 4. Constructivism (Education)—United States.
I. Title.   II. Series: Language and literacy series (New York, N.Y.)
LB1632.H95   1997
428.4'071'2—dc21   97-34284

ISBN 0-8077-3687-2 (paper)
ISBN 0-8077-3688-0 (cloth)
IRA Inventory Number 9102

Printed on acid-free paper
Manufactured in the United States of America

04 03 02 01 00 99 98 97   8 7 6 5 4 3 2 1

For Elizabeth Marie

—my hope,

—our future

In Which I Am Legally Excused from Class

*the sunlight filters down through the unbreakable windows. i have
come with my hall pass and my wish for something more on this, my
journey to solitude. it's the moments i manage to snatch out of the air
as they fly by, the wild sweet notes of music you hear in crowds but
never find the origin of, the brief flash of a face momentarily beautiful,
as the sharpness and realness of the sun and the grass gets reflected for
just a second. in this building the outlines get blurry and the shapes
waver and gray. the skin tones of all the people look faded and washed
out and tongues get too thick to push ideas out with. in this flourescent
dream chamber the walls seem to move in to cradle you in a sleep of
forgetting. the grownup people seem lulled and complacent, nestling
down in great beds of computer paper, clutching files to their breasts as
a toddler her favorite blanket, as in sleep—and it is a sleep. each day
that we manage to laugh with reality, stay awake, or feel some kind of
roughness or edge is a miracle. every touch is worth something more. in
the library, although the students bend to the shape of bookshelves
and chairs, there is a space at the top of a short flight of stairs that
leads nowhere else. i curl up in that space, a mole trying to bury
beneath the carpet and the dust that chokes originality. i would not fit
into a chair now. by becoming my own shape i am breaking a rule. i
am breaking a rule in the gym, a wooden womb of conquest and
shame as i stand close to a friend and embrace him, in a simple tired
hug. but touch, it seems, breeds reality and closeness, and We Must
Not Have That Here. i am breaking a rule as i stand here with my pass,
letting the sun wash over me, diluted by plastic. This is my moment,
non-standardized, unique, and vaguely illegal. mine alone in pleasure
and defiant victory, far exceeding my allottment of Real Life Per
Schoolday.*

—Dalia Sapon-Shevin, Age 14

Contents

Foreword *by Judith A. Langer*   xi

Acknowledgments   xv

Introduction   1
Back to the Middle: Negotiating Adolescence   2
My English Education   4
Negotiating This Book   12

1. **Literature and Literacy as Sociopolitical Practices**   14
   The Setting   14
   The Evolution of This Study   16
   Phase One: Social Cognition with a Capital "C"   20
   Phase Two: Social Construing with a Capital "S"   22
   One Step Beyond   25

2. **On Schools Bells and Bumblebees:**
   The World of the Young Adolescent   28
   "Waiting for a stupid little bell to ring": Welcome to Our World   29
   From "Mini High" to Middle School: The Growth of Adolescence   30
   The World of Logan Middle School   33
   Navigating the Depths: Discovering Our Literate Lives   35
   "Don't teach as much": Teaching Like a Reader   45
   The Flight of the Bumblebee:
   Teaching Middle School at the Millennium   51

3. **Falling Apart and Coming Together: Constructing**
   a Literate Community in the Middle Grades   56
   "My Own 'School'-World":
   Balancing the Personal and the Social   57
   "This ping pong thing": Falling Apart   59
   "Giving up my style for a while": One Step Backward   68
   Lightning Strikes: Coming Together   70
   Teacher on the Brink   72
   Challenging Learner-Centered Constructivism   73

4. Kianna:
    "If you look hard enough, you will see a butterfly"   78
    "Trying to read on my own"   80
    "Two minds working together":
        Literacy as Social Collaboration   89
    Literacy as Performance   95

5. Jason: "Strong as a pencil"   104
    "Romancing the shade": Jason in the Classroom   105
    "We've never had a garage sale so they're still there":
        Jason on Reading   108
    Transformations:
        "The more I read them, the less scared I get"   115
    Stephen Who?   120
    "An overload of busywork":
        Cheating Our Students in the American High School   125

6. Another First Day:
    Revising the Learner-Centered Classroom   133
    "This feels like home": Familiar Roadblocks in New Terrain 133
    Visions and Revisions:
        Complexities of the Constructivist Classroom   136
    "One black dot in the class": Race and Resistance   144
    "Phantoms in the opera": Race, Gender, and Exclusion   148
    "Sick of reading from reading class":
        Broadening the Canon of Control   152
    "I have always been a buzzard":
        Reading and Teaching Like a Writer   157
    Toward a Pedagogy of Literary Reading   159

7. Is There an "A" Reader in This Class?:
    Angel and Samantha   162
    Is There an "A" Reader in This Class?   166
    Surviving the "Performance-Based" Curriculum   167
    "Diving Off" and Stepping Back:
        Critical and Aesthetic Reading   168
    Reading for Success: Socialized to Schooling   173
    "Can Do" or "Will Do":
        Reading for School and Reading for Life   176
    Getting Through: Reading at Home and School   177
    Another Brink: Four Years Later   184

8. "Can 'the gifted' play football?": Luis   193

    Count Luis   *194*
    Joining "The Gifted"   *199*
    "People seemed to listen": Literacy as Social Action   *200*
    "Reading use to be nice"   *201*
    Meeting on the Threshold   *202*
    His "Moving Life": Living on the Edges   *205*

9. Reconstructing Constructivism   225

    "They're not 'a class,' but individuals":
        The Power of Personal Choice   *225*
    "Learning by osmosis"   *228*
    Revising the Performance-Centered Curriculum   *231*
    "Losing control to gain it": Shifting Power Relations   *238*
    Extending the Classroom Walls   *241*
    Reconstructing Learner-Centered Constructivism   *253*

10. Aftermath   256

    On the Personal, the Social, and the Political   *256*
    The Politics of Political Neutrality: Words Left Unspoken   *258*
    Toward a Multiplicity of Multiculturalisms   *260*
    Revising Resistance: Power Relations
        in the Classroom and World   *262*
    The Myth of the Safe Haven: Coalition or Community?   *264*
    Sharing Spaces   *266*
    Toward a Critical Constructivism   *267*
    Toward a Critical Pedagogy of Literary Reading   *269*

    Afterword: Meg, 1997   279

    Appendix   281

    References   285

    Index   295

    About the Author   303

Foreword

In our personal and professional lives, we are constantly reminded that the United States of America, the land inscribed with ethnic and cultural diversity from its early roots, is growing more diverse day by day. In some urban schools, "minority" groups already constitute the largest part of the student body and more schools are joining these ranks each year. Some predict that before long in the United States, the minority will become the majority. But what does this mean? Who are the majorities and minorities? And what does it all mean for education? And for our country? And for the world? For all our futures? These are essential questions teachers and educational policymakers must face, but we need new lenses with which to see today and plan ahead. In this book, Susan Hynds helps us develop the lenses we need.

Until a few years ago it all seemed clear, at least to our less critical eyes: minorities were people of color and Latinos. And they were considered "at risk" for success, less likely to do "well" in school and work than the majority. Research showed that people from these groups were not only doing poorly but were being treated differentially, living lives of unequal access, experience, reward, and justice. Since the 1960s notions of equity have served as the cornerstone of social reform efforts in both communities and schools. If we could understand the various cultures, learn to appreciate the accumulated knowledge, shared values, interaction styles, and linguistic forms, and find ways to link these to schooling, we would be better able to help the "at risk" achieve academic success. This seemed to make good theoretical as well as everyday sense. But too often it didn't work.

It has been only since the mid 1980s that we have become aware of blatant oversights inherent in notions of group identity. Just this morning over my coffee, before I sat down to write this foreword, I read an article in the *New York Times* about Ward Connerly, a California businessman who has become a vocal anti-affirmative action advocate.

> "One drop of blood does it," he said, reviewing the computation: 25 percent black plus 37.5 percent Irish plus 25 percent French plus 12.5 percent Choctaw equals 100 percent black. (Bearak, 1997, p. 1)

More and more of us are the progeny of cross-cultural and inter-racial unions somewhere in our ancestral lineage; and many of us just don't know it. Too often, distinctions regarding cultural heritage don't work. Even the U.S. Census Bureau has found the act of categorizing people to be a very thorny problem, and are currently in the throes of rethinking their system, although new categories are unlikely to help much.

Research and scholarship are complicating our notions of social and cultural identity, reminding us that we are all members of many cultures and subcultures (family, religious groups, friends, hobby groups, work, and school) each with its own set of beliefs, ways of communicating, and behaving (Dyson, 1994; Langer, 1995; Minnick, 1990). We do not behave or act or feel the same in each of these different cultural settings, and we use different knowledge and ways of communicating—different kinds of expertise—to get on in each setting in which we participate. Gender, economics, political and sexual orientation make a difference. Our collective subcultures and past experiences are part of us; we bring our many voices (Bakhtin, 1981) to each experience and we use these to complicate our thinking in highly interesting and literate ways. From this perspective, treating people as if they have a common background, expecting common understandings, or moving them to consensus strips them of their knowledge and renders them invisible (Barbules & Rice, 1991), less rather than more able to learn.

In contrast, Bruner (1996), Langer (1995), and Lemke (1995) suggest various ways to conceptualize classrooms as communities of individuals who come to find solidarity in difference. Bruner calls them "mutual learning cultures," Langer "envisionment-building communities," and Lemke "organized heterogeneity"; each sees classrooms as places where difference is not only expected, but is seen as an advantage—a way for students not merely to cooperatively share knowledge, but as an opportunity to hear others' ideas, to interact about them, and through interaction and exploration to gain perspective and vision. Here, issues of knowledge, power, and cooperation take on new meaning.

You are about to read an unusual book. It is rare that a study spans five years, examining an urban teacher and her students in such depth that you can trace ways in which they interact, react, and change over so much time; and it is rarer yet that it is so well written. We follow Meg as she comes to see her students through the perspectives of their individual lives, watch her attempts to change her instructional approaches in ways that acknowledge who they are, and learn from her students' responses to those attempts. Meg's and her students' stories are important to hear, and Susan Hynds tells their tale and her own with sensitivity and grace. She shares her concerns and revelations about teaching and the social politics of schooling, offers us an in-depth view of Meg's changes over time, and invites us into diverse students' lives as the connections among their in and out of school selves unfold. In each case, she takes us into whole lives, and with her the reader explores interrelationships among literacy, learning, and life. We come to understand Hynd's view of "critical constructivism," where the political and social dimensions of schooling become central to learning, and we gain insights into what English classrooms might look like and the ways we need to rethink what counts as learning. She gives us new lenses through which to examine issues of education and diversity.

All teachers who have tried something new will see their students and themselves (as well as their younger selves) in Meg and her students. I did. They will also find themselves drawn into Meg's situation, and use this as an invitation to rethink their own classrooms as environments that honor the diverse knowledge and experiences of the students by putting these at the center of each class meeting, thus making their classrooms more effective learning communities.

—Judith A. Langer

REFERENCES

Bakhtin, M. (1981). *The dialogic imagination* (C. Emerson & M. Helquist, Trans.). Austin, TX: University of Texas Press.

Barbules, N. C., & Rice, S. (1991). Dialogue across difference: Continuing the conversation. *Harvard Education Review, 61*(4), 393–416.

Bearak, B. (1997, July 27). Questions of race run deep for foe of preferences, *New York Times*, p. 1.

Bruner, J. (1996). *The culture of education.* Cambridge, MA: Harvard University Press.

Dyson, A. (1994). Confronting the split between "the child" and children. *English Education, 26*, 12–28.

Langer, J. A. (1995). *Envisioning literature: Literary understanding and literature instruction.* New York: Teachers College Press.

Lemke, J. L. (1995). *Textual politics.* London: Taylor & Francis.

Minnick, E. (1990). *Transforming knowledge.* Philadelphia: Temple University Press.

Acknowledgments

"Alone? All one.
What is this multitude of a few good friends?"

—J.P.

There is an old saying that "when the student is ready, the teacher will appear." Many friends and family members have been my teachers, before, during, and after this project. Here are just a few of them.

First, I owe a great debt of gratitude to those who contributed ideas during the years of writing this manuscript. To the anonymous reviewers, and to Peter Smagorinsky, for your rich and insightful comments. Your responses inspired me to completely rethink and recast the ideas in this book from first draft to last. To my colleague, Celia Oyler, for the constant intellectual challenge of our morning runs. Most of all, to Carol Chambers Collins, painstaking editor, advocate, and all-around great person, for bringing this manuscript to publication.

My sincere gratitude to the Syracuse University Senate Research Fund and the National Council of Teachers of English Research Committee for providing the generous funding for the years of this study.

Thanks to my "family of friends" in the profession: Arthur Applebee, Rick Beach, Sheridan Blau, Judith Langer, Jim Marshall, Bonnie Sunstein, and especially Deborah Appleman, my "conference co-conspirator" and dear friend. To these professional colleagues, and so many more, thanks for giving me an academic home base, and for teaching me that the scholar's life does not have to be a lonely business.

To my departmental family: Carol Baxter, Benita Blachman, Marlene Blumin, Barbara Combs, David Graham, Kathy Hinchman, Hal Herber, and, of course, our "departmental daddy," Peter Mosenthal, for giving me so many reasons to come to work each day. To Joan Simonetta, longtime friend, for your great sense of humor and painstaking typing of the transcripts. Thank you all for teaching me that universities can be places of laughter and good cheer.

To my "real family," either by blood or by commitment. First, to my mother and father, Leone and Charles Hynds. Thank you for your enduring belief in me, and for attending every one of my high school plays. To my late grandmother, Marie Just, for "roses in December." To Maria DiTullio and Debbie Mahaney, for your constant personal support. And especially, to

Susan Scharoun, for the countless acts of love "behind the scenes" that make our lives secure and happy.

Of course, the greatest thanks go to the members of Meg's classroom family, especially:

> To Angel, for teaching me that young women can start out strong and end up that way.
>
> To Jason, for teaching me that boys can be poets, and proud of it.
>
> To Kianna, for teaching me to "look hard" and see the butterfly.
>
> To Luis, for teaching me that strength, tenacity, and sensitivity can all live in the heart of a man.
>
> To Samantha, for the cover photograph, and for reminding me of the mysterious and pleasurable art of reading.

Finally, and most of all, to "Meg"—friend, colleague, confidante, and now, fellow mother. Thank you for the years spent in your "classroom home" and for sharing with me the heart and soul of a born teacher.

To this "multitude of a few good friends," I offer my deepest gratitude. I can never repay you in words, but perhaps I can in good works for all of our children, now and in the years to come.

Introduction

I'm a writing teacher. In order to get [my students] to write, I get them to trust me. They trust me with so much of their lives, but then I am powerless to do anything about their pain. I guess what I can do is be a good listener, encourage them to channel their feelings into something safe and productive, and be a role model for them—sharing my true self when I can. My new program allows them to write about whatever they want. So many of them are using their writing as a vehicle to cry for help. It's not just an expression of how they feel—but I see, stamped over the words, HELP ME—in invisible ink. To help them—not to lose myself—I need to remain objective. But how do I do that? Last year at this time my biggest concerns were their grades and if my plans were being written correctly and carried out. This year I fall asleep wondering if so-and-so got into a fight with their dad, or did so-and-so eat right today? Or is so-and-so pregnant? The stories of their lives are unfolding in my classroom. They will unfold and unfold and then these kids will move on—and a new batch will come.

I'm beginning to sound like them.

—Meg

When she wrote these words in her teaching journal, Meg was an eighth-grade teacher for the second time.* Just 2 years earlier, she was safely situated in her life as an eighth-grade English and drama teacher in an urban middle school. This was a world within which Meg was not only comfortable, but also successful and admired by the many eighth-grade students who passed through the doors of her classroom. Then she decided to take what she thought would be only a small detour in her career. She became part of a pilot program where she would start with a group of seventh-grade students just entering middle school and teach them for 2 years, until they were ready to graduate from eighth grade and enter high school.

What she expected would be a small detour actually took her to the brink of what would be a long and sometimes painful journey to a new vision of

---

*All names of informants, the name of the school, and locations in the study are pseudonyms. Throughout the book, all written data will appear in italics.

1

herself as teacher and a deeper understanding of the varied and unique ways that her young students came to envision themselves as literate people.

This book chronicles Meg's story from the time she met her brand-new crop of seventh-grade students until the time she saw them off to graduation and to their new lives as high school students. Nested within this story of Meg, the stories of several of her students also unfold in the chapters of this book. While Meg's story tells a larger tale of how teachers cope with and define themselves through curricular change, her students' stories reveal just how complex and unpredictable this process of "becoming literate" really is, particularly in the fluid and tentative world of the young adolescent.

In a sense, whether we set out to teach these young learners or to study them in the daily life of their classroom, we bring ourselves to the brink of new understandings, new insights, and sometimes new definitions of our work. I hope that as I take you down the halls of Logan Middle School and into Meg's classroom, you will see how, over time, her students began to see themselves as readers and authors, and how the entire experience changed not only them, but also Meg and, I must admit, even me in the process.

Our stories form the essence of a much larger story—one that tells how unique and individualized, and yet how socially and politically situated, this process of becoming literate is. In Meg's classroom, the process never seemed to happen the same way for any two students. Much of it was in fits and starts, and there was a lot of cycling backward before going forward. Not only that, but it didn't always happen before our eyes. Much of their growth as readers, writers, and language users seemed to happen at odd moments, as they careened over the horizon, just out of sight—so that they might come back to class one day changed, as if by magic. But I'm getting ahead of myself. Let me explain how I first became interested in this project, and how this work fits within the larger context of my experiences as a student, teacher, teacher educator, and researcher.

BACK TO THE MIDDLE: NEGOTIATING ADOLESCENCE

A while back, I was trying to think of a metaphor that might capture the way middle school students move through their few short years between elementary school and high school. I happened to be taking a walk in my neighborhood that morning and pondering the remarkable lives of these young adolescents, the incredible growth spurts they experience in such a short time, and all of the chaos that surrounds that place between childhood and young adulthood where they seem to dwell. Suddenly I heard a great clatter and turned around just in time to see a young man sailing down the street on a skateboard. He cruised toward the sidewalk with his mop of hair flying in the wind, hit the curb with a bang, then teetered momentarily on the edge, before pushing away down the street and out of my view.

That day it occurred to me how much middle school learners are like that skateboarder, cruising along through life and school, often literally at breakneck speeds. There are those inevitable inclines and dips, and just as inevitably, what goes up must come down. No matter how many knee pads and helmets their teachers try to provide for them, there is really no guarantee as to how the whole ride is going to turn out. So often, middle school learners are poised on the edge of childhood and young adulthood, just like that skateboarder, rocking back and forth on the edge of a curb, before pushing off into the horizon of high school and eventually adulthood. Not that they are in some nether world in the middle of adolescence, mind you! On the contrary, they are always teetering between the world of the child and the world of the young adult, so that sometimes they tip to the side of irrepressible immaturity, and at other times they right themselves again, astounding their teachers with their depth and sensitivity.

As I entered T. Samuel Logan Middle School on the first day of what would turn out to be a 3-year study, I felt a bit like an adolescent myself. I had been a middle school teacher for only 2 years of my 9-year career as a high school English, speech, and drama teacher. My brief time teaching sixth through twelfth grade happened at the end of my secondary teaching career, just before I graduated with my doctorate in English education and moved on to become a teacher educator in a university setting.

Although much of my middle school teaching experience was a blur, I remember assuming when I took the job that these new students were probably just a smaller version of the high school students I had taught. After all, kids between 12 and 18 were all technically adolescents, weren't they? I can remember my astonishment when the "clever" activities that had always succeeded with my eleventh and twelfth graders disintegrated into noise and chaos in a matter of minutes, and I had to abandon an entire unit plan on my first day as a sixth-grade teacher. I learned how silly it had been of me to envision middle school learners either as mini high school students or as overgrown elementary students. This, of course, is why the concept of the "junior high school" has been steadily replaced by the middle school movement over the past decades, and why so much emphasis over the past several years has been focused on the unique qualities of middle school learners (George & Oldaker, 1985–86; Hornbeck, 1989; Lipsitz, 1984; Strahan, 1983).

As I embarked on my study in the fall of 1988, I couldn't explain my anxiety. I'd been at Logan Middle School many times before. Four years earlier, I had met Meg, a lively and effervescent eighth-grade teacher, as she took the first course of her masters program with me. Among other things, we realized that we both had been drama and English teachers. Over the next few years, we developed a friendship. I had supervised student teachers in Meg's classroom many times, had been to her house for dinner, knew her husband and young daughter, and was ecstatic when she invited me to come into her classroom and conduct a research project. So what explained the butterflies in my stomach as I carried my pile of dittoed questionnaires into her classroom as a researcher for the very first time?

I didn't realize it then, but I was going back into a world that I had left several years earlier, and this time as an observer in someone else's classroom. Would the students like me? Would they trust me enough to be honest? Had I forgotten everything I knew about teaching young adolescents, or would some of it come back to me? And more important, would Meg's and my friendship survive this dramatic change in our relationship? I had only a few minutes to ponder these questions, as the bell for the change of classes had rung. As I was swept into the blur of young bodies moving toward their next classes, I knew that, no matter how hard I wished I was back in the safety and security of my classroom at the university, I was now entering the chaotic and unpredictable world of an urban middle school. What I didn't realize at the time was that I would be in this world for a total of 3 years, and that I would leave it 3 years later never able to look at middle school students or research and teaching in the literacy classroom the same way again.

MY ENGLISH EDUCATION

To place this study and its core issues into a larger context, I'll try to explain some of the philosophical approaches to teaching that surrounded and informed my early years as a student, and later as a secondary English teacher and teacher educator.

"Knowledge" and "Growth": Tensions in Teaching

I began my career as a secondary English teacher in the early 1970s with a desire to give my students important literacy skills, coupled with a strong intuitive sense that the best way to teach those skills was not necessarily the way they had been taught to me. Although I have fond memories of many of my English and language arts teachers, most of them operated from a "transmission" viewpoint (Barnes & Barnes, 1984), where knowledge was a sort of commodity that could be transmitted from teacher to student. For the most part, my teachers selected the texts I would read and the topics I would write about. Activities were tightly controlled, and there was little opportunity for me to explore ideas with a group of peers, to read literature of my own choosing, or to experiment with a variety of writing genres and topics. Typical of teachers during the late 1950s and early 1960s, most of mine operated from a *building blocks* perspective, where lessons proceeded from sentence level to paragraph level skills, or from memorization of literary terms to writing essays on the questions in the literature anthology, for example.

Later, in my own undergraduate teacher education program during the late 1960s, I encountered the work of theorists such as Dewey (1900), Bruner (1960), and Piaget (Piaget & Inhelder, 1969). I'd also read just enough of the current educational innovators and critics, such as Kozol (1967), Macrorie (1970), and Moffett (1968), so that I felt torn between the skills-based view of language learning embraced by my early teachers and the more learner-centered notions about the worth and dignity of individual students that I'd been taught in my college methods classes. I was told by my professors in the late 1960s and early 1970s that astounding changes were afoot in the teaching of English. The Dartmouth Conference of 1966 had just begun to make its mark on the profession, and I was impassioned by the spirit of optimism and progressivism that seemed to be sweeping university education programs at the time. I was soon disappointed, however, when I took my first job and discovered that no such movement had swept through the English departments in which I was to work over the next 9 years.

Joseph Harris (1991) has noted this stark contrast between what I learned in my teacher education program and the daily realities of the schools where I taught. He argues that this "heroic view" (p. 631) of Dartmouth as the catalyst for progressive education in America was inaccurate. In fact, there was a noticeable difference between the basic philosophies of the Americans and the British participants at the conference—a difference that was at the core of my uneasiness as a novice teacher, and one that I believe is still alive in the profession today. Harris (1991) argues that the British educators at Dartmouth largely supported a "growth model," informed by developmentalists such as Piaget, Vygotsky, and Bruner. This view celebrated the personal experiences of students and the expressive nature of language. The Americans, on the other hand, still reeling from the effects of Sputnik, and deeply engaged in the work of "Project English," were trying to define English as an academic discipline. Inspired by the work of linguists such as Noam Chomsky (1957) and literary critics such as Northrop Frye (1967), they were attempting to establish the legitimacy of English as a formal subject of study, with distinct bodies of knowledge and subsets of skills to be mastered.

Although there were notable departures from these views on either side of the Atlantic (James Squire, James Miller, and James Moffett from the United States embraced the growth movement, for example), the conflict between "knowledge" and "growth" models is still present in American educational theory and practice today. Harris (1991) suggests that "one reason why recent conservative attacks on teaching have met with success is that they have claimed to provide students with access to power—usually in some form of 'cultural literacy'—that an emphasis on individual growth and expression cannot offer" (p. 643).

It is little wonder that this tension I felt in the early days of my career is still very much alive today. On the one hand, approaches such as "whole language," "process-centered teaching," and "reader response pedagogy" have gained ground in many classrooms. These approaches, grouped under the rubric of "The New Literacy" by John Willinsky (1990), are in striking contrast to the "transmission" views of behaviorist psychology that presume learning to be a process of imparting facts to passive learners. By contrast, pedagogies of the New Literacy follow a "constructivist" model, defined by Hiebert (1991) as one that

> views learners as active participants in the creation of their own knowledge. Because learners interact with and interpret the world, knowledge is a function of the learner's background and purposes. Learning often occurs in social contexts, and, therefore, the learner's relationships with other persons serve a vital function in the interpretation process. The social aspects of learning are especially relevant in homes and schools, where interaction between adults and children has a strong influence on what, how, and how much children learn. (p. 2)

Although there has been much written in the professional literature and tremendous enthusiasm on the part of some teachers for constructivist, learner-centered views of pedagogy, these models simply do not offer the same kind of rewards or "currency" in the larger world of American schooling as do the more knowledge- or skills-based approaches. When teachers choose constructivist approaches, they usually do so because these approaches seem to make intuitive sense, or because they are willing to stand up against administrators, school boards, or parents, most of whom adhere to a more knowledge-based model. Thus, the tension persists. As Harris (1991) has observed:

> On the one hand, there is a continuing need to legitimize English as an academic field with its own specialized subject and methods of study. On the other hand, English has long been valued precisely because it seems more than yet another specialized area of concern, because it offers a place where different kinds of knowledge can be brought together and related to personal experience. (p. 635)

Complexities and Contradictions of the Constructivist Classroom

In the literacy classroom, this tension between knowledge and growth perspectives still plagues many teachers, even those committed to a more learner-centered, constructivist philosophy. The result is often a kind of schizophrenia, where teachers may adopt holistic, learner-centered approaches to writing, for example, but still cling to transmissionist approaches to literature teaching, such as basal readers at the elementary level and worksheets or study questions at the secondary level. Or perhaps they may teach literature from a "response-centered" perspective, but then fall back on transmissionist approaches such as multiple choice testing or prefabricated study guides when it comes to evaluation.

There also seem to be few models to help teachers with the very real problems they face with parents, administrators, and even some of their own students when they attempt to implement constructivist approaches within an educational climate where knowledge and skills are still considered paramount. A great many teachers from a "whole language," "integrated language arts," or "reader response" perspective borrow heavily from articles and books about teaching that seem to ignore the difficulties of implementing learner-centered constructivist practices in the culturally diverse and complex world of modern classrooms. The early works of Nancie Atwell (1987), Lucy Calkins (1986), and Donald Graves (1983), for example, often have been translated into a rather romanticized view of language learning that many teachers cannot embrace because it so concretely contradicts the very real world of their classrooms. For example, after a decade of teaching fifth grade by rather traditional methods, Peg Sudol (Sudol & Sudol, 1991) adopted a workshop model, based largely on the early writings of Graves, Calkins, and Atwell. In describing her year-long experience, she and her co-author argued:

> Graves, Calkins, and Atwell seem to present teachers as free agents who can operate independently of administrative or curricular constraints. Only Atwell discusses changing the curriculum, but she had the freedom to develop her own curriculum and the luxury of a supportive principal. . . . Although Graves, Calkins, and Atwell inspired [Peg, she] had a nagging suspicion that something wasn't quite right. They never discussed failures: Their workshops ran so smoothly; everyone achieved success. She also noticed that problems, though mentioned, were quickly glossed over or easily solved. She'd been teaching too long to believe these stories; they sounded too good to be true. (pp. 293–294)

The Limits of Learner-Centered Constructivism

Although much of the practical literature on teaching English from constructivist perspectives acknowledges and supports the importance of social activities such as collaborative learning and teacher–student conferring, the real emphasis, and perhaps the lure of these texts, is in their insistence on the *personally* liberating aspects of expressive language, freedom of topic choice, and student control of learning. Even collaborative learning often is presented as a way for *individual learners* to develop tolerance, value diversity, and share their personal understandings with peers and teachers. This learner-centered, individualistic view has led to many healthy reforms of transmissionist curricula. At the same time, many teachers have interpreted it, rather religiously, as a "hands-off" approach that eschews any interference whatsoever in the process of student learning. Student choice is usually a linchpin of the learner-centered classroom. There is an underlying premise that if teachers simply get out of the way and provide relatively unrestrained choices, students eventually will take charge of their own learning and unleash their authentic personal voices in writing, talk, and response to literature.

An unfortunate effect of this strong emphasis on student choice has been that teachers, swept up in the enthusiasm of creating a learner-centered curriculum, often feel guilty when their instincts tell them to take some control over the structure of their classrooms or the content of student learning. While on the one hand teachers can never place too much emphasis on the worth and dignity of the individual learner and the empowering effects of personal choice, there are times when the curriculum should be negotiated and teachers must be empowered to lead students in directions they might not take on their own. There are currently few models to assist teachers in knowing when to let students have open choice and when to step in and become more active participants in the decisions of the classroom.

By the same token, although learner-centered constructivist approaches acknowledge the importance of social language processes such as collaborative learning, conferring, publishing, and performing, teachers often come away with the rather simplistic belief that these activities in themselves are inherently motivating and liberating for all students. The early literature from a learner-centered perspective seems to presume that students naturally will gravitate toward sharing their private lives and publishing their personal writing. Beneath this perspective is an individualistic "achievement ideal," or the assumption that, given equal opportunities and a "safe" classroom climate, all students have the same chance to succeed. This assumption is particularly problematic when students don't all come from ethnically or racially homogeneous backgrounds. What happens, for instance, when students come from cultures where sharing is not a comfortable or a common act? What about students who fear that their private lives would be misunderstood or misinterpreted across the cultural divides that separate them from others in the diverse world of the urban classroom? And what happens when teachers and other students view the lively and sometimes raucous oral interchange of students from "nonmainstream" cultures as disruptive and disrespectful to others? Finally, what about students who know that no amount of literacy skills will give them social and economic equity in a world that is still socially and politically rigged against them?

Because there is so little acknowledgment of the political and social dimensions of collaborative work and sharing, many teachers are disappointed when small groups degenerate into aimless chatter, conferences with students seem to have little direction or substance, and otherwise capable students belligerently refuse to share their work with others whom they perceive as different from themselves.

Finally, although more is being written about alternative methods of evaluation each day, teachers in the learner-centered classroom still struggle with issues of evaluation. Encouraged to become co-learners and confidantes in their daily interactions with students, they experience great discomfort as they must step back into the role of grade giver or evaluator.

Palincsar and David (1991) have summed up the dilemma of what they call "natural literacy" approaches to teaching.

> The teacher is left dangling in the natural literacy argument. What is the place of conscious teaching of the means to deal with written text? Is the teacher merely the facilitator for the activities of rather autonomous learners? Or, should classrooms be the place where the teacher, by virtue of relative expertise, with deliberate intention, enables the learner to acquire knowledge and procedures? (p. 124)

We also might ask, beyond the responsibility for developing skills and organizing the classroom, what is the teacher's role in confronting some of the political and social inequities in our increasingly diverse literacy classrooms?

Beyond the Psychological: Toward a Sociopolitical Constructivism

The complications that arose—between the political and the personal, between student choice and teacher expertise—lingered at the edges of my consciousness, not only for the 3 years I spent in Meg's classroom, but during the intervening years, as I prepared to write this book. They remained with me during the summer of 1995, when I invited some of Meg's students back to reflect on their middle school experience, as they stood on the brink of their years beyond high school.

Although neither of us used these terms when I first entered Logan Middle School in 1988, it seems to me now that Meg was trying to balance two versions of constructivism in her English classroom: one based largely on the work of Piaget, and the other on the work of Vygotsky. In its early version, what has come to be called "psychological constructivism" (Cobb,

1995) was a reaction to the behavioristic, transmissionist views of teaching and learning that Meg and I both had experienced as students. Based largely on the theories of Piaget (1950) and Dewey (1900), as well as early research in cognitive psychology, psychological constructivism posits that learners are active and not passive, constructing their own knowledge out of the "stuff" of their personal lives and their learning experiences.

During her masters degree program, Meg had been introduced to several teaching approaches based on a learner-centered view, compatible with the tenets of psychological constructivism. In her course in adolescent literature, she had learned about "response-centered" teaching (Probst, 1984; Purves, 1972), and in her other courses, she learned about "process-centered" views of writing and oral language (Barnes, 1975; Britton, Burgess, Martin, McLeod, & Rosen, 1975; Calkins, 1983; Graves, 1983). Writers like Nancie Atwell (1987), Robert Probst (1984), Donald Graves (1983), and Lucy Calkins (1983) painted a rather enticing portrait of individual learners as capable, active creatures, entitled to choices in the products and processes of their own learning. Their writings reinforced Meg's view that schools, following a repressive bureaucratic model, tend to fragment students' knowledge, both controlling and trivializing the topics and texts of the language classroom. In its humanistic focus on the individual child, Meg resonated with this philosophy. However, as a teacher in a diverse urban setting, she often found herself struggling with her role as teacher in this rather individualistic version of the constructivist classroom.

At the same time as she valued the growth of the individual, Meg also realized the value of collaboration and community in her English classroom. As had many of her mentors in the published literature, she had begun to move toward a more "sociocultural" or "social constructivist" position (Phillips, 1995), based largely on the work of Vygotsky (1962, 1987). Unfortunately, the work of Piaget and some of the early work of cognitive psychologists had been translated rather simplistically by curriculum planners and test makers into the belief that individual learners proceed through rather hard-and-fast developmental stages, from egocentrism to a more "decentered" or socially involved position. By this notion, children at the lower (egocentric) levels of this spectrum were viewed as somehow deficient. Many of Meg's colleagues, as well as the standardized testing system and language curriculum in her state, seemed to follow this rather rigid developmental path. In Tom Newkirk's (1985) words, such simplistic developmental notions amount to the belief "that one must pass through the lower levels in the act of producing higher level discourse—like having to pass through Atlanta, Georgia to get to Daytona Beach" (p. 595).

In contrast to Piaget's view that learning proceeds from the private to the public sphere, literacy researchers and educators were beginning to embrace the Vygotskian (1962, 1987) argument that learning begins not privately, but through social interaction; only gradually does knowledge become internalized. Meg was attracted to many social constructivist teaching approaches, inspired by Vygotsky and his followers, including collaborative learning (Bruffee, 1984), the negotiation of classroom authority (Boomer, 1982), the creation of "safe" learning communities, and the communal sharing of personal stories (Atwell, 1987). Believing in the value of social collaboration, she wished to create a "multicultural" classroom community, where differences were celebrated and all students' voices could be shared equally.

It was several years after I left Meg's classroom before I began to realize that neither Piagetian nor Vygotskian constructivism had provided the necessary framework to understand the complex social and political issues that arose in Meg's urban classroom. Both Piaget and Vygotsky were psychologists. And although they differed in their arguments about the origins of knowledge, both Vygotskian and Piagetian constructivism were heavily focused on how *individual* learners construct knowledge. In that sense, both Vygotsky and Piaget fit comfortably into what I have been calling a "learner-centered" pedagogy. Even though literacy educators were beginning to recognize the role of social interaction in learning, there was still little acknowledgment of the political forces that surrounded and suffused those interactions. Along these lines, Jim Cummins (1993) has argued:

> Minority students are disabled or disempowered by schools in very much the same way that their communities are disempowered by interactions with societal institutions. Since equality of opportunity is believed to be a given, it is assumed that individuals are responsible for their own failure and are, therefore, made to feel that they have failed because of their own inferiority, despite the best efforts of dominant-group institutions and individuals to help them. (pp. 107–108)

This "pull-yourself-up-by-your-bootstraps," individual achievement ideal is simply no longer viable for marginalized students, who know that the economic and political deck is stacked against them. As this book will reveal, a move from Piagetian to Vygotskian constructivism (recognizing that learning is essentially social in origin) still did not explain the *sociopolitical* relationships that so strongly influenced the daily events of Meg's classroom. Even today, in the development of constructivist teaching models, there is still little acknowledgment of the complicated social, cultural, and political milieu of today's classrooms. This book is devoted to exploring one urban classroom, not only in terms of its personal and social dimensions, but in terms of the larger sociopolitical sphere in which the literate lives of Meg and her students unfolded and evolved.

NEGOTIATING THIS BOOK

In Chapter One, I will explain how this study grew out of my early experiences as a secondary teacher, teacher educator, and researcher. In many ways, as a beginning teacher, I struggled with many of the same issues and tensions that Meg struggled with as she moved into this new phase of her career. In this chapter, I will explore some of the early theoretical frameworks that influenced my work with adolescent readers and my later visions of the social nature of literary reading. The chapter will conclude with a discussion of the setting, participants, data collection, and procedures of the study.

In Chapter Two, I will explore the literate lives of Meg's middle school students, including their early experiences with reading and writing, their views of the reading process, and their perceptions of reading at home and for school. This chapter will draw a rough sketch of the different ways in which these middle school learners viewed not only the reading of literature, but their own development as literate persons.

Chapter Three will tell the story of Meg's early struggle as she moved from the safe, familiar world of her eighth-grade classroom and into the world of her seventh-grade students, who were entering middle school for the first time. Much to her surprise, Meg found that the learner-centered constructivist model that she had used so successfully with her eighth-grade students in the past was frightening and confusing for her new students, many of whom came from elementary schools that relied heavily on more traditional forms of instruction. After much private agonizing, she decided that, to help herself and her students during this frightening transition, she needed to move temporarily into the safety of routine and structure, before leading them into new territory of choice and responsibility. This decision was not without struggle, as Meg had to question her own identity as an "innovative teacher" in the process.

The case studies of Kianna in Chapter Four and Jason in Chapter Five will chronicle the ways in which students came to define and redefine themselves as literate people over the 2 years of their middle school career. As the chapters will reveal, this process of self-definition was deeply intertwined with issues of race and gender.

In Chapter Six, we return to Meg's classroom, as she begins the final year of the study and tries to move from a more learner-centered view of constructivism to a view that encompasses the social and political realities in which she and her students operated.

The stories of Angel and Samantha in Chapter Seven and Luis in Chapter Eight will further highlight the ways in which Meg's students dealt with these social and political exigencies.

Eventually, by the time her students reached the eighth grade, Meg was able to offer them even more choices than she had ever offered at any other point in her teaching career. The final saga in the story of Meg's changes unfolds in Chapter Nine.

Chapter Ten is an attempt to redefine both the reading of literature and the concept of literacy through the lens of what I will call "critical constructivism." In this chapter, I will trace the changes in my own thinking as a researcher and teacher educator, as a result of spending these 3 years in Meg's classroom.

In a sense, all of us—Meg, her students, and I—stood on the brink of our own personal changes at several points during our time together. However, rather than tipping safely over that brink into a better or safer place, we all seemed to rock back and forth between our past and future identities, whether these identities were as teacher, researcher, or literate person. This process of identity change, like the process of literacy development, is neither neat nor tidy. As Maxine Greene (1995) has observed:

> Neither my self nor my narrative can have . . . a single strand. I stand at the crossing point of too many social and cultural forces; and, in any case, I am forever on my way. My identity has to be perceived as multiple, even as I strive towards some coherent notion of what is human and decent and just. (p. 1)

The negotiation of these social and cultural forces both complicates and enriches the stories in this book.

CHAPTER 1

Literature and Literacy as Sociopolitical Practices

What stands out for me is just how emotional and adolescent I've felt of late. Is it from spending so much time in this bloodstream called middle school? The kids are no longer names on questionnaires. They have lives in and outside of school. Their stories are unfolding on—and yet apart from—the papers in my file drawer. I fear their rejection. I am moved by their relentless hopes, their graveyard walks at midnight, or their fight for life in a hospital or a jail cell. I am swept away by their feelings of abandonment and isolation, because, with each child comes a little unwanted glimpse back into my own childhood. (Analytic memo, October 7, 1990)

When I wrote this memo to myself during the second phase of this study, I was facing the consequences of moving from the safety of my anonymous questionnaires and becoming swept into the lives of Meg and her students. I hadn't realized, when I moved into the observational phase of my study, just how demanding it was to study these young adolescents, not only as they developed their literate identities, but as they grappled with aspects of their personal lives within and beyond the classroom walls. As I became immersed in the daily routines of Meg's classroom, my notion of the social nature of literacy development was being gradually expanded and enlarged. Toward the end of the study, I began to look beyond the psychological aspects of social collaboration and through the sociopolitical lenses of race, class, and gender. In this chapter, I will introduce the study's setting and participants, and then trace some of my changing perspectives on the nature of literature teaching and literacy development.

THE SETTING

Located near a large northeastern private university in a city of roughly 170,000, Logan Middle School is a two-story dark brick structure with entrances and parking lots on two sides of the building. The school serves students that range from upper to lower socioeconomic status, who are racially, ethnically, and academically integrated.

Due to space limitations of the building, this middle school has only two grade levels: seventh and eighth. The students at Logan include children of professors from the nearby university, as well as students from the public housing projects a few blocks away and students whose parents live in the "Wellesley Street" area, which is populated by a colorful mix of artists, students, professionals, and college professors. On the streets immediately surrounding the school are several rather large, two-story frame or brick houses, built in the early part of the century. A few blocks to the east of the school are the Maple Knoll apartments, a public assistance housing project where many of the students from Logan live.

Spanning roughly two blocks of Wellesley Street itself are a variety of "ethnic" restaurants (Middle Eastern, Greek, Chinese, Ethiopian), a bakery, "new age" bookstore, used clothing store, bar, liquor store, and an assortment of pizza and fast food restaurants. At the time of the study, the street also had a small movie theatre that showed second-run movies and attracted many of the students from Logan during the evening hours.

In the first year of the study, the school population consisted of 587 students in the following racial categories: European American (53.5%), African American (39%), Native American (2%), Asian or Pacific Islander (1.4%), Latino/Latina (5.9%). According to the city school district office, 50% of the students at Logan were eligible for the free or reduced cost lunch program in 1988. Although the school had no official tracking system, on the basis of test scores, students sometimes were placed in special "reading" classes or sent to a resource room in addition to their regular academic classes. There was also a "gifted" program, which provided special assemblies and enrichment activities for students who had high grade point averages and scored well on standardized tests.

During the first phase of this project, Meg, a European-American teacher in her 30s, was completing her masters degree in the English Education program at the university where I taught. As part of her graduate work, she had been introduced to several books and articles from a learner-centered constructivist perspective. At the start of phase one, Meg had been at Logan for 5 years, teaching eighth-grade English and directing the school drama program. Before coming to Logan, she had taught first and second grade in a parochial school for a total of 5 years, and eighth grade in another public school for 1 year.

For the 3 years of the study, Meg was assisted part of the time by Ed Jackson, an African-American teacher in his 30s. Ed had come to Logan as the director of Arts and Education. Previously he had been an actor and director with a professional theatre company. Meg and Ed did quite a bit of team teaching during the 2 years he was at Logan, usually involving creative dramatics and other kinds of performance activities. For roughly 11 weeks of the study, Meg also had a student teacher from the university where I taught.

THE EVOLUTION OF THIS STUDY

> It may seem a minor distinction to insist on viewing literacy as a social as well as a cognitive practice, a political and personal act as well as a measurable capability, that can also shed new light on the study of literature. . . . To shift some part of our educational energies in this way means exploring how literacy reaches out into the world, rather than treating it as simply a testable cognitive capacity that needs practicing. (Willinsky, 1991, p. 4)

In *The Triumph of Literature/The Fate of Literacy* (1991), John Willinsky argues that Louise Rosenblatt wrote her landmark book, *Literature as Exploration* (1995, originally published in 1938) during the Progressive era of the 1930s with two aims in mind: One was to argue the importance of the individual reader's response in the literary transaction; the other was to highlight the social and political role of literature in a democracy. While the first purpose has been reflected in much current work on literature teaching, Willinsky argues that the second has been largely neglected. Although even in her recent work Rosenblatt has argued persuasively for the social and socializing role of literature, her most famous contribution, and the one most clearly influential in the teaching of literature, is the private, personal nature of the literary reading process.

In distinguishing between "efferent reading" (appropriate for nonliterary or informational reading) and "aesthetic reading" (appropriate for literary reading), Louise Rosenblatt (1994) has helped to move literature teaching from a New Critical focus on texts, to a recognition of the highly divergent responses of individual readers. More than any other scholar in the past 6 decades, Rosenblatt has inspired a vision of literary reading as a self-enhancing, humanizing, liberatory process (Probst, 1984). Willinsky argues, however, that what has been lost in this approach to teaching is the social and socializing potential of literature that Rosenblatt first wrote about in 1938. The more individualized view of literary reading most often associated with Rosenblatt conjures up the image of the lone reader, sitting with a book and engaged in a private, aesthetic transaction of his or her own making. Willinsky (1990) challenges this individualistic view, proposing instead that

> The self takes its meaning from what is said about it; we constitute ourselves out of what we overhear in the language and imagery of our culture, as our

identity is wrested from the symbolic values of such elements as gender, color, ethnicity, vocation, and the words that have become common to this symbolization. (p. 221)

Thus, Willinsky argues for a reconceptualization of literature and its teaching to encompass the social and political, as well as the private dimensions of literary reading.

Teaching Adolescents: Learning as a Social Event

It was in my own career as a high school teacher that I first apprehended the incredibly social nature of language learning. It quickly became obvious to me that many of my adolescent students seemed to learn best in collaboration with others. Their reading, writing, speaking, and listening seemed most enriched when they engaged in meaningful tasks, and when these very different language acts were allowed to intersect and intermix. As my confidence in teaching grew, I discovered that through participating collaboratively in oral interpretation, readers' theatre, and project-centered instruction, my high school and middle school students could create a social climate within which they discovered things about their lives (Beach, 1983), developed a social support system for reading, and began to understand more about social (Beach, 1983), cultural (Purves, 1986), and literary conventions (Culler, 1975; Fish, 1976).

Even as a novice teacher, I knew that simply giving students the skills to comprehend literature was not the same as teaching them to understand the "why" of literature in the context of their personal and social experiences. I grew to believe, as Shirley Brice Heath (1985) argues, that more than "literacy skills," my students needed to develop "literate behaviors." That is, they needed to see themselves as literate persons and to develop literate practices that would last beyond their years of formal schooling.

Since I was a teacher of English, speech, and drama, I centered much of my curriculum around oral interpretation of literature and readers' theatre. I saw firsthand the power of dramatic performance in helping my students to develop rich resources for understanding and interpreting literature. At the same time, there were students who, although academically competent, failed to make these connections between "literature and life" (Hynds, 1989). I began to believe that simply learning to read (in the sense of decoding, or even interpreting literary texts) was not enough; beyond the general intellectual ability of comprehending literature, readers needed a kind of social competence in order to understand the cultural and interpersonal dynamics of texts (Hynds, 1990). I assumed at the time that if I could ask students "higher-level" questions about characters and their motivations, or if I could help them to make connections between literature and their real lives, I would somehow bring them to this social competence.

Because my concept of reading still envisioned the reader as a "universe of one," I failed to realize that it was these daily social interactions, rather than my "higher-level" learning strategies, that both developed their social competence for reading and gave them the confidence to envision themselves as literate people. I was to make that discovery much later, after I left my own classroom, and began to study the students in Meg's.

Studying Adolescent Readers: The Inner Drama

As I entered a university setting in the mid-1980s, I began to explore the questions that had fascinated me as a secondary teacher. For example, why did some people seem to have rich and complex perceptions of characters in literature, while others had only vague or stereotypic notions of what people in stories or poems were all about? I knew that some adolescents could immediately "step inside the heads" of literary characters and transport themselves into imaginary worlds. These students, not surprisingly, were the most able performers in the readers' theatres and plays I directed. Other students, although intelligent and capable, had to be taught, through intensive discussion and dramatic role playing, to take those perspectives.

Inspired by the work of Louise Rosenblatt (1968), I believed that each reader creates a uniquely personal interpretation of a literary text out of the realm of experiences and perspectives that she or he brings to the reading event. Despite all the anthologies and textbooks that presumed a "one correct answer" approach to literary reading, I knew that each of my students created a highly personal interpretation, so that none of us had exactly the same perceptions of the books, stories, and poems that we had read together. Was it possible, I wondered, that the reading of literature might involve a sort of *inner drama* that was more rich and vivid for some readers than for others?

About this time, I also had begun to read the work of George Kelly (1955), who suggested that people in the social world operate like amateur scientists, always interested in influencing others around them. As they try to predict and control the actions of others, people develop a repertoire of "interpersonal constructs" upon which to represent people they know. Young children, for example, might begin by believing that all teachers are "good." As they go through life, they discover that teachers can be "bad" as well as "good," or that there are more discriminating ways to describe teachers that don't involve the polarities of good and bad. Teachers can be described as "demanding," "strict," or "encouraging," or in terms of a whole host of other interpersonal constructs.

What was most interesting to me was that this social construing ability was not connected to general intelligence or verbal abilities (Burleson, Applegate, & Neuwirth, 1981; Hale, 1980). Some people could be intellectually gifted, but impoverished in the world of interpersonal relations. At the time, the work on social construing inspired by George Kelly seemed to explain why so many of my "able" readers were unable to create this inner drama that I had suspected was so essential to the literary reading process. I also had a hunch that this ability to dramatically envision the events of literature was connected to the motivation and maturity to read throughout a lifetime. I remembered the special times when I was able to entice an otherwise reluctant student into the world of literature through the power of dramatic performance. Often, a few weeks later, I'd see that same student with a book of poetry or a novel under his or her arm. I was intrigued, not just by what adolescents chose *to read*, but also what made them choose to view themselves *as readers* in the classroom and in the larger world.

Thus, inspired by the views of Kelly and Rosenblatt, my very first notion of the social nature of literary reading was situated largely in the individual reader. That is, I was interested in the process of *social cognition*, essential to thinking deeply about characters in literature and people in the social world. I wondered whether students' attitudes toward reading, their social support for reading in school and home, and their experiences in classrooms had something to do with their tendencies to bring these social cognitive abilities to reading.

In the tradition of many early researchers from a *reader response* perspective, I presumed that I could study readers apart from the contexts within which they read. So I took them out of their classroom, to libraries or conference rooms, set up my tape recorder, and asked them to talk about the role of reading in their lives or to "think aloud" as they read a story for my benefit. The study of readers in this rather decontextualized way was typical of a great many early studies of literary response, as Judith Langer (1991) observes.

> Although there was an active line of research on general classroom practices . . . in the 1970s and early 1980s, process-oriented literacy research tended to focus on cognitive behaviors alone, not also on what to teach and how to teach it, nor on the conditions that affect the learning enterprise; there was little direct concern about societal uses of literacy or about literacy instruction. (p. 10)

During my early work (Hynds, 1983, 1985), I used a relatively simple, yet reliable method for determining "interpersonal cognitive complexity" (Crockett, 1965), in which I would ask informants to describe, in writing, someone their own age whom they liked and someone their own age whom they disliked. These open-ended written impressions, called "Role Category Questionnaires" (see Crockett, Press, Delia, & Kenny, 1974), then could be coded for the numbers of interpersonal constructs in the impressions and converted into an index of "peer complexity." By modifying this procedure slightly, I could ask informants to describe, in writing, the protagonists in selected short stories. These impressions then could be coded in order to assess each informant's "character complexity" (Hynds, 1989). In my earlier studies, I had discovered that readers seemed to fall within one of four profiles in understanding story characters and people in their social worlds (see Table 1.1). Although these four profiles eventually bore little relevance to this study, they served as an organizing framework for my initial research questions, as I will explain in the following section.

PHASE ONE: SOCIAL COGNITION WITH A CAPITAL "C"

In the first phase of this study (1988–1989), I relied on questionnaire and interview data to explore the following questions:

1. What factors in students' reading backgrounds and overall story ratings appear to distinguish students in the four social construing profiles?
2. What do the students within each social construing profile perceive to be the factors that motivate them to bring interpersonal understandings to literary texts?

Influenced by a tradition of research in cognitive psychology and communication studies, I wanted to see how students thought about peers and literary characters. I began by asking 124 of Meg's eighth-grade students to respond to 10 questionnaires over a period of several weeks in the fall of 1988. These measures included a "Literary Interest Questionnaire," which assesses how many literary works they have read for pleasure in the past year (Purves, 1973), a "Reading Interest and Background Questionnaire," which assesses previous reading experiences within and outside of schools, and a "structural-affect" story rating scale (Jose & Brewer, 1984) for each of two short stories that I read aloud to them on separate occasions. The "structural-affect" scale explored how readers' perceptions of story structures, characters, and text conventions influenced their liking or disliking of stories. For example, informants were asked to what extent they felt similar to or positive toward characters in the story they had read, and to what extent they were satisfied by the ending. Scores on these scales then could be compared with their overall "story liking" ratings.

I placed each participating student into one of the four profile groups described in Table 1.1, according to "high" or "low" ratings on the peer and character Role Category Questionnaires (see Appendix for a more complete description of how students were assigned to each profile group).

Of the original group, 86 students completed all 10 questionnaires and were included in the pool of students for the study. In addition, over the course of the 1988–89 academic year, an assistant and I conducted a series of 40 interviews with 10 student volunteers from each profile group, to determine in a more qualitative way whether particular aspects of their reading interests, backgrounds, and attitudes toward reading related to the four social construing patterns in Table 1.1.

In the spring of 1990, I chose eight focal informants (two in each profile group) and asked them to engage in more in-depth interviews outside of the regular classroom setting. Informants were chosen first on the basis of their scores on the peer and character Role Category Questionnaires. If a student declined to participate, I selected another informant from the same profile group, until I had two representatives from each group. The interviews focused on various aspects of students' responses to and perceptions of literature. In the early interviews, I asked them to share with me their memories of learning to read and their attitudes toward reading at home and in school. In later interviews, I asked them to read some short stories and to "think aloud" as they read. After they read these stories, I sometimes asked them to draw cognitive maps, which helped them to discuss various characters and their relationships. In the final interview, these focal students were

TABLE 1.1: Social Construing Patterns of Readers

Profile One	Socially Complex	These readers exhibit a high degree of social complexity for both peers and characters.
Profile Two	Socially Unelaborated	These readers exhibit a low degree of social complexity for both peers and characters.
Profile Three	Peer Complex	These readers exhibit a high degree of social complexity for peers and a low degree for characters.
Profile Four	Character Complex	These readers exhibit a high degree of social complexity for characters and a low degree for peers.

asked to choose, from among 40 selections covered in class, "those works that relate to your life," and to discuss reasons why these texts seemed more personally relevant than other texts.

I performed a series of factor analyses on the questionnaire data from phase one. Although there were some interesting trends, subsequent analyses of variance comparing students in the four profile groups revealed no significant differences on factors of: (a) reading interest and background, (b) literary interest and transfer, or (c) influences of affective response to characters and aspects of story structure on overall story liking. The most interesting trend was a tendency among readers with high peer complexity ratings to read more novels and books outside of the classroom than did readers with low peer complexity ratings. This trend was consistent with my earlier research (Hynds, 1983, 1985, 1989), which indicated that people who demonstrated elaborate perceptions of both peers and characters were those who also read for pleasure outside of school.

Generally, however, I was disappointed by the rather slim findings from the mounds of questionnaire data I had collected and analyzed in this first phase of the study. The most provocative patterns and themes seemed to emerge in the interview data and in my visits to Meg's classroom. By the end of this preliminary phase, I had begun to question the *psychological* notion of social cognition with a capital "C" and wondered if moving from the cognitive toward the *social* might be the key to an understanding of both literary reading and literacy development.

Thus, I began to adopt a more *social* constructivist perspective (Driver, Asoko, Leach, Mortimer, & Scott, 1994; E. Smith, 1995), realizing that a focus on the reader alone (through questionnaires and interviews) could provide only partial information about this complex social act called reading. I wanted to follow a group of students and their teacher through their daily classroom experiences, studying reading not only within the classroom context, as it interrelates with other language acts, but beyond the classroom as well, as it functions in readers' lives.

PHASE TWO: SOCIAL CONSTRUING WITH A CAPITAL "S"

[Fred] pretty much refuses to do anything except draw. When he does write it always has to be illustrated or he will not write at all, and all his reading is about drawing or from comic books. But he has such a creative mind! I really feel that somehow I could tap into that creativity and show him that it can spill into many other areas besides drawing. It happens occasionally, but then something always seems to happen that scares him back into his silence. Today, however, he was doing so

> *well, and was so involved! His group was working on a horror movie scene, and he was fashioning the characters on paper. What a reader and writer he must be if he can see characters in so much detail! While the others were writing he was throwing in his "two cents' worth" about how the characters would react and what they would say or do in a particular situation. Sometimes kids work so well as a piece of the whole. Don't we all? (Meg, Journal, 1990)*

Just as Meg discovered that her students learned to become readers within the rich social milieu of her classroom, at the end of phase one of the study, I had greatly redefined my notion of the social nature of literary reading. During the next phase, I moved from a focus on the reader as a universe of one, to a focus on readers as they interacted with other readers, with their teachers, and occasionally with others outside of the classroom walls. Thus, I moved beyond my initial interest in how individual readers develop social construing ability (a *psychological* constructivist position), and into a broader interest in how readers, in interaction with others, develop identities as readers and literate persons (a *social* constructivist position).

I also discovered that it was difficult, if not misleading, to attempt to study the literary reading process in the absence of other language processes. Often, students in Meg's classroom became readers through their engagement with writing. Others became readers first, then developed identities as writers. Students like Fred came to reading through drawing or oral language, while still others never came to see themselves as readers at all. I felt the need to study these middle school learners, not in one snapshot moment of their eighth-grade year, but over time, as their definitions of themselves as literate people and readers of literature developed and transformed throughout their entire middle school experience.

As I broadened my focus on individual readers to a study of readers within a classroom community, I became intrigued with Meg's changes, particularly during the last 2 years of the study. Throughout this period, I was able to gather many insights about the complicated process of implementing curricular change in the teaching of literature, as described by Arthur Applebee (1992a). Applebee argues that although there have been significant advances in writing pedagogy, largely through the efforts of such groups as the National Writing Project, there have been few such advances in the teaching of literature. He concludes:

> What is lacking is a well-articulated overall theory of the teaching and learning of literature that will give a degree of order and coherence to the day-to-day decisions that teachers make about what and how to teach. . . . Relatively well-established traditions have begun to provide such frameworks for read-

ing and writing within the English language arts. The teaching of literature, however, has until recently remained largely outside of recent movements in those fields. (pp. 13–14)

Throughout the first phase of the study, I was beginning to develop some understanding about why the curricular changes in literature teaching on the national level that Applebee has called for have been so slow in coming. In the next phase of the study, through a combination of fortunate events, I was able to explore these and other insights generated in phase one.

In the fall of 1989, Meg consented to participating in a pilot project, where she was assigned five classes of seventh-grade students, who would continue with her for a 2-year period until their graduation from middle school. That same fall, I was awarded a grant from the NCTE Research Foundation to continue my study. Thus, I had the opportunity to study a group of students in their crucial middle school years, as they read and responded to a variety of literary texts within a classroom setting. Equally important, the 2-year extension would allow me to follow one teacher as she attempted to create a learner-centered, constructivist classroom.

Beginning in the fall of 1989, I distributed the same questionnaires I had used in phase one of the study to the seventh-grade students in all five of Meg's classes. Rather than conducting statistical analyses of these measures, however, I decided that results from this initial assessment would act as a sort of "purposeful sampling" (see Bogdan & Biklen, 1992), or a way to ensure that students with a variety of social construing patterns would be included in the interviews and observations. During that fall semester, an assistant and I conducted preliminary interviews with 58 of Meg's students (representing the four profile groups in Table 1.1. in a roughly equal way). As they had in phase one, these preliminary interviews allowed me to explore particular aspects of these middle school students' interests, backgrounds, and attitudes toward reading.

Focal and Case Study Students

By the spring semester of 1990, I chose eight focal informants (two in each of the four profile groups) and asked them to participate in more focused interviews outside of the normal classroom setting. That spring, I continued to observe Meg's classes, but now was able to focus my observations on the interactions of four of these focal informants. My assistant observed the remaining four informants, while I continued to interview them on a regular basis throughout the 2 years of phase two. Data from the four informants I did not directly observe, together with data from the eight focal students in phase one of the study, would be analyzed primarily for evidence of participants' perspectives on and experiences with literacy, presented in Chapter Two.

Finally, another student, Luis, was in one of the classrooms I observed for both years of the study. Although I did not have "official" permission to include him in the case study group, I had been particularly intrigued by him and decided to continue my close observations, in the hope that I might eventually persuade him to be a part of the project. In 1988, Luis had refused to fill out any of the questionnaires I had handed out. I learned much later that, because of a slight speech impediment, he also refused to be audio taped. However, as I observed the many changes in this young man over the 2-year period, I felt it important to contact him later, to see if he would be willing to be included in this study. Luis represents students who, for one reason or another, are not often the subject of classroom research. Because they seem to drift around the periphery of a classroom and are not often eager to speak with outsiders, it is easy for researchers to dismiss students like these. I pursued Luis, and eventually was able to garner permission to include him, because I think he has a valuable story to tell about adolescents who are not firmly situated in the academic mainstream.

Thus, by the end of phase two, I had collected data from nine focal informants (five females and four males). Five members of this original group of nine became the subject of in-depth case studies: Jason, Kianna, Samantha, Angel, and Luis. These case studies will be presented in Chapters Four, Five, Seven and Eight (see Appendix for a more complete description of how case study informants were chosen). Information about the nine focal informants, including the five case study informants, is presented in Table 1.2.

ONE STEP BEYOND

Finally, 4 years after their graduation from middle school, in the summer of 1995, I contacted Jason, Samantha, Angel, and Luis, as they prepared to enter their years beyond high school. Each agreed to participate in an interview of approximately 90 minutes. To my delight, Luis not only agreed to be interviewed and to release his written work from middle school for the study, but he also brought a portfolio of writings that he had saved throughout his high school career. I have been in touch with him by mail and telephone several times since then. These conversations, although retrospective, have helped me to fill in some of the missing details that had puzzled and intrigued me 4 years earlier when I observed him in Meg's classroom. As of this writing, although I tried to track her down several times, beginning in the summer of 1995, I have not received a response from Kianna.

TABLE 1.2: Focal Informants

Name	Peer Complexity Rating	Character Complexity Rating	Gender	Race/Ethnicity
Angel*	High	High	Female	European American
Samantha*	Low	Low	Female	Biracial (African American and European American)
Kianna*	High	Low	Female	African American
Jason*	High	Low	Male	European American
Luis*	n.a.	n.a.	Male	African American
Mark	Low	High	Male	European American
Cassie	High	High	Female	European American
Daniel	Low	High	Male	Lebanese American
Jessie	Low	Low	Female	European American

*indicates case study informant

In all, over the 3-year period, a total of 110 student interviews were taped and transcribed. Complete questionnaires were collected on a voluntary basis from 167 students, and written texts, including journals and imaginative pieces, were collected on a voluntary basis from 117 students. Data sources for the 3-year period are presented in Table 1.3 (for a more detailed discussion of analytic procedures, see Appendix).

In Chapter Two, I will discuss the impressions I gathered from my interviews of the 16 focal informants and their classmates during the 3-year period of the study. I will try to paint, in rather broad strokes, a portrait of these middle school students' views of literacy in general and literary reading in particular. In many ways, what I learned confirmed my earlier hunches as a teacher: Rather than mastering a set of discrete, decontextualized skills, students engaged in a complex array of social practices that defined and developed their identities as readers, writers, and language users. In another sense, however, I learned more than I had bargained for. The social and political realities that eventually emerged between the lines of my observational notes and memos caused me to reconsider and revise my former perspectives as both teacher and researcher.

TABLE 1.3: Data Sources

Phase One: 1988-1989

	Participating Students	Questionnaires	Preliminary Interviews	In-Depth Interviews
	48	10		
	40	10	1	
	8 focal	10	1	3
Totals	96	960	48	24

Phase Two: 1989-1991

Participating Students	Questionnaires	Preliminary Interviews	In-Depth Interviews		Classroom Observations	Journals	Other Written Texts
			89-91	'95			
59	10					voluntary basis	voluntary basis
50	10	1				voluntary basis	voluntary basis
3 focal	10	1	4		assistant observed	X	X
5 case study	10	1	4	1	personally observed	X	X
Totals 117	1,170	58	32	4			

CHAPTER 2

On School Bells and Bumblebees: The World of the Young Adolescent

I stand at the top of the polished stairs as the bell clangs through the halls of Logan Middle School. There is a vacant pause—almost a holding of collective breath—before the cacophony of a thousand young bodies crashing out of doorways, shouting insults and greetings to friends, slamming lockers, and pushing steadily toward the highlight of the young adolescent's day: lunch. For Meg's students, as for so many others, middle school is a constant balancing of chaos and constraint.

For a few moments, I think back to my days as a middle school teacher. Over a decade earlier, I had decided to leave the familiarity of my urban high school classroom and begin a doctoral program in English Education. Knowing that I couldn't be a full-time teacher and graduate student, I took a part-time position in a girls' Catholic school, teaching speech and drama to students from sixth through twelfth grade.

I remember vividly the first time I faced my high-spirited group of sixth-grade girls. Earlier that morning, I had taken my classes of eleventh- and twelfth-grade students onto the theatre stage, introduced them to where they would be working for the next several months, and begun some creative dramatics exercises. They loved it. Naively, I assumed that my sixth-grade students would as well. And they did. In the space of a few minutes, though, they were clambering over the scaffolding, attacking the dimmer switches, and holding a contest to see who could jump the farthest off the 5-foot high stage and onto the gymnasium floor below! I knew immediately I had to go back to my curricular drawing board.

The "drama room" at Saint Bernard Academy in Nashville, Tennessee, wasn't actually a classroom, but a dressing room, right across the hall from the auditorium and gym. As such, it was too small to accommodate 30 chairs without squeezing them into traditional rows. Rather than conduct creative dramatics exercises in a lecture arrangement, I had asked the janitor to get rid of the chairs so that I could hold classes on the floor. The day after the debacle in the auditorium, I walked into my classroom and announced that we wouldn't be returning to the stage for a while. Amidst the groans of disappointment, I suggested that we try something even more fun: "theatre of the mind." I took a deep breath, as my sixth-grade girls settled around me on the patchwork of shag carpeting.

The rules for theatre of the mind were simple, I explained: There could be no shoving or pinching, shouting or moving around the room. As soon as everyone got quiet, we could begin. I turned off the lights and waited. Then I whispered tentatively: "We're going on a trip. Where shall we go?" "The moon!" one girl immediately shouted. "Okay! The moon. What should we take with us?" "My boyfriend!" another chimed in. And so it went. For days, we traveled in our imaginations to nearly unimaginable locations—from the center of the sea to the jungles of Africa. We crossed the great prairie in a Conestoga wagon and traveled with our ancestors across the ocean to America. Each day we sat in my darkened classroom, traveling as far as our voices and our imaginations would carry us. Best of all, from my vantage point, we did so with a minimum of noise and damage. It would be several months before I could venture out with them to more daring locations like the theatre stage, with all of its mesmerizing switches and pulleys and scaffolds.

"WAITING FOR A STUPID LITTLE BELL TO RING": WELCOME TO OUR WORLD

One of the delightful things I found out about middle school students in those first few weeks is that they are incredibly open and receptive to imaginary flights of fancy. Although interested in their peers, they aren't quite as inhibited by social pressures as high school students. Physically and emotionally, middle school students have three main characteristics: energy, energy, and more energy. But this need for physical activity is sporadic and changeable. At the sound of the school bell, girls as well as boys tumble into a room, hitting and poking each other. A few minutes later, you'll see the same kids lounging in their seats in what seems like a permanent state of catatonia. Between the ages of 10 and 14, young adolescents have a strong need for physical activity. They need frequent breaks, chances to move around the room and collaborate with others. Perhaps Mark, a young man in Meg's class, best describes what goes on in a typical young adolescent's mind during the school day. Listen to this rap he wrote:

> Sitting here watching the clock tick away
> Tick-tock-tick-tock every day
> Waiting for a stupid little bell to ring
> So I can go home and do my thing.
> Which is playing lacrosse, and riding in the park

And if you don't know me my name is Mark
Sparks is my last name and don't forget it
If you mess with me you're gonna regret it
My next class is french, and that's okay
But I think we're having a test today
Then comes science, and that's pretty fun
But science ain't for everyone
Then is lunch, and that is great
But you're in trouble if you are late
6th period gym is the best
It is better than all the rest
Then we have to go to t.a.
That is boring unless we play
I get on the bus and I go home
Then I call my girlfriend on the phone
That's one day in a normal week
To me it's dull, it's boring, and it's weak.

"Mark, oh Mark," I want to ask. "How can so much chaos be so boring?" And yet it's precisely this balancing—this negotiating between maturity and childhood—that marks the middle school experience. Young adolescents like Mark are bundles of energy. At the same time, they can be easily bored and distracted. It is in this world of middle school, where identities and energies shift whimsically from moment to moment, that Mark and his classmates must learn to navigate the complex routines and rituals of growing up and developing identities as literate persons.

FROM "MINI HIGH" TO MIDDLE SCHOOL: THE GROWTH OF ADOLESCENCE

The fact is that adolescence itself is not a biological truism, but a social construct, born in the shift from an agrarian to an industrial society. While a century ago, teenagers were needed in the fields and villages, today, as far as the American economy is concerned, young men like Mark are, quite literally, useless, except as consumers of junk food, designer clothes, and trendy, extravagant sports equipment. No wonder they are portrayed in the media as materialistic, self-indulgent pleasure-seekers, captivated only by the mindlessness of television and video games.

In the early part of the twentieth century, G. Stanley Hall (1904) wrote his famous book on adolescence, in which he argued that teenagers were not just miniature adults, but had special needs and characteristics. As the concept of adolescence took hold, American educators tried to create a kind of schooling that would meet these special needs. Several social and economic factors led to the growth of the junior high school in the late nineteenth century. For one, there was a huge dropout rate prior to eighth grade, which was attributed to the fact that the later elementary grades were repetitive and boring. In addition, curriculum planners began to look for a way to introduce students to the structure of high schools, with their specialized subjects and content-oriented curriculum. For students not planning to go to high school, junior high schools would provide an opportunity to explore possible employment paths. Thus, out of these varied and somewhat unrelated factors, the junior high school appeared on the landscape of American education.

By the early 1970s, however, we became disenchanted with the junior high school model for a variety of reasons. Perhaps I can best explain this general disenchantment by describing my own particular experience in junior high school. In the late 1950s, when I entered junior high school, the launching of Sputnik had created a new focus on education as a matter of national security. Federally funded curriculum projects such as the "New Math" and "New English" had just made their way onto the American scene. With the sudden push to "beat the Russians" came concepts like homogeneous grouping, "gifted and talented" education, and a more competitive high school-like model of schooling.

Until I entered seventh grade in 1959, school had always come easily to me. My only dilemma seemed to be getting my hand in the air and waving it wildly enough to be recognized by my teachers. Junior high school, I was soon to learn, was another story. I remember standing outside of the building on that first day of my seventh-grade year, trying to see my name on one of three lists: "the A class," "the B class," and "the C class." I had taken a test at the end of the sixth grade and become paralyzed by a few tough questions right at the beginning. Not wanting to risk a mistake, I got stuck on these few questions and failed to finish the rest of the test. Little did I know that my lack of test-taking savvy would relegate me to the "B" class. Watching so many of my childhood friends file into the "A" class that day was devastating to me. But my status was brought home even more painfully at the end of each 6 weeks, as the principal would enter my classroom and make this announcement:

> Boys and girls, as you know, each term, there are a few students who have worked very hard. As a result of their hard work, these students have been promoted to the "A" class. Will the students whose names I call please take your books and line up at the door?

As the new recruits filed across the hall to the "A" class, the principal's bright smile seemed to curl into a sneer, as he announced:

> Now, I'm sad to say that there are some students who did not work hard enough this term to remain in the "B" class. Will these students please take your books and move to the "C" class across the hall?

For my entire seventh-grade year, until I too was able to prove myself worthy of the "A" class, I lived in dreaded fear of being one of the unlucky students relegated to the "C" class.

After that first immersion in the intellectually competitive world of academic tracking, we were left to wend our way through another complicated array of social relationships and structures. For example, the sock hop in the gym each day after lunch was a testing ground for what later would become the elaborate routines of dating and, presumably, marriage. I had never been taught to dance and was too shy to learn in front of my peers. I spent my free time trying to eat my lunch slowly enough so that I wouldn't have to deal with the pressures of the daily sock hop. In addition, the shifting from one class, subject, and teacher to the next every hour demanded intellectual and social skills for which the insulated world of my elementary school had left me ill prepared.

By the late 1950s, many junior high schools like mine had become mini high schools, with an overemphasis on social activities and a strong competitive spirit, both intellectually and socially. Because there were few interdisciplinary connections, young adolescents had to adapt quickly to the separateness of subject matter. There was little in the way of guidance and support for children like me, who were constantly shifting between childhood and young adulthood. Both academically—with its homogeneous grouping—and socially—with its "high school-like" activities—the great American junior high school failed me and, I suspect, so many others. Rather than guiding me through this threatening situation, my teachers assigned "write offs" about the perils of misbehaving, and lectured me about not being mature enough for high school.

In response to the growing dissatisfaction with the junior high school model, the middle school movement began in the 1970s and 1980s. The newly established National Middle School Association argued for a move away from specialized "miniature high schools," which failed to provide the sort of support that young adolescents seemed to need in the passage between elementary and high school.

In addition, several social and economic factors had rendered much of the rationale behind the junior high school movement irrelevant. For example, by the 1970s, compulsory schooling laws in most states had made it impossible for children to drop out at eighth grade. So, keeping students in school was no longer an issue. In addition, the mean age of puberty had dropped approximately one year from where it was at the turn of the century. Hargreaves, Earl, and Ryan (1996) have noted that within the past 150 years, the average onset of puberty in girls has lowered from 16 to 12.5 years of age. Considering this shift, we began to believe that sixth-grade students were more like junior high kids than they were like children of elementary age. As a result, many districts moved sixth-grade students (and sometimes fifth-grade students) into middle school, and ninth-grade students into high school.

Through the work of developmental psychologists, we began to realize that young adolescents are very different from older adolescents. They are undergoing phenomenal changes: moving away from the family, yet still tied to it; developing physically, but still child-like emotionally; tied to peers, and yet feeling like social misfits most of the time. Leaders of the middle school movement called for a more "student-centered" agenda, with an emphasis on heterogeneous grouping, multiculturalism, and interdisciplinary team teaching. In addition, middle school teachers were expected to act in quasi-parental roles, in order to ease the transition into high school.

In urban areas, two social developments further influenced the creation of middle schools. The baby boom of the 1950s and 1960s had caused enrollments to skyrocket. Since city schools were financially strapped, school planners decided that it was cheaper to house children in one big school rather than several small ones. In addition, there was a push to end the de facto segregation of the neighborhood elementary school. In some communities and states, federal courts mandated equality of opportunity for all students. Therefore, creating larger middle schools that included sixth (and occasionally fifth) grades seemed to be a good way to mandate racial integration in the earlier grades.

THE WORLD OF LOGAN MIDDLE SCHOOL

The middle school model adopted by Logan differed from my junior high school in several ways. Teachers like Meg created curricula that were learner-centered, rather than teacher-centered or content-centered. The focus at Logan, in principle at least, was on kids and their development, rather than on generic "skills" or "content" that all students were supposed to master by a certain age. The administration recognized the young adolescent's need for nurturing, parenting, and guidance. Meg and her colleagues worked in teams, where one small group of students were placed with the same inter-disciplinary group of teachers, who tried to plan thematic, integrated ways for the curriculum to seem more coherent from one subject area to another. Logan began each day with a "T.A." (Team Advisement) period, different from a homeroom, in that students and their advisors met individually and sometimes planned activities to make the school seem more family-like. Although some students were placed into "reading" classes or "resource rooms" for extra help during part of the day, Logan based its philosophy on fostering the achievement of all kids, rather than labeling them or putting them into special classes on the basis of their ability to succeed at standardized tasks.

In some ways, then, Logan Middle School seemed like it should be a safer place than Lincoln Junior High School, where I made my way painfully through early adolescence. The corridors of Logan reflected the diversity of its students, as well as a strong community spirit. Posters and photographs for Black Pride Week lined the display cases, and slogans like "We Are Family" surrounded the many colorful photographs of students from various racial and ethnic backgrounds, engaged in various school activities.

And yet, as I stood at the top of the stairs on this particular morning, in some ways Logan felt more scary and alien than my early memories of junior high school. The noise and chaos, for one thing, would not have been permitted in the old brick building where each day we lined up, separated by gender, at one of two doorways on opposite sides of the building, with the words "girls" and "boys" permanently inscribed in the concrete. When the bell rang, our teachers led us quietly, in single file, to homeroom and the beginning of our school day.

At Logan, boys and girls slammed through the halls together, rough and playful, slapping or pushing each other in highly charged and sometimes sexual ways. Young teenagers congregated around lockers in social cliques often bounded by gender, skin color, and class. At the end of each day, they boarded buses and went home to a colorful panoply of family structures, neighborhoods, and cultural traditions, many of which didn't exist in my White, working class midwestern town.

And in the midst of all this cultural richness was the curiously detached world of school, where Meg's students moved each day in lines and bunches at 40-minute intervals to the sound of a bell. Within this strange place, there lived a peculiar hybrid of creativity and ritual, written words and implicit rules, called "the English classroom." Meg's room, nested within the larger worlds of home, school, community, and country, was the setting for the 2-year journey that she and her students would take as they negotiated their way toward their literate identities. It is within this world that I learned more about the unique and varied lives of young adolescents than I did in my years as a middle school teacher myself.

In the following pages, I will step back a bit from the particular lives of

Meg and her students, before zooming close again in the case studies of individual students and the story of Meg in the chapters to follow. In a sort of montage of her students' written and spoken words, I will try to portray the incredible complexity that teachers like Meg encounter as they enter their urban English classrooms each day. The subtext of their words also suggests the larger social and political realities that surround and shape her students' attitudes toward literature, literacy, and the tricky process of teaching and learning. This chapter foreshadows some of the core issues in the chapters to follow.

NAVIGATING THE DEPTHS: DISCOVERING OUR LITERATE LIVES

In 1989, as Meg embarked on the pilot program that would take her and her students through their middle school years, she stood in the doorway of her carefully created classroom, waiting for the inevitable rush of new students. In place of desks were six rectangular tables, set up to accommodate five students apiece. To the left of the doorway, almost as an afterthought, Meg's desk sat in the corner. Across the cramped room was a small makeshift stage, painted black and draped with dark cloth. At the foot of this stage was an overstuffed plaid couch, some plants, and a set of colorful throw pillows that Meg had bought with her own money. Each day, as nearly 40 students bounded into a classroom set up for 30, I got a vivid glimpse of this strange and intriguing creature called the young adolescent.

In the literacy autobiographies Meg asked her students to write those first few weeks, I was surprised that nearly every student had fond memories of reading as a young child. Even the most reluctant readers described being read to as children or having family members (most often, mothers, but also fathers, siblings, and other relatives like aunts and grandmothers) who read for pleasure. For example, Shante remembered being given a book about spelling from her Aunt Delores, which she read over and over. Later, her father would read to her from books for "older children." She explained, "These books had no pictures and were about 100 pages long." Shante always wanted to be able to read like her father. "Now," she explains, "I can and I passed all my reading levels through ninth grade in sixth grade."

Shante and her classmates remember their children's books fondly: *The Frog Prince*, *Green Eggs and Ham* (Seuss, 1960), *Goodnight Moon* (Brown, 1947), *The Three Bears*, *Cinderella*, *Are You There God? It's Me, Margaret* (Blume, 1974), *Curious George* (Ray, 1973), *Jack and the Beanstalk*, *The Cat in the Hat* (Seuss, 1957), to name a few. Reading during childhood is often remembered as a cozy affair, where mothers or older sisters (less often fathers or male relatives) cuddle up in bed or settle into a comfortable spot in order to read to their eager children. Reading at home is often a ritual performance, where kids know just when adults have skipped a page, or complain when parents lapse into monotone instead of changing voices with each new character. Most of all, reading at home is marked by the absence of evaluation. As children struggle through the complicated maze of print, adults who are not teachers offer encouragement and guidance, delighted at each of their children's small steps toward literacy. Belinda's mother, for example, taught her everything she knows about reading. She recalls:

> *[My mother] would say to me, "Belinda, look at the picture and tell me what you see. I would say, "I see a dog, ect." My mother was very pretty, she had long pretty hair. And she would always say to me when I got a question wrong, "great job try again."*

Often, reading for school was a different story. For example, Kristen was always shy as a young child. In first grade, her teacher asked her to read a story aloud to the class. When Kristen stumbled over a word, her teacher became angry that Kristen "couldn't read as good" as her teacher could. She called Kristen an "unintelligent reader" and made her stand in the corner. Kristen wanted to cry, but instead "held it in." She remembered her teacher as "the meanest teacher [she] ever had." Kristen was humiliated, as "the class laughed and talked about" her. Today, Kristen doesn't "like to read out loud a lot," but she still reads to herself.

Given the gloss of memory, I suspect that these stories of early reading are not entirely accurate. But in another sense, they're absolutely true. They are, after all, the remembered context, against which Meg's young adolescents measure and judge their early school experiences. For some, even in the early elementary grades, these memories of school reading are bittersweet. Amy recalls:

> *I really remember being asked a question out of my reading work book and becoming so sweaty and completely nerves because of the excitement made by the other classmates. All I could hear was, 0000000, 0000000 pick on me Mrs. O, pick on me! That class always made me feel like I was the biggest dummy because for some reason I never remember answering a question.*

Even academically successful students have bad memories of reading for school, with its hierarchies of skills and homogeneous groups. Melissa captures her recollections of reading groups in this poem:

Reading Groups

I listen to others read,
I listen to how they sound.
It's like they knew how to read,
How to read since they were born.
And me sitting there by myself,
Feeling all alone.
One person away,
From my appointment with doom.
Then it was my turn to read,
With sweat dripping down my neck I started to read
After a while I started to get used to it.
That's what got me interested in reading!

Fortunately, since Melissa is an academically successful student, the competition of reading groups proved to be an incentive, and not a barrier to reading. Melissa's classmate, Kimantha, is another story. Kim describes warm memories of reading *The Three Bears* and *Cinderella* with her mother as a small child. By the time she entered kindergarten, however, she encountered the monotonous basal readers "that said things like, 'Jane and Sam went to the store.'" In first grade, Kim was in the blue reading group, yet always longed to be in the prestigious yellow group. Although she was in the lowest group, she explained, "we were not stupid, just kind of slow." By the time she reached fifth grade, Kimantha had been suspended six times, each time for hitting or threatening a teacher. She admitted, "I really didn't read a lot that year because I was too busy being bad."

In the world of the young adolescent, there is more variation across children intellectually, and more variation in one child across time, than at any other age. It does no good to put them into "homogeneous" groups, because they change so swiftly, and because a child may be brilliant in one area and in great need of help in another. Melissa was lucky. She developed the social savvy to "read" not only her textbooks, but also her teacher's hidden agenda. Kimantha wasn't so lucky. And neither was Ben.

"A Perpose I Didn't Understand": Negotiating the Hidden Curriculum

Ben transferred into Meg's classroom in eighth grade. By outward appearances, he was the epitome of the adolescent outcast—"nerd," "dweeb," "dork"—the label changes over the years, but the social marginalization doesn't. Ben was taller than most kids his age, was a bit overweight, and wore glasses. He seemed more comfortable interacting with adults than with other students. He was also, I came to discover, a budding novelist. Some days as I sat near Meg's desk with my tape recorder, Ben would slide a chair up to mine and demand: "Turn that thing on. I have something to say." As the reels turned, Ben would proceed to fill me in on his novel in progress, a futuristic story about a handsome and fearless fighter pilot. His story, "Alpha Force," was, it seemed to me, a fictionalized dream world where Ben could escape the earthbound life of a middle school outcast. It began:

Alpha Force

It was a cold, damp morning. I was awoken by the sound of my airplane shaped phone. I was thinking of all the possible people who would call me at this time of the morning. I got to the bottom of my list of names and thought peter. I quickly grabbed the phone and said "hello".

I was right, it was peter and he was telling me that a formation of russian war jets had entered american air space and were heading for washington, d.c. I quickly tried to get my clothes on without waking up my fiance. I got on my shirt. When I was pulling on my pants I fell onto the bed and she woke up.

"Where are you going?" she asked.

"I just got a call from peter and I have to go: I answered

"At least tell me where you're going" she said [as] I was putting on my shoes.

"You know my business, I can't reveal where I'm going." I answered back as I grabbed for my jacket.

I kissed her good-bye and swung open the front door and ran to my ferrari. I jumped in and started the engine and took off like a shot.

Ben explained to my tape recorder that his father, a computer buff, had taught him to use a word processor a year earlier. Since that time, he wrote most of his stories on the computer, where he wasn't distracted by the mess and drudgery of handwriting. Several weeks later, in the middle of a casual conversation, Ben slipped in the fact that his father died a few months earlier. I was flabbergasted, as Ben reported this fact without the least sign of emotion. There were other surprises as well.

The creativity and sophistication of his novel (which grew, over time, to several chapters) led me to believe that Ben was somewhat verbally gifted. Imagine my shock when I was chatting casually with Ben in the hall one day, and I asked what class he had just come from. He replied without a blink,

"The resource room." Apparently, Ben had failed several tests and was placed in the resource room for special help. I sensed (although I had no permission to inquire at the time) that he might be labeled "learning disabled." Evidence of this possibility surfaced at the end of his eighth-grade year, when Meg gave her "final examination." She asked all of her students to pick one of two texts and write a short response to it. Ben picked the poem, "Oranges," by Gary Soto (1990). His response to this more formal school task, where he could not compose on a computer, and where he had a limited time to respond, was a sharp contrast with the competencies he demonstrated in his "Alpha Force" piece. In response to Gary Soto's poem, Ben wrote this short, pained paragraph, full of misspellings and sentence fragments:

> *I felt that this poem had a perpose that I didn't understand. I think it was good but confusing to read. The auther might have seen this or just thought. I think it had great description of everything. I liked how he sawed "he thumbed a nickel in his pocket."*

Like Ben, so many of Meg's middle-school kids are a curious mix of contradictions. Many have private lives that would astound their teachers if they knew. There's Adiata, who was inspired to become a writer by her grandmother, who used to be a journalist for the *Chicago Tribune*. Adiata is teaching her own father to read, since he never learned when he was her age. And there's Karen, who wants to be an astronaut. If you ask her, she will tell you about the importance of reading "fictional, as well as nonfictional, works" to prepare for one's career.

Throughout the 3 years I spent in her classroom, Meg was challenged to provide a whole range of learning experiences in different language modalities, where young people like Ben could succeed, alongside students like Adiata and Karen. Ben taught me that often their emotional, as well as their intellectual, lives float beneath the surface of their school performance like glaciers. Teachers like Meg must be crafty navigators, sounding the depths of their students' hidden literate lives. For Ben, reading (and the writing that grew from it) was a way out of a painful existence. For others, it was a practical requirement for future success. For still others, it was a secret passion, an escape from the mundaneness of everyday life.

"A Couch Potato Like Everybody Else": Why, How, and When We Read

Max got a bad report card a few weeks earlier. Dismayed at his reading grade, his mother urged him to read more, and Max complied. Since that time, Max has been reading "more and more every day." For Max, reading is "what you need in life." A pragmatist to the core, Max lumps literary reading with textbooks and newspapers. Reading, for Max, is for getting "a better understanding of some subjects." Tommell agrees. He reads "for something to do, to learn . . . for information." Readers like Max and Tommell see reading as work, not pleasure—information, not aesthetic absorption. Max believes that other people read in lieu of anything better to do, "just to catch up on their reading and . . . [so that school] just doesn't drag on." Meg's challenge is to help Max and Tommell to see reading as more than just gathering information or a sort of workout for "real life." The intense, aesthetic experience of literature has not yet happened for Max and Tommell. Meg must be a catalyst for this absorbing, aesthetic experience. But considering the push for "skills and knowledge" by parents, administrators, and test makers, this will prove difficult.

Kathleen and Libby don't share this rather instrumental view of reading. Both avid readers in their spare time, they often have books by their beds and stowed away in their backpacks and lockers. Kathleen loves the "pictures in [her] head" that books afford—imaginary dramas, enacted on the mind's stage that allow pleasure readers like her to go even "more in depth than movies." Kathleen will tell you about what it's like to read for pleasure: "If you get into a good book . . . you don't want to put it down. . . . It takes up all your time 'cause the book's so good."

Time is just what the average middle school student has little of. Perhaps for this reason, readers like Kathleen are rare and elusive. Meg would like a whole classroom of them. Unfortunately, because reading is so intensely private and personal, they often balk at "bogus" activities designed to convince English teachers that they read—activities like reading journals, papers, tests, and quizzes. Pleasure readers like Kathleen and Libby often get so wrapped up in books that they forget characters' names, titles, and textual minutiae—the very details that demonstrate academic competence to teachers. Meg will have to look deeper for subtle signs of these "closet readers," lest they drift to the academic margins, where they may spend their days labeled as "mediocre" or disinterested.

A great many of Meg's students find their time crammed too full of an active life to spare time for reading. In literature, as in life, their interests and enthusiasms are sporadic and changeable. What they often see as a dull and lonely pursuit comes last on a long list of other, more active preoccupations. Dan explains, "When I get a good book, I can't put it down. But then when I get a book that's not so good, I just stop. You know, . . . I watch TV more than I read." Along the same lines, Harvena observes:

I read when I am bored on Sundays when there is nothing on T.V. I read the new books that came from the new book packet that comes to my house. . . . I read more comics and magazines because they are more fun to read. . . . When I get in the eighth grade I will read more than I do now.

Kim agrees: "I like reading. Nothing's wrong with it. I mean, I do it some-times, you know." Perhaps Jerrod sums it up best: "I can [read] but I don't usually. I've become a couch potato, like everybody else."

Heidi has developed a sort of "thumb test" for literature. "If it's not good in the beginning," she explains, "I'll read a little bit more, and then if it's not getting any better, I'll just stop reading it." Tommell agrees: "If I read the first page and I like it, then it's a good book." Despite the limits of his patience, Tommell does consider himself a reader, often becoming deeply involved in books during the summer and in the evenings before bed, when there are fewer demands on his time. When he manages to become involved in reading, he admits, "it'll take a lot to get me out of my daze." As with many young adolescents, other people are a distraction, but noise is not; Tommell likes to read with the radio on.

Middle school students are mercurial and passionate about their likes and dislikes. They make snap decisions and sharp turns in the road to aca-demic success. Meg must help some students to stick with a book or story, even when it doesn't immediately entice them. Because they have so little free time, she must provide open spaces in her classroom for free reading. At other times, because "real readers" often reject what they don't like, Meg must provide the freedom to abandon books that serve only to dull and dampen their fragile enthusiasm for reading.

"Cliquey" with a Capital C: Nerds, Geeks, and Closet Readers

Perhaps because they have just left the safety of elementary school, where they stayed with one teacher throughout the day, middle school students want desperately to belong. They are needy of little touches that say they are cared about. Teachers like Meg are always dispensing paper clips, pencils, hall passes, and band-aids. Young adolescents need to belong in another way as well. In the middle school years, small groups of students begin to form within the classroom. They're beginning to be what I call "cliquey" with a capital C. For this reason, they will not collaborate readily with people whom they view as outside their social circle. Students will listen with rapt attention to their friends during Sharing Time, and absolutely ignore others whom they do not see as a part of their particular social group. Often this "cliqueyness" is along the lines of race or gender. But it could be along any kinds of lines, really: jocks, preppies, "straight-edged punks," or any of the other "special interest groups" that seem to form at this age. By the time students reach middle school, the friends of elementary school are forgotten quickly. All young adolescents, but especially girls, are beginning in middle school to forge the bonds that lead to long-term friendships.

Interestingly, while most of Meg's students saw themselves as surrounded by family members who like to read, few saw their friends as readers. Many were afraid to reveal their reading interests to friends, for fear of looking "nerdy." Harvena admits, "When I got to Logan, I was sort of scared that I would be considered a nerd because I always had a book with me." A few avid readers (mostly girls) talked fondly about going to libraries and trading books with friends. However, most of Meg's students would rather not reveal their reading interests to friends.

Emily, for example, described herself as an "average" reader and writer. She didn't start out feeling average, but by the time she reached second grade, she remembered being paralyzed by her reading teacher's dittoed sheets because she didn't want to risk a mistake in front of her classmates. Typical of so many young girls as they move toward adolescence, Emily took the safe route, carefully avoiding books or stories that might be "confusing" and preferring what she called "everyday typical books" like *Sweet Valley High* (Pascal, 1992a) and *Sweet Valley Twins* (Pascal, 1992b). In her first year of middle school, Emily would not share her reading interest with friends, because, in their words, only "nerds read." She explained:

> A lot of my friends are in the popular group, and they think that everyone who reads is "nerdy" or "geeks," whatever. . . . I don't know why they don't read. I guess . . . they think it's for nerds. I bet they read at home.

It took Emily most of her seventh-grade year to wean herself from the need to be safely situated "in the norm." She began to see that there was more to people than their surface appearance. Interestingly, Rosa Guy's novel, *The Friends* (1973) helped to move Emily toward this realization. She related strongly to the ambivalence of the main character, Phylissia, about making friends with Edith Jackson, a poorly dressed girl from the streets of Harlem. Emily explained:

> When I was little, I used to misjudge my friends and used to hang out with the popular crowd and I used to let go of the kids that were poor or didn't dress right. My friends would tell me not to hang out with them because they were a nerd.

As she began to look beneath the surface of her relationships with other people, she also became more relaxed and adventurous as a reader, seeking out more complex books and stories in the process. By eighth grade, Emily had become less conscious of appearances in her social relationships, as well as her relationships with books. She ventured beyond what she had come to call "teeny bop" books and into more challenging genres like mysteries and poetry.

So many young adolescent girls like Emily start out life full of energy and spunk. Unfortunately, by the time they reach adolescence, they adopt rigid gender roles, taking the safe route in everything from the friends to the books they choose. By the same token, adolescent males are reluctant to reveal their reading behaviors to friends, for fear of looking like "sissies" or, worse yet, "girls." As Carlos writes, "When I was in the first grade I did not like reading. I did not learn to read then or now. I learned to do things by myself. I look at *hot rod magazine*." Meg will be challenged to convince students like Emily and Carlos that becoming a lifetime reader will not relegate them to the ranks of the social misfit.

"Real Life Isn't That Special": Reading as Action

I saw scant evidence in Meg's classroom of what teachers might call "critical reading," "reading for theme," or what Vipond and Hunt (1984) call "point-driven" reading. This didn't surprise me, since I've found little evidence of this kind of reading among adult pleasure readers, or anyone else who is not specifically directed to read this way for school. Above all else, middle school readers like strong plots with lots of suspense, action, and/or humor.

Their preferences often run along gender lines. Girls tend to choose mysteries, books about families, and occasionally adventure or horror stories. They are avid readers of what Margaret Finders (1997) calls "Teen Zines," magazines directed toward the insatiable curiosity of adolescents for the latest news about fashion, sex, and relationships. Maria, like so many of Meg's students, loves Stephen King, with his fast-moving plots and simple characters. In fact, girls in general talk more about characters than do boys; and those characters have to be believable and realistic. For example, Maria prefers "story characters that you can actually, like, visualize." Libby likes characters "that aren't too weird"; Rebecca explains that "you have to believe in the characters. . . . They can't all of a sudden in the middle of the book change." Like their male counterparts, girls read fantasy and mystery, and often see reading as an escape from the mundaneness of teenage life. As Kathy says, "Real life isn't that special. . . . I mean, you can make up more exciting things." At the same time, where realistic fiction is concerned, in literature, if not in life, girls have their feet planted firmly in the real world. For example, Heidi likes any book that seems "real—like it really happened, [not too much] fantasizing and stuff like that." Similarly, Maria prefers realistic stories, as opposed to literature that is "so far-fetched . . . it's really stupid." For Libby as well, characters have to be "normal people."

Boys tend to like humorous books, adventure stories, and horror stories, but their clear preference is for anything to do with sports. They read some sports novels and stories, but gravitate more toward nonfiction—newspapers and magazines like *Sports Illustrated*. Many young men in Meg's class read sports "stats" the way adults read Danielle Steele or Sidney Sheldon. Perhaps because boys tend not to seek intimate friendships during early adolescence (Messner, 1992; Salisbury & Jackson, 1996), they seem to focus more on the action of a story than on the characters. As Max says, "A book has to be easy to read and have a good plot and everything."

Terrence collects comic books. The way comics build suspense from issue to issue—placing a "to be continued" frame just at the point of a character's impending death—keeps Terrence engaged. None of the books or stories he has read for English this year related to his life, although he wishes they had. He explains, "I'm really into comics. If there [were] such a thing as superheroes and stuff like that [in literature], then I'd want to be a part of [reading]." To Terrence, as to many of Meg's male students, events and characters that are larger than life are more engaging than subtle characters or true-to-life stories.

Regardless of gender, Meg's students all agree that good books should be fairly easy, yet somewhat complicated in plot. They should not be too long or have a lot of big words, and yet they should be long enough to piqué and hold their adolescent interest. Stephen King, the clear front-runner in Meg's classroom, writes long novels. Yet boys and girls alike tend to look past the length or even take a certain pride in tackling his books, with their compelling plots and simple language. The death knell for any piece of literature is too much description. As Tiffany explains, books with "totally irrelevant" description, "like what the person is wearing," are grounds for immediate dismissal. Kathy hates books that are "all facts, where you have to get information." So do most of her classmates, both male and female. Meg's challenge will be to make reading and writing connections, so that students learn how vivid description can help to build strong plots and compelling characters. Shante has discovered the power of these connections.

> *Something happened over the summer I don't know what. All I know is that when I came back to school I was a good writer and I enjoyed writing. I am now working on a book inspired by Stephen King. About two months ago I started to read Stephen King. I loved him and decided to read all his books. I then decided to write like him. I want it to be real good and something every horror lover can enjoy.*

It is the almost addictive enthusiasm for a favorite author or genre that helps kids like Shante to "read like a writer" (Smith, 1984), noticing and appreciating the subtle nuance, as well as the compelling plot, of a good story. As Kathleen, Terrence, and their classmates learn to become writers of fiction, hopefully they will become more sensitive and critical readers in the process.

"DON'T TEACH AS MUCH": TEACHING LIKE A READER

The fact is that reading is just plain hard work for a good many young adolescents—I daresay, for a good many adults. It is an activity with little tangible payoff and one often associated with failure or ridicule. Some of Meg's students are incredibly articulate about their reading problems. One day I asked Libby to meet me in a library conference room, to read a short story silently, and to stop wherever she could to give me a "think-aloud" of what was going through her mind as she read. After several minutes of painful silence, I asked her what was going on. She admitted how easy it is for her to get distracted as she reads: "Sometimes when I read I kind of get the picture of something else that doesn't have anything to do with the story. . . . Usually, I just don't only think about people in the story."

Libby's comments remind me that in "real life," books often take us on tangents. They cause us to reflect on a thousand personal experiences, things done and left undone; dreams imagined or realized; problems that puzzle or inspire. I watch Libby in the library conference room as she struggles to articulate her response for my benefit, and I realize that there is someone else in the room with us right now—an imaginary evaluator, perhaps a former teacher, whose impatience renders Libby inarticulate when her mind takes her on inevitable detours. Another student, Tiffany, reminds me: "People have to take a rest! . . . [My mind] just stops where it wants to." "Yes, Tiffany," I want to say, "so does everyone's." Kim echoes Tiffany's observation: "Sometimes when I'm reading, I start doing all these things and I can't help it, and then I'll have to read that part over again [especially] when I'm bored."

Meg will have to teach readers like Libby, Tiffany, and Kim that their detours and momentary rest stops are productive strategies that lifetime readers use. As I ponder their comments, I wonder what it is about school that makes these young people so guilty for the divergent response, for the moments spent "off track." I want to ask, "Whose track is it, and what is the great value of staying on it," when there are other, more enticing or personally liberating tracks to follow or perhaps no tracks at all? Just read what Meg's students would teach English teachers if they could.

- *Cut down on reading . . . 'cause sometimes the kids don't really like to read; they just go through stories and don't really read them.* (Max)
- *Pick better stories. . . . I know [teachers] are trying to teach us, like, to get the meaning across and everything, but the stories are just so boring!* (Heidi)

Sometimes, their remarks reflect the offbeat humor of the young adolescent, not yet dimmed by impending adulthood.

- *Cut down on homework, have more parties, and don't teach as much!* (Tommell)

And sometimes they reflect confusion and ambivalence between a real need for engaging work and a serious concern about the social value of correct language.

- *I would tell english teachers to drill thare students on basic english skills.* (Max)

"They Force You to Read It! They Wanna Kill You": Playing the School Game

Outside the zoo of American schooling, I am convinced that "School Reading" is a rare or nonexistent species. Unfortunately, within the walls of the typical American classroom, School Reading seems to be the only animal around. Despite our best hopes, this peculiar breed of reading behavior is far from endangered. Notice how these middle school students write about the convolutions and contortions of reading for school.

- *[In school] I worry about not finishing [a book] in time and getting the details and everything. . . . I look for key words and stuff like that.* (Libby)
- *If you're reading for a report or something in school, you maybe skim through until you find the answers.* (Kim)
- *[In school] they're usually, like, ten page stories and then [there'll] be a whole list of questions, comprehension check book, and you know . . . I just remember it was such a pain . . . when you have to read something and then answer questions.* (Margaret)
- *When I was in kindergarten I had a teacher who's nickname was mrs. Bucktooth because of her two front teeth. I don't really remember learning how to read at such an early age exept when we worked in these workbooks. The thing I mostly remember was writing my name down*

on the thick lined paper all the time. I'm pretty sure that's where I got my bad thumb from. (Brittany)

Often, the very strategies that help students become successful readers in school are precisely the strategies that keep them from experiencing the aesthetic, absorbing aspects of reading literature. For example, Tonyal is an avid reader with plenty of support for reading at home. Proudly, he explains that it took him a month to count all of the books in his house, and there were "somewhere between 20 and 25 thousand." Tonyal reads at least 2 hours a day—everything from *All Quiet on the Western Front* (Remarque, 1984) to Stephen King's *Talisman* (King & Straub, 1984). Easily distracted by the presence of others in the classroom, Tonyal often re-reads school-assigned books in the quiet of his home. Yet, listen as Tonyal describes the reading strategy he uses, even for reading literature.

> If you speed read, you pick up the main topic of each paragraph and sometimes, that's the only important point in the whole paragraph. . . . [Authors] draw everything out. They say the most important thing and then they describe it, and some of the describing parts are real boring.

When I asked if strategies like speed reading might be inappropriate for reading literature, Tonyal countered that it was an especially handy way to read when he had to write a book report afterward. Besides, he remarked, even in a Stephen King novel, "some of the thought you can skip over, 'cuz it's just real boring."

Meg needs to *un-teach* kids like Libby, Brittany, Jacob, and Kim the part-to-whole strategies they learned in the scope and sequence of their early reading classes. They need to discover ways to make reading literature in school more like reading at home. As Jerrod says, "It takes all the fun out of reading when you have to answer questions about it. They force you to read it. They wanna kill you!"

In contrast to these negative perceptions of school reading, Meg's students describe their nonschool reading positively.

- *The [books] I read in school are better literature, but the ones I read at home are for enjoyment. . . . If I'm reading for enjoyment . . . I'll listen to what I'm reading. I'll visualize what's going on.* (Maria)
- *I loved to read so much that when I used to walk home from school . . . I could be seen reading books while I walked down the street. I still do that. Sometimes on the weekend I stay up till 3 o'clock reading a 200 page book. The reason I am so smart is because I read so much. I even*

ask for books on Christmas . . . my hobbie is . . . you guessed it—READING!
(Brianna)

- *If you read [books] outside of class, it'd be great. . . . But in class with
  all these people around . . . there's too many distractions, so you really
  don't get the whole concept of the book. So, I usually try to read stuff
  over again that I have to read in class, because it gives me a better understanding of the story.* (Tonyal)
- *I read now constantly. I'm addicted to books. . . . I'm a very solitary
  person, I don't like it when people bug me or interfer in my life. I think
  reading made that happen. No one thinks like I do, no one can relate
  to my thought or feelings although they say they can, there lying. . . .
  I'm attracted to books because they don't talk back, they don't pretend that they understand. That's the appeal.* (Xantippe)

In over a decade of talking with adolescents and young adults about their
reading, two requests stick with me: "Let us read what we want to read."
And, to paraphrase several students: "If you want us to read aesthetically,
pleasurably, and for a lifetime, please stop giving TESTS on literature." Kathleen
says it best: "I HATE *tests* & homework because I can study on my own!"

In a rather tongue-in-cheek example, Kieran Egan (1992) points out the
kind of damage our testing mentality can wreak on the literature curriculum.

> Imagine that you are going to see a newly released film that you are sure you
> will enjoy. You are told that, on coming out of the cinema, you will be given a
> test to make sure you have learned the names of the characters and their main
> characteristics, details of their backgrounds and of the events and the locations
> in which they take place. Your salary will be adjusted according to your per-
> formance in the test. Do you imagine that you would straightforwardly enjoy
> the film? . . . Yet we do this to students constantly after they read a work of
> literature. Shakespeare's plays were written to enlarge experience and give plea-
> sure, not to provide detail for exam questions. (p. 149)

How many of us grew up "studying" literature? And when is this perverse practice going to stop? How many decades of children (and even teachers) will grow up hating reading at about fourth grade, when the classroom
"canon" shifts from books written for and about children to books originally written for adults—when "literature" gets abstracted and parceled (or
partialed) out into literary terms and techniques, and school reading becomes
a game of mistrust and suspicion? In these crucial years, unfortunately, the
intellectual proving ground for so many young people is the sit-down exam
or the formal literary paper.

Meg's academically successful students can tell you how to play the game
of school, shifting easily from one teacher-selected response medium to

another. The trouble is that neither teachers nor students can agree on one brand of responding that allows all students to succeed. There are subtle differences in the way students perceive various forms of public responding; unfortunately, these differences often reflect powerfully on their classroom performance.

Kathleen, for example, prefers to respond in journals, where she can write "her opinion on a story." Class papers, however, call for her to "mix . . . criticism with the work, and come up with something that's, like, intermixed with both of them." Kathleen is savvy to what most teachers look for in class papers. She explains that the teacher "wants information about the books, so I'll write a little bit about the book and what I think about the book, and a little bit of how it could have been improved." When she knows she has to write a paper afterward, Kathleen reads literature for information. When there is a test, she reads with anticipation of the inevitable questions that follow her reading. She explains: "All the work that we're given in school is usually for information because we have tests and questions and answers on our project."

While Kathy prefers journals, Heidi describes them as "not one of the fun things," like class discussions or the opportunity to write her own children's books. In contrast to these purposeful activities, Heidi sees journals as perfunctory. She explains: "[Journals are] like, 'I read this book and I also did this.'" Heidi knows that in journals, most teachers look for some very specific information that has little to do with lifetime reading and seldom inspires critical or complex thought. Heidi has learned to read the implicit question behind her teachers' questions. In her words, most of them want to know one very simple thing: "Do you know what this book is about, and the author and everything?"

In her time with these students, Meg must find a way to end this game of mistrust and suspicion. If reading is so meaningless and boring in schools, assigning tests and papers will only make it more so. And if students must be coerced to marshal textual trivia in order to prove that they are reading, then just maybe it is our reading agenda, and not our students' lack of commitment, that's in serious need of overhaul. In some ways, Meg's challenge in her 2 years with these students will have more to do with *un-teaching* than with teaching.

Just as teachers' words convey many lessons about succeeding in school, they also teach about scraping by. I'd wager that if our students put as much thought into finding and enjoying books as they put into pleasing teachers or, conversely, resisting school tasks, pleasure reading statistics would skyrocket. Tommell explains his view of the system: "If I write in my journal, then I'll just make it plain, but if I'm gonna write a paper, then I'll spruce it up." Tommell prefers reading journals because they're "easier . . . [and don't] take that much work." Libby explains that journals call for her ideas, while class papers are more organized, requiring an outline and making her "more cautious of what [she's] doing." Libby doesn't like class discussions, where she's usually too shy to say anything.

Jackson informed me in an interview one day that he liked to "make up stories about people." In fact, he boasted, "I could make up a story about you." For the next 5 minutes I listened, spellbound, as Jackson wove an impromptu story about a woman named "Susan," who lived in a forest and had a "castle all to herself." By the end of the story, "Susan" had found a husband, ended up pregnant, had a baby named Carol, and lived to the ripe old age of 87. A bit winded by my whirlwind tour of Jackson's imagination, I asked if he wrote stories like these for English class. He replied, "I can make up [a story] out of my head, but when I go to put it on paper, then I say "No, no, no. It don't sound right."

I could go on about the myriad ways that Meg's students view supposedly neutral techniques like journals, class discussions, oral reports, and imaginative and more formal writings. The fact is that, because no two students can agree on their most comfortable medium for proving their competence, Meg must always offer multiple options so that all students can have a chance to succeed. Unlike the writing process, reading offers no tangible product, beyond the forms of public responding that teachers create. *Private response* is often inchoate, although socially influenced. *Public responding* gives shape and substance to private response; outside of school, it is what we do when we share our opinions of books with friends. In school, it is far more contrived, surfacing in the form of reading journals, class papers, and discussions. Each kind of public responding is perceived in vastly divergent ways by Meg's students.

Journals, for instance, can be an informal and personal place to play with ideas, assert an opinion, or discover new aspects of reading. They also can be bogus and perfunctory, a thinly disguised book report, designed to convince teachers that students are keeping up with their reading. Papers can be a way of synthesizing ideas, searching for theme and coherence, articulating a critical reaction. More often, they are the formal, carefully embellished artifacts of higher learning, devoted more to mastering form than marshaling critical response. Class discussions can be tentative, exploratory, a chance to hash out and argue about ideas. For shy students, however, they are intellectual booby traps, occasions to fall on one's face in front of teachers and peers. One thing is certain: Whatever form of public responding a teacher favors, students' attitudes toward both reading and response are powerfully shaped. Some students will learn appropriate ways of responding in school, while others will not, or cannot.

THE FLIGHT OF THE BUMBLEBEE:
TEACHING MIDDLE SCHOOL AT THE MILLENNIUM

It's an old truism that, considering the aerodynamics of the bumblebee's body and the requirements of flight, it should be theoretically impossible for bumblebees to fly. And yet, as if by magic, somehow the whole thing works. Considering all of the demands of a teaching life, on top of the incredible complexity and chaos of the young adolescent, teaching in an urban middle school like Logan often seemed theoretically impossible from my observer's vantage point. And yet, at the end of each year, I watched Meg stand wistfully by her classroom door as another group of young learners moved out to the ease of summer vacation or the broad horizons of high school and beyond. Today I marvel, as I consider all of the complexities and uncertainties that Meg managed so smoothly in the pressured world of her urban classroom.

Throughout the 3 years I spent with her, Meg constantly balanced the needs of her students to make emotional and personal connections in their reading and writing, and her guilt over not teaching them a set of objective skills. Years ago, when junior high schools dominated the American scene, it was assumed that students between 10 and 14 were moving from Piaget's (1950) "concrete operations" into "formal operations." That is, they were beginning to think abstractly about themselves and the world. For that reason, many instructional materials for junior high school students were designed to lead students up through the ranks from concrete to more abstract, "higher levels" of thinking.

Today, we know that most middle school students (and many high school students, and even adults, for that matter) have not yet moved into formal operational thinking, in the strictest sense of the term. Most middle school students need concrete connections between abstract ideas and their own personal experiences. Meg's students would read one of the Greek myths, for example, and remark: "He's just a male chauvinist!" or "She's stupid!" They seldom gravitated toward the more abstract comments on Piaget's hierarchy, like: "People shouldn't be greedy," or "Lying doesn't pay." Or, "If everybody disobeyed their parents, nothing would work right."

Meg's students may have been egocentric, but they were not egotistical. Much of the time, they seemed to believe that all eyes were on them; most felt oddly out-of-place, trying desperately to be normal and "fit in." As a result, they often had trouble looking past their own viewpoints. In reading a story, for instance, kids might shout out statements like, "She's just dumb!" or "I hated her!" rather than more reflective comments like, "I think she really cares about her daughter, even though she's mean to her." It's not that middle school students can't think abstractly; it's that they have to be helped to make connections between what is directly experienced in their lives and what might be, or what is generally true. They need to be led by caring, committed teachers like Meg into the realm of imagining, speculating, and hypothesizing. In the lore of teaching, I often hear that middle school students tire easily of abstract, intellectual tasks. Teachers like Meg will tell you, though, that lessons shouldn't be simplified, broken into manageable tasks on dittoed sheets.

Meg had to find a way to make tasks personally meaningful and related to the personal worlds of her young adolescent students. She had to capitalize on their gregarious nature and give them chances to work collaboratively with others. Experienced middle school teachers like Meg know that often what looks like hyperactivity—giggling, whispering, punching, and shouting—is actually a young adolescent's very real need to socialize and to make connections with others in the course of a school day. There is a great deal of connection between their physical and social development; both are in a perpetual and dramatic state of flux.

At the same time as Meg's students were forming important friendships, they were beginning to think of themselves as members of a larger society. Some of them were just becoming conscious of issues of race, poverty, crime, and substance abuse. For example, many of Meg's African-American students loved to write plays and poems about life in the ghetto. Interestingly, some of them came from relatively middle class homes, not the ghetto. But there seemed to be a kind of racial solidarity in writing about the problems of inner city life, so often portrayed in rap music, videos, and popular movies. All middle school students, but particularly students of color, are just beginning to articulate their experiences with prejudice, poverty, and crime. Many focus on topics of race in their personal writing. At the same time, their public schools often have limited budgets and an outdated collection of White, male, ethnically homogeneous literature. Unless teachers like Meg spend their own money on alternative books and stories, many students go all the way through middle and high school never having the chance to "see themselves in the mirror."

Lovlee, for example, likes to read "about Black history and stuff like that because you don't really learn about it in school." As a result, she does most of her reading outside of school, where both of her parents are avid readers of Black history, as well as of magazines like *Ebony*, *Jet*, and *Essence*. In her seventh-grade year, Lovlee related to only one book in Meg's classroom: Rosa Guy's novel, *The Friends*. In a situation typical of many urban schools with limited budgets and scant resources, Meg had found the only copy of this book in the Logan library and was forced to read it aloud each day to the students, because there were not enough copies for a classroom set. Meg's predicament speaks loudly and forcibly to the fact that, while we may have made a small stab toward desegregation in the early 1970s, for most students of color, public schools remain "desegregated, but unequal." Where reading materials and topics for discussion and writing are concerned, we simply must do better for students like Lovlee.

Shekia, Lovlee's classmate, is also an avid reader in her spare time, often reading books and their sequels by Black authors from Virginia Hamilton and Langston Hughes to Oprah Winfrey and Diana Ross. She explains:

> I'm not prejudiced or anything but I like for my kind [of people] to see Black families. . . . It's not that I don't like reading books, like, on White families. I read a lot of those. But mainly I like to focus on Black families.

Every 2 weeks, Shekia and her mother visit the public library. Unfortunately, the Logan library doesn't suit her needs, since it has mostly "everything . . . that you've read already." I assume, although Shekia doesn't say it, that the public library has more books by and about African-American people than her school library. On a limited budget, Meg must find a way to introduce readers like Shekia and Lovlee, as well as their White classmates, to books and stories by and about people from a variety of cultural backgrounds. Furthermore, since she is able to afford only a few books by authors outside the Eurocentric tradition, it is important for Meg's students not to "essentialize" other races and cultures on the basis of the one or two pieces of literature they read from nonmainstream cultures.

Just as Meg needs to expand her literary canon to include works from a variety of cultures, she must learn how to respond sensitively and tactfully to issues that young adolescents of her generation would have never voiced. For example, as I mentioned earlier in this chapter, young adolescents are reaching puberty earlier than a century ago, and, as a friend of mine is fond of saying, many are "using" their puberty. They are both intrigued and embarrassed by sex. They sometimes will bring it up in discussion or write about it in journals, just to see what an adult will do. Any mention of it will send them into giggles. As Meg discovered, her students want teachers to set limits where sex is concerned. And yet, they are ambivalent; they want to talk about it, and they want to forget it at the same time.

Emotionally, Meg's students seek intensity in everything they do. Part of this intensity stems from the phenomenal physical, social, and personal changes they are experiencing. Perhaps because life seems so intense for them, Meg's students have a powerful need to be recognized and listened to by others. They need opportunities to perform, to be at center stage. They also need comic relief and appreciate occasions when teachers and other students can laugh *with* them, not *at* them. Humor provides a welcome release from the humdrum of the classroom as well as the intensity of their lives outside of school.

This intensity gives them a very strong need for routine. There is a fine line, though, between comfortable structures and boring drills. In Meg's room, structures like Sharing Time and Literature Circle provided familiar and comfortable rituals, which gave her students the stability and predictability to go out on a limb and be creative. Often these rituals seemed to say, "We are a classroom family." The need for a sense of family is perhaps so acute because few of Meg's students have what would be considered a traditional family structure. Young adolescents today must face some harsh realities that did not surface as often in the days when I or even Meg went to junior high school.

For one thing, parental neglect and abuse are becoming more visible in urban, as well as rural and suburban, areas. In areas stricken by poverty, as well as more affluent settings, parental substance abuse leaves lasting intellectual and emotional scars. Today, middle school teachers must deal with a confusing array of learning disabilities and emotional problems that had no labels in previous generations. I suspect that these issues and problems were always with us, but that through more sensitive diagnosis, as well as the openness of the popular media, our society has become more attuned to these problems than ever before. Certainly, child abuse reporting laws have made these problems much more visible.

Because of our changing economy and the need for both parents to work, a good many kids live in households with parents who don't have time for them. They let themselves in each night and spend much time alone, wandering the streets, consuming junk food and video games, or finding comfort in gangs. Others are from families where one parent struggles to stay out of poverty and has little left over for nurturance or support. As Meg discovered, parental neglect and abuse know no racial, ethnic, or socioeconomic lines.

Finally, there is a great deal of media openness, which treats virginity as a social disease and makes middle school students increasingly aware of topics that would have been taboo in earlier times. There are advertisements, TV programs, and movies that promote materialism and make a life of crime seem like a glamourous occupation. For these and so many other reasons, Meg must provide opportunities for her students not only to understand but to tackle larger social problems in the community and the world.

From the top of the stairs, I look down on the swirl of young adolescents making their way toward their next classes and, eventually, their futures as literate people. I wonder if, like the bumblebee, so many of Meg's students aren't their own kind of theoretical impossibility: child-like, yet exposed brutally and too soon to the harshness of adult life; wanting to believe in the value of school, yet knowing that literacy alone will not make them successful in the world; seeking intensity in all they do, yet reaching backward always for the safety and security of a classroom family.

The following chapters take you inside the theoretically impossible, yet magically real, world of one teacher's classroom in an urban middle school. In the stories that follow are probably more dilemmas than solutions, more particularities than universal truths. Yet, Carl Rogers (1986) once said, "What is most personal is most general" (p. 110). My hope is that the particular stories of Meg and her students will invite you to reconsider and perhaps even revise your view of the broader issues of learning, literacy, and teaching in the twenty-first century.

CHAPTER 3

Falling Apart and Coming Together: Constructing a Literate Community in the Middle Grades

I always wanted to be a teacher. From the time I was old enough to pretend, I was a teacher to stuffed animals, or dolls, or anyone that I thought was teachable in my little girl world where anything was possible. (Meg, masters thesis, 1990)

From "her little girl world where anything was possible" to her early experiences as a student and eventually her career as a middle school teacher, the theme of teaching wove its way through Meg Andrews's life. During the first year I spent in her classroom, Meg was a successful and well-respected eighth-grade teacher. During the second year, this comfortable world seemed to turn on its end, as she moved into the unfamiliar terrain of her new seventh-grade classroom. In 1989, as a teacher in the school's new pilot program, Meg had agreed to begin with a group of seventh-grade students just entering Logan and to remain with them through their eighth-grade year until they graduated from middle school. What seemed at first like a minor and temporary change ended up being a year of turmoil and self-doubt for Meg, as she not only encountered a brand-new group of younger students, but attempted to introduce them to a more learner-centered constructivist classroom, based on collaborative learning, integrated language experiences, and student choice.

For some time, Meg had been reading the early work of Nancie Atwell (1987), Donald Graves (1983), Donald Murray (1985), and Lucy Calkins (1983), among many other advocates of a learner-centered classroom. As an eighth-grade teacher, she had successfully adapted and used techniques such as writing conferences, collaborative groups, independent reading, and individualized learning centers. Now was her chance to become more reflective about the process, firming up what her experiences as an eighth-grade teacher had taught her, and trying out her new curriculum with a younger group of students. She envisioned that she and her students would work together, creating their own comfortable learning community for their entire 2 years of middle school. After all, these were the promises of the learner-centered classroom in the journals and books she had been reading. Little did she realize, however, what these seemingly simple revisions would mean, for her image of herself not only as a teacher, but as a literate person as well. As this chapter will reveal, Meg constantly grappled with the many conflicts among personal choice, social collaboration, and their larger political implications in the course of her teaching for the next 2 years.

"MY OWN 'SCHOOL'-WORLD": BALANCING THE PERSONAL AND THE SOCIAL

Throughout her teaching career, Meg had tried to do more for her students than many of her early teachers had done for her. Although she had always dreamed of becoming a teacher, that dream had little to do with what actually happened in her own elementary and secondary school years. Most of her teachers were "boring or scary" and most of her work was "tedious or without meaning." Still, she wanted to be a teacher. She explained:

> I'd sit through a typical school day, and then race home to my own "school"-world, where learning was fun. If I wanted to read, I chose the books. I chose how long I would read, and then I would dream up ways to share that with my "students." If I wanted to write, I could write whatever I wanted, however I wanted, and I could choose when it was time to make that final copy and display it in my room. I put on plays in my room, had art displays, and read aloud to myself. I wrote songs, and danced, and experienced all that was good about school primarily at home.

Like mine, Meg's own experiences as a student were marked by a transmissionist view of teaching, focused largely on students' mastery in creating and comprehending texts. She was judged on how many books she read and how many language forms she could master. Realizing that this was not what she wished for her students, she turned to the many advocates of a learner-centered classroom in the professional literature. Beyond a concern for individual learners, however, Meg also embraced the notion that students develop best when allowed to collaborate with teachers and peers. Thus, borrowing from both individualistic and social perspectives, she tried to balance opportunities for independent learning with more collaborative experiences, where students could learn with and from each other.

Eventually, as a high school student in a Catholic girl's academy, she met a teacher, Sister Miriam, who successfully negotiated this balance between the individual and the social that Meg so admired. She remembered:

She was the first teacher that I had ever had who brought the kind of school that I had created for myself into the real classroom. . . . The way she taught made me feel intoxicated with all the possibilities of learning and growing. . . . We were infatuated when we read sonnets by Elizabeth Barrett Browning, angered by 1984 and its social implications, intrigued by Our Town *and the doubts that we all shared about death and the afterlife, and were truly horrified by the evil in* Lord of the Flies.*

And then we'd write, whatever we wanted, and she would sit and talk with us. There would be no red pen, and sometimes, no grade. We read and we wrote because we somehow felt that we would miss a vibrant part of life without doing so.

I will remember her forever.

In Sister Miriam's classroom, Meg discovered a talent for sharing and performing, as well as the wonder and possibility of connecting reading and writing to her own private world. Several years later, she began her own teaching career, determined to be neither boring nor scary, but to do for her own students what Sister Miriam had done for her. "My students would become engaged," she hoped, "and come to love reading and writing as much as I did. I would teach, and then, they would remember me forever. It just has not been that simple."

One day early in her teaching career, Meg was disappointed to discover that she had become more teacher-centered than she had ever imagined. She had just asked her students to write a poem about one of the gods they were studying in Greek mythology. Martin, one of the students, grew increasingly restless, then announced, "I can't do this!" She tried for several minutes to reassure him that he had the creativity for the assignment. Still he insisted, "You don't understand; I can't do this." After several minutes of Meg's cajoling, Martin stood up and headed for the door. As she tried to stop him, he wheeled around and said, "If you'd listen for 2 minutes instead of trying to be my mother with this poem thing, I'll tell you. Just listen, okay? I can't do the stupid poem because I have to go to the dentist. See." As he handed her his excuse and left the room, she knew that she had just fallen victim to his adolescent joke. At the same time, Meg thought long and hard about his last words to her: "Just listen, okay?" She wondered, "Had I become boring and scary?" She reflected on the contrast between the student she had been and the teacher she had become.

My experience as a student had told me that I should be student-centered, that I should guide and not dictate, and that my students' choices were more important than my teacher-made decisions. My experience as a teacher, however, had told me that I knew best about what my students should learn, that firm control of the classroom and the lesson led to more learning, and that my students might not always make good decisions. I had moved away from the very things that had led me to teaching.

After ten years, my first class of seventh graders changed all that. "Just listen, okay?" I'm listening now.

"THIS PING PONG THING": FALLING APART

Just as Meg's students struggled toward their own literate identities during their middle school careers, she seemed to move to a place of doubt and uncertainty, before finally moving toward a vision of teaching that balanced the social and the individual needs of her students. In the 2 years she remained with them, her journey was neither swift nor without struggle. I can remember so clearly one of the first days I visited Meg's classroom after she had begun teaching in the pilot program. I'd been in her classroom many times in the past, supervising student teachers from our program who had been placed with her. I'd always found her to be a powerful teacher: dramatic, engaging, and an endless source of creative, entertaining projects for reading and writing. Her students loved her. Usually, I'd enter her classroom and see eighth-grade students scattered around the room, engaged in various reading, writing, and oral language experiences. As students worked independently or together in learning centers around her colorful classroom, Meg was in constant motion—keeping a small group on track or holding individual conferences with struggling writers who needed her help. When she first entered her new seventh-grade classroom, neither she nor I were prepared for what it meant to leave the familiar world of eighth grade.

One of Meg's first adjustments was the fact that her classroom had moved to the seventh-grade wing of the building. She had given up the larger, carpeted room with the small stage platform in the eighth-grade wing that she had always enjoyed as the school's drama director. Normally, her commitment to the pilot program would not have necessitated a change in classroom. However, Meg's years of work as a teacher leader, offering inservice workshops for the district, and her involvement in grant projects with the university had rendered her suspect by other teachers, who had been spreading the rumor that she was favored by the administration. She suspected that her move to the new classroom was precipitated by some jealous colleagues, who had insisted that she give up the drama room and join the other seventh-grade teachers. These suspicions left her feeling vulnerable, as though all eyes were on her and her fellow teachers were hoping she would fail.

Although she didn't want to appear more entitled than the other teachers, she had to admit that the new classroom added to her vulnerability and discomfort. Not only was the room smaller, but since it had no carpeting, the noise level often became almost unbearable. In addition, since the wing was on the top floor, the windows had to be left open in the September heat, an invitation to wasps and other flying creatures, who constantly disrupted her attempts to keep order in her new room. Despite these discomforts, she tried to make her new classroom as inviting as the old, with many of the same comfortable structures and arrangements that her eighth-grade students had enjoyed.

"I Wanted It Not to Look Like a Classroom": Constructing a Collaborative Space

Expecting her seventh-grade students to be even more active and energetic than her eighth-grade students, Meg planned her new curriculum around a great deal of collaborative work. She realized that the old "desks in rows" arrangement would not work for this approach. After a good deal of coaxing, she finally was able to negotiate with the custodian to get tables and chairs to replace the desks in her room. She arranged them in cozy little clusters so that each table could comfortably accommodate five or six students as they worked together on projects. In one corner of the room, she placed her desk, and in another corner, a makeshift stage, made of black blocks of wood, with a comfortable couch and pillows for students to sit on while they watched their classmates perform.

When her noisy seventh-grade students spilled in on that first day of school, she expected them to take their seats at the tables, excited about the prospect of sitting next to and working with their peers. She wasn't prepared for what happened. The moment they hit the room, everything fell apart. Their reactions ranged from mildly hysterical to downright hostile. Years in classrooms where teachers had given them rigid structures and rules had not prepared them for the loose, collaborative structures that Meg had created. Some students interpreted the room arrangement as "party time," while others just plain resented sitting that close to people they barely knew. Meg recalled those first few difficult days.

> I can remember I had the summer to prepare and I had never taught seventh grade and wasn't familiar with the text and went all through and picked out fabulous stories. [I thought] my learning centers will work great with seventh graders because they love the hands on. I just had this picture that they'd even

be younger and maybe more enchanted with the way that I did things. Even though I moved into a classroom that was much smaller, I spent a lot of time with space and planning out. . . . I wanted it not to look like a classroom. I wanted it to look more inviting. So when they walked in they knew right away that something different was going to happen. Maybe different from what they had before but also different from the other subjects that they had during the day.

What she described on that first day shattered her expectations.

From day one it wasn't a happy, "Oh look at this!" It was more like: "This isn't a classroom!" "This isn't a real room!" And the guys were like, "This is a girls' room!" . . . They were immediately disrespectful to things. They were pulling parts off the plants! They were writing on the pillows. I was shouting, "Wait a minute! Those were 19 dollars!"

During those early weeks, Meg recalled her nagging self-doubts: "Each day I would walk in with some "tried-and-true" strategy from my eighth-grade experience, and each day I would fall on my face. . . . It got to the point where I was going home every day in tears, and I was beginning to doubt that I had ever been an effective teacher."

Despite her doubts, she tried to maintain an enthusiastic attitude. During the first week, she carefully explained her class procedures, her philosophy of reading and writing "not being separate things," and her belief that the teacher's role was to "give the students the environment in which they see themselves as readers and writers." For the first few days, as she passed out descriptions of her procedures, the students appeared relatively quiet. She took their silence to mean that they had understood and accepted her goals for them; unfortunately, they hadn't.

Her frustration grew as students continued to complain: "Why are we doing this?" "I don't want to do that!" "Where are the workbooks?" Her students had come from three different elementary schools. Only one had adopted what she called a "process-centered" view of language. Students from that school were somewhat familiar with her approach, while the other students were accustomed to traditional approaches such as ability groups in reading, worksheets, spelling books, skill drills, and memorization activities. Even when she tried some simple "get acquainted" activities, the students were resistant. In her view, they saw these activities as "touchy-feely" and were saying to her, "Let's start with page one. Stop talking to us, and getting us to know each other!" To make matters worse, Meg graded some of their work on a pass/fail basis. This further intensified their resistance. "They hated that," she said.

> [They complained], "I want to see a grade!" "I want to know whether I got a 97 or a 72 because that means something different to me." I think my initial feeling was that I worked so hard to make this work. And everything was falling apart.

What Meg and I came to call this "falling apartness" marked the first several weeks that she spent with her new group of seventh-grade students. We both watched in discomfort as she tried first one approach, and then another, to build a classroom community.

Like Meg, I believed that all children will blossom if allowed to take risks, to create and explore. Yet, obviously many of these young adolescents had spent their elementary grades in classrooms dominated by what Martin Haberman (1996) calls the "pedagogy of poverty"—a curriculum based on "teacher direction and student compliance" (p. 121). Rather than resisting such mundanity, Haberman contends that students, perhaps unwittingly, often perpetuate it. He argues, "Any teacher who believes that he or she can take on an urban teaching assignment and ignore the pedagogy of poverty will be quickly rushed by the students themselves" (p. 122). "In their own knowing but crafty way," he argues,

> students do not want to trade a system in which they can make their teachers ineffective for one in which they would themselves become accountable and responsible for what they learn. It would be risky for students to swap a "try and make me" system for one that says, "Let's see how well and how much you really can do." (pp. 124–125)

Unfortunately, Meg's students seemed most resistant to the collaborative learning tables she had fought so hard to procure. Originally, she expected to have 25 students per class. Due to a scheduling mistake, however, she was assigned nearly 40 students per class for 3 weeks, right at the beginning of the year when she was trying to establish her procedures. With too many students and too few tables, the students were right on top of each other. The space issue was only the tip of a much larger problem. Meg had failed to anticipate the distrust and fear lurking in the minds of young adolescents just entering middle school. To her disappointment, this fear often surfaced in violent and antisocial ways. At first, she couldn't help comparing these students with the eighth-grade students she was so fond of.

> In eighth grade I was used to kids walking in, they'd sit down when the bell rang, you'd say, "Open to page such and such." They'd do

> it. . . . Basically they had enough common sense to at least look like they were paying attention. And they were polite, for the most part. These [seventh-grade] kids were not polite. . . . It took me the first 10 minutes to get them settled down. . . . It was always, "You fag," "Your mother's this"—tons of name calling and explosive little things—and not only with kids around them but with kids across the room.

As Meg quickly realized, much of this offensive behavior had roots in fear. The unfamiliarity of Meg's room arrangement and her constantly changing procedures further intensified their fears as well as her own. Worried that her students didn't like her, and meeting increasing resistance to each day's carefully planned activity, she had fallen into what she called this "ping pong thing."

> I think that I was really fumbling, trying something new every day. And the kids were very aware of that. . . . They would say, "We never do the same things." They would say, "You're always trying something new." And I think they felt an unrest. I would say to them, "From now on" (I had made up this weekly schedule), we'll do this on Mondays, this on Tuesdays" . . . and then I'd come in the next day and say, "Well, scratch that, we're going to do this." And 2 days later I'd come in and say, "Well no, we're going to do it this way," because I couldn't bear one more day doing it the way it didn't work. . . . But they didn't like it. . . . They couldn't handle the switching back and forth.

Reflecting a year later on that painful period in her teaching, Meg observed: "If I had to do it over again, I'd give up some of my own personal style and start with things that were more familiar to them and gradually take them from there. But I didn't know that then." Instead, she tried to do too much, too soon. Based on her experiences with eighth-grade students, she mistakenly thought: "[They're] going to be able to work in groups beautifully, they're going to be able to get up in front of the classroom and speak. They're going to be all these on the second day of school."

Turning (in) the Tables: Collaboration and Resistance

One of the hardest things for Meg to give up in those early days were her collaborative learning tables. At first, she tried various arrangements. She had started with a U-shape, then decided to break things up a bit and arrange the tables more randomly. This only made her job more difficult:

"I was just all over the room and never knew who was looking at me."
Finally, in a rather ironic conciliation to the traditional classroom, she created rows of tables. This time, the room just felt more cramped and uncomfortable. It wasn't just the physical discomfort, however, that made
Meg's students resist the collaborative learning tables. She came to realize
that a certain level of trust would have to be built before students would
be comfortable even sitting next to each other, much less working on a
collaborative project.

> You can't ask kids to learn together if they can't even sit next to
> each other. I thought [that] . . . they would get so engaged in an
> activity that they would learn to like each other through the
> activity. And that was all backwards. They had to come to the point
> that they had to feel comfortable with each other first before they
> could even attempt a learning activity.

These overwhelming fears—hers and her students'—made it impossible
to introduce what she called "content" in the early weeks of classes. Not
only were students being assigned more work than in elementary school, but
they were even having trouble moving from one class to another. On top of
this, Meg explained that they were barraged with all kinds of social dilemmas, continually asking themselves, "Where do I sit in the cafeteria?" "Look
at all these kids I don't know." "I can't use my locker. What if I have to be
to class in 3 minutes? My locker's down on first floor so how do they expect
me to do this?"

Meg saw these social issues as "bigger than any kind of content" she
was trying to cover. Their transition to middle school meant accepting the
fact that they were not elementary students any more. "While they resented
being treated at all like babies," Meg complained, "they liked it. . . . It just
seemed like no matter what you did you just couldn't make them happy."
Instead of using her room as she had intended, the students simply wanted
to "sleep and trash the place." Rather than taking their behavior personally,
Meg attributed much of her difficulty to the perpetually chaotic lives of young
adolescents just entering middle school. She mused:

> That's how they are. Their bodies are changing. Their minds are
> changing. Their boyfriends are changing. Their hair—one day
> their hair is this way, the next day, that. The next day they say
> they'll never wear makeup and the next day they have tons of
> makeup on. That's who they are. . . . So, I just have to sit back and
> realize that . . . as soon as I think that "this is the way it's going to
> be," then I lose it.

The vulnerable and unpredictable personalities of her young students eventually led Meg to revise the collaborative environment she was trying to create. She discovered other problems with her constructivist classroom as well.

"Doing It for Me": The Performance-Based Curriculum

Since her conversion to the learner-centered classroom several years earlier, Meg had invested heavily in the idea of personal sharing and performing. Because she was a drama teacher and had always enjoyed sharing and performing herself, it seemed natural that her middle school students, with their incredible creativity and energy, would gravitate toward a performance-based curriculum. She hadn't bargained, however, on how her young students would view techniques as seemingly innocuous as dramatic performance and collaborative groups.

In the early part of the year, performing and sharing—acts she thought would be so natural and enjoyable for younger children—turned into a perverse kind of "demonstrating"—an activity performed only in schools for the benefit of grade givers, and often resulting in censure and ridicule. Meg's attempt to involve students in dramatic activities also came to a crashing halt. To her disappointment, her small stage area was rarely used for anything but a place for students to lounge and fight before class started. She remembered: "[I'd] try to get kids up on [the stage] and they didn't want to go up on it, let alone make anything for it. The day I did try to get them to make scenery, we brought out the paints. There was just no place to put anything and then they'd paint each other's faces."

Although the eighth-grade students had loved acting on the stage, the seventh-grade students were uncomfortable being set apart and asked to perform in front of others. I thought it curious that her students weren't shy about yelling comments across the room to each other in the middle of class, yet seemed to resent being asked to go up on a stage platform. Meg explained: "When they yell across the room they're still part of a whole. [But] when they'd get up there [on stage] everyone's attention [was] focused on them." She admitted:

> I lost the trust in the beginning. They kind of liked me and all that, but they weren't putting themselves in my hands and saying, "She knows exactly what she's doing." It was more like, "Who is this kooky messed up lady who never knows what she's doing? She's kind of funny but . . ."

By constantly changing the room setup, as well as her assignments and expectations each day, Meg had undercut the very trust she was trying to build. Assuming that all students would be comfortable with sharing and performing, she placed them in awkward social situations and further increased the distance among them. In retrospect, Meg admitted her confusion: "I was thinking that they're going to do this for themselves, and that's what I really want[ed]. What I really wanted then was for them to do this for me and all the rest of the kids in the class."

The double-edged sword of performing and sharing came crashing down on Meg and her colleague, Ed Jackson, one day during a mythology unit. Up to this point, Meg had always felt comfortable prodding students to perform in front of others, whether they wanted to or not. It took a bizarre and profoundly painful incident to convince her that she would never again force students to share against their will. She recalled the incident with a mix of embarrassment and humor.

> One of the guys didn't want to go up there. . . . He had to read this thing on mythology that he had done. But he didn't want to go up there. . . . Ed Jackson was in the classroom at the time. And we were both egging this kid on. We went through the stage where [we said], "This isn't a decision. You have to do this." And so finally the kid did it, and he was standing, holding the paper over his face, and all of a sudden his shorts started to grow. Well, Ed noticed it first and he kept looking at me and looking at the kid's pants. Then I noticed it and this kid is like trailing off of what he was saying. And everybody is starting to snicker. Finally the kid said he just couldn't do this anymore and he sat down. . . . Although it's a funny story, I don't think I have ever felt more sorry for a kid or more upset at myself for forcing a kid to do something. And I think that it speaks to listening to kids. Sometimes kids are being jerks and they don't want to do something because they don't feel like it. But you never know, and you don't have the right to force a kid to do something that he doesn't want to do.

Although she saw student choice and personal sharing as a key to creating a classroom community, Meg found herself in a quandary. So many young adolescents love to share and perform. But what is the fine line between personal sharing and public embarrassment? What if students *choose* not to sit next to and work collaboratively with each other, and their choices separate them along racial or gender lines? Or what if students choose to limit their choices and demand that she, as teacher, give them familiar hoops to jump through? Meg wondered, what were the limits of personal choice, and when did she, as teacher, need to step in and nudge students into what seemed like uncomfortable places?

"Write Down Your Deepest Darkest":
The Perils of Personal Sharing

Just as her approach to collaboration began to fall apart, more personal and private aspects of her curriculum, such as reading response journals, also were met with much resistance, particularly from the boys, who felt that "only girls keep journals." In addition, many of the students felt that their lives were either uninteresting or too personal to share with others they hardly knew. For many, writing of any kind had always been associated with some form of grading or evaluation (often negative) in the past. On the one hand, since the journal wouldn't be graded, many students saw no point in doing it. On the other hand, years of being evaluated by teachers for their public performances and writings had left many of them wary of sharing personal information with teachers or peers. As Meg explained, asking them to write in journals was like saying,

> write down your deepest darkest [secret] and we're all going to sit and talk about it. And then I wondered why they didn't want to do it. It was almost this hippie kind of "Let's all love one another" [approach], and they weren't into all this stuff.

Her students weren't the only ones who struggled with journals. As I observed her during those early weeks, I discovered that Meg herself was not entirely clear about what purpose journals would serve in her classroom. For example, as part of our research project, Meg and I had agreed to ask students to keep reading response journals, to which I and two graduate students would respond each week. The day that Meg set up the activity, I looked on with great anticipation. We had planned the journal exchange as a way for students to respond, not to a teacher, but to an older "pen pal" in an informal and honest way about their reactions to books.

That day, after I thought we had agreed that the journals should be ungraded and uncensored, I was shocked as Meg introduced the project by placing five different ways of responding to journals on the board and instructed her students to choose one way of responding for each entry. Predictably, the response journal turned into just another academic exercise. As the weeks wore on, students often began each entry with a label such as "paraphrase" or "analysis" at the top of their perfunctory paragraph. After a few months, we gave up on the response journal project, when it became obvious that most students were treating it like a meaningless exercise. In looking back on the situation a year later, Meg was able to find some humor in it. "They must have thought I was psychowoman!" she laughed. "Kids have the ability to forget, so I'm hoping that's how it was."

"GIVING UP MY STYLE FOR A WHILE":
ONE STEP BACKWARD

One day in the fall semester, I walked into Meg's classroom to drop something off. By this time, she had given up every shred of her usually casual demeanor, as she agonized over the ever-changing table arrangement. After commiserating with her, I said, "Maybe you should just move the desks back in." Oddly, this seemed to give Meg a sort of absolution she was looking for. Reflecting on the situation a year later, she mused:

> You were right . . . getting rid of the tables was a big step for me. That was like [admitting] "I'm giving up my style for a while." It was almost in a way like saying to other teachers who walked into the room, "It didn't work." And I wasn't ready to say that to myself or anyone else. But then I put that aside and went to the poor custodian and told him that these tables that I begged for I didn't want anymore. So then he got me these desks. The kids acted like I bought them lollipops or something. . . . The kids would go around and say, "Is this my desk?" "Is this where I can sit?" . . . What they wanted was: "This [desk] is mine and when I walk in here every day, this is where I sit. I'm not going to get challenged and nobody's going to say, 'I don't want to sit with you.'"

Unfortunately, in those first few weeks, one of the things that fell apart—and quickly—was Meg's image of herself as an innovative educator, who had no need for desks in straight lines or any of the other paraphernalia of the traditional English classroom.

At the same time that Meg realized the need to bring her students back to some of the accoutrements of a more traditional classroom, she also realized that she had begun to retreat into a traditional view of lesson planning and teaching that hung on her like an ill-fitting coat. Like a great many veteran teachers, Meg had come to rely mostly on her storehouse of experience and intuition as she planned her lessons. Traditional written plans, in her view, were usually "for someone else, not for me." Taking on the pilot program in front of her doubting colleagues, and, undoubtedly, having me in her classroom to document the whole thing, made her feel as on-the-spot as her students must have felt. She remembered:

> The thing that scared me the most was the reason that I had volunteered to teach seventh grade in the first place: I was taking part in a 2-year follow-through program. I would not only have these students for one year—allowing me to fail miserably and then

hand them over to someone who would be much better at teaching than I was—but I was going to be their English teacher for the next year also. If I made mistakes, all of us were going to live with them for a long time.

Cast in the spotlight, Meg began to doubt even her most familiar routines and practices. For example, although her informal planning process had always worked for her, she secretly had always wished that her planning book would look "like so and so's." This particular year, she saw herself as "very much into 'supposed to,'" and figured, "I've got these kids for 2 years; now I have to make sure I do it right." Unfortunately, adopting this more traditional persona only made matters worse for her and her students: "I thought I wanted to move in that direction [of] being organized. What I did was, I got much too teacher-focused. If I spent 2 hours creating a lesson plan and they didn't like it, I was pissed. It was like 'I spent all this time.'"

Ironically, however, moving to a more traditional approach not only made her students feel more comfortable, but assuaged some of Meg's fears as well. As she began to assign writing and reading that were "pretty much out of the book," she admitted, "It made me feel so much more organized in a way because I had these papers to collect and they were all on the same topic." After so many years of throwing off the yoke of traditional instruction, Meg had allowed herself to drift back to it. This move toward the comfortable and familiar trappings of organization and teacher control is somewhat predictable, considering the kind of overwhelming personal change that the New Literacy seems to demand from teachers. John Willinsky (1990) has argued:

> [The] new literacy is about more than instructional techniques for reading and writing, just as literacy is about more than the ability to score at or above the mean on standardized tests. . . . It moves teacher and student out of traditional patterns of classroom behavior. Even as the teacher must have doubts about the wisdom and workability of these new plans, she can be surprised and often hurt to find that these self-doubts are becoming a public, staffroom concern. (pp. xvi–xvii)

Fortunately, this retreat into the familiar was a temporary step backward that allowed students to build the necessary trust to move into the less familiar environment that Meg was asking them to accept. In giving up her "style for a while," Meg was able to learn something very valuable about students who are just entering a middle school from an elementary school, as these seventh-grade students were: They needed comfortable, predictable structures within which to be safe and, eventually, to be creative. Meg discovered that part of creating this safe environment involved warning the students when the seating arrangement would be changed. After trying a myriad of different and unworkable arrangements, she learned to give students a day's notice when the room was going to be rearranged for a special activity or project. Sometimes in the middle of an activity, she could rearrange the room without protest, but students still expected her to assign seats. On the occasional day when she would forget to warn them, students would complain: "Why are the desks in groups?" "What are we doing?" "You didn't tell us."

Even though students began to feel more at ease, Meg was still disappointed. Not only did she feel guilty about going against her basic beliefs about teaching and learning, but she also felt that students were in a sort of holding pattern—not as fearful as they once had been, but not really moving ahead either. Although students were busier and more on-task, they weren't doing much more than filling in answers to workbook-like exercises and answering questions in the back of the literature book. She complained, "I didn't have to fight my way through class . . . but I really wasn't getting anywhere. It wasn't doing either of us any good except making the kids calmer."

LIGHTNING STRIKES: COMING TOGETHER

Eventually, several weeks into the semester, Meg reached a turning point. She ran headlong into a literal and figurative "power failure." Eloquently and painfully, she described this incident in her masters thesis, written the following summer. Her story, as revealed in this excerpt, is a moving and poignant account of her transformation that year.

In my curriculum-laden approach to teaching my seventh graders, I had been neglecting to listen to the tremendous needs of these unique students. I had been giving them all the room in the world they needed to fail, but very little room to succeed.

Then the lightning struck, literally.

I was teaching second period when it happened. Our classroom, which is walled on one entire side by floor to ceiling windows, was surrounded, suddenly, by heavy rain, lightning and very loud thunder. The lesson that I had so meticulously planned was over. The students were laughing and screaming, and I was getting nervous, feeling that I was quickly losing control. As I was standing there, thinking about what I should do next, all the lights went out in the building. We found ourselves in a sudden, startling nighttime, except for the electric lightshow just beyond the windows. Someone yelled, "Close the shades; it's too scary." So we pulled the shades, and were enveloped in darkness.

Jason said, "I have a little flashlight." He took it out of his pocket and turned it on. I looked around the room, at each face. They were scared, or quiet, or mischievous, or pensive. But they were all listening to the storm, and staring at the light that Jason had propped on his desk.

I said, "Let's go over to the reading area." They moved over to the "living room" section of the classroom and huddled on the couches and chairs. Some students sat on the floor, leaning against the pillows. They were all around me. I could feel the heat from their bodies, and I could hear them breathing. When lightning streaked in through the openings around the shades, I could feel us all tense, bracing ourselves for the thunder that would follow. And when the thunder roared, we instantly gasped.

An administrator came to the door and told us that we would not be moving to the next class until the lights came back on. The class looked at me. I looked at them. We were not teacher and students; we were people who were beginning to enjoy the scary yet cozy situation that the storm and the power failure had created.

"Let's tell ghost stories," I whispered.

For the next hour that is exactly what we did. Everyone took turns telling his or her favorite scary story, and sharing anecdotes about where we first heard them. We were speaking and listening in a way that I had never experienced in class with my seventh graders before that day. We heard about camping trips, and how some of the kids hang out in the back of movie theatres after horror movies. We heard of terrifying stories of babysitting, and about how frightening some of the kids' neighborhoods are. Their stories were humorous and suspenseful, fascinating and just plain silly. The time flew by. The storm continued, but was now a simple punctuation to each of the stories.

After a while there was a silence. We were storied out, and everyone just sat there. I said, "Do you think it would be fun if we wrote about this?" The words were out of my mouth before I realized the possible danger of what I was saying. What if I was ruining the moment? What if I was becoming teacher again after the close time we had just shared? The question I asked put a fear in me that the storm never could have. I waited for their response.

Nicole said, "Well, if we are going to write, we need some real light. Let's pull the shades up." Two students moved toward the windows and snapped the shades into place. Everyone went to get a pencil and paper. Brian gave me a piece of his paper and a pen. Then

my students scattered themselves all over the room. Some had returned
to their seats; others sprawled on the soft furniture.
    And then they wrote. The storm raged on and the lights remained
off for another half an hour. Students wrote silently, and then began to
trade their pieces with those around them. I was passing my piece
around, and reading one after another.
    The lightning was still brilliant; the thunder, powerful. The rain
beat heavily on our windows. But there was no more fear.
    I learned that day that a very important part of teaching has to do
with validating and calming fear. And which students, I wondered, deal
with more fear than the ones who are brand new to middle school?

TEACHER ON THE BRINK

Meg learned a great many things over the remaining two years I spent
with her, as her vulnerable seventh graders eventually grew up, graduated,
and made their way to high school. By the end of the summer, she had decided to make several changes to her curriculum, allowing students choices
in whether they wished to work independently or collaboratively, in pairs or
small groups. She planned to organize her classroom into six learning centers: *Getting Started* (for students to begin writing pieces); *Drafting* (for students to work on writing alone or with others); *Publishing and Performing*
(for students to generate final copies or to combine writing with some other
art form such as drawing or acting); *Reading and Responding* (a comfortable place for students to read books of their own choosing); *Sharing* (a space
in the center of the room where Meg and her students could read and discuss literature or share their writings together); and *Conferencing* (a place
where students could meet with Meg to discuss their general progress each
week). Realizing that for most of their seventh-grade year, she "was the one
who assigned literature and writing topics, and [she] was the one who evaluated their work based on [her] perceptions of the perfect English student,"
Meg decided to give them more choices in the processes and products of their
learning.

As Chapter Six will reveal, Meg eventually moved the desks back out of
their rows and into little clusters. Her students came to value the learning
centers she set up. In eighth grade, they were given a great deal more inde-
pendence and a great many personal choices in the books they read, the topics they wrote about, and what they did each day. Her bulletin boards became laden with student texts, and her students found interested audiences
for their writing in the school and in the larger world. And just as her students found their own pathways to literacy, Meg made her way to a vision

of herself as teacher—one that rendered her more receptive and able to help her students to craft their own unique visions of themselves as literate persons.

CHALLENGING LEARNER-CENTERED CONSTRUCTIVISM

In the typical learner-centered success story of the genre Meg and I had been reading in the professional literature for the past several years, her journey should end right about here: students and teacher coming together in a tight, cohesive learning community, learning tolerance of others, and at the same time striving toward their own "personal best." During the next year, however, Meg was often disappointed to discover that the success stories of learner-centered teaching that she had read in books and journals still seldom unfolded in her own classroom in the same smooth and seamless way.

As a participant observer in Meg's classroom, and as a former English teacher myself, I resonated with her struggle. Throughout the years, I too had found myself noticing the stark contrast between learner-centered classrooms like those portrayed in the pages of *English Journal* or *Language Arts* and classrooms like Meg's and others I'd visited, or even my own classroom years earlier.

As an undergraduate major in English education in the 1960s, I had cut my teeth on Louise Rosenblatt's *Literature as Exploration* (1968) and Postman and Weingartner's *Teaching as a Subversive Activity* (1969). As a preservice teacher in the early 1970s, I protested the war in Viet Nam and the New Criticism with the same vengeance. Early in my career I had been weaned on a version of curriculum based largely on the writings of Piaget (1950), underscored by the notion that young children move from a place of egocentrism to one of increasing social involvement. I believed that individual learners actively construct their own knowledge and that one of my primary goals was to know when to "step out of the way" and allow my students to develop naturally and independently.

To me, as to Meg, the learner-centered classroom seemed a welcome alternative to the text-centered, transmissionist view of learning that so many of my own teachers had modeled and that I still saw in many of the classrooms I visited as a teacher educator. In my early days at the university, I argued passionately against an obsession with skills and texts, and pushed for a more humanistic focus on the personal growth of all students. I must admit, though, that it was no easy matter—for me or the teachers with whom I worked—to shift roles from "knowledge-giver" to "co-learner" or "facilitator," gently coaxing out each student's potential.

Throughout the 3 years I spent with her, Meg seemed to draw from both psychological and social constructivist positions in her teaching. Envisioning individual learners as active creators of their own knowledge, she tried to provide her students with the sort of personal freedom of expression she had enjoyed in her "own 'school'-world" at home. On the other hand, she recognized the inherently social nature of learning and the value of creating a safe and supportive learning community where students learned from and with each other.

In the published literature on literacy and its teaching, lines between psychological and social constructivism are not neatly drawn. Some of the most influential voices in what John Willinsky (1990) calls "the New Literacy" borrow heavily from both perspectives. In Willinsky's view, the New Literacy maintains a perpetual "dialogue or dialectic between personal meaning and public display" (p. 211). As I have argued in the introduction to this book, however, both Vygotsky and Piaget focused on the ways in which *individual learners* create knowledge. Phillips (1995), for example, has argued that "some constructivists—Piaget and Vygotsky would be quintessential figures here—have been concerned with how the individual learner goes about the construction of knowledge in his or her own cognitive apparatus" (p. 7). Thus, while Vygotsky often has been associated with the position known as "social constructivism," Phillips associates Vygotsky with what he calls an "Individual creation" view of constructivism, in contrast with what he calls a "Sociopolitical" view, or the notion that even the "rules and criteria" of knowledge construction "[are] constructed by social processes, and thus [are] influenced by power relations, partisan interests, and so forth" (p. 9).

Like Meg, I found myself shifting gradually from a psychological constructivist to a more social constructivist position in my research methods. I had broadened my focus from the individualistic perspective of questionnaires and interviews, and immersed myself in the complicated social arena of Meg's classroom. However, I found that what happened each day could not be fully explained by studying either the perspectives of individuals or the social interactions of a group. As I pored over the voluminous scripts of talk and writing I had gathered, I discovered that the places of greatest interest, tension, and contradiction were not openly articulated by the participants, but seemed to lie in the nonverbal negotiations beneath the "official" classroom text of writing or speech. These negotiations seemed to point to *sociopolitical* forces that seldom surfaced in the *words* of teacher and students, but seemed to permeate every aspect of the classroom *world*.

As I analyzed my data, a nagging voice began to warn me that the tale of the learner-centered classroom, whether based on the work of Piaget or Vygotsky, had become too much like a bedtime story—comfortable and cozy, but no longer inclusive of the diverse classroom of the 1990s. Like Meg, I was left with more questions than answers about learner-centered teaching as it relates to the social and political complexities of today's classrooms. Here are just a few: Does my responsibility as literature teacher end with enlarging the canon of literature available to students? Must I go further than letting each student see her- or himself in the mirror? Rather than promoting multiculturalism and building "tolerance" of diversity, should I not take up the business of creating an *anti-bias* classroom? Does successful teaching mean simply stepping out of the way and allowing students to reach their full potential, or must I occasionally step into the center of things, sharing what I know or intervening in the face of unfairness? And more than this, should I expand my role as bookpeddler and fellow reader toward a more political stance, bringing issues like race, class, gender, ability, or sexual orientation to the surface of reading, writing, and talk in the classroom? As Patricia Bizzell (1991) has argued, simply providing multicultural materials is not enough to create a truly multicultural consciousness among students.

> I do not mean to suggest that the pluralism of our reading material is not praiseworthy. But I do think we have perhaps been a little inclined to take it for granted that if the available material is pluralistic, then left-oriented or liberatory issues are bound to be addressed. Yet we often leave the choice and handling of this material entirely up to the students, with the result that they are often stunningly successful at normalizing or defusing material that we might have thought was politically explosive. . . . This really should not surprise us, since leaving so much up to them sends the message that what one does with politically explosive material is entirely a matter of personal choice. (p. 66)

In the area of literature teaching, "the response-based classroom" (Probst, 1984; Purves, Rogers, & Soter, 1995) presents itself as a seemingly neutral zone where each individual response is valued equally and each student's voice has an equal opportunity to be heard. But teachers and students, particularly in urban classrooms, know the fallacy of expecting all students to make the same journey over what is often strikingly uneven terrain. Just what does it mean, for example, to "give" each student a "voice"? Should the few students of color in some classrooms always bear the burden of voicing issues about racial justice and equity? As Mimi Orner (1992) has argued:

> Historically, the demand by academics and other powerful groups for an "authentic" people's voice or culture to be heard has been received by disenfranchised groups with a great deal of suspicion. Why must the "oppressed" speak? For whose benefit do we/do they speak? . . . What use is made of the "people's voice" after it is heard? (p. 76)

What, then, is the teacher's role when students don't voice larger social issues at all? What are the limits of personal choice when the social and political playing field is unequal and uneven? When Meg's students chose to segregate themselves on the basis of gender or race, what were her responsibilities to bring the topic of their chosen segregation into the center of the discussion? And is it enough to create a "safe" climate where students can "take risks," when the penalty for sharing personal stories is much greater for some students than for others? For example, no matter how comfortable my students are in my classroom, can I guarantee safe passage in the hallways or on the streets for the gay child or the victim of sexual abuse who, in the seemingly safe context of a literature discussion, discloses these personal secrets?

While both the psychological and social models of constructivism were a necessary alternative to text-based, transmissionist teaching, they still fell short in addressing these complex questions. Meg found little solace—in fact, felt increasingly guilty—when the published portraits of the learner-centered classroom failed to materialize in her own. The rather uncomplicated picture of learning and teaching in these books and articles was of little help to her, especially when the classrooms presented were often racially and ethnically homogeneous, and the learners were often above-average or verbally gifted students.

As the next year unfolded, I watched Meg struggle with the contrast between the reality of her classroom and the promises of learner-centered pedagogy. Although her curriculum moved steadily in the direction of more personal choice for students, she learned the complexities of personal choice within the web of social and political relations in her urban classroom, where students seldom behaved in ways that were egalitarian, safe, or respectful of others. Meg learned that her responsibilities involved far more than setting up classroom structures like learning centers and Sharing Circles, and letting students do the rest. As Chapter Six will reveal, she found herself implicated in the social, political, and power relations of her classroom in new and often unsettling ways. Toward the end of her year as a seventh-grade teacher, she wrote:

> When I began looking at my students, and listening to them, I saw that they form a beautiful and intricate collage. This artwork is created daily out of shapes, textures, and colors. Because of their individual experiences, these young adults have become sharp, yet lovely pieces of cut glass, wadded paper, strings of soft yarn, jagged strips of metal, opaque cloth, sparks of glitter, chunks of worn tires, splashes of paint, blocks of smoothed wood, dried flowers, and hardened plaster. And although they see me as their teacher, I am also the artist, and it is my privilege to recognize their beauty and to arrange it, just as it is, into a performance piece. In order to do this, I must study them carefully. I

also can't wish that yarn was metal, or wood was paint. I must not only accept them as they are, but also guide them to their own special place in the classroom collage.

Perhaps that's true for all of us who have had the privilege of spending a few short moments in the lives of these young students as they make their way in that long, and sometimes frightful, passage between childhood and young adulthood. Like Meg, I often found myself reading the success stories of learner-centered teaching in textbooks and journals and suddenly wishing that "yarn was metal, or wood was paint." Today, I wish for the wisdom to hold any teaching model up to the constantly changing realities of the students and schools as they are, rather than those as I wish they might be. As Johnson (1995) has argued, "Whether we as teachers choose to address it or not, students' lives come into our classrooms. Instead of wishing for other students, let us gear our work towards the students we have" (p. 229). This, of course, is a supreme balancing act—one that requires what Ayers and Ford (1996b) describe as

> an environment for learning that is wide enough and deep enough to nurture and challenge the huge range of students who actually walk through the classroom door (as opposed to the fantasy students, the stereotypes, ingrained in our consciousness from too many years of *Leave It to Beaver* or *Beverly Hills 90210*). (p. xxi)

For Meg, it meant learning to accept her students completely as individuals, while providing them with everything they needed to create their own special vision of themselves as literate people, not only in school but in the larger world beyond. Sometimes it meant stepping over that fine and precarious line between teacher as knowledge giver or even facilitator, and teacher as social activist, helping students not only to understand but to challenge and change the political and social realities that surrounded them.

CHAPTER 4

Kianna: "If You Look Hard Enough, You Will See a Butterfly"

> A young child can enter the world of a story as easily as Cinderella stepping into the pumpkin carriage. Yet the adult, attempting to capture the child's response to literature, is left peering into the carriage window and wondering how to get inside. How can adults negotiate the winding paths of children's play, talk, emotions, and movements to understand what and how they learn from literature? How can adults move their attention from the act of reading to the experience of reading? (Wolf & Heath, 1992, p. 1)

It is a few minutes after 9:00 on an October morning. Second period has just begun, and Kianna is standing impatiently at her teacher's desk. Promptness is not Kianna's strong suit, but I can almost set my watch each morning by what I have come to call her "routine." In a megaphone voice that cuts through the morning chaos, she asks permission to go anywhere outside of the classroom: to the library, to guidance, to her locker. The destination doesn't seem to matter much; Kianna is simply trying to get out of her seat and out of the classroom by any means possible. She is also trying her teacher's patience in the bargain. Kianna does this to break up the boredom, to satisfy her adolescent need for constant activity, and perhaps to place herself at the center of Meg's attention in a backhanded way.

Today, Kianna is wearing sandals, a purple, red, and blue turtleneck, and matching skirt. Gold bracelets dangle from her wrist and complement a pair of small gold earrings. Her hair is arranged in a row of bangs on her forehead and combed back into a neat wedge. Most mornings, I can spot her from across the room by her red Reebok shoes with iridescent laces. On the back pocket of today's "fashion statement" is a small scrap of paper, hanging by a piece of tape. It reads, "K-Mart: America's film developer." I can't figure out whether this touch is accidental or planned. You never know with Kianna.

This morning, Meg begins the class with a choice: "Raise your hand if you would like sharing day to be on Thursday." Surveying the raised hands, she responds, "Okay, majority rules." Before getting her Literature Circle into motion, Meg must attend to Kianna. There is a touch of irritation in her expression as she seems to be setting a boundary. It is obvious that she doesn't want to grant Kianna's request, which is some variant of "Can I get out of here and go somewhere else?" She argues, "If I say 'Okay, Kianna, you can do that,' then I have to say that for everyone." Kianna sulks slowly back to her seat. A few minutes later, I notice her leaving the room with a hall pass and wonder whether Meg gave her the pass because the request was legitimate or because it was simply easier to get Kianna out of the classroom and out of her hair.

When Kianna returns, Meg, Tommell, Martin, and Abe have started to read "Casey at the Bat" for this morning's Literature Circle. The three boys are lying on the floor, feet radiating outward like spokes of a wheel. Other students are working independently at learning centers around the room. The reading has just gotten started when Kianna storms back into the room, slamming the door and claiming to have cut her finger. She demands another pass from Meg, then strides toward the door, making sure to slam it on her way out.

Such incidents are typical of Kianna. For most of her seventh-grade year and well into eighth grade, Kianna seemed fixated on getting out of the classroom by any means possible. She rarely seemed motivated to begin, much less complete, a school task. Often I'd see her lurking along the periphery of the room; at other times, she might be leaning on another student's desk, rapt in conversation; at still other times, like this morning, she places herself squarely at the center of attention. One of her most common attention-getting devices is to begin every sentence with: "But I don't want to . . ." (go to Literature Circle, read, sit by the window, or whatever Meg just asked the class to do). Again, the content of these negations doesn't really seem to matter; they seem to be a way of resisting whatever procedures or arrangements Meg is trying to set up. Often there is a not-so-subtle manipulation in these forms of resistance. Today, for instance, Meg can hardly refuse when Kianna claims to have cut her finger, or asks to go to the bathroom, as she did earlier this morning.

Once, after a particularly long day, I asked Meg to share her impressions of Kianna. "You really want to know the truth?" she said with a wry smile. "Of course," I chuckled, waiting for the joke I knew would follow. "Oh please, please, Kianna," Meg intoned, with hands clasped together and eyes turned heavenward. "Please get sent to Allen School so I don't have to deal with you anymore!" Allen is a special school for what the district calls "at-risk" students—those who have been arrested, are pregnant, or are otherwise, in the opinion of the district, not appropriate for the "regular" school setting. Of course, Meg's remark is tongue-in-cheek; but having watched Kianna for several weeks, I can understand her frustration.

Meg and I both knew, however, that Kianna wasn't easily pigeonholed. Just when I thought I had captured her onto my tape recorder or the pages of my notebook, she'd do something to challenge and complicate my impressions. And even then, her changes were rarely lasting. Like many of the young adolescents I came to know, she seemed to linger on the edge of young adulthood, almost slipping over, then pulling herself safely back into childhood at the last minute.

As I came to discover, her relationship with reading was equally sporadic and elusive. In the early part of her eighth-grade year, I began to believe that she had, indeed, stepped into the imaginative world of literature at some time point in her life; yet, more often than not, I found myself, in the words of Wolf and Heath at the beginning of this chapter, "peering into the carriage window and wondering how to get inside." As an adult, and therefore an authority figure to her, I often found myself on the outside looking in, as I pondered if she would ever come to consider herself a lifetime reader. I began by exploring her memories of reading as a young child.

"TRYING TO READ ON MY OWN"

My name is Kianna Moore and I'm going to [write] about how I felt in my past years reading and writing.

When I was around the ages of 3–6 my mom use to read me bedtime stories every night and I really enjoyed that a lot. I would say I enjoy people reading to me instead of reading myself. I would say I like for people to read to me instead of reading to myself because I like to relax and sit back while listening to a story instead of being frustrated trying to read on my own.

When I reached the age of 10 I had learned how to read on my own well and I began to read to myself. Every once in a while I would get stuck on a word and I would be scared to ask my teachers for help because I thought she would try to make fun of me but when I was home reading I could always ask my mother to help because I knew she would never make fun of me, she would only try to encourage me to try harder and I would suceed. (from "Me, Myself as a Reader and Writer,"
5/30/1990)

In hundreds of interviews with adolescents over the past decade, I've begun to expect many of them to register a dislike for reading and writing around fourth or fifth grade. National studies of literacy (Applebee, Langer, Jenkins, Mullis, & Foertsch, 1990; Langer, Applebee, Mullis, & Foertsch, 1990) have reported similar findings on a larger scale. In Kianna's case, I wondered whether the fact that she was an African-American student might have made her particularly sensitive to criticism from her reading teachers.

Research has demonstrated that as students are reading aloud in elementary school, teachers often stop them to correct dialectical miscues, such as "He be going," while they tend to ignore nondialectical miscues (e.g., "Put it over there," instead of "Put it over here.") (Cunningham, 1976–77). This kind of intrusive criticism has dire consequences for many students who do not naturally speak or write in a standard dialect. Keith Gilyard (1991), for example, has observed:

> The third grade is cited as a critical juncture in the elementary school education of African-American, urban, public school students. . . . These children for the most part enter public school with normal to high levels of self-esteem and a matching eagerness to learn, but typically fall behind academically by the end of the third grade, as they have found academic pursuit unfulfilling and have begun to retreat from the process. . . . African-American students will indeed develop the academic ability to succeed throughout public school if they can but weather the early years, can but get over the hump. (p. 61)

In all the time I spent with Kianna, I was never sure whether she would ever get over "the hump" that Gilyard describes. Early in her seventh-grade year, she observed, "I don't do a lot of reading but I like reading." Reading at home was usually a warm and pleasant experience for her. She explained that her sister, who has a handicapping condition, "reads a lot . . . she'll read any kind of book." Her mother "reads a whole lot of different books, [for example] *The Color Purple* and *Flowers in the Attic*." Although Kianna says that "everybody in [her] family likes to read," her family members rarely trade or suggest books to each other. With the exception of the two books she mentioned, she is hard pressed to recall what her mother or her sister might be reading at any time. Except for her friend Brenda, Kianna's peers don't appear to read at all. She explains, "They probably think like they're too cool to read."

On her own bookshelves, Kianna has mostly mysteries, "like *Encyclopedia Brown* and stuff." Mysteries, especially those about girls, are her favorite genre; Lois Duncan is her favorite author. When asked what is so special about mysteries, she replied, "Probably because when I read [them] I try to figure what's going on." Kianna is a very plot-focused reader, who abhors what she calls "dull" or "dead" books (usually those she reads in school). "In school," she says, "I read because I have no choice but to read, or I get a bad grade."

I don't like reading in school. Like on Fridays we have to do that silent reading stuff. I don't like that . . . because it be dead. You just sit and read and read for a whole 25 minutes. Sometimes I don't have my book and we have to read what the teacher gives you to read. Mrs. Andrews will give us stuff about baseball. It be dead!

To Kianna, "dead" literature is "a story with no excitement in it, like *Old Yeller* or something like that. . . . It's dead! It's about a dog!" In seventh grade, reading for the classroom and, I suspect, most school activities fell into the "dead" category. Besides the lack of interesting reading materials, there was also the threat of being evaluated that seemed noticeably absent from her memories of reading at home. When I asked about the differences between home and school, she replied:

> *Kianna*: I read more carefully.
> *Susan*: In which situation?
> *Kianna*: When I have to take a test, when I have to read, whether it be a paragraph or whatever, and then have to take a test on it the next day, I have to read it carefully the first time.
> *Susan*: What about for class discussion? Do you read differently?
> *Kianna*: No, I read the same way.
> *Susan*: Why do you have to be careful in that situation?
> *Kianna*: Because the teacher might penalize you and you might look stupid shouting out the wrong answer.

I find it interesting that Kianna seems to have no qualms about openly challenging the procedures and rules of Meg's classroom, yet she seems afraid of going out on a limb with a response that might be viewed as a "wrong answer." This fear of looking stupid in a school task, where she might be expected to demonstrate competence or intelligence, surfaced in other situations as well, as I began to search for other explanations about why Kianna seemed so uninvolved with reading for school. Toward the end of her seventh-grade year, I asked her what pieces of literature seemed to relate most to her life. Although stories read for school rarely engaged her, those that did usually had characters that reminded her of herself or friends. She described one story, for instance, about a girl who "felt left out of her family and everything. And I used to feel like that, but I talked to my mom about it and stuff and now everything's OK." In the same vein, she enjoyed a chapter from Richard Wright's *Black Boy* (1945) because it reminded her of a time when her mother forced her to "act tough" with a bunch of children in a new neighborhood. She described another favorite story about a girl who, in her words, "was real quiet [but] like, when you mess with her, though, she could fight and everything. And, I'm a quiet person, but I keep like everything to myself and then when I let it out, I just go off."

I was astounded to hear Kianna describe herself as a "quiet person," and immediately thought about what a surprise this would be to her teacher. Why did she see herself so differently than we did? And why, so much of the time, did she appear to be losing her composure and "going off" in Meg's classroom? Kianna appeared to have mastered the art of being "bad"; being a good student and succeeding in school seemed much more frightening and tricky for her.

I also began to wonder whether what Meg and I perceived as "acting out" actually might be a form of resistance to losing what Kianna saw as an important part of her identity. Banks (1993), noting the work of Fordham and Ogbu (1986), observes that

> African American students often experience academic difficulties in the school because of the ways that cultural knowledge within their community conflicts with school knowledge, norms and expectations. . . . These students believe that if they master the knowledge taught in schools they will violate fictive kinship norms and run the risk of "acting White." (p. 7)

Obviously, Kianna is both Black and female. Unfortunately, the issues surrounding this dual identity often have been glossed over in the literature on race and gender. As McCarthy (1996) has argued: "Minority women and girls have radically different experiences of racial inequality than their male counterparts, because of the issue of gender" (p. 39). Similarly, Giroux (1991) argues that current theories of resistance "rarely take into account issues of gender and race," focusing "instead on males and class issues" (p. 287). He contends that "the failure to include women and racial minorities in such studies has resulted in a rather uncritical theoretical tendency to romanticize modes of resistance even when they contain reactionary racial and gender views" (p. 287).

In her study of a predominantly African-American high school in Washington, DC, Signithia Fordham (1993) concluded that Black teenage girls are more likely than any other group to be shunted to the margins of the classroom. As a result, they typically try to achieve academic success by being "phantoms in the opera." That is, they either remain "voiceless" or, like Kianna, they impersonate "a male image" (p. 10). Citing a term coined by Grace Evans (1988), Fordham argues that "those loud Black girls" often unwittingly participate in their own exclusion by engaging in behaviors that alienate their teachers. In Fordham's study, "loud Black girls" were marked by "striking visibility and presence—(these young women were known by everyone at the school and did not try to minimize the disruption that their visibility implied)" (p. 11). For example, Rita, a young woman in Fordham's study, refused to conform to her teacher's standards of good behavior. Instead, like Kianna, she "live[d] on the edge, self-consciously stretching legitimate school rules to help her retrieve a safe cultural space" (p. 16). Unfortunately, Fordham notes:

> Rita's consistent practice of breaking the cultural assumptions so valued in the school context often [led] her teachers to erase their perception of her as a bright, intelligent person. Also, the "slam dunking" part of her persona that propels her to the margins of good behavior, without actually forcing her into the realm of "bad behavior," makes "shrinking lilies" out of most adults who interact with her or, alternatively, motivates them to avoid contact with her, if that is an option. (p. 17)

Unfortunately, I did not fully explore these issues personally with Kianna, since she was often reticent to talk openly with me, and I felt that bringing up the topic of race might further alienate her. Perhaps I too had become a "shrinking lily" in her presence. I did, however, observe what seemed like a constant struggle between behaving in school-sanctioned ways and disrupting Meg's classroom routines. At the heart of both kinds of behavior seemed to be a constant thread: putting herself at the center of attention, one way or the other. Of course, much of this need for attention is typical of a good many young adolescents. I sensed, however, that in Kianna's case it had something to do with refusing to be relegated to the margins of the classroom, as well as the boredom she associated with most school tasks.

In her book, *Unbank the Fire: Visions for the Education of African American Children* (1994), Janice Hale argues that schools often fail African-American children by misinterpreting their sociability and need for constant activity as signs of poor academic ability. Hale argues that rooted in traditional West African culture is a strong performance orientation. She observes, "African American children learn at an early age how to perfect performer roles. They see this expressiveness in African American preachers, athletes, singers, and dancers and also among ordinary African Americans" (p. 202).

Often, however, students like Kianna frustrate teachers because their behaviors do not conform to traditional notions of the peaceable classroom. These "pariah behaviors," as Hale terms them, set up a damaging cycle for African-American children. Teachers interpret them as signs of poor attention or academic inadequacies; and as a result, students, sensitive to nonverbal cues, view their teachers as unfair and oppressive. Hale argues that "the miscommunication between the teacher and the child breaks down the relations between them until the child begins to form an alternative to the teacher's organization of the classroom in an attempt to become visible" (pp. 156–157). Often, this "alternative" involves ignoring the teacher's authority and turning to peer groups for attention and support. Citing McDermott (1987), Hale argues:

> In pariah classrooms, to attend to the teacher is to give the teacher a leader-ship role; to attend to the peer group is to challenge the teacher's authority. Those who attend learn to read; those who do not attend do not learn to read. (p. 161)

Hale suggests that White children may be more successful in school because of their "greater tolerance for monotony" (p. 203). She argues:

> White children might not perform as well if they were faced with format varia-tion and stimulation or if they were asked to utilize movement more. Likewise, perhaps, African American children are not as successful in school because they are more intolerant of monotonous, boring tasks and the sterile, unstimulating school environment. (pp. 203–204)

I suspected that being corrected in class, as well as some earlier negative experiences with White teachers, might be one reason why reading for school seemed to have little or no fascination for Kianna.

"They're Not Really Real": Story Characters and "Real People"

Eventually, I came to learn that Kianna placed the most importance on her interactions with people in her social world. By contrast, characters in the imaginary world of literature were not nearly as compelling. I first no-ticed this distinction between "real people" and characters in literature as I compared her description of someone she knew with her description of a character from a story she had read. Early in Kianna's seventh-grade year, I had asked all of Meg's students to write a brief description of someone their own age whom they liked. This was followed by a brief description of some-one their own age whom they disliked. Later, I asked each student to listen, on separate occasions, to two short stories being read aloud and to write impressions of the characters they liked most and least. Analyzing these open-ended responses gave me an idea of any differences that might emerge be-tween the depth and complexity of their perceptions of peers and characters (see the explanation of "cognitive complexity" in Chapter One).

In describing her friend, Kianna seemed to focus on a number of inter-nal attributes. She wrote:

_____ *is a nice girl. She is very nice [to] others. If she does not like you she will not agree and fight you. She will just ignore you.*

She's one of my best friends. Every time I need her she is there for me.
She is black. She dislikes rude and snotty people. She cheerleads with
me. Sometimes she comes to my house after school.

Although neither is particularly long, I noticed a rather striking contrast between Kianna's description of her friend and her rather cursory description of Chuck, the protagonist in Robin Brancato's short story, "The Fourth of July" (1985): "Chuck is a person who somehow lost a amount of money and he says someone stole it witch that might be true"

Kianna is typical of many readers who describe story characters in rather cursory, external terms, yet seem to describe people they know in terms of more internal personal attributes and characteristics. In an interview during the spring of Kianna's seventh-grade year, I explained that sometimes we look at other people "on the outside" and sometimes we look "inside" for explanations of why they do what they do, or for information about their personalities. I then asked her to look over her descriptions of peers and story characters and talk about the differences.

> *Kianna*: People in the real world you can really find out things about them and you really know how they are. Characters in the story you don't know them. You just know them by what you read.
> *Susan*: So the author doesn't really give you a key to what's inside of them. Do you think authors meant for you just to look on the outside?
> *Kianna*: I don't know.

I pondered why Kianna found real people so much more compelling than story characters. I had noticed a similar attitude on the part of a great many adolescents and young adults in my previous studies, and I'd experienced this same attitude among some of my students as a secondary teacher as well. What made some readers who had the capacity to think about the inner qualities of others, unable or unwilling to do so in the world of literature? One possibility may be that they are not taught to do so; another may be that they belong to a culture that places more value on real-world experiences than on experiences in the imaginary world of literature. Wolf and Heath (1992) have suggested that

> in some cultures, children learn to attend to the expectations of human inter-actions and the logic of real-world actions as primary; these children found questions about fictionalized plots of stories in books curiously framed in a world of rules peculiar to learning to read in school. (p. 179)

Somehow, during her years as a student, Kianna had learned to view most reading, but particularly reading for school, as divorced from her real life and therefore largely uninteresting. Gradually, through participation in the varied activities of Meg's classroom over the course of 2 years, Kianna discovered her own particular way of bringing her own personal experiences and viewpoints into her school life. However, she was able to make this connection through writing and oral language more often than through reading. Only occasionally was she able to make personal connections with the literature that she read for school. When she did, it was usually because the reading had been presented in a dramatic way, much like the events of real life.

Reading as a Dramatic Event

Kianna was able to connect with literature when someone read it aloud to her or when she participated in dramatic activities as part of her reading. I recalled her comment in her "Myself as a Reader and Writer" piece: "I like for people to read to me instead of reading to myself because I like to relax and sit back while listening to a story instead of being frustrated trying to read on my own."

Over the years, Kianna had equated reading for school with the fear of being wrong. Even at the age of 10, when she had learned to read on her own, she remembered getting "stuck on a word" and being scared to ask her teacher for help for fear of being ridiculed. At home, on the other hand, her mother would encourage her to "try harder," and she "would succeed." Of her elementary school experience, Kianna remembered: "In my past grades my teachers always read to us. Like last year, I didn't have a reading book. We read stories. At _____ [her elementary school] we'd read one book and then change to another book."

This dramatizing or reading aloud seemed essential in helping Kianna to relate to literature in school. For example, in seventh grade, Kianna's class read "All Summer in a Day" by Ray Bradbury (1987) and "Nancy" by Elizabeth Enright (1987). Interestingly, even though Kianna described these stories as not particularly relating to her life, she liked them both. "Probably the main reason I liked them," she explained, "is the way Mrs. Andrews read them. She didn't read them all dead. She put feeling into it." In contrast, she saw reading on her own as "just reading," a process in which "there was just nothing."

Kianna's favorite book during her middle school years was *The Friends* by Rosa Guy (1973). This is a book about two young girls growing up in Harlem. One of the characters, Phylissia, has moved to New York from the West Indies and has great difficulty adjusting to her new life. She is befriended by a tough young girl named Edith, who has become the sole support of her large family, since her mother died and her father disappeared. For once, Kianna seemed to relate to the characters in this book. She described Edith as "really bummy and nobody liked her." Phylissia, Kianna explained, was "embarrassed to be with the girl [Edith] but she really liked the girl." It helped that Edith reminded Kianna of someone she knew at Logan.

Since she had only one copy of the novel, Meg read aloud several chapters of *The Friends*, rather than asking students to read it on their own. Kianna remembered this oral reading fondly; but she was actually enticed into the book through a creative dramatics activity. One day, Meg had asked groups of students to role play different versions of a scene where Phylissia is being bullied by a girl in her class and Edith comes to her rescue. This dramatic enactment helped Kianna to make a personal connection with the novel. In an interview, she described how she had read *The Friends*: "At first [I read it] just for the story, because Mrs. Andrews read this to us, and we didn't pay much attention to it at first. . . . When I first started liking it was when Edith first walked into the class [in the book]. We did a lot with this, acted it out." The raucous enactment of the fight scene in the book seemed to appeal to Kianna's energy level, as well as her need to relate literature to real-life situations.

I decided to explore Kianna's general approach to reading, in terms of Vipond and Hunt's (1984) three orientations: "story-driven" (for action and plot), "information-driven" (for information), or "point-driven" (with a concern for the author's intentions or meaning).

> *Susan:* Sometimes [when] we're reading, we read for different purposes. In other words, sometimes . . . we just read for information. We want some information on [what we're reading]. Or sometimes we read to get the point of it—why the author is telling you this. Sometimes we just read for the story—just for the reading. . . . Generally, when you read, do you read [for the story, for the point, for information] or for a combination of all three?
> *Kianna:* Most of the time, when I'm reading in class, I read for information.
> *Susan:* Do you really? What about when you're not in class?
> *Kianna:* [I read for them] all.

Kianna seems to be both "story-driven" and "point-driven" in her reading when she can connect it with something in the real world, or when important adults recommend literature to her. Reading for school, as opposed to reading at home, offers very few of these personal connections. When she did occasionally become interested in school-sponsored reading, it was because adults like the librarian or her teacher had somehow managed to interest her in a particular novel or story. For example, Kianna and many of her classmates admired and respected Ed Jackson, the artist in residence at Logan, who was a frequent visitor and co-teacher in Meg's class. He managed to entice Kianna into reading a chapter from Richard Wright's *Black Boy* (1945). This was one of a very few school-sponsored stories that she had recalled reading in a point-driven, as well as a story-driven, way. She explained: "Mr. Jackson had told us a story that had happened to him. And so, we didn't have to read this, but I read this because I thought the story was interesting." Apparently, her admiration for Ed Jackson, a charismatic African-American actor and teacher, contributed to her enjoyment of the story. During the 2 years that I observed him, Ed Jackson served as a role model for many of the students, but particularly for African-American students like Kianna, whose race was often underrepresented in the literature being read and who often felt on the margins of academic success.

Out of nearly 40 pieces of literature that she had read in Meg's classroom during her seventh-grade year, Kianna chose only three texts that "related to her life:" *The Friends* by Rosa Guy (1973), the chapter from Richard Wright's *Black Boy* (1945), and "All Summer in a Day" by Ray Bradbury (1987). Again, it did not surprise me that two out of these three texts had African-American protagonists and the third was female. During my time at Logan, I was continually struck by how important it is for middle school students to see themselves in what they read and to represent their real lives in their writing and speaking. This observation seems crucial in view of the findings from national studies that, despite many calls for multicultural and student-centered approaches to literature, the curriculum remains traditional in nature, typically excluding non-White and women authors (Applebee, 1992b). Kianna seemed to typify the young adolescent's need to make strong connections between her own life and her school activities. Eventually, she was able to make some of these connections, but not without the help of her teachers and peers.

"TWO MINDS WORKING TOGETHER": LITERACY AS SOCIAL COLLABORATION

It was in October of Kianna's eighth-grade year that I first began to notice a change in her attitude and classroom demeanor. I had just walked into the classroom one morning to see Meg, Tamesha, Lovlee, Angie, Matthew, George, and Sandra in Literature Circle, engaged in an animated discussion about whether Pygmalion in the Greek myth hated women. Angie was shouting, "There are lots of guys that think they don't like women, but they do!" George countered, "Why didn't he turn gay?"

In the midst of this discussion, my attention turned to Kianna. She had chosen not to go to Literature Circle that morning and seemed to be handing me a note from her desk. At the last minute, she pulled it back and, with a wry smile, tore it up. I noticed that she and Brandy had pushed their desks together and were whispering furiously. As usual, I assumed they were talking about something unrelated to school, perhaps an incident with a boyfriend or a tasty bit of gossip. I was surprised to discover that Kianna had seated herself in the "Getting Started" Center and that the two girls were actually writing something. After a few minutes, I sidled over to Kianna's desk, hoping not to break the spell of the moment. Both girls appeared pleased to have been noticed. I asked them if I might see what they were writing whenever they got to a stopping place.

A few minutes later, Brandy walked shyly over to my desk and handed me a poem. It was a piece about teenage pregnancy, titled, appropriately enough, "Affection Versus Protection." I could see that Brandy and Kianna were waiting for my response, and perhaps my embarrassment, which I tried desperately to hide. Without missing too many beats, I replied, "I like this poem. I think it may send a message to girls who might be thinking about this sort of thing." After a brief conversation, Brandy walked proudly back to her desk, where Kianna was waiting for my "very good" sign. From across the room, I whispered, "I'd like to have a copy of that poem when you're done."

It was several minutes before I looked up to find Brandy again at my desk. Instead of the "Affection Versus Protection" piece, she handed me a neatly computer-typed copy of a poem that Kianna had written several days earlier. I had heard it in Sharing Time and had complimented her on it afterward. Apparently Kianna hadn't forgotten the compliment. I wondered, though, why she sent Brandy over to my desk with the poem, rather than coming to me herself. Her poem, entitled "Colors," would be my first brush with the riddle of contradictions that was to become my impression of Kianna over the 2 years I came to know her.

Colors!

Colors—
The color white is just right
For everything good—
A wedding for example—
The brides dress would most likely be white.
Colors—
The color black is just right
for sad times—
a funeral for example—

black is most likely worn at funerals
a funeral of course black is worn
Colors—
Those two colors Black = N = White just
don't seem right.

Kianna felt a special pride in this particular poem. She had received many compliments, including mine, when she read it the week before in Sharing Circle. More important, it had sparked a good discussion with her classmates about racial stereotyping. In a note to Meg at the end of her eighth-grade year, Kianna recalled that it was the best piece she had written all year.

> *I really enjoyed writing and sharing my piece (called "Colors"). I got to express feelings toward the situation I was writing about and it also made people realize the truth about the two colors black and white. . . . I was very proud of my poem. Others really like it. (6/14/91)*

Later that year, Kianna had a chance to read this poem aloud to 200 of her classmates at an assembly. Interestingly, despite her brash and animated behavior in Meg's classroom, Kianna chose to ask Samantha, one of her class-mates, to read it aloud for her. I began to realize that, although Kianna was perfectly comfortable disrupting the classroom routine, it was difficult for her to share something that she was invested in. Being disruptive seemed to come naturally to her; putting herself "out there" as a writer was much more difficult. In a conversation with me much later, she observed that perform-ing in the assembly "was scary for [her] because [she didn't] like getting up and talking."

Kianna is typical of a great many middle school students who can be so irritatingly outspoken in one situation and so withdrawn and shy in another. Interestingly, it was through the support and encouragement of her peers that she would come to see herself as a writer and begin to channel some of her incredible energy into her fledgling identity as a literate person. As she began writing collaboratively with friends, I noticed a shift in her enthusiasm for school tasks. When I asked her about this, she replied, "It was easier with two minds working together. If I was doing it by myself I probably would have gotten stuck."

"Colors Such as a Rainbow": Developing a Literate Identity

After her success with her poem "Colors," Kianna tried other poems about colors in the coming months. This piece called "The Colors of the Puddle" is an example of what I came to call her "color" poems.

The Colors of the Puddle

These colors of this puddle
are ordinary colors you see everyday
          —but to me they're very important
they're important to me because
these are the colors of life
          If I had no life I wouldn't be able to see these colors everyday.
So, of course I give thianks to God everynight before I ly my head
          down to sleep for letting me see these colors another day
colors of the puddle

Throughout her middle school years, Kianna seemed in a state of sporadic, but steady transformation. At first blush, an observer might sum her
up as a rather typical, highly energized young adolescent, trying desperately
to get attention. Looking closely, however, I saw that behind these "ordinary colors you see everyday" was a young woman of great complexity. She
was outspoken in her classroom interactions with teachers and peers, yet
could turn incredibly shy when asked to share something that was important to her. I began to suspect that she used her noisy persona to mask a great
deal of sensitivity and insight. "The Butterfly" tells the story of just how
elusive this sensitivity was.

The Butterfly

You may see it—
You may not—
if you look hard enough you will see a butterfly
made up of colors—
colors such as a rainbow are in this butterfly
just look hard and you shall see
this certain butterfly
created by me

As I came to know her, I realized that Kianna was indeed a "butterfly made
up of colors." From her neon shoelaces to her lightning transformations of
personality and mood, she posed a constant challenge to her teacher to "look
hard," past the booming voice and the clever manipulations to discover the
shy young adolescent, just waiting to transform into a writer.

From Poet to Playwright

In her eighth-grade year, as Kianna's theme of colors wove its way into
poem after poem, her theme of teenage motherhood eventually wended its

way from poem to play script. One day, as I was waiting for second period to start, 21 students, as usual, came streaming and screaming into Meg's classroom. Gary stormed through the door in iridescent jeans and a university tee shirt, announcing in full view of Meg, "I hate this class. It's so boring!" Rameka stormed in next, demanding, "Where is my pass?" I had to laugh at the candor with which these students had started to relate to Meg, since she had opened up so many of the choices in her room. If Meg was bothered by this, she didn't let it show. She began with an announcement: "I found a really good documentary to show you but I couldn't get it for today. I'd like to switch days. I'd like to have individual conferences for today. What I'd like is for everyone to have a seat. . . ."

As Meg was making her announcement, Kianna was standing with Maisha, Shavonne, Donnell, Matthew, and Brandy. In the middle of Meg's announcement, Kianna registered a loud complaint: "But we have to work on our play!" I hadn't realized until this morning that this group had been writing a play. It turned out to be a spinoff on Brandy and Kianna's "Affection Versus Protection" poem, now called "Tina has a Problem." I could see the disappointment on all of their faces, as Meg explained that their group couldn't go to the library today because it was closed. Reluctantly, they walked over to the Writing Center, where they soon were involved in an animated discussion. Meg had just stapled Mark's poem onto the bulletin board when she noticed a loud commotion in the Writing Center. She walked over and began giving Kianna's group directions for how to break up the task. "Kianna can write the dialogue," she said. "Matthew writes/designs the stage; someone else does costumes." Barely stopping to notice Meg's directives, the group pushed on noisily, grabbing for the pencil and shouting instructions to each other. I sat there amazed that Kianna was not only participating, but seemed to be actually directing other students, in a school-related task.

A few days later, I came to observe the Friday Sharing Time. Meg had just introduced the procedure, offering some options to students: Those with finished pieces could read them aloud, while those with pieces-in-process could read a draft and ask for feedback. She continued to talk about the purpose of Sharing Time: "It's not about me. It should be more focused on you." Barely holding back her excitement, Kianna interrupted: "Please, can we go first!" This was the first time I observed her getting excited about sharing her writing. She began to read the "Affection Versus Protection" poem, now titled "Teenage Mom's":

Teenage Mom's

Young ladys today.
just want to get laid
think about affection

with no protection
end up 3 months pregnant
knowing now she regrets it
the babies now 4 months
and the mom is going nutts
O—how she hates taking care of this kid
but only if she would have thought
about the kid
back then

I suspected that Kianna's fascination with teenage pregnancy was not an idle preoccupation, considering the fact that the highest number of babies born in the African-American community are to mothers between the ages of 12 and 20. As Hale (1994) explains:

The greatest barrier I see to success among African American girls is a high fertility rate at a young age. . . . Girls give birth at a time when they are unable to be financially independent and at a time when their bodies are not well pre-pared for childbirth. These young mothers do not receive adequate prenatal care, and their children do not receive adequate postnatal care. (pp. 196–197)

Along the same lines, Sadker and Sadker (1994) have noted that

More than a million teenage girls become pregnant every year. The Alan Guttmacher Institute says that approximately 44 percent of all teenage girls in the United States and 63 percent of African-American teenage girls will become pregnant at least once. (p. 115)

Obviously this social reality was not lost on Kianna, as she continued to explore the topic of teen pregnancy in writing throughout the rest of the semester. During Sharing Time that day, she seemed so engaged in reading her piece aloud that she didn't even notice Marcus giggling at all of the sen-sitive spots. At the end of her performance, Meg asked, "What are you read-ing now?" There was a silence, then Kianna mumbled something unintelli-gible. She didn't seem to want to talk about her reading with the same enthusiasm as she had just shared her writing. Changing the topic somewhat, Kianna blurted out that Meg should give Ms. Randolph, her reading teacher, "some tips on letting us read our own stuff."

Instead of pushing Kianna about her reading, Meg moved on. After several students had the chance to share, Maisha yelled, "Me and Shavonne wrote a play." In a few moments, they were assigning parts. Apparently, they had written some of their classmates, as well as Meg, into the cast of charac-ters. Maisha directed the action: "Ms. Andrews, you be the teacher, Kianna, you be . . ." The parts were assigned and the play script was read aloud after much pushing and many false starts. During the reading, students forgot to read, bungled their lines, and read too quickly to be heard, but their enthusiasm was undeniable.

LITERACY AS PERFORMANCE

Around this time, I noticed that several groups of African-American students in Meg's classroom had been organizing themselves into play writing groups. Many of the plays were more prose narratives than dialogues, and most were reminiscent of television movies or commercials, based on "real-world" problems and issues. Typical topics were drug abuse, teen pregnancy, and crime. Often, stage directions were interspersed as part of the dialogue, making the scenes difficult to stage. In one part of "Tina Has a Problem," for instance, students were perplexed at just how to stage the line, "Tina and her boyfriend make love on the living room couch." They solved the problem by having a male student push "Tina" off the stage, presumably into another room. I noticed that students often mixed prose and dramatic dialogue in their play scripts, seemingly caught up in details of plot, yet not always sure how to move it along by pure dialogue and action.

In contrast to Literature Circle, an activity created and sponsored by Meg, these collaborative writing groups seemed to have sprung up on their own. It was in this informal social situation that Kianna began to bloom. In these groups, her natural leadership abilities and her need for activity and motion were satisfied, consuming much of the energy that used to go toward distracting behaviors like pestering Meg for the hall pass. One day, for instance, I walked into the room to see Kianna noisily directing the members of her play writing group in a rehearsal on the small stage platform in Meg's room.

These informal writing/performing groups seemed to be a student-sponsored version of what Meg had begun to model with her Literature Circles. However, since Meg was not a focal part of them, the talk in these groups seemed much less restrained and more student-centered, although often appearing to fall into noise and chaos. These groups were far from misdirected or off-task, however. As students worked together, I overheard real decisions being made: whether a character's lines were realistic, how an action could actually be staged, or where the plot should move next.

When I asked Meg whether these student-directed groups were more popular with African-American students than with others, she agreed.

I think that [African-American students' participation in groups] has something to do with insecurity on their own. And I also think—

and Ed [Jackson] and I have conversations about this all the time—
part of their culture is much more—they want to do something
where they can talk; they want to do something where they can be
active. I think that's part of it.

The importance of oral dialogue in all classrooms, but particularly in urban
settings, has been noted by Cureton (1985).

> The inner-city student's learning style depends on oral involvement. The stu-
> dent needs to talk out, with a group, the rationale for a particular choice. This
> oral exchange of reasons and answers also helps to provide the less apt stu-
> dent with strategies for selecting answers. Most "individualized" programs
> cannot provide this kind of support. (p. 106)

Perhaps, also, the talk in these groups seemed more invested than the
talk in a typical classroom discussion because Meg's role in these groups was
more advisor than leader. When she did step in, it was usually to "direct
traffic" or to settle a heated argument, not to direct the content or flow of
the talk. In the midst of this kind of work, Kianna was likely to make requests that seemed more purposeful than the subtle forms of resistance that
were once a part of her "routine." Rather than saying, "Can I go down to
guidance," or "But I don't want to . . ." she was more likely to shout, "We
need to practice!" or "We need to go to the library today!" There was an air
of importance, of dedication to a task, that was not apparent at other times
when Kianna was working individually. The lure of collaborative group
activities, particularly for African-American students, has been noted by
Labov (1982).

> The kind of close cooperation that is best represented in a rock group would
> be called institutionalized cheating if it were done in examinations. We can
> find the same patterns of group interaction in the highly developed patterns of
> use of language in the black community: in church or in the street. Vernacular
> skills are not developed in the quiet of the study chamber, but in close exchange
> of group members. (p. 169)

Exploring the World Through Writing

As Kianna was given more opportunities for collaboration and oral interaction, she began to develop an identity as actress and playwright. At the
same time, she continued to cultivate an image of herself as a poet. She had
begun to follow the lead of other writers in the classroom, creating a series
of what I came to call "world issues" poems. Often these poems sounded a
bit like advertisements or public service announcements that students like

Kianna may have borrowed from their television watching. In her poem, "The World," for instance, Kianna lamented some problems common in the inner cities.

The World!

The World—
The world around us—we live in today
        isnt very safe for the kids to play
out in the front yard
without being harassed
by junkies, drug sellers, just people who pass
The World—
In this world today
you can't walk down the street
with a nice pair of sneakers
without getting beat
in the head
over sneakers—I said
This world today is the Pitts
Now what could we do
about all these young crews
who walk around fighting
with guns and knives
that's no way to survive
in the game of life

In contrast to her reading, Kianna's poetry writing revealed her considerable ability to think deeply about other people. She wrote a series of "people poems" that were similar to her "world issues" poems, in that she described people who contributed to the ills of society. In her poem "Names," she reveals her frustrations over people who stereotype and generalize.

Names

Why do people have names?
I would like to know
When it's the person itself
that really shows.
what I mean by that is
the name does[n't] mean a thing
It's the way a person acts or look

that gives them a name.
for example: if I had a big head
or a big nose
people would say I'm ugly
that's how it gos
Why do people have names?
I would like to know (2/91)

Similarly, in her poem, "Talkers," Kianna reveals a fairly typical adolescent frustration over the backbiting and gossip of supposed friends.

Talkers

People who talk
and show no action
talk for their friends
first for satisfaction
lie about this—lie about that
always taking behind someones back
its mostly girls who do these things
jealous Cause the other has a ring
all of this madness needs to stop
people talking about others and the way they talk
people just stop—
talking about each other
and try to get along with one another
                    By Kianna Moore (1/91)

Through reading her poetry, I began to realize that Kianna was certainly capable of looking deeply into the inner qualities of others. In fact, when asked to respond to two short pieces of literature on her "final examination" at the end of her eighth-grade year, she revealed her understanding and empathy toward the characters in the pieces Meg had selected. For example, in response to "Oranges" by Gary Soto (1990) (a poem about a young man who silently barters with a shopkeeper for a piece of candy for his girlfriend in exchange for an orange), Kianna wrote:

I liked this poem. I like the way it was written—the way he started off with a flashback and focused on it throughout the whole poem. I felt that he was a pretty nice young man to give up his orange to buy her something. The saleslady was very nice to ecept all he had to give her for exchange of the cholate. I liked the boys character because he was a nice and unselfish young man.

Similarly, in response to the short story, "The Colt," by Wallace Stegner (1976), Kianna showed obvious empathy toward the characters' feelings.

> This short story was O.K. I felt sorry for the broken leged colt. I think Bruce really cared about the colt. I also think Bruces mom cared about it a little—but she really cared about Bruce and the way he felt towards the colt. The father acted like he didn't really care about the colt or there was really no hope for it. This was the longest short story I've ever read in my life. But it was an O.K. short story to me.

I couldn't help but notice how much more richly detailed these character impressions were than those Kianna had written for me early in her seventh-grade year. By Kianna's eighth-grade year, Meg's new curriculum allowed Kianna more opportunities to go to the library and pick out her own books. She had engaged in many collaborative activities with her classmates and had begun to take great pride in her developing identity as a writer. I wondered, would this opportunity for more choice in reading, coupled with her successes as a writer, cause Kianna to feel differently about reading this year? Would she make the reading/writing connections that are often touted as the hallmark of classrooms where reading, writing, speaking, and listening are allowed to intersect in creative ways? In our final interview, I decided to explore these questions.

"If Someone . . . Is About to Shoot You": Literature and Life

Just before her graduation from middle school, I again asked Kianna whether people in the real world or characters in books were more interesting to her. Apparently, despite her growing enthusiasm for writing, not much had changed in her attitude toward reading. Once again, she replied that people in the real world were far more interesting than characters in literature. She reasoned:

> People in life are real. If you're reading a book and people are doing some action, you can't really see what they're doing. And if someone in the real world is about to shoot you, you're going to see it.

Interestingly, if she had changed at all, Kianna seemed to be moving away from reading, in favor of writing. Although in seventh grade she didn't like to write, in the eighth grade she had discovered a fascination for writing poetry. When I asked whether she had changed as a reader, she replied:

Toward the beginning of the year I liked to read. Before I started writing a lot I used to like to read a lot. I don't read that much anymore. . . . [Reading is] boring. Books are boring. . . . In the beginning of the year we didn't have a librarian to pick me out good books, and she tried to pick me out ones that I read [before].

Obviously, adults played a significant role in developing or discouraging Kianna's reading interests. My conversations with her reminded me again of the many demands in the busy world of the young adolescent. As teachers, many of us have come to believe that growth in one of the language arts will stimulate and nurture growth in others. While this is often the case, young adolescents like Kianna can become preoccupied with one language activity, to the exclusion of another. One day middle school students are reading a book a week, and other times they have no time for reading at all. Their attention turns to writing, to drama, or to the many outside interests that surround their lives in school: dating, sports, or other personal concerns.

In Kianna's case, she seemed to see writing as a chance to perform in front of others, to collaborate with her peers, and to be admired by her teacher and classmates. The poems and other pieces of writing that began to pile up in her portfolio were evidence of her success. Reading simply did not offer this kind of tangible gratification. In addition, as she was allowed choices in writing topics and some latitude for following her own preferences during English class, she felt some measure of control in devoting her energies to writing.

> *Kianna*: . . . I started writing because I wasn't forced to do [it]. I just started to do it on my own.
> *Susan*: How do think reading and writing for you are different, or are they different?
> *Kianna*: They're different. I feel different about them. I like writing more than reading.
> *Susan*: So you like reading a little less. Do you think that will change as you go through school and you go through life?
> *Kianna*: It probably will.

I had a feeling that this last statement was made mostly for my benefit, considering the fact that I was an adult who obviously valued reading, as well as an authority figure to Kianna. In fact, she did try to reassure me that reading hadn't entirely disappeared from her life. Although she still rarely enjoyed reading for school, and never read with friends, she did admit, "When I go home I read. My mother has a lot of good books and I read sometimes when I'm at home. Everybody in my family likes to read."

As I walked away from my last interview with Kianna, I wondered what it would take for her to enjoy reading for school and, more important, to become a lifetime reader. What kind of teaching would she encounter in her high school English classes, after the relative freedom she had been given in her 2 years with Meg? And if 2 years of freedom were not enough to turn her into a reader, what would be?

First, she would need teachers in high school who could continue to nurture her budding development as a writer. I am convinced that one of the reasons why teachers in "integrated language arts" or "whole language" classrooms often are criticized for not producing "measurable" growth in all of their students is because some students, steeped in the skills-based, atomistic curricula of their early schooling, cannot make the kind of leaps they are expected to make in 1 or 2 short years. It took Kianna 6 years of schooling to develop her negative attitudes toward reading. Was it fair to expect that these attitudes would be erased in only 2? If she had any prospects of making reading and writing a fundamental part of her life beyond her middle school years, she would need teachers who could help her to make connections between her experiences as an author and the experiences of other authors. Reading might become a way of appreciating and even borrowing the techniques of published writers for her own poetry.

Her reading experiences also would need to be surrounded and enriched by many oral language opportunities to perform and collaborate. Geneva Smitherman (1986) has discussed the importance of the "call–response" pattern of African-American oral discourse, or the "spontaneous verbal and non-verbal interaction between speaker and listener in which all of the speaker's statements ('calls') are punctuated by expressions ('responses') from the listener" (p. 104). Smitherman argues that this communicative dynamic is "essential to the communication system of Black English" (p. 219). She observes:

> Since black communication works in this interactive way, then maybe it means that black students who are passively listening aren't really learning. Teachers can capitalize on this dynamic by recognizing that they should expect—indeed, be desirous of—some "noisy" behavior from black kids. It means they diggin on what you sayin. . . . Just as blacks aren't passive communicators or listeners, they aren't passive learners. . . . Since blacks communicate best by interacting with one another, they can also *learn* best by interacting with one another. Thus students might be paired or grouped and allowed to talk and move about freely as they learn new information and practice educational skills. (pp. 219–220)

Beyond the chance to capitalize on her natural abilities as a performer and classroom leader, Kianna also would need to learn how to balance her own need for activity as a creative young adolescent with the needs of her teacher and classmates for some order and structure. She needs to adopt productive forms of resistance, rather than adopting the persona of a "loud Black girl." Along these lines, Giroux (1983) cites the example of young girls who aggressively assert their own femininity by flaunting their interest in boys and older men. He argues, "This type of oppositional behavior, rather than suggesting resistance, primarily displays an oppressive mode of sexism . . . [and] is informed by a dominating, rather than liberating, logic" (p. 286). By contrast, Giroux (1983) suggests "modes of resistance that are quietly subversive in the most immediate sense, but that have the potential to be politically progressive in the long run . . . [and] will not make them powerless in the future" (p. 288). Students like Kianna must first stay in school, thus gaining "access to knowledge and skills . . . [to avoid] positions of dead-end, alienating labor that most of the showy rebels will eventually occupy" (p. 288).

As teachers, we need to become more critical about the concept of resistance, recognizing its damaging as well as its liberating forms. For Kianna to discover productive forms of resistance, I believe that she will have to become more fully convinced of her own self-worth as a learner and a literate person. I suspect that if Kianna had been more confident of her abilities to succeed in school, she might have channeled her considerable energies into productive tasks more willingly and enthusiastically. I am not sure, however, that Meg could be expected to erase all of Kianna's bad memories of school in their 2 short years together.

Students like Kianna need teachers who can lead them gently toward their own particular visions of themselves as literate people. When they pursue classroom tasks perfunctorily, or not at all, they need teachers who can support and coax them toward reading, writing, and oral language experiences that will capture and hold their interest. When they come to school hardened, wary, or disrespectful, they need teachers who can accept their resistance as a challenge and not a personal threat—teachers who can be patient when growth seems doubtful and the daily rewards of teaching are few. Maxine Greene (1992) describes how such teachers might help not only students like Kianna, but all students to pursue a fully literate life.

> To help . . . the diverse students we know, articulate their stories is not only to help them pursue the meanings of their lives—to find out how things are happening, to keep posing questions about the why. . . . It is . . . to reach out for the proficiencies and capacities, the craft required to be fully participant in society, and to do so without losing the consciousness of who they are. . . . We want our classrooms to be just and caring, full of various conceptions of the good. We want them to be articulate, with the dialogue involving as many persons as possible, opening to one another, opening to the world. And we

want them to be concerned for one another, as we learn to be concerned for them. We want them to achieve friendships among one another, as each one moves to a heightened sense of craft and wide-awakeness, to a renewed consciousness of worth and possibility. (p. 259)

It is nurturing this "consciousness of worth and possibility" that remains the task of Kianna's future teachers. Hopefully, she will find adults who inspire and support her as she cultivates the sense of "craft and wide-awakeness" so necessary to a literate life in her years of schooling and beyond.

CHAPTER 5

Jason: "Strong as a Pencil"

> Just below the swaggering, boastful public face [of boys] are often suppressed, alternative identities demanding to be heard. At unexpected moments, in the awkward breaks in heroic performances, you can often hear these other identities struggling to get out. . . . The range and variety of these hidden boys' identities need to be more explicitly acknowledged in public. Underneath boys' brave mouthing you can hear the other choked voices straining to come through. (Salisbury & Jackson, 1996, pp. 8–9)

On a stifling afternoon in the late summer of 1995, Meg and I were taking a breather in her darkened classroom. For the past few weeks, we had been interviewing some of her former students, who were then at the age when most people were graduating from high school. The halls of Logan were strangely silent, as the new fall crop of middle school students was not due to arrive for another 2 weeks. The day before, Jason Kernfeldt, tall, mature, and almost ready for college, had come in for an interview. I was talking about the remarkable transformation in Jason over his 4 years of high school, when I noticed that Meg had a perplexed, almost guilty look on her face. Almost reading my mind, she said:

> I've been thinking about this all morning. When you first asked me to help locate Jason a couple of months ago, I had absolutely no recollection of him. I feel terrible about this, but I didn't remember ever having him in my classroom. Looking back over his work from middle school, I'm impressed by his ability; and the fact that he's continued reading and writing all these years just blows me away. I can't believe I didn't remember him!

Considering how many times he had tried her patience in their 2 years together, I could understand how Meg might have wanted to push Jason to the edges of her memory as soon as he left her classroom. At the same time, I wondered how many Jasons had come and gone in my own lifetime as a teacher. How many young boys and girls, immature and incessantly vying for attention, had slipped (or been pushed) through the cracks of my memory? Generally more mischievous than devious, they were not the official "troublemakers," who wound up in the principal's office or out on the streets. They were smart, but not academically outstanding, often preferring to do the minimum and "get by." As a result, like Meg, I tended to file them in my "lost child" basket and move on to my next crop of students.

I had to admit, though, that Jason had stuck in my mind over the years, not only because I had made it a point to follow him through middle school, but because he reminded me a bit of myself in seventh grade. For a variety of reasons, I too had earned the title of "class pest" in seventh grade. Like Jason, I could resist no opportunity to disrupt class with a joke or an inappropriately snide comment. I seldom made it to the principal's office, but a few months into the school year, my homeroom teacher installed my desk permanently in the cloak room, so I couldn't disrupt the other students with my antics. It was probably my own short-lived career as a class clown and "teacher's pest" that first drew me to Jason. Because, in so many ways, he reminded me of myself as a young adolescent, I was probably more tolerant of his high-strung immaturity than Meg was. I was also, fortunately, not responsible for keeping his irritating behaviors in tow.

"ROMANCING THE SHADE": JASON IN THE CLASSROOM

For most of Jason's seventh-grade year, you could find him either teasing an unlucky girl or "romancing" the cord of the window shade, for which he seemed to have a passionate fascination. At nearly any given moment on a typical day, I'd catch sight of Jason as he tied the cord into knots, anchored it to his desk, or snapped it high into the air, sending the shade flapping upward at some (always) inappropriate time. In seventh grade, Jason read very little that was not related to sports. An avid athlete, he preferred reading what he called "stats" over almost anything else. Typical of many energetic, athletic young adolescent boys, Jason was in constant motion, both intellectually and physically.

One day, for example, I observed him working with three girls in a collaborative group. The room was still a bit stifling, as the cool October days had not set in. Jason was wearing red shorts, wire-rimmed glasses, and a Chicago Bulls tee shirt. His dark shiny hair was cropped in a fashionable "skater cut." Jason had what I called a "Leave It to Beaver" face. He was freckled, smiling, yet (unlike "The Beav") devilish beyond belief! You can't imagine—or maybe you can—what a boy like Jason could do to Meg's carefully planned collaborative learning lesson. On this particular day, his group's assignment was to find a grammar rule in the handbook and decide on a way to teach it to the rest of the class. That day, I wrote in my observer's notebook:

Jason is fiddling with his shirt laces and teasing Angel as she blows
bubbles with her gum. Suddenly, Jason points at Angel and shouts,
"Look, she's got a (pencil?) between her legs!" He begins to giggle
uncontrollably, as the girls roll their eyes. Meg walks by and tries to put
the situation back in order. She gives an extended explanation of what
the group is supposed to be doing. She asks some questions. Angel
answers all of them. Jason is playing with the blind cord, still giggling.
After Meg leaves, Jason begins reading examples from the book aloud
as the group listens. After a few minutes, Jason screams, "Oh, I poked
myself in the eye! With a pencil!" When he gets no response from this,
he tries a joke, looking all the time at the girls. In her own "polite" way,
Angel tries to bring the group back on track, yelling at the top of her
lungs, "Jason! Shut up!"

Such encounters were typical of Jason, especially in the presence of young girls. Unfortunately for him, although girls seemed to occupy much of his attention, he had little finesse with them. He had even less grace when it came to dealing with Meg.

In my privileged position as observer rather than teacher, I was able to see past most of Jason's off-putting behaviors. Eventually, between seventh and eighth grade, I witnessed a slow but striking transformation in Jason's self-concept as a reader. My access to focused observations and private interviews, in addition to his "official" classroom work, such as reading journals, papers, and imaginative writings, perhaps gave me a more balanced perspective that Meg didn't have. By the end of his eighth-grade year, I was convinced that, with a little maturing, Jason would move out of his "jock" role and embrace the more intellectual, sensitive side that Salisbury and Jackson mention in the beginning of this chapter. I must admit, though, that there was little foreshadowing of this transformation in Jason's seventh-grade year.

Although Jason was fairly good-natured, I witnessed him openly confronting Meg's authority many times. For example, a few days after this collaborative learning experience, Jason had been chosen by his fellow group members to teach the lesson on grammar that they had prepared. At the time, I thought it interesting that, although Jason was clearly off-task during his group preparation time, he was still chosen as the spokesperson when it came time to share what they had learned. This phenomenon transpired many times in Meg's classroom, and was consistent with research demonstrating that typically, mixed groups of males and females will choose a male as spokesperson, even though females may have done most of the work. Salisbury and Jackson (1996) have observed that

> boys in group discussion situations reveal all the traits of not listening, which
> adult males in groups are noted for. . . . In mixed sex discussion groups . . . a

minority of girls in the group were almost entirely silenced by the dominant use of space and sound by the boys in the group. . . . The boys groaned when girls made contributions or asked questions or just simply made rude comments about them. (p. 169)

In the same vein, Sadker and Sadker (1994) argue that teachers often have seen cooperative learning as a way to encourage gender equity and friendships across cultural boundaries. Unfortunately, this is not always the outcome. In supposedly cooperative groups, they found that "aggressive students, who were more likely to be male, were taking the speaking parts and the leadership roles" (p. 270).

True to form that day, Jason sat twirling on a stool at the front of the class as he waited for his turn to teach. Finally, Meg gave him permission to write some sentences on the board. He began to write, "Her dog is brown she ate the apple"—presumably a prelude to a discussion of run-on sentences. As soon as he was finished, Jason began to read each sentence aloud, calling on students to identify which were complete sentences and which were fragments.

Suddenly Meg interrupted: "I know I came in late, Mr. Kernfeldt . . ." She then proceeded to explain that one of the sentences was really two separate sentences. Jason, in turn, interrupted her: "Mrs. Andrews, we're the teachers. Can we call on people?" Meg answered, "Yes, but you have to stand up." Jason complained: "Who's the teacher here, anyway?" Sufficiently chastened, she smiled and let him go on with lesson.

Later in the fall term, Jason again confronted Meg's authority. For several days, the class had been reading Rosa Guy's novel, *The Friends* (1973). Meg had assigned a paragraph character description the night before. She explained that even though she had asked for a paragraph, she still got abbreviated lists from some students. To model what she meant by a paragraph, she asked Jason to read his character description of Edith Jackson. As Jason read his description, Munjed remarked: "Jason described the things around Edith, but he didn't describe her." Alexis added, "It wasn't to the point enough." Meg explained, "Jason had an excellent topic sentence, but that kind of broke down." She then called on Munjed to read his paragraph. It was obvious that Jason didn't like being criticized by Meg or his classmates. He interrupted the discussion: "Can I make a quick comment? Personally, I don't like constructive criticism. I feel uncomfortable doing it."

As Jason began jiggling around in his chair, Meg tried to lure him back into the discussion: "Let's do a little example. Let's have Jason tell us about one of these characters." Jason ignored her, continuing to squirm in his seat. Meg complained: "Jason, you are the one who brought this up!" When Jason again failed to respond, Meg started a mini-lecture about character description. Derailing her explanation, Jason broke in: "Are we going to get to talk about the fight sometime?" Apparently there had been a fight in the halls earlier, and Meg had promised the students some time to discuss it in class. Later, I wrote:

> *Jason is the most vocal in the class about questioning Meg's authority. He frequently responds (bluntly, and negatively) to any attempt on her part to give him (or the other students) criticism. . . . Jason responds negatively to what he calls "constructive criticism," and Meg responds by making that the agenda for the rest of the period. Sometimes I feel that Jason knows about Meg's sincere desire to have students feel consulted and in control, and he takes advantage of that to a certain extent. As soon as she started (in earnest) to deal with the issue he brought up, he began to engage in some distracting behaviors that let her know he wasn't quite sincere.*

As a young adolescent, Jason clearly demanded control of everything from his reading and writing choices to the activities in which Meg tried to engage him. In the early part of his seventh-grade year, it was hard to tell whether he was bored by school or simply hyperactive and immature. Perhaps because of his high energy level and short attention span, he seemed to have little interest in writing and even less in reading.

"WE'VE NEVER HAD A GARAGE SALE SO THEY'RE STILL THERE": JASON ON READING

Interestingly, in seventh grade, Jason described a good deal of support for reading at home: "My dad loves reading and so does my sister. My sister takes three different books and reads part of it each day, a little of each one each day. I don't understand how she can do that." Jason's father read everything from Gary Larson, "Far Side," and "Doonesbury" cartoons to business books and what Jason called "joy books" (books just for fun). He explained, "I've seen him with four books in his car and like every day he's picking up a different one." Jason's mother, a teacher, managed to read a novel a month. An Agatha Christie buff, she had read every one in the series, except for one she could not locate. She often read these novels more than once. Jason, on the other hand, admitted to reading very little at home. When I asked what I might find on his bookshelves, he replied that his mom is a teacher "so you'd find dictionaries." In addition, Jason still had some of his childhood books: "We've never had a garage sale so they're still there." Mostly, though, Jason seemed proud of the fact that his family had more records on their shelves than books.

Only one of Jason's friends, Ian, knew that Jason read at all. He explained, "Sometimes we read the same book. We read them at the same time, we race." Given Jason's fascination for sports, it wasn't surprising that he made a competitive game, even out of his pleasure reading. Occasionally, Jason would read a book, see the movie, then discuss both with Ian. He explained, "It's kind of fun to read the same book as one of your friends; you can talk about it." For the most part, however, his friends had no idea that Jason read. Perhaps this was because of his "jock" reputation, as well as the fact that reading was last on a long list of other preoccupations. He explained, "I like reading if it's something I like to read but if it's not, I don't like to read." In a piece called "Myself as a Reader and Writer," Jason wrote:

> *When I was young I hated to read. I wouldn't even pick up a book until I found out I was in the highest reading grade. I started to like reading better, but I still did not enjoy reading or writing enough. . . . In the second grade I was in the highest reading class until Mr. Crabbe sent me back a reading level for turning around in class. That sucked, but that didn't hurt me for more than four years.*

Four whole years! How little it took to turn Jason off to reading. From what I had observed in Meg's class, I wondered if "turning around in class" was Jason's only offense. At the same time, I couldn't help wondering what these, admittedly distracting, behaviors had to do with his reading level in Mr. Crabbe's class. It was also interesting to me that he rarely picked up a book until he discovered he was in the highest reading group. In the classroom, as on the playing field, Jason struck me as someone who would not compete, unless he was sure of winning. In time, I learned a great many other things about Jason's reading habits and preferences.

Reading Better with the Lights Out

By the time he reached middle school, Jason clearly learned to see reading as a kind of last resort. Early in his seventh-grade year, he remarked, "I think TV overrules [reading], playing sports overrules it, and my computer overrules it, but it's better than doing nothing." He explained further:

> It depends on how busy I am. Two weeks ago was the busiest week of my life. I had an after-school activity every single day and three times I had two after-school activities. So I didn't get much time. I had a lot of homework, so I didn't read at all. And last week was real relaxing so I read a lot.

In addition to adequate time for reading, the freedom to choose his own reading materials was crucial to Jason. When I asked him what he would tell English teachers if he could, he answered: "Not to assign me books!" Later, in his journal, he wrote:

> I think that reading is OK, but only when I get to pick the subject and book. I really don't like being assigned to read a book or story. It's not that I don't like the book or story, but that I some-times feel I'm being pushed into reading when I don't need to be. I feel the same about writing. When I can write about anything, I write good, but when I'm assigned a topic I don't get interested in it.

Seldom did Jason feel free to choose his own books in school. Yet, occasion-ally he seemed to appreciate teachers' choices, admitting:

> Usually the school will assign books that I like. Like the book that we're reading now, *The Friends*, I like that book. And I was assigned *The Call of the Wild* and I read that. There was two other books that I was assigned that I liked: *The Red Badge of Courage* and *The Prince and the Pauper*.

Although he occasionally enjoyed reading literature in school, Jason was reluctant to call himself "a reader."

> I guess I don't call myself a reader because it takes so long for me to read things. And a lot of times I get lost when I'm reading something I don't like. I see the words and I can read them a hundred times but I have to think about the words, which is hard for me to do.

Not surprisingly, Jason found reading less laborious when he discovered a book that interested him: "It's better when I like it." Reading within the typical school schedule was difficult, however. Because he considered him-self a slow reader, Jason was extremely resistant to deadlines.

> I'd rather take a month to read a book that I don't like than to take a book that I like and try to read it in a week . . . because I like going slow and thinking about what's going on for a while. When you just have one week to read a book, even if you like it, . . . it's not really going to be the same as when you take your time.

Jason was clearly limited in his reading preferences: "I like reading sports stories but I don't really like adventure kind of books. . . . I'm always doing something that has to do with sports . . . sports and stats. I've always been good at stats." The only time Jason seemed to read literature was when it was assigned for school. At home, he read mostly the sports pages in the newspaper. What Jason saw as his slow reading pace and his limited vocabulary may have contributed to his tenuous relationship with books. He explained:

> I don't read fast like other people. I can't read half a book in one night. Other people can do that. And there are times when I'll go for a week and not read a book. But then the next week I'll read 20 pages every night.

Because of what he saw as his reading difficulties, he resisted most novels, claiming they were too long and had "a lot of words I've never heard before." Short stories, on the other hand, weren't long enough. When he did read at home, it was usually on Tuesday and Wednesday nights after dinner, and only when there was nothing more interesting on television. He detested books that "just have facts and . . . don't have any excitement," and books that sounded "like a computer made them up." On the other hand, in contrast to other active, athletic young adolescents, Jason found most adventure books "too obvious." Even when he watched television, Jason explained that he was always commenting, "This is so obvious, watch, I bet this happens."

Perhaps because of his high energy level, Jason preferred a certain amount of noise when he read. He explained, "Sometimes I have trouble reading, if there's no sound on." Although his parents didn't believe him, he preferred to listen to his radio when he read. Perhaps for the same reasons, he preferred reading in groups to reading silently and alone: "I like reading in groups; that way there's nothing else to put my mind on. I like reading while I hear the reading; that helps me a lot." On the other hand, Jason was susceptible to visual distractions, remarking, "As weird as it may be, I usually can't have too much light. I can read better in the dark . . . because I don't see things around me that make me distracted."

Reading as Sport: "It's Only Boring If I'm Out of the Action"

Jason saw reading much like playing basketball. Books that made him feel "part of the action," he explained, were likely to sustain his interest, even if he didn't particularly like them.

> I got bored in gym today because nobody ever passed me the ball.
> The first time I got the ball I scored. It's only boring if I'm out of the
> action. And I don't like to sit still. I don't like books where it's just
> calm for an hour. I'm never sitting still, I'm always doing some-
> thing. People always ask me am I nervous. I'm not nervous. I always
> do things like this.

In literature and life, feeling that he was "part of the action" helped Jason to "stay in the game."

I was surprised one day, however, when Jason overturned one of my hunches about the reading process. I had always assumed that adolescents—particularly active young men like Jason—would become most involved with the reading process if they could learn to think deeply about characters, exploring the "why" of their behaviors and beliefs. In an interview, I explained my thinking to Jason: "[I have this theory that] when you . . . come up against a character, you kind of wonder, what makes this person tick, what is this person doing this for? Do you think that's true?" Jason replied, "I don't think it's true with me really. . . . I don't think [reading characters' minds] is good. I don't like that." He explained:

> I like it when it feels like I'm part of the book. Like [if] a character
> [is] there watching me, I wouldn't know what they're thinking. . . .
> In this book The Mummy, they don't say "as Elliot thinks this" or
> stuff like that. . . . [Anne Rice] didn't say, "His nephew feels this,"
> [she] said "His nephew looks like he feels this."

According to Jason, "You can describe one of your friends, but you don't know what's going on in their mind because you can't read their minds." When characters are presented by their behaviors rather than their feelings or thoughts, Jason feels more like "the observer," looking at the story's scene. Somewhat paradoxically, in feeling like an observer, he becomes a more willing *participant* in the unfolding literary drama. He maintained this disinterest in character motivations, even in an interview during eighth grade, when he admitted:

> It's not interesting to me . . . to figure out the person. I like to
> figure out what's going to happen. It feels good when you guess
> what's going to happen. The book Tommyknockers—it was kind of
> obvious, predictable. I knew what was going to happen the whole
> book, thing after thing after thing. There was one part where this
> guy gets electrocuted by a TV and they talk about his eyes pop out
> of his head, and as soon as they said eyes, I was thinking they were
> going to pop out of his head.

In eighth grade, he enjoyed Stephen King, who, according to Jason, didn't "really get deep into most characters. . . . Most of the characters are just characters. He just tells you what happened."

Just as he rarely explored characters' motivations as a young adolescent, Jason rarely considered how other people in his social world thought about him. Perhaps because he was more focused on himself than on others, Jason explained that he didn't really need to know what his classmates thought. It wasn't until late in his high school years that Jason began to form what he called "true friendships" and to think more deeply about others in his social world. Along these lines, Messner (1992) has speculated on why many adolescent males involved with athletics fail to form true friendships during their secondary schooling.

> Young boys may initially find that playing competitively gives them the opportunity to experience emotionally "safe" connections with others. But once enmeshed in sport as an institution, they are confronted by two interrelated realities—hierarchy and homophobia—that undermine the possibility of boys' transcending their fears of intimacy and developing truly close relationships with others. (p. 33)

In addition to competing with his time for reading and writing, his participation in sports may have taken its toll on Jason in other ways. As Salisbury and Jackson (1996) explain:

> In order to achieve this fantasy state of heroic virility, boys have to learn to go for aggressive performance, success, superiority over women, emotional stoicism, physical strength and goal-directedness in their sporting activities. However, they often learn to do this at the expense of their capacity to act as human beings. Their abilities to relate to other people, to feel for others, to trust, to cooperate, to link together their bodies with their hearts, are all damaged and severely limited by such sporting practices. (p. 205)

Like Jason, many young adolescent males get caught up in the competitiveness of organized sports and fail to establish close relationships with peers. Although perhaps schools have most flagrantly failed their female students, in many ways they have failed boys like Jason as well, not only in supporting rather rigid gender roles, but in failing to address the limitations of these roles as a conscious part of the curriculum. As it turned out, many of Jason's former and current teachers were guilty of another kind of benign neglect as well; they failed to recognize that Jason had learned enough of the system to "get by" and, in the process, often felt cheated out of opportunities for meaningful learning.

"Half I Didn't Read and the Other Half I Don't Remember": Reading and Responding

In seventh grade, Jason earned fairly good grades. I got the sense, however, that school, like reading, was at the bottom of his list of priorities. In classroom settings, he saw himself as more of a talker than a reader or writer. Writing in his response journal was an exercise in futility to him. He complained: "I don't really like [journals]. . . . I mean if you're so interested in what's happening in the book, then why don't you read it? [In my response journal] I'm just practically writing the whole book over." Generally, he saw writing of any kind as a perfunctory exercise in demonstrating knowledge to teachers. Writing in response journals frustrated him because "every word has to be just about perfect when you're writing." Talking in class was much easier for him because "when you're talking you can mumble, you can make it last longer." Talking about a book, he explained, "makes the remembering of the book last longer." Talking informally about reading was, for Jason, a way of "going slow and thinking about what's going on for a while" as he read.

At the end of his seventh-grade year, I brought Jason to a table where I had laid out copies of some 40 pieces of literature that Meg's class had read that year, and asked him to pick out those selections that had "related to his life." After several minutes, he admitted that he could not pick out a single title. When I asked why, he replied candidly, "Mostly because half of them I didn't read and the other half I don't remember."

Despite his enjoyment of books about sports or books with fast-moving plots, he felt that the latter didn't relate to his life because he didn't "lead an adventurous life." When books "relate to my life," Jason explained, "then I've already been there and I don't need that." Jason, like so many young people his age, is fascinated by what Kieran Egan (1992) calls "the extremes and limits of human experience" (p. 72). Young adolescents are intrigued by what Egan calls

> the most courageous or the cruellest acts, the strangest and the most bizarre natural phenomena, the most terrible or the most wonderful events. These are staples of the TV shows, books, and films that exploit this prominent characteristic of students' imaginations. . . . Students are interested in limits and extremes because such exotica provide the context within which their daily lives and experience are meaningful. (pp. 72–73)

Occasionally, when a book captured his interest, Jason managed to find time for reading, and admitted that books could be a pleasant counterpoint to what he considered his unadventurous life. When he occasionally found a book he liked, he would read it again. "Some things are better the second time," he explained, "like lasagna."

Jason, like so many young adolescent males, was a "binge reader" in seventh grade. Outside forces—sports, his other schoolwork, girls, and all of the other temptations of middle school life—lured him away from reading and writing. Because of his highly social nature, outside people—teachers like Meg and Mr. Crabbe—were strong influences on how he felt about himself as a reader and a writer. He looked for the approval of adults, just as, in a backhanded way, he sought approval from the girls he teased. But the most important thing for Jason, in terms of his identity as a reader and a writer, was having some control over his literate life.

TRANSFORMATIONS: "THE MORE I READ THEM, THE LESS SCARED I GET."

I didn't see Jason as much during his eighth-grade year, because he had been moved to a period much later in the day that conflicted with a class I was teaching at the university. Much to my surprise, however, late in his eighth-grade year, he arrived for an interview several inches taller and handsome in a boyish way. I suspected that he'd given up "romancing" the window shade and had now turned his attention to real live girls. But something else had changed as well. Somewhere in the months since I had last observed him, Jason had discovered Stephen King. And that, in the words of Jason, had "made all the difference." He wrote this about *Tommyknockers* (King, 1993) in his reading journal:

> *I've been reading a book called "The Tommyknockers" by Stephen King. It's sick and twisted and probably the best book I have ever read. I like the greusome parts of this book. I like the way the book seasaws back and forth, from good to bad, greusome to subtle, scary to boring. When this happens in a book usully it's not very good. But this is different. Its a total difference from the real world. The way this book make me feal is unusual. It makes me feel good when a persons eyes explod or a person gets shot through the ear with an arrow. Is that good or bad. I don't know, and I don't care; it's just a* BOOK.

Behind the gory descriptive language and the fascination with what Jason had learned to call "the macabre," I could see the first glimmer of a budding literary critic. I read with pleasure as Jason described the way "the book seesaws back and forth, from good to bad, gruesome to subtle, scary to boring."

Meg too had noticed this transformation. In an interview late in Jason's eighth-grade year, she remarked:

> Last year [Jason was] constantly playing around, fooling around, staring out the window, falling asleep, unengaged, rolling the eyes all the time. This year, [he's] just reading so much on his own. Reading, reading, reading. . . . And writing some very good things. It's still pulling teeth to get him to write, but it's kind of like "I need your attention, so I'm not gonna turn this in when you want it. I'm gonna make you come and get it." . . . But when he hands something in, it's just so good. It's so good.

That year, Jason seemed to bloom within the learner-centered curriculum that Meg had established. When I reminded him of his sporadic reading patterns in seventh grade, he remarked that he was "looking at reading as something that [he] had to do, not wanted to do, last year." I asked him if there was a moment when he could remember changing his opinion. With an almost reverential attitude, he replied, "Yeah, my first Stephen King book." He added:

> Last year I just read anything. I'd read an *Encyclopedia Brown* book if I had one. It really didn't matter. But this year, I read just about nothing but Stephen King books. I read one Anne Rice book, *The Queen of the Damned*, but I read about six Stephen King books.

Earlier that year, Jason's friend Ian had introduced him to Stephen King. He read *Misery* (King, 1987), then went to see the movie, which was "really different" from the book. In the movie, he explained, "they took out the really gruesome parts, like, she doesn't have any candles so she cuts off his thumbs. She runs over this guy's head with a lawn mower." He admitted that his encounters with Stephen King in eighth grade started him on a horror story binge: "I haven't read anything but horror books since my first Stephen King book."

Suddenly, Jason was no longer daunted by long books. In fact, he seemed to prefer them. For example, *Tommyknockers* (King, 1993) was his all-time favorite. Not only did he read the 700-page book in 1 week, but he turned around and read it again a week later. Jason spoke with pride about the long books he had read that year: "I read less books but bigger books. . . . *Tommyknocker* was 750 pages. I'm reading [another Stephen King book] now and it's over 1,000. After that I'm going to read *The Stand*, which is 1,500."

When I shared my amazement over his newfound passion for long books, Jason remarked, "Yeah, big ones. I like the big ones." To Jason, King's simple writing style made reading much easier: "I can just skim through [a Stephen King book]—not skim, but go really fast and do a page in like 50 seconds." When I asked Jason why, in my survey of his classmates, so many of them had preferred writing over reading, he remarked, "They're young. They haven't read Stephen King books."

Despite what seemed like a fascination for gore and suspense, Jason told me that literature gave him a sort of distance that helped calm his fears. He explained, "I don't always like to watch [horror]. I like to read about it. I never really liked horror movies. I used to rent them at my birthday parties, but then I'd go and watch something else." Toward the end of his eighth-grade year, he wrote:

> I feel that most or all of the literature I read is horror stories. I think I read them because the more I read them, the less scared I get. I feel that if I read something in a horror story, it's almost impossible for it to happen.

At the end of his eighth-grade year, Jason and I sat down to compare the questionnaires he had completed in seventh grade with those he had filled out in eighth grade. I pointed out that in eighth grade, he reported bringing his knowledge of real people into his reading of literature, whereas in seventh grade he had not. Here again, his fascination with Stephen King had allowed him to connect characters with real people from his social world. "When I read [Stephen King], Jason explained, "I was seeing if I could find which one of my friends would be like the characters."

"It's so free! It's so 60s!": Jason on Choice

Although his passion for Stephen King was certainly a turning point for Jason, the changes in Meg's curriculum also had much to do with his transformation as a reader. During Jason's seventh-grade year, as Meg groped her own way to the teaching style and the classroom routines that best fit her irrepressible seventh graders, students had very little choice in the texts they read. Most were selected by Meg herself and read as a whole class. In eighth grade, Meg changed the curriculum to provide many more options for self-selected, independent reading. The move toward independent learning centers and self-selected reading was perfect for students like Jason, who demanded control in the books and writing topics they chose. Toward the end of the year, as he surveyed Meg's classroom, Jason remarked, half joking, "I love it like this. I love not being assigned to do a certain thing every day. . . . It's so free! It's so 60s!" At the same time, Jason admitted that the open atmosphere sometimes allowed him to get off-track. Although he appreciated Meg's learning center arrangement, he observed:

> It's nice being able to choose where you want to go, but I think it would be better if we got assigned when you got to [go to a particular learning center] . . . because you forget how many times you've gone.

Jason's comment seems to echo David Elkind's (1994) observation that, despite our postmodern belief that young adults are more sophisticated than their predecessors in other generations, they remain in need of boundaries and limits. Elkind argues:

> Children are the young of the species and, like the young of all species, they need adult guidance, direction, and protection. . . . Asserting our adultness does not mean being an ogre or drill sergeant. It does mean that we appreciate that children, adolescents, and even young adults may not yet have a set of internalized rules and standards, nor a good set of controls over their emotions and behavior. The only way they are going to get these internalized rules and standards is from us. Yes, young people may not like us when we set rules and standards, and that is too bad. When we worry about our children liking us, however, we put our needs ahead of our children's needs. (pp. 226–227)

Interestingly, although he enjoyed his private, independent reading, Jason did not particularly enjoy attending Literature Circles. This surprised me, since I expected that Jason's highly social personality would have made him a perfect candidate for these small, informal reading groups. Instead, he described Literature Circles as an exercise in talking about books that "no one else has ever heard of except for the people in this class." By contrast, he enjoyed Reading/Writing Circles, especially when Meg occasionally shared what she was writing and asked for feedback. Because Jason witnessed his comments making an impact on a "real writer," he discovered a kind of reading response that was active, not passive. In contrast to reading journals (which in Jason's mind were to prove that he had read something), responding orally to a fellow author—his teacher at that—was a purposeful form of reading response and appealed to his need to be "part of the action."

In addition to more freedom in his personal reading, Jason also appreciated the chance to do homework for other classes in Meg's room. He remembered, "A lot of times I didn't have my homework done and I'd do my homework in this class. That got me about 10 points for the entire year." Somewhat tongue-in-cheek, I asked him if he was "learning English" in this rather nontraditional setting. He replied, "I am learning English because I'm learning that English isn't something that should be forced. It's like reading. You shouldn't be forced to read something. It should really be your choice as to what you want to read." Jason explained that this opportunity to do other work in Meg's classroom had an effect on his other grades as well: "My grades say it all. Last year I was an 85 average and this year I've been on honor roll every time."

The physical structures of Meg's new classroom also appealed to Jason. "It's my favorite class," he remarked. "Last year she wouldn't let us sit on the couches every day." In eighth grade, Jason seemed to have replaced his fascination for the window shade with a newfound infatuation with the couch. In fact, he spent so much time there that I wasn't surprised when, 5 years later, as he returned to Meg's classroom for a follow-up interview, he dove onto the familiar brown plaid couch and exclaimed, "I almost forgot! I spent my whole eighth-grade year on this thing!" As an energetic young adolescent, Jason was grateful for the chance "to get up and walk around and visit different places." Late in his eighth-grade year, I reminded Jason of his relationship with the window shade the previous year and asked him why he no longer seemed interested in tying the cord into knots. He replied, "I don't know. It's too immature."

We talked for a few more moments in that final interview of 1991 about Steven King's other books—some of them, in Jason's words, "900 pages!" He mentioned that he hoped to attend King's personal appearance in a few weeks and planned to get an autograph. When I asked if he thought he'd be a lifetime reader, Jason replied: "Yeah, sure." "Would you have said that last year, in seventh grade?" I asked. Jason replied, "Definitely not." When I asked if Stephen King had made the difference for him, he responded, "Not really the author, the subject." "Which is?" I asked. Jason explained, "I guess the best word for it is 'macabre.'" Impressed by his growing vocabulary, I remarked, "That's a pretty big word for a person your age to know." Jason beamed. "It took me a while to learn it. At first I thought it was pronounced differently. [I saw it first in] his book *Danse Macabre*." As a parting thought, I said:

> Jason, I've really seen you change a lot. I think it's all for the better. And I'm going to hold you to that lifetime reading promise. [Someday maybe I'll find you when you go to high school] and ask you, "What are you reading?"

Jason just smiled: "I hope it will still be Stephen King."

I chuckle when I think of how often teachers are admonished to break middle school learners of those obsessive addictions to authors we may not consider of "literary merit." Students like Jason teach me that often these reading binges—these obsessions with a favorite writer or a favorite genre—give young adolescents a certain sense of stability, of predictability, as they're balancing on that narrow gulf between childhood and young adulthood. Hopefully, they give young adolescents the self-confidence to extend their horizons and their reading tastes, and to become, like Jason, self-proclaimed "lifetime readers."

STEPHEN WHO?

Having witnessed this transformation in Jason, I was somewhat prepared for the tall athletic young man with the hint of a beard who walked into Meg's room, along with his friend, Jaquille, that summer day in 1995. Somehow I had expected the deepening of voice, the calmness of manner, and the other physical and emotional contrasts with the hyperactive boy who first entered Meg's classroom in 1989. What I did not anticipate was discovering that all through middle school and high school, Jason had been a "closet poet," keeping a secret journal the entire time.

Some time during that afternoon, he offered to go out to his car and bring his poetry journal to share with us. As he left the room, Meg and I looked at each other, flabbergasted. Unbeknown to us, poetry had been a "kind of free thought" that got Jason through his middle school and high school years. He explained, "I have a friend that writes a lot too and I guess we call it 'flowing.' We just flow." In middle school, Jason had kept this secret carefully guarded, since poetry "just wasn't something that guys are supposed to do in seventh and eighth grade." Jason's comment reminded me of Tony, a young man in Sadker and Sadker's (1994) study, who served as co-editor of his high school literary magazine. Tony listed five rules that "must be followed by boys who want to fit the standard code of behavior" (p. 206).

> Be a good student but not too good—any better than B+ is a nerd. Play three varsity sports—or two with weight training. Party and get drunk. Brag about sexual accomplishments and refer to girls as bitches in casual conversation. And never show your feelings. (p. 206)

Like Jason, Tony talked about the sensitive side that adolescent boys had to keep carefully hidden. He remarked:

> Tough guys and jocks hand in these incredible poems. They're usually the seniors who will never see anyone again—or they make it anonymous. They're so afraid if they mess with their macho appearance, people will think less of them. (p. 209)

As both a "tough guy" and a jock, Jason knew all too well the consequences of revealing this sensitive side to his peers. Fortunately, by the time of our interview, he had found a way to embrace his poetic side. I took his journal home that evening and pored over it. His first entry reveals something of the elusive, sensitive side of this young man who took us both by surprise that afternoon.

10/29/93 Friday

It's Friday night and this is my first entry. I'm not at the Halloween dance with Vel, like I should be, because I was too scared to ask her last week, and she did not like me very much this week. I think that I'm falling in love with someone who probably doesn't care for me. I don't see her all day, I just hear her voice. It's such a beautiful voice, I cannot stop hearing it.

You know, but you don't
your voice feeds my eyes
my eyes block my hearing
why are you so good
almost perfect, it kills my thoughts
I feel confined in my name
while your name confines my heart.
I can't love you yet
but I can't help to think
what it would be like
to hear you at night
Your voice untangles my heart
while my fear retangles it
but I can't help to think, what it would be like
to hear you at night.

Jason had changed in other ways as well. By his senior year of high school, he admitted that sports no longer dominated his life. That week, he had just finished his "last ever high school basketball game." Jason is typical of a great many middle to upper class young men who realize in later adolescence the futility of a career in sports. Middle class White males like Jason typically see a wider range of alternatives open to them than do poorer students. As Messner (1992) observes:

Where the middle class boy once found sport to be a convenient institution in which to construct masculine identity and status, the young adult simply transfers these same strivings to other institutional contexts: education and careers. As a result, as we examine the higher levels of the sport career hierarchy, we find that an increasingly disproportionate number of the athletes come from lower-class and minority families. (p. 60)

Although he still liked athletics, they just didn't seem as important to Jason as they had in middle school when he read nothing but sports books and Stephen King novels.

Also, surprisingly, he could no longer stand to watch television. He chuckled about his middle school obsession with re-runs of "Charles in Charge" and "Full House." "How I watched that stuff," he remarked, "[I don't know!] Terrible! It's so bad!" While television had exited the scene, playing guitar and listening to music, as well as spending time with friends, now competed with reading for him. Still an incredibly social person, Jason didn't spend much time alone, admitting: "I really don't read as much as I should, because I'm always out, hanging out with my friends or something." Still, even in the midst of his highly social life, he had not lost the image of himself as a lifetime reader.

When I asked if he was still reading Stephen King, he gave me a blank look, until I showed him the old interview transcripts, where he had raved about King's writing. He chuckled, "Stephen King probably got me reading now that I think about it. I totally forgot that part. . . . I'm not surprised I liked him. He has such an eighth grader's vocabulary."

How odd, yet how fitting, it is that, in our reading lifetimes, favorite authors fade with time, so that only their imprints remain. Could it be that we never remember what authors write, only how we *read* them? As a senior in high school, Jason was reading Henry Miller, Oscar Wilde, and even Robert Pirsig, and was planning to read Hermann Hesse over the summer. Interestingly, as his reading tastes expanded, Jason had become more comfortable with letting teachers make choices for him. He remarked:

> These days when I get assigned something to read, it's something that I'd want to read anyhow. When I had a very select, few things that I enjoyed reading, and it wasn't usually what the school offered, I liked to choose . . . but nowadays I got assigned Oscar Wilde and I am enjoying that, and you know, the assigned books I get aren't that bad. *1984* was great; it was great fun to read. So, hum, I suppose choice is important to me only when . . . I am not given a choice and have something pushed on me that I just don't want.

Similarly, Jason explained that he needed less control over his writing topics. "These days I am getting better and better at just writing what I'm told to write."

Jason's reading processes also seemed to have changed considerably since eighth grade. While he was incredibly social in middle school, he rarely thought of how other people saw him. Four years later, he admitted that he had had many friends in middle school but no "real friends." It wasn't until his later years in high school that he finally made a true friend. As his relationships with friends deepened, apparently his ability to reflect upon and shape his behavior to others' expectations had come to him in what seemed like a perfect Piagetian sequence. In our interview, I reminded Jason that in middle school he seemed more interested in plot than complex characterization. He agreed: "All of a sudden at some point in my career [I began to think about] what's going on in other people's heads. . . . I just started . . . looking into people deeper than just what they do. Try[ing] to figure out why people did certain things."

Just as Meg had been troubled by not remembering Jason, he too seemed unable to remember many of the details of his middle school life. For example, after several interviews with him and my frequent presence in Meg's classroom, he had not remembered my being there at all. Yet what seemed like an amnesia of small details was balanced by a remarkable ability to step outside himself and reflect upon (even laugh at) the immature boy he had been. He recalled, "I had like funny nervous ticks. I was always tapping my feet or going like this (fidgeting nervously)."

High school had not dampened his high spirits and his tendency to challenge his teachers' authority. He explained that during his senior year, he had run into a problem in an English class.

> We read the poem "Do Not Go Gentle into That Good Night," and me and my teacher got into an argument. . . . We had two different opinions. I wasn't saying that he was wrong; I was just saying, well, "This is what I got [my interpretation] from." And he said, "Well, okay, well, that's wrong." . . . [And then] I would give another burning comment about backing up what I thought. And he was like, "Well, we are going to move on now. I think you are missing the point." . . . I eventually shut down, but I was mad that he would tell me that my interpretation of something literary was wrong. 'Cause I always thought that it was whatever you got out of it.

On another occasion, Jason got into a long argument with his Latin teacher about the past tense of "set." Not content with her explanation, he sought out two of his English teachers and got them to write notes, supporting his viewpoint. Eventually the Latin teacher apologized, admitting that she had looked up the word in her dictionary and discovered that Jason was right.

Even in high school, Jason still chafed at what he called "constructive criticism" of his writing. One day, he had shared a poem with his father, who suggested that Jason delete a verse. Later that day, he sought a second opinion from his English teacher, who suggested that Jason "put something more into the rhythm or the rhyming or something." He thought:

> I don't know why I asked you to look at it. I wrote it the way I wanted to write it. I mean, I didn't say that to him, but that's the way I felt. I get annoyed when I get criticized in a way like that. . . . I can take grammatical criticism and I can take criticism on my punctuation; I can't take criticism on the way I choose to write something.

As I thought back about my years in Meg's classroom, I realized that both Jason and Kianna resisted the structures and strictures of schooling, yet Jason had maintained a fairly high grade point average and was on his way to college, while Kianna's brand of resistance often relegated her to the margins of academic success. In describing the limits of certain forms of academic resistance, such as disrupting classes or dropping out of school, Giroux (1991) observes:

> There is a certain irony here: while students [who resisted in these ways] were capable of challenging the dominant ideology of the school, they failed to recognize the limits of their own resistance. By leaving school, these students placed themselves in a structural position that cut them off from political and social avenues conducive to the task of radical reconstruction. (p. 284)

Giroux contrasts these unproductive forms of resistance with those practiced by more academically successful students. He explains:

> These students may use humor to disrupt a class, use collective pressure to draw teachers away from class lessons, or purposely ignore the teacher's directions while attempting to develop collective spaces that allow them to escape the ethos of individualism permeating school life. . . . These students are resisting school ideology in a manner that gives them power to reject the system on a level that will not make them powerless in the future. (1985, pp. 287–288)

In middle school, Jason's brand of resistance had been a bit like Kianna's in some ways. His jittery, off-task behaviors probably contributed to Meg's tendency to want to ignore him. As with most male students, however, Jason refused to be ignored, taking up much of the air time in Meg's class and, unlike Kianna, often shouting out answers to Meg's questions or volunteering to be group spokesperson for collaborative projects. So, while Meg may have wanted to ignore his off-putting behaviors, by openly challenging her authority in front of the class, yet also participating actively and vocally in lessons, he made sure to keep her attention focused on him in positive as well as negative ways.

Jason brought this practice of challenging teachers' authority to high school. However, it seemed that he had perfected his game, making sure his challenges always had an intellectual content that could hardly be grounds for teachers' retaliation or academic retribution. Jason had two things going for him that Kianna did not: He had made academic resistance into a fine art, and he was a White male. Presumably, this combination of factors kept him out of the "official troublemaker" role with school authorities. Still, while he managed to maintain a respectable grade point average and had earned the respect of most of his teachers, Jason talked bitterly about the mindlessness of his high school experience.

"AN OVERLOAD OF BUSYWORK": CHEATING OUR STUDENTS IN THE AMERICAN HIGH SCHOOL

Jason's memories of high school revealed many things, not only about his development as a reader and writer, but about how our nation's high schools are, literally and figuratively, failing our students. As you will discover in later chapters of this book, of the original group of five focal students in this study, four eventually escaped their public high school by one means or another, either dropping out, taking the GED, getting expelled, or transferring to a private school. Ironically, "bad boy" Jason was the only one to graduate from his original high school. What was it about these public high schools that failed to keep young people like these within its walls?

Jason was all too happy to speculate on the problem. At one point in the interview, Meg had to leave for another appointment. As soon as she left, Jason seemed to become more candid about his high school experiences, intimating, "If I thought you were coming here to talk just about education in general, I could really tell you about things that are just screwed up in high school." Intrigued, I encouraged him to go on. He began by describing his typical high school English curriculum. In secondary school, teachers rarely assigned what he called "creative writing." Instead, there was what he called a "steady progression" of academic writing through his high school years. Tests and quizzes were a staple of the literature curriculum. With a mix of disgust and pity, Jason described one of his student teachers.

She would give us tests with questions like "what was the name of this obscure person who has no importance whatsoever to the plot.

Tell me the address of this person who . . ." just dumb things that
didn't make any sense. And to have to pick apart a book like that,
you'd lose like the rhythm of the book—any excitement of the
book—you'd lose it. But she's a student teacher, so she'll get
better.

Perhaps because of his experiences in Meg's middle school classroom, Jason
saw all too clearly the travesty of a "one correct response" approach to literature, arguing, "The way I see it in school, the only thing you learn that is
absolute fact is math, because numbers are man-made. . . . With every other
class, [even] science is just man's absolute best guess."

"In English," he observed, "there are rules to follow," but "things are
never right or wrong. It's a totally free, artistic thing, where you can write
whatever you want and it can be whatever you want." Even in a book report, where teachers supposedly solicit students' honest evaluations, Jason
mused, "You're really not allowed to write, 'This book is terrible, I didn't
enjoy it. I thought it was stupid.' . . . You're supposed to write about how
good the book was." In high school, Jason complained that teachers taught
"everything as fact, when the only thing that you can learn as fact is math."

Not only did teachers seem to seek out "safe," narrow responses in the
various subject areas, but there was what Jason called an "overload of
busywork."

I'll tell you that three of four classes that every student has, every
year are total busywork. . . . You can learn all the information there
is, not do a single thing of homework, ace every test, and the way
it is set up you could fail the class. . . . And teachers really don't
reward kids for paying attention; they reward them solely for doing
busywork.

In his first year of high school, Jason was enrolled in "gifted English,"
which, in his view, "just wasn't a class." He explained:

It was poorly structured and we weren't disciplined to do anything.
Basically we got away . . . without reading a single page in a book.
. . . I didn't do any work all year, and got by—actually I almost
failed the class, but I was just really annoyed with the teacher, how
dumb the work was. . . . Well [she] picked on me 'cause I didn't do
my work, and I guess I didn't do my work 'cause she picked on me.

To Jason, "getting by" seemed to be the most popular pastime at Briarcliff
High School.

People could skip. You could just walk out of school and nothing would happen. There was one hall monitor who was immobile. He would sit down in one place, and you could walk out any door in the building. So, school wasn't taken seriously by most people, including myself.

In his junior year, Jason again took an honors English class. He explained, "I hated the teacher, 'cause she assigned us *The Scarlet Letter.* That's harder to read than Shakespeare! It's terrible! I had no fun reading that whatsoever." This time, he had a first-year English teacher, who, despite what Jason saw as a momentary lapse of taste with *The Scarlet Letter* (Hawthorne, 1995), did manage to interest Jason in several other books, including *The Jungle* (Sinclair, 1981) and *The Catcher in the Rye* (Salinger, 1991). He was assigned Thoreau's *Walden,* but "didn't realize how complex the thinking you have to put in to read that book." It took him 2 days to read 10 pages, and he abandoned the book. Nevertheless, he earned a 97 on the essay. I asked Jason what it meant that he could read only 10 pages of the book, yet get a 97. He replied candidly, "It is so easy to b.s. your way through English, because it's just a theoretical class—there is no right or wrong answers."

In Jason's mind, most teachers were simply too lazy to try to "read" their students. In his opinion, teachers focused on getting students to follow directions and fell back on busywork as a way of "lessening their job." In middle school, Jason observed that students are younger and teachers can "read" whether they are learning or not. In high school, on the other hand, "it is so much easier to hide . . . when you have the tools to hide whether or not you are learning."

Only one teacher in Jason's entire high school career—a math teacher—was "teaching to teach you, to make you learn things. He's not teaching you because it's his job or whatever." This math teacher would "do a problem out" if a student got it wrong, and avoided "these meaningless little quizzes every week that you can study for in 3 minutes before." High school, in Jason's opinion, is set up "for people that just want to get busy and get good grades."

Although cynical about his high school experience, Jason didn't seem damaged by it. Still, I sensed that it would stay with him for the rest of his life. As Sadker and Sadker (1994) have argued:

Many adults carry high school around with them always. It is a unique, eccentric, and insulated social system, a pressure cooker where teenagers rush from one class to another, shoved into close quarters with twenty-five or thirty others their age they may love, hate, care little about, or hardly know at all. It has its own norms, rituals, vocabulary, and even its own way to tell time—not by the minute and hour, but . . . by periods. . . . There is life after high school, but what we do as adults is powerfully shaped by those years. (p. 99)

Jason had the insight, and perhaps a bit of the insensitivity, to make a mockery out of his high school years. But I thought about the many young people and adults I've met who have been deeply scarred by the criticisms and the mindless busywork they've suffered in high school English classes. Ironically, some of them end up in my teacher education classes at the university, so timid about former teachers' negative evaluation that it takes a whole semester to discover their writing voices and claim authorship of their own ideas. Sadly, some of them never reach this point. Many of them are English teachers, and good ones at that! I'd like to blame outmoded approaches to literacy like New Criticism and atomistic grammar drills for their bad experiences. But even today, when such approaches are beginning to wane, there remains an overemphasis on "objective" evaluation and a disconnection between the routines of schooling and the real world of today's diverse students. It is this disconnection and irrelevance in our secondary classrooms that should be our first priority, not—as the politicians and test makers argue—our students' scores on standardized tests. Hargreaves, Earl, and Ryan (1996) echo these sentiments about the modern high school.

> Secondary schools may suffer from a *culture of individualism.* . . . They are places where teachers own the classrooms and students move around the school like passengers in a crowded airport. . . . The lack of a sense of home or collective responsibility leads to a weak sense of institutional pride. . . . [Secondary schooling] is a "curiously fragmented experience" for students; of school bells sounding every forty minutes or to signal a changing of the guard. Isolation is still the norm for secondary school students' experience. . . . And the world in which they are isolated can be a large, complex, and intimidating one. This is particularly disturbing for young adolescent students whose needs for care, security and group attachment . . . are exceptionally strong at this stage of their development. (p. 31, emphasis in original)

We may believe our students are failing to reach our standards, but young people like Jason teach me that, in fundamental ways, we are failing them.

"Make [Reading] Mysterious to This Kid"

Only once in his sophomore year did Jason get excited about anything in an English classroom. During a unit on Shakespeare's *Julius Caesar*, the teacher had asked the class to rewrite their own version of the ending. This particular activity, where Jason could exercise his imagination, helped him to rediscover the "enjoyment in writing things" that he had experienced in

Meg's class years earlier. He was supposed to do the project with a group of his classmates, who wanted to rewrite the ending in what he called "basic English." Jason, however, wanted to rewrite it in "Shakespeare's English." When the other group members put down his idea, Jason said, "Fine. I'll do it myself." On his own, he wrote two scenes in Elizabethan dialect, and remembered that one project as "the single thing that got me into reading and writing."

Toward the end of my interview, I asked Jason how he would teach a student like himself. At first, he replied with a chuckle: "Make him grow up a little. I was pretty immature." Then he added:

> Make [reading] mysterious to this kid, like give him part of the story, read the character and ask him to finish the story the way he'd think it should end. I think that would be the best way . . . to get a kid to try to get inside a character's head.

I asked him once again whether he thought of himself as a lifetime reader. Without hesitation, he replied, "Oh yeah," adding:

> If I never got interested in anything other than sports, I probably wouldn't be a lifetime reader . . . The only thing I'd read in the rest of my life would be scores. That's about it. But it's just the way things worked out, as I happened to have my interests change.

"Strong as a Pencil": His "Nonapplication Process"

As with many other aspects of his life in high school, Jason seemed to have a fairly lackadaisical attitude toward the college application process. Apparently, he had let the deadlines slip by and admitted, "I really messed up at application time. I only applied to [state] schools, and that's it actually. No private schools, no private universities." He planned to live with an uncle in Santa Barbara, where he could establish residency before applying to a California school. He still was not sure what his major might be, but felt somewhat constrained by the fact that his math SATs were 760, while his verbal score was 560. Although he would probably major in mathematics or psychology, he wanted to continue his hobby as a poet by taking a creative writing course. He had just recently discovered that Emerson College had an entire creative writing program. With a chuckle, he admitted, "I didn't know any of this stuff while I was 'not applying' for colleges."

After our interview that day, I sat in the quiet of my living room and read Jason's journal. Toward the end, I discovered this poem, in which he pondered life beyond high school.

This summer.
After graduation, after the prom, after a million cigarettes
after my last school lunch,
My next life will begin.
I'll sleep ten hours every night,
and I'll be in constant awareness of the bright and clear sky.
The wheather will be mine!
I'll love through the summer, breaking all my ties,
and revealing all my lies.
And then one day, at the end of August, I'll jump in my car and
     drive on out to California.
Then another live will start.
I'll drive through L.A. to see my dad's sister and her husband, Eddie
Then I'll drive out to Santa Barbara, out of city, out of the smog
     and air pollution.
I'll live on a mountain with my dad's brother and his wife Story,
     with their two kids Day Bird and Natty and there puppy Maisy.
I'll deal with the bears by trying to make friends,
And the ocean won't intimidate me because I'll offer her my hand.
I'll run around all day, dancing with the sun, and I'll get strong as a
     pencil.

At first blush, I'm inclined not to worry about the Jasons of the world.
I suspect that he will go to college, despite his "nonapplication" process. Yet,
whatever the details of his future career—whether he pursues academics or
some other vocation—whether he becomes a mathematician (I doubt it), a
poet (as he already is), or a psychologist, I believe he will succeed in his own
time and on his own terms—always on his own terms.

In the literate underground, where Jason has always been comfortable,
despite and not because of school, he has found his way to Arthur Miller,
Oscar Wilde, and even Robert Pirsig. He still will not finish a book if it fails
to capture him. Yet today, he will try a book, even if a teacher assigns it.
When Jason can shape reading and writing to suit his agile mind, rewriting
a scene from Shakespeare in Elizabethan prose, he discovers a sort of alchemy
of words. No longer content to confine himself to sports stories (the easy
choice), or driven by the "eighth-grade vocabulary" of Stephen King, he
prefers to take apart a story and put it back together in his own way. In this
way, he makes both reading and writing acts of composing, and stays "in
the action" of a literate life.

In my final interview with him, I slip in the word "catharsis," because I
know he will not understand the meaning. I catch the glimmer in his eye as
he files it permanently, alongside "macabre" in his memory bank. I suspect

Jason has never thought about becoming a teacher, although he probably should. He resists the walls and boundaries, the hierarchies and banalities of formal schooling, the conformities of the high school classroom. Yet he, like so many young people, disenchanted with the mundane aspects of school, is probably just the right candidate for teaching. He could be a mentor for students outside the mainstream, knowing, as he does, all the escape routes in our formal education system. During this very interview, he was getting out of an in-school suspension at Briarcliff. A note from his father explained his prior commitment to meet with me. The elaborate process of punishment and reward rolls easily off Jason's back, as he has learned how to manipulate the system. He could become a teacher. He could even like it. But his disdain for the incessant busywork of high school makes me doubt it somehow.

What I do know is that Jason will go out into the world, challenging and reshaping it when it doesn't suit him. He will do so, as he always has, with sense and passion and eventually, perhaps, a certain artfulness.

Jason's story provokes many questions about the practices of American secondary schooling, however. What are we doing in the American public high school that so many of our students escape its confines? Even when we build safe places of choice and trust and openness, when we provide students with resources and find ways for them to lead the way, they elude us. I fear that, in our zeal to reach an overly simplified and neat version of Piaget's cognitive stages, we miss students' unique and subtle signs of maturity. At the same time, in our hybridized Vygotskian versions of "collaborative learning," we risk depriving students like Jason of those private spaces where he can safely nurture his identity as poet and reader, apart from the glare and scrutiny of his peers who believe that "boys" don't do that sort of thing. More seriously, in our religiously apolitical stance, we fail to challenge gender stereotypes like these as a conscious part of our curriculum.

I suspect that, despite his irritating behaviors, most of Jason's teachers didn't worry about him. He had mastered the art of "getting by," demonstrating just enough intellectual ability to get them off his back. In my own temptation to dismiss him, however, I hear another voice—a warning that we'd best worry about the Jasons of the world—those who never learn to break free of oppressive gender stereotypes that limit young males, especially those involved in athletics. As Sadker and Sadker (1994) have argued:

> To all the world boys appear to be the favored gender, heirs apparent to society's rewards. They are the recipients of the lion's share of teacher time and attention and the featured figures in most textbooks. Sitting atop high standardized test scores, they haul in the majority of scholarship dollars, claim more than half of the openings in the most prestigious colleges, and are destined for high

salaries and honored professions. Few would consider boys "miseducated," but gender bias is a two-edged sword. Girls are shortchanged, but males pay a price as well. (p. 197)

Jason had become adept at "taking on the teacher"; yet, throughout his middle and high school career, he found few teachers willing to take him on—to challenge his temptation to backslide, or to ask for, and expect, his best efforts. Like a great many male students, he took up much of the space and much of the air time in his classes. Furthermore, his athletic prowess had taught him well how to compete on the playing field, as well as the intellectual scene. Sports did little, however, to teach him about the spirit of caring, connectedness, and cooperation necessary for making true friends and sharing his sensitive side. These things he had to learn on his own.

Salisbury and Jackson (1996) comment on how schools cheat boys like Jason: "At the moment, too many schools just passively react to boys' disruption. A policy of containment or just getting by seems to be the order of the day" (p. 3). Just as girls are silenced in schools, students like Jason, while visible and vocal in the official classroom arena, are silenced in another way. It remains a challenge for all of us to look beyond Jason's "brave mouthing" and to help him bring forth these other "choked voices that reveal his multifaced identities" (Salisbury & Jackson, 1996, pp. 8–9). The future of our schools and our society rests on this responsibility.

CHAPTER 6

Another First Day: Revising the Learner-Centered Classroom

I'm really nervous, sitting here at my desk looking out at my empty classroom on the first day of school. Well, I guess it's not empty. It's filled with desks, posters, furniture, rugs—everything set in place with a lot of hope, planning, and anticipation. It's so quiet. . . . I hear them outside. If I walked over to the windows I would look down and see them—a moving blur of new clothes, notebooks, book bags, and laughing nervous faces. They're scared too. But we all pretend that we're not. . . . So—I have my course outline sheets, this beautiful classroom—and me. What if, even after last year, even after all the reading, soul searching, and planning—what if this new reading and writing program doesn't work? Stop it, Meg. Smile. Fix your skirt. Let them know you're glad to be back. There's the bell. Oh shit! (Meg, Journal, 1990)

"THIS FEELS LIKE HOME": FAMILIAR ROADBLOCKS IN NEW TERRAIN

As her students spilled in the door of her new classroom on their second "first day," many of Meg's worries began to evaporate. Her eighth-grade students had returned, not only more mature, but more at home with Meg and their classmates. In her journal after that first day, she rejoiced:

It was great—just like "old home's week"—whatever that means! Hugs, kisses, fast conversations about our summers. They like the room. They love the carpet and all the space. I look around—this feels like home. My nervous feeling is still there—but now it's more like nervous energy, the good kind.

Despite the easy familiarity with each other, however, there were still the "new and improved" structures and procedures that Meg had to sell to her wary students. She began her handout for the eighth-grade year with the motto: "We'll do our best. We can't do anymore, and we shouldn't do any less." Further down the page, she listed brief descriptions of her classroom learning centers:

- GETTING STARTED: *A center where you can begin writing pieces of your choice based on imagination, personal experiences, and individual or class reading, using any process that best suits your writing needs.*
- DRAFTING: *A center where you can work on creating your writing alone, or with the help of other students.*
- PUBLISHING AND PERFORMING: *A center where you can make final copies of your writing, while possibly combining them with other art forms such as drawing or acting.*
- READING AND RESPONDING: *A comfortable center to read whatever you choose and to write letters of response in your composition notebook.*
- SHARING (LITERATURE CIRCLE): *A space in the center of the room where we can read and discuss literature together on a voluntary basis, and where you can perform readings of your own writing.*
- CONFERENCING: *A center where you can meet with me to discuss your general progress each week.*

In an attempt to balance independent and collaborative learning experiences, Meg arranged her curriculum along the lines of Nancie Atwell's (1987) model of reading and writing workshop. Much of her students' time during the week would be spent reading or writing independently or in small groups. This freed Meg up from days of whole-class instruction to act more as mentor or guide while her students pursued independent activities. She reasoned:

> It goes back to my theory, when you have a large group, no matter what you're doing, you have [a third of the students] with you, a third going either way, and a third who don't want to do it. And the third that's bored—the third that definitely will not do it and will become belligerent—those personalities come out in a full group. And I don't know if the [problems with whole-class instruction are because of the] dynamics of "I'm going to show off for my friends" or "I'm not special anymore. I'm one of 25 instead of one of 6 or 7." [or] "This is something that I've been told to do rather than something that I've chosen to do. . . ." They're special when they're in a small group and when they've chosen what they're going to do.

Although Meg would still choose certain texts for students to read, she replaced mandatory whole-group reading with what she called Literature

Circles twice a week. In this arrangement, a small group of student volunteers would gather on the rug to read and talk about short pieces of literature with Meg. According to her weekly schedule, 4 days a week would begin with a mini-lesson on spelling or writing skills. Mondays through Thursdays were available for students to choose particular learning centers in which to work. On Mondays and Wednesdays, Meg would hold Literature Circles; on Fridays, the whole class would gather together for "Sharing Time," where they could share a piece of their writing or discuss something they were reading. For homework, students were expected to complete two entries in their "Independent Reading and Responding" logs and one piece of independent writing per week. Participation in Literature Circle was not specified, but was noted for each student in Meg's class record book. When students failed to attend Literature Circle, Meg planned to gently encourage them to join. Each week, and at the end of each quarter, students would meet with Meg for evaluation conferences, based on materials gathered in their notebooks and their own appraisal of their work.

Despite her carefully planned curriculum, as the days of the fall semester wore on, Meg again grew a bit disenchanted. Although students were certainly more comfortable on a personal and social level this year, she was distressed that they again seemed to resist the curricular changes she had planned for them. During the first week of classes, she wrote in her journal:

> *I was calm today. My voice was even. My movements relaxed. But I expected them to rave about this program—but they just kind of sat there—blank. I bet they were thinking, "Here she goes again—trying out her new ideas that won't work": We'll see—*

Even after an entire year of getting to know her students, and after moving once again to the familiar territory of the eighth-grade classroom, Meg hadn't bargained on the consequences of incorporating a learner-centered curriculum into the socially complex world of her urban classroom. She envisioned her classroom as a place for individual students to have more personal choices in the texts they read and wrote, and even in the activities they chose each day. Her new curriculum, however, was hardly a neutral array of rules and techniques, but a vision of teaching and learning that would continue to challenge not only her beliefs as a teacher, but also her very identity as a literate person.

As this chapter will reveal, the personal sharing she encouraged in journals and class discussions brought her into areas of her students' lives that hardly felt like "safe spaces." In addition, the seemingly neutral zone of Sharing Time became an occasion for racial and other social conflicts to surface in hurtful and divisive ways. As these conflicts emerged, Meg came to question her identity as a White female teacher and to feel somewhat powerless to effectively teach the students of color in her classroom. Finally, her new role in her independent reading program as "fellow reader," rather than "textual authority," stirred up some painful memories of reading and brought her very identity as a reader into question.

Once again, Meg's curriculum borrowed heavily from the Piagetian ideal of individual students reaching their own potential, as well as Vygotsky's notion of the inextricable relationship between the social and the personal. It was in this balancing act that she encountered the stubborn tensions that would appear and reappear on the horizon of her classroom as the days unfolded.

VISIONS AND REVISIONS:
COMPLEXITIES OF THE CONSTRUCTIVIST CLASSROOM

I work with students who are so thin I can wrap my thumb and index finger around their shoulders. . . . These are twelve and thirteen-year-old children. Children who should be eating constantly, moving constantly, and thinking constantly. Are they supposed to shut up and listen? Am I supposed to talk about nouns and verbs in the abstract? How about: "Harry is too thin!" "Society should not allow guys to get this thin!" Now go back and circle the verbs. (Rehak, 1996, p. 282)

Just as Jay Rehak, a Chicago high school English teacher, constantly examined his teaching against the harsh backdrop of his students' lives, Meg discovered that with more time devoted to personal reading, writing, and sharing in her new curriculum, she too was treading far outside the familiar topics of language and literacy teaching. In previous years, she had worried about whether her students were learning about reading, writing, and the connections between them. Now she found herself implicated more intimately in their lives, worrying about issues like teenage pregnancy, sexual abuse, drugs, poverty, and crime in highly personal terms. In her journal, she wrote, "To help them—to not lose myself—I need to remain objective. But how do I do that?"

"Cries for Help": The Challenge of Personal Sharing

Although she was now in a better position to help and understand her students, there were times when she seemed to regret her journey inside the boundaries of their private lives. For example, early in the year, Meg learned from a student that Rebecca, another student, was being sexually abused by her father. Upon hearing about it, Meg was legally and ethically bound to report it to the authorities. Unfortunately, rather than removing Rebecca immediately from the household, the officials from the local child protective agency arrived at 5:00 in the evening, confronted the father, then left Rebecca to spend the night with her outraged family. Meg was appalled by the misery her actions unwittingly had caused Rebecca. For several weeks, as the case wore on, Meg was continually drawn into the situation, sometimes to the neglect of her classes. One day she wrote:

> *Today I missed two periods because Rebecca's case worker came to talk to us again. . . . We got her to be a little more open, but there is still nothing that we can do. You know, Rebecca has never written about this at all—she writes very "up" pieces—until the last one, I guess. It was about a little boy whom no one liked. He is going to school for a field trip and the end of the world happens. Only the children survive because they are the "innocent." I think that is very telling.*

As she opened up the options for student writing topics, Meg unlocked a Pandora's box of disturbing issues within the walls of her classroom. The students she had read about in the popular literature on literacy teaching had focused on rather general struggles in growing up and moving through adolescence. Meg's students were writing about far more serious issues: alcoholism, drug addiction, crime, and teenage pregnancy. Although she admitted that it was burdensome for her to read the "depressing" writing her students were handing in, she also saw it as a rare opportunity to learn about the issues that many of them dealt with on a daily basis. She wrote in her journal, "There is so much pain, boredom, ambivalence and insecurity. They take all that, and because they are adolescents, they magnify their situations with the drama of it all."

Unfortunately, not all of her students' stories were magnified out of proportion. Some were both life threatening and terrifying. For example, early in November, Meg was chaperoning a school dance. At some point in the evening she noticed that some of her students had come in drunk. Samantha, one of the group members, told her that earlier that evening, they had lied to their parents and had gone to a nearby park to drink, rather than going directly to the dance. Not only oblivious to the dangers of hanging out in a city park after dark, they were also unaware that Ariel, one of Meg's students, had begun to lose consciousness because of the combination of alcohol in her body and the cold weather. Afraid of going for help, and not realizing that Ariel was slipping into hypothermia, they tried to help her themselves, pushing her perilously close to death.

The Monday after the incident, shaken and saddened, Meg clipped a poem that Ariel had written about the incident inside her teaching journal.

The poem began with a bleak description of Ariel's fear and loneliness, ending with the lines: "Black as night/Hollowness fills my heart/With an enemy called life/But I stay still." Meg's personal involvement in these and other situations threw her into understandable turmoil. She complained, "My new program allows them to write about whatever they want. So many of them are using their writing as a vehicle to cry for help."

Throughout that year, Meg continued to struggle between detachment and involvement in her students' personal lives. One day, for example, Frank confided that he had just come from family court because a friend of his was shoplifting and Frank was found guilty by association. He asked Meg for advice on how to convince his parents he was innocent. She wrestled back and forth: "He is an innocent kid who is being punished for something he didn't do—and he's carrying that around with him all by himself. But then I think—what if he's lying to me? But why would he—I'm not involved."

By opening up students' independent reading choices, she also opened up the possibilities for talk in Sharing Time to include some of the formerly "taboo" topics now making their way into the popular literature available to adolescents and young adults. One day, for instance, Rameka decided to share an excerpt from Alice Walker's *The Color Purple* (1995).

> *Rameka* (exclaiming suddenly): Oh, wait a minute. You probably
>   don't know about this part. She's talking about how sex looks.
> *Amy*: How what looks?
> *Rameka*: Like how her vagina looks.
> *Bekka*: She hasn't looked at it?
> *Amy*: Stop!
> *Bekka*: She never washed it before?
> *Doreen*: Read every word!

As Rameka started to read, students began to giggle and shift uncomfortably in their seats. When a student yelled, "That's gross!" Meg stepped out onto the shaky tightrope between her students' freedom of speech and her need to set the boundaries of appropriateness. She began:

> Let's talk for a minute . . . now my position as a teacher [is that] we
> have a mixed group of people. I think that, especially at your age,
> it's important to read things about sex that end up showing you
> what a really marvelous part of life it can be. I think that, I would
> never be one to talk about pornography. . . . Like in a *Penthouse*
> letter, where it's written as something cheap and merely for
> entertainment. But I think there's a lot of literature that deals with

sex in a very beautiful way, especially at your ages when this is something that you're making decisions about. I think that [sex can be] something that is very beautiful to read about. You need to make sure that you're reading about it in a way that shows how beautiful it is, or [that teaches you] not to let yourself be taken advantage of or things like that. I think my position as a teacher is that I've got people sitting here at different ages, different backgrounds; some people have experimented with sex, other people haven't yet. Some people are very well-informed about it; others aren't. And that's really something that starts with the home or your private life, as far as how much you're into it or how much you know about it and all that. So I have to make sure that when we talk about it, we talk about it in general terms and not specific terms. Do you know what I mean? Because some people know a lot and other people don't. And people have to learn in their own way in their own time. And so I have to be mindful of the many types of people we have here.

Although Meg's boundary setting was necessary to establish a safe space for Sharing Time, it was difficult for her, especially since she had few role models in her own teachers for how to broach such issues. She was caught between a desire to allow all students freedom of expression, and protecting some of them from the pseudo-sophistication that some young adults adopt in an era of overt sexuality, physical violence, and other residues of advertising, music, television programs, and movies specifically targeted toward their age group. David Elkind (1994) has explained that "in the postmodern era, we have come to see youths as sophisticated and knowledgeable in sexual matters" (p. 157). Unfortunately, this largely uninformed perception has had a negative impact on young adolescents who choose not to be sexually active. As Elkind explains, "Peer group pressure is such that they are forced to accept and condone the suggestive language and behavior of their sexually active peers, even if it makes them uncomfortable" (p. 157).

On the other hand, the free-flowing conversation during Sharing Time was not without its humorous moments. One day, Luis read a Nikki Giovanni poem that compared the rain to "god's sperm falling." After a moment of silence, Kendra mused, "No wonder rain smells so funny!" Meg wrote in her journal that day, "I was in over my head once again, and we all moved on. The things I leave myself open for when they pick what they want to share! But—I love it." Although at times it seemed as if she was treading in dangerous territory, it began to dawn on Meg how much this personal involvement with her students had become tied in with her self-esteem as a teacher and human being.

I've known all along that this is more than a job—but today something hit me that never really has before—I need them! I need to lose myself in them. . . . My teaching is probably my greatest source of positive self-esteem. Is that why I work so hard at it? Is some of this selfish? If so—is that wrong?

As I watched Meg struggle with the balance between detachment and involvement in her students' lives, I realized that my new stance as a qualitative researcher in Meg's classroom had implicated me in a similar balancing act between participant and observer. Sometimes, as I watched her teaching, I longed to be back in my own middle school classroom. I'd find myself thinking, "Just let me get in there and teach! Here's what I'd do. . . ." One day after visiting her class, I reflected in an analytic memo that "I struggle to stay away from [a participant role] and to enter into it at the same time." I wrote:

I struggle to stay out . . . watching the wheels of my recorder turn, I dutifully keep my notes in separate columns on the page. I sit at the beginning of class, nodding recognition, but not really recognizing the kids. I struggle to enter in . . . dropping comments and questions during share time, occasionally engaging in casual conversation with a kid or two who happens to recognize me from 2nd period. But there is still a wall, a holding back. I want to say it's respect for Meg and the kids—for their territory. But I think there's an element of insecurity in there as well. Like when somebody hands you a baby, and you don't quite know what to do with it. . . . These kids are not my kids, so I relate to them from a distance, if at all. Am I being too hard on myself? Perhaps. . . . Now, I return to my "other" life . . . my appointments and meetings at the university. . . . Why do I feel so adolescent *these days?*

My new role as both participant and observer left me with many questions about when I should watch the events in Meg's classroom unfold from the sidelines, and when I should step in and give my advice or opinion. It occurred to me then that, whether for teachers or researchers, the move toward a social constructivist perspective demands more than a simple change in procedure. Neither teachers nor researchers can simply step aside and let events unfold before their eyes. I thought back to the days when questionnaires and interviews were the mainstay of my research. Afterward, in the private space of my office at the university, alone with only another "rater," I could feed anonymous data into a computer program. There were few struggles then between participant and observer. In my new role as classroom researcher, I faced a much deeper personal, social, and ethical issue: how to present Meg's classroom in all of its complexity, rather than reducing it to the simplicity of charts and numbers.

I thought back to JoBeth Allen's (1990) remarks at a workshop I'd attended a few years back: "Our new roles as qualitative researchers are demanding that we arrive earlier and stay later in classrooms these days." As Meg and I learned, we not only arrived earlier and stayed later, but we were encountering and sharing our whole selves with others in the process. Like Meg, I struggled between my "lives" as researcher and university professor. One day, I wrote in my notes:

> If I don't know who I am in this research project, perhaps it's because I'm expected to wear so many hats and run in so many different directions in my "other" life at the university. Strangely, this school is beginning to feel like "the real world" and [the university] is becoming the distraction.

"I Don't Have No Civilization": The Politics of Collaboration

The year she started the pilot project, Meg's school district had invested heavily in collaborative learning as an instructional strategy. As part of this district-wide initiative, Meg had volunteered her classroom as a site for a university grant project, based on collaborative learning as a way of creating an "inclusive" classroom. This meant that she would serve as a teacher leader, offering workshops on collaborative learning for other teachers in the district, and would open up her classroom to visits by members of the research team.

Although it was not an explicit stipulation of the research team, Meg felt great pressure to make collaborative learning "work" in her classroom. Although publicly supporting and even teaching the model to other teachers in workshops, Meg struggled privately with the day-to-day realities of collaborative learning and sharing in her diverse urban classroom. In an interview with me, she observed:

> A lot of the stuff they tell you about [the notion that] "cooperative learning is the key to making your class work together"—I just think that your kids have to be at a certain point before that can happen. I became very aware this year of the levels of trust that have to be there before you can do a lot of these things.

Much of the literature she had read on collaborative learning, and what the research team seemed to be espousing, rested largely on a set of neat structures for placing students into defined task roles. Meg, however, encountered a great deal of resistance whenever her collaborative tasks became too structured. For example, in her students' seventh-grade year, she had placed them into teams, asked them to find a grammar rule, and instructed them to "teach" this rule to the rest of the class. She recalled, "I tried to make it too organized. [I said] 'this is your group, and this is the schedule for the week. This is color-coded with this and . . .'" Meg felt that this tight structure, combined with the expectation that students were to "be creative," sent them a mixed message. On the one hand, she was saying to students, "You're going to have freedom to read what you want, write what you want, and I'm going to follow your lead." On the other hand, so much emphasis on the structure of groups made the process very teacher-controlled. She mused, "I was saying one thing and doing another. I think that's probably how they got confused."

This year, she had tried to shed the rather restrictive set of group roles and allow students to collaborate in more informal ways: in self-selected small groups or pairs, writing or performing together, or in teacher-led small groups, responding to literature or sharing their reading and writing. Unfortunately, these changes in classroom structure still did not eliminate the interpersonal conflict and intolerance that often surfaced during collaborative activities. Students would sit in tight little groups, listening only when their friends were sharing, and falling into rude chatter when someone from another group spoke. Whenever the entire group gathered together, she felt as though one-third of the class was "engaged," one-third was "sometimes engaged," and one-third was "totally unengaged." "I know this can work," she wrote in her journal, "but on [learning center days] I'm used to seeing *everyone* into what they're doing. I'm so spoiled." After a particularly frustrating experience during Sharing Time one day, Meg wrote in her journal:

> *This is going to be a difficult thing to say, but I think that the main reason that I feel a lot of tension on sharing days is because many of the students really don't like each other. Ben read the opening of this story—and it was really excellent— . . . But just because BEN wrote it, the feeling in the room was that it wasn't worth listening to. All day long I noticed this happening. The opposite is true also. "Cool" kids can read stuff that is not so good and everyone will praise it.*

Ben had entered Meg's classroom during the second year of the pilot project. At least by his physical appearance, and by the standards of his middle school classmates, he was the classic "nerd." He was also a promising fiction writer. As I explained in Chapter Two, many times Ben would come over to where I was sitting, turn on my tape recorder, and engage in an on-the-spot interview about his budding career as a young novelist. Many times, he would slip me the latest computer-generated draft of *Alpha Force*, a science fiction novel he was writing. Students like Ben often were excluded from the "in" cliques in Sharing Time, as his classmates would degenerate into rude whispering and idle chatter when he tried to share his writing.

Increasingly frustrated with the insensitivity during Sharing Time, Meg opened one Friday session with a "class meeting," in which she invited students to share their honest reactions to the class procedures. She began:

> This is the time if you feel things have been unfair in any way or you didn't like the way something was done, or if you have a suggestion, a new way something can be done or whatever, anything that's on your mind, this is the time and the place to speak your mind. Anyone have anything to say? Everybody happy?

Rasheen broke the silence with a firm "No." When other students tried to silence him, he responded angrily, "No, I'm not happy and if I'm not happy I don't have to say yes if I don't want to, so I'm not happy and don't tell me I am!" Meg tried to draw out some of Rasheen's feelings.

Meg: Is it just life in general, Rasheen, or is it this class you're unhappy with?
Rasheen: This class.
Meg: Can you speak more specifically?
Rasheen: The people in the class, some of the people.
Meg: Okay, Rasheen, there's a real easy solution for that and that is that you could separate [from people you don't like and sit by me] because I don't bite.
Rasheen: No, I have a seat right here and I'm going to stay.
Anthea: We are civilized.
Rasheen: People used to be very cool last year but they're . . .
Anthea: People change.
Meg: I happen to like the change, and I am waiting for the civilization to dawn on you.
Rasheen: I don't have no civilization.

Later in the discussion, Rasheen mentioned that he'd like to do a rap. Still trying to draw him into the discussion, Meg said, "Why don't you make one up for us, Rasheen? You haven't shared anything with us today." He refused, saying only that "sharing [is] boring." Meg pushed on: "What have you been working on?" "Women," Rasheen replied. Although more openly

hostile and sarcastic than his classmates, Rasheen demonstrated an intolerance that was typical of many of his classmates toward spending time with
anyone outside of their small social circle. During Sharing Time one day, Meg
tried to break through some of this resistance by explaining to the students:

> We had an unfortunate incident second period where someone
> started to share her poem and it was a really good poem but it was
> a difficult poem, and a couple [of] people started laughing and
> rolling their eyes and all that. That's the kind of thing that can't
> happen. We have to be really attentive to each other and respectful
> of each other's work or no one's going to want to share. I wouldn't
> bring in my stuff if I looked around and saw people whispering to
> each other and making comments or laughing. I wouldn't bring it
> in. No one wants to go through that. Let's try and be real respect-
> ful to each other.

Still, the intolerance and rudeness continued. Often, to Meg's frustration,
this intolerance ran along racial lines.

"ONE BLACK DOT IN THE CLASS": RACE AND RESISTANCE

I had been noticing for a long time that students often segregated themselves into racial groups when given the opportunity to sit where they chose.
As early as January of the year before, I wrote in a memo:

> *There seems to be racial solidarity in the ways that kids hang out
> together, though it doesn't exactly play itself out in predictable ways.
> Sometimes (only occasionally) I see a Black student asking a White
> student to read her piece aloud (once, actually). But usually, kids of the
> same race tend to sit and to work together. So much for "great strides
> in integration."*

Although she rarely brought the topic up in our informal talks, Meg mentioned this fact in her journal. Once, after another trying day in Sharing Time,
she wrote:

> *Today was sharing day. I like sharing day, but in a way [sharing days]
> give me back the bad feeling of 25 against one. First period was great!
> They shared their pieces—reacted well to each other, etc. Second period
> was good too—but one thing really bothered me. The kids came in and
> chose their own places to sit like this:*

Whites (who were only interested when a white student shared)	Blacks (who were only interested when a black student shared)

Me

Blacks & Whites (who listened to everyone)

I felt like there was a subtle race war going on. I want the kids to choose where they sit—but what do I do when it ends up like this?

Throughout the year, Meg continued to puzzle over the limitations of a learner-centered pedagogy in her diverse classroom where racial tensions made the need for solidarity uppermost in students' minds. What happens when "personal choice" turns into the choice to exclude or separate from others on the basis of race? This tension played itself out in many ways during my time in Meg's classroom. One day, for instance, Meg was pleasantly surprised to discover that a group of students had written a play with her in the starring role; at the same time, she was disappointed, writing in her journal, "I loved it. (But again—two black girls wrote it and only chose other black kids to act it out) kind of a theme of the day."

Interestingly, although Meg privately agonized about the racial segregation in her classroom, I seldom witnessed her directly addressing the issue in her talks with students. More often, she referred to rudeness and lack of cooperation as general traits, shared by all students, rather than articulating the racial issues that seemed to lie just beneath the surface of the classroom dynamics.

This racial segregation continued in subtle ways. For example, that spring, Meg organized a play writing group where students were responsible for writing and producing their own original drama. I noticed that after a few weeks of rehearsal there were more White students in the group than students of color. When I brought this up to Meg in an interview, she explained:

> It didn't start out like that. I made a conscious effort for it to be 50/50. Now we have this rule in our school it has to be 35/[65]. Or should. Anything should be, that's your goal. And then I had four black kids drop out. And every kid that dropped out were black kids. And I think that some of them—a lot of those kids have to

babysit young kids and couldn't make it. There were two girls who didn't have large enough parts and were very upset that they didn't have more of a part so they dropped out. Some I lost to sports. . . . I felt really bad because it was so obvious it was those kids. And I really didn't think it had anything to do with me. For a minute I thought it was because I was white, and [that] the black kids that stayed in there were "white" black kids. But no. [There was] Luis [for example].

Although there were a number of plausible reasons for the deteriorating racial balance in Meg's play writing group, I too wondered if Meg's identity as a White woman teacher might have had something to do with the situation. I had noticed that the school held a number of talent shows and assemblies, organized by Janet Edwards, the Assistant Principal, and Ed Jackson, the artist in residence, who were both African American. The racial balance in these activities heavily favored African-American students. At one assembly, I noticed that a large group of Black students read their pieces first, followed by a handful of White students. Halfway through the assembly, I wrote in my notes:

> I notice that almost all of the readers [so far] have been Black. I wonder if the fact that Ed Jackson is organizing things makes the African-American students feel more comfortable in getting up in front of their peers. I also wonder how the White kids feel about being a minority, for once.

Meg explained that, historically at Logan, the play was seen as "an upper . . . preppy boy activity. And it's very hard to break through that." Although disappointed that more students of color weren't involved in her play writing group, she was happy with small victories, pointing out, "I don't think a Black kid was in a play when I got here."

Although I had no tangible proof for my hunches, I also wondered whether her increased involvement in students' personal lives had made Meg more acutely aware of her identity as a White woman teacher and her sometimes strained relationships with the African-American students, particularly the males, in her classroom. Her negative encounters with them, some of which bordered on verbal or physical violence, left her frustrated and emotionally exhausted. In the midst of her frustration and fear, she struggled over her ability to reach these young men, empathizing deeply with their circumstances and occasionally writing poems like these in her journal:

When i come to school
my family comes with me, tucked in my mind.
My street is my heart

My dog, Ralphie, is my soul
My brother travels with me in my pocket
and my neighbors are always hangin out, watching me.
Kids in school are different,
but i don't want them to be.
i need a second home.
i need to be respected
i need to tell my stories.
i need people to know it's my birthday
keep my doubts and secrets safe.
But
Sometimes i sit in class
and let my brother crawl from my pocket
and walk across my desk
He knows when i am bored with almighty teacher
I watch her and think
She should walk herself down my street
peel plaster off my rotting walls
listen to my father brag about the bets
and reach past the cold math problems to me.
But sometimes i go to her room.
the nice teacher
who knows she ain't the world
who shows me friend
who helps bring my street to school
who helps white people see
pride in my black eyes
who helps me ask questions
and feel like
it's okay to be lost
who helps me be apart of something
    bigger than myself
who helps me learn
    not just
        good boy
        respectful student
        hard worker
    but playful brother
        street fighter
        lonely child
I could not learn just as one
black dot in the class.

Meg's struggle with her identity as "White teacher" surfaced in a journal entry she wrote one day when Ed Jackson had taken over her classes. Many times, I myself had witnessed Ed's charisma with African-American males. I'd look on, awestruck, as he'd grab a rowdy student like Jaquille by the arm and poke him sharply in the chest with a warning: "You think this is a joke, but this is the real world! You can't go around acting like this all your life!" I'd watch as the very same students who were noisy and disruptive in Meg's class would look to Ed with respect and admiration, almost enjoying his rough boundary setting and his piercing honesty. Although certainly grateful for his presence in her classroom, Meg couldn't help worrying about her ability to reach her African-American males as Ed was able to. She wrote in her journal:

Ed Jackson started with us today. He talked to the kids who were not in literature circle. I watched him move around the room—from one kid to the next, a very quiet, reassuring presence. All I kept thinking was that he was reaching kids that I haven't really. It's not that I'm jealous or anything, but his being a successful black man who is a writer/actor acts as magic to the black males in my room. It's too bad that we can't always teach together. I watched him with Tommell, Jerome, Alvin, Tony—he was getting them to talk, making pointed suggestions for their writing—giving them material to read. They can identify so much with people reacting to people to make learning happen.

"PHANTOMS IN THE OPERA": RACE, GENDER, AND EXCLUSION

I must admit that I didn't notice it at the time I was observing in Meg's classroom, but later, upon sifting through the data, I saw few instances where Meg focused on African-American female students in her journal. Although she noted a few times when they had written exceptional poetry, her own poems and reflections about the lives of her Black students typically centered on the males. On the surface, it would seem that her female identity amplified the distance from the males in a way that it did not for the females. It also may have been that her negative encounters with Black male students were potentially more violent than those with Black female students, and therefore stood out more vividly for her. Nevertheless, some time after my data had been collected, I ran across a study of first-grade students by Linda Grant (1984), who observed:

Black girls' orientations toward teachers ranged from apple-polishing to wary avoidance, with most falling in between. Although generally compliant with teacher rules, black females were less tied to teachers than white girls were and approached them only when they had a specific need to do so. White girls spent more time with teachers, prolonging questions into chats about personal issues. Black girls' contacts were briefer, more task-related, and often on behalf of a peer rather than self. (p. 107)

Grant later concluded that "peer interchanges, as well as student–teacher relationships, put a premium on black girls' social, rather than academic, skills" (p. 109).

As I read this observation, I thought particularly about Kianna. Although she certainly had captured Meg's attention (often in negative ways), and although she had written poetry of great depth, and had even organized her own play writing group, Kianna was never the topic of Meg's journal. Considering Grant's findings, I realized that I never witnessed Kianna taking time to chat or share personal issues with Meg the way many of her White female students had. Instead, Kianna's encounters with Meg usually revolved around some scheme for getting out of the classroom or, as I observed one morning, loudly protesting when she thought that Meg had been unfair to a friend of hers. One day in April of Kianna's eighth-grade year, Meg seemed reluctant to issue a pass to the nurse for Kianna's friend Tippi. Kianna challenged in an accusing tone, "You put Tippi on the pass list, Mrs. Andrews?" Even though Meg replied "Yes," Kianna muttered, "We need to beat you up." Noticing that I had been watching, Kianna smiled wryly at me and asked, "Why do you keep looking at me and writing?" Caught off guard, I replied, somewhat untruthfully, "I'm looking at everyone, Kianna; you only think I'm looking just at you." Meg then tried to get Kianna interested in some private freewriting. After a few minutes, Kianna shouted, "This stuff is stupid, Mrs. Andrews!"

It would be unfair of me to make judgments about how Meg treated her female African-American students on the basis of so few observations and such spotty data. However, recent work on the tenuous status of African-American females in school and society (e.g., Fine, 1995; Fordham, 1988, 1993, 1996; Grant, 1984; hooks, 1989; McCarthy, 1996; Sadker & Sadker, 1994; Williams, 1991) causes me to look at not only Meg's classroom but my own in a different light.

Meg's male students, like Luis and Montell, lived on the margins of academic success and challenged her authority, just as Kianna did. But unlike Kianna, these male students made it into the pages of Meg's journal, seeming to garner more of her focused attention and reflection. One day, for instance, Montell had been unusually disruptive, forcing Meg to send him down to guidance. When he got there and no one was in, he came back visibly and vocally agitated, making it difficult for Meg to focus on her teaching. In desperation that afternoon, Meg remarked in her journal, "Why is it that some days I take everything that happens to me personally? Every time I do that I overreact. Some days I have a sense of humor about everything. Not today. But this Montell thing will be in my mind for a long time." That afternoon, Meg converted her frustration into a poem.

The boy looked at me
through swollen eyes,
a challenge for me
to be less than
I am.
White woman,
trying to understand
black boy
who says
that
fighting is a way of
life
around
small apartments
that try to be
homes
His mother holds
eight kids to her
like startled birds,
and fear
holds them
all together,
the way love should
white cops
slap proud black
from young boy's faces,
pipes,
knives,
chains,
all trying to protect
who they are.
I looked at the boy
through swollen eyes,
a challenge for him
to be more
than any boy
should have to be.

On Monday after the incident, Montell came back into class and astounded Meg by writing a piece called "getto boy" that ended with the line, "I just want a family from god, not from hell, and someday I'll have it." This piece so moved Meg that she reflected in her journal:

> *Kids do listen to the things we say as teacher—and they do internalize them. Also—there is a fine line between caring about students, and becoming too personally involved. There has to be some objectivity. I lost that with Montell last Friday. . . . Prisons are filled with people who were forced to learn curriculum until they quit school maybe, but not so filled with people who know who they are and who have learned how to unleash all their potential. Every kid I teach is a writer and a reader. They are all in different places and have different futures. . . . If they all go to high school with . . . the belief that reading and writing has a purpose in their lives . . . then that is what will determine whether or not they have really learned and whether or not I have really taught!*

I think of Meg's statement, meant to be humorous, a year earlier, when I asked her to talk about Kianna: "Oh please, please Kianna, get sent to Allen School, so I don't have to deal with you any more!" Why, I wondered, did Kianna not make it into the pages of Meg's journal, when Montell and Luis did? Sadker and Sadker (1994) have observed this same phenomenon.

> When teachers are asked to remember their most outstanding students, boys' names dominate the list. . . . But boys are on another roster. When teachers remember their worst students—the discipline problems, the ones most likely to create a classroom disturbance or to flunk out of school—they still list boys. (p. 198)

Despite these compelling findings, it is often hardest for teachers, swept up in the daily routines of their classroom, to detect patterns of gender bias. Sadker and Sadker concur:

> It is difficult to detect sexism unless you know precisely how to observe. And if a lifetime of socialization makes it difficult to spot gender bias even when you're looking for it, how much harder is it to avoid the traps when you are the one doing the teaching. (p. 4)

In response to this dilemma, Sadker and Sadker suggest: "Given the hectic pace of classroom life, clocked at several hundred to a thousand interactions daily, most teachers cannot monitor accurately who receives their attention. An outside observer—a colleague, parent, or even a student—must help" (p. 267).

As that "outside observer," I was, at the time, of little help to Meg. Although I considered myself sharply attuned to gender issues, I now wonder why this disparity between males and females of color in Meg's room didn't dawn on me until long after my data had been collected. In my research, I had moved from the safety and distance of my questionnaires—from a psychological to a social constructivist position. And yet, an issue that often had been the very subject of my university methods classes, had managed to slip right past me: gender exclusion. Although I had allowed myself to be swept into the complex social dynamics of this urban classroom, in order to fully understand those dynamics, I needed a perspective that went beyond both Piagetian and Vygotskian constructivism, with their focus on the individual learner.

As Chapter Nine will reveal, several years later, I have only begun to explore a "critical constructivism" (Kincheloe & Steinberg, 1993) that affords the richness of perspective to understand both the political and personal dimensions of those 3 years I spent with Meg and her students. I came to believe that Meg needed a similar framework within which to understand the perplexities and complexities of her teaching decisions.

"SICK OF READING FROM READING CLASS": BROADENING THE CANON OF CONTROL

As she struggled to create a collaborative climate in her classroom, Meg also fought to maintain a balance between reading and writing, in both her curriculum and her personal life. Although I hadn't noticed the difference in her "official" talk about the role of reading and writing in her curriculum, I gradually began to notice that reading and writing were *treated* differently in Meg's room. Freeing up students to make more choices in the books they read and making Literature Circle an optional activity certainly had improved her students' attitudes toward reading. But I noticed that Meg herself seemed to turn nearly every moment in the classroom into an occasion for focusing on writing. During Literature Circle and Sharing Time, Meg often broke off a discussion about books and stories to deliver a mini-lecture on some aspect of writing technique. For example, she began one of her first Literature Circles with a discussion of narrative poetry. Notice how she follows a rather typical "Initiation" and "Reply" pattern (Mehan, 1979), in which each reply to students is actually a mini-lecture about writing technique.

> *Meg:* One thing that I want you to notice is that this is a narrative poem. Do you know what the word narrative means?
> *Angel:* The narrator's talking.

Meg: Someone's talking. That comes from the word narrator, someone telling a story. The narrative poem is a poem that tells a story. This doesn't just, a lot of the poems that we are reading, give us like one clear feeling or they paint one picture and usually the poems are shorter than this.

Harvena: This paints a couple pictures.

Meg: There's definitely description in here. This does paint a picture. In fact there's description all the way through it. But the poem itself, if you didn't have this picture to look at, if you read through this poem you could get a picture of what's happening in your mind. So this poem does paint a picture. But what it also does is tells a story, from beginning to end. It has characters in it, just like if you were to write a short story you'd have characters and you'd have settings of places and all of that. That's what this does. It develops things a little bit more than a regular poem does. So this is something that you can think about, the different kind of form that we haven't really done much with writing this year and that's the narrative poem. You say, "I have this thing that I want to turn into a story." You can turn it into a narrative poem. It would be a different kind of form that you could write in. Okay. What I'd like to do is do a reading with this for you and then we're going to talk about it a little.

In her early Literature Circles, Meg often did much of the talking and usually relied on four kinds of comments: mini-lectures about literary technique, questions about the literal meaning of the text, requests for students' personal stories related to the text, or reminiscences about her own personal experiences.

As I read over the Literature Circle transcripts, it began to occur to me why it has been so difficult over the years to create a pedagogy of literary reading. Teachers have models for the composing process; they know roughly the stages of the process, what revising strategies to use, and how to set up a system for monitoring student progress. But what do you do when students have finished reading a story, besides giving tests or asking questions to which you already know the answers? I watched Meg struggle with this issue in the daily activities of her Literature Circle. Even in this more informal small-group context, Meg talked more than her students, asked rather limited questions about plot or personal experience, or shared a story of her own. But beyond these rather rudimentary response strategies, she seemed to be grasping at straws. In an October memo I wrote, "I notice that talk in one situation [writing] is more exploratory and open-ended while the other is more fixed. Does Meg have more of an agenda for reading than writing?"

Meg herself noticed the differences between her reading and writing curriculum in her journal.

> *I have been concerned about the reading my students have been doing, and not doing. The writing aspect of the program is so successful. But the students still seem reluctant to read. Not only are they reluctant—I have even sensed some hostility concerning the responses to their reading.*

This hostility toward reading (and particularly sharing what they read with others) became apparent in both indirect and more blatant ways. When not openly disrespectful, students often demonstrated resistance to Meg's reading program more subtly, by "forgetting" their reading response notebook or refusing to participate in Literature Circle. In the early months of their eighth-grade year, I often heard Meg say to students, "You owe me two reading responses" or "You haven't been to Literature Circle in weeks."

These not-so-gentle nudgings sometimes surfaced in her conferences with students. Once, for instance, Rasheen started a conference with Meg by stating that he had "forgotten" his reading response notebook. Frustrated and angry, Meg decided to forbid him to work with other students until he could learn to use his time productively. She complained:

> You come in here and I'd say you spend about 75% of your time playing around and 25% of your time working. And I need to see what Rasheen can do all by himself for a while. So I don't want you working with somebody else. I want you to come in here and decide whether you're going to read or going to write. Sit down and write or read all by yourself. And be responsible about your deadlines. And maybe if I see that for a while I can let you go back to working with other people.

Later in the same class period, when Conrad "couldn't find" his reading response notebook, Meg invited him to sit down and tell her about his reading. Although he'd started *The Cat Ate My Gymsuit* (Danziger, 1975), he hadn't come close to finishing it. Meg asked in exasperation:

> Do you ever choose to read it in here? See this is part of your problem. At least once a week you should go to the reading center, and you can write the rest of the time. If you're not getting it done at home and all that, then you need to say, "One day a week I'm going to go to reading response." Then you do your reading and you write your response and then it's done. You need to make a

choice to go to the reading center one day a week. Half of this program is trying to get you to be a better writer. The other half is trying to get you to be a better reader. We're making all kinds of connections between what you read and how you read and what makes you a better writer and back and forth. . . . You obviously need to do more than just the 10 minutes a day reading in reading class. . . . Because you need to get those reading responses in to me. Okay?

But although she had envisioned her curriculum as half reading and half writing, it didn't seem to play out that way in practice. While students like Rasheen and Conrad clearly frustrated Meg with their sarcastic comments and irresponsibility, she reflected in her journal that, regardless of the students with whom she conferred, talking about writing was simply easier and more pleasurable than talking about reading.

I find my (writing) conferences going so much better than I had originally planned, because I always have so many questions for them. It's so fascinating to find out what they were thinking of or what happened to cause them to write. I must admit that I am not so interested in their reading. Part of that has to do with time, I think. There's just not always enough time to talk about both, although I'm always trying to make connections between their reading and writing. Another thing is that so many of them are reading things that I haven't read. I think, though, if I just discipline myself to set the time aside each conference, that it will get better. I am personally more of a reader (oops) writer than I am a reader—so I tend to want to talk about the writing more. I also need to do more reading. When?

Clearly, several aspects of her new literature curriculum demanded more of Meg than she was willing or able to give. First, she did not see herself as an avid reader, preferring to write rather than settling down with a book. Second, her new independent reading program suddenly cast her into the role of fellow reader, rather than textual authority. She was terrified of reading less than her students or being unable to talk to them about books that she had not read herself. She admitted that, given the choice of glossing over reading or glossing over writing, she often "let reading go over letting writing go." Privately, she agonized in her journal:

Maybe they don't see me as an avid reader. I know they perceive me as a writer. Well—reading will have to be a real focus now. I want to get

to the point where I do both equally. I mean, I preach the reading/
writing connection all the time, but somehow the message isn't getting
across. I will have to find more time for personal reading—discuss
books I've read on sharing days—and find a way to make reading
conferences more fruitful. Not too much to ask myself—huh?

Although she often resolved to "find more time" for reading, Meg was still left with the nagging self-doubt that accompanied her new independent reading program and the changes it demanded in her role as textual authority. Privately, she empathized with her students.

Ken was all excited about *Catcher in the Rye.* I have never read
Catcher in the Rye. I have never read it. And I said, "Here I am, Ms.
English teacher, masters degree at X University, and I have never
read *Catcher in the Rye. . . ."* I can admit that I haven't read *Sweet
Valley High* or some of these other things; I can't admit that I
haven't read *Catcher in the Rye.* Well, luckily, the bell rang or
something like that. [I experienced] total fear. It's like this is what
the kids must feel like when they haven't done their homework or
something.

In truth, many of her students echoed Meg's discomfort with reading, particularly when they had to write in response logs. One day she opened Sharing Time with a class meeting, in which she asked them to write her a note about how they felt about reading response logs. Their comments were mostly negative. One student wrote, "Reading is bad enough—then when I have to write about it, it's even worse." Another commented, "I can't read in class—there's too much going on. Then when I read at home—I forget to respond." Another student, presumably in the remedial reading program, lamented, "I'm too sick of reading from reading class." As a response to their discomfort, Meg decided to expand the requirement of the reading logs to include five different options: writing in response journals, response talks in conferences, talking about books on sharing days, writing "book reports" from a menu of 50 options available in the reading center, and writing about topics generated in Literature Circles.

Unfortunately, although these changes in procedure might have helped her students, they did little for Meg's own relationship with reading. What we were both soon to learn was that her very identity as a reader would have to change before her reading curriculum could fall into pace with her writing curriculum.

"I HAVE ALWAYS BEEN A BUZZARD":
READING AND TEACHING LIKE A WRITER

One afternoon in late October, Meg and I were seated on the floor around my coffee table with a tape recorder poised between us. We had been talking for nearly an hour about several of her students, when Meg observed, "I notice that when you ask me about a kid, I talk about their writing, I don't talk about their reading." For several weeks, I had been noticing the differences between reading and writing in her classroom, but hadn't thought of a way to bring that up without making her unduly self-conscious. I was glad she finally had broached the topic. Her explanation surprised me, though:

> I was always in the lowest reading groups in school and I have horrible memories of that. And my mother was always "read, read, read!" She'd buy me all these books and magazines and I always wanted to write instead of read. I didn't like to read because I didn't think I was a good reader. So I went through a lot of that when I was a kid. I was probably more praised for the writing than the reading. Reading was something that I had to do and writing was something that I liked to do.

As she spoke, I couldn't help but think of students like Kianna and Jason, who had made nearly identical statements about reading. Like so many of her students, Meg had endured the agony of being made to read in public and placed in reading groups. She remembered painfully:

> You know, [in first grade you] used to have the blue jays, the robins, and the buzzards. . . . And I was always a buzzard. . . . I have nightmares about reading classes. . . . Being told to stand in the corner because you didn't know the words, always being in the buzzard reading group. Having my mother sit there night after night with all these flash cards. And I'd know them one night, and forget them the next night and cry.

Like Kianna, Meg saw herself as a writer rather than a reader. Unlike Kianna, however, Meg had decided to become an English teacher, carefully guarding her secret, and courageously trying to make reading a fundamental part of her curriculum. In the many years I had visited Meg's classroom, I had never been aware of her poor self-image as a reader. I learned that, to Meg, reading was simply a means to an end: understanding and appreciating what other writers do. For example, she had thoroughly enjoyed *The Story of My Life* by Jay McInerney (1989) because of its effect on her writing.

> That book had an effect on me as a writer. In style, in many ways I thought that I would use this as a writer. I will write like this someday. I will give this a try. If he can do this maybe I can do that.

At the time of this interview, Meg had begun writing her own young adult novel, *Before the Leaves Change*. She fondly remembered two young adult books from her graduate course in adolescent literature that had a profound influence on her novel.

> [When I read] *Bridge* [*to Terabithia*] . . . and *Tuck Everlasting*, that's where my whole book came from, almost. This is the kind of book I see myself writing. . . . Most books I read—and it takes a couple of months and I really don't like it but I feel like I should be doing it because I'm this reading/writing person—so I push myself through it. But every once in a while there's this book . . . *Summer of My German Soldier* was like that. . . . [These books make me] feel like writing. [They make] me feel like a writer.

As the first semester of her students' eighth-grade year drew to a close, Meg had made great strides in creating a classroom that equally encompassed writing, talk, and listening. By this time, many of her students had come to see themselves as writers. Evidence of this transformation was appearing in the form of "published" student texts on her bulletin boards and in the lively talk about writing during Sharing Time and Conference Days. Creative talk about books, collaborative group activities, and occasions for active, respectful listening and response to literature seemed far less evident in her classroom, however.

Although she blamed herself for the contrast between reading and writing in her classroom, it seemed to me that this discrepancy was more than a matter of Meg's own negative relationship with reading. There was, quite simply, an absence of guidelines for how to teach literature, similar to those available for teaching "process-centered" writing that had germinated from the National Writing Project Centers several years earlier. Meg was not only fearful of reading less than her students, but was also clueless as to how to generate a discussion about books and to move her students past their rather simple "good–bad" pronouncements about books and stories. In her own teaching, she had few strategies beyond her own teacher-generated questions or mini-lectures on literary techniques. As Chapter Nine will demonstrate, it was not until she began to join the Literature Circle as an author herself that she discovered ways of responding to texts beyond the "questions at the back of the book," and began to make those "reading/writing connections" she had sought in her curriculum.

TOWARD A PEDAGOGY OF LITERARY READING

In his report of a national survey of English classrooms, sponsored by the Center for the Learning and Teaching of Literature, Arthur Applebee (1992a) concluded that

> The patterns of instruction revealed in the national survey reflect an English classroom divided against itself. . . . Even if not fully accepted, process-oriented approaches to writing are at least widely understood. But in the teaching of literature, on the other hand, the focus on the student is likely to stop after an initial emphasis on developing motivation and interest. At that point, a focus on the text, with the attendant concern with common interpretations, the "right answers" of literary study, comes to the fore. (pp. 13–14)

Similarly, Judith Langer (1992) has observed that

> A unified way of conceptualizing the goals of literature instruction still eludes us. By and large, the teaching of literature is "rudderless," espousing a focus on thinking and reasoning without a strong and stable conception of what this means in response to literature and without the conceptual anchor that can be provided by a clear understanding of the relationships among the nature of literary understandings and the instructional contexts in which such understandings develop. (p. 51)

Meg needed not only concrete strategies for her literature curriculum, but also a kind of intellectual freedom from so many of the strictures and expectations about literature she had experienced over the years from parents, administrators, and students themselves. Caught in a political climate based on a "return" to the "basics," Meg needed a way to shed her lingering guilt about not inculcating students into the "great tradition of Western literature" or initiating them into the academic mainstream through a knowledge of literary terminology and technique.

In her writing curriculum, she had a storehouse of concrete classroom strategies from the published work of teachers and teacher educators affiliated with the National Writing Project network. In her literature classroom, she had few, if any, concrete models. Since the work of organizations like the National Literature Project had not yet reached the walls of Logan Middle School, Meg was left with memories of her own negative experiences as a reader and an oppressive sense of guilt about not being the classroom "expert" about books. While she had resolved the debate in her writing curriculum, her literature curriculum was still mired in the struggle between what Harris (1991) has called "knowledge" and "growth" models of teaching. It seemed to me that more traditional approaches like New Critical "close reading" and a "Great Books" philosophy, based on an established canon of Eurocentric texts, simply offered more powerful currency in the marketplace of schooling than the more learner-centered perspectives of Reader Response and process-centered teaching.

Beyond the struggle between transmissionist and constructivist versions of teaching, Meg also was caught between social and sociopolitical models of the constructivist classroom. As political issues like racism, classism, and gender stereotyping surrounded her students' interactions, Meg also found herself caught between the personal and the political in the "official" classroom talk that surrounded her students' literary reading. The published literature on Reader Response teaching had underscored the value of helping her students to make personal connections with the texts they read. She also was beginning to broaden and expand the canon of books, stories, and poems in her classroom beyond the typical European and American variety. Rarely, however, did she or her students venture beyond the personal and into the political repercussions of the books and stories they were reading. While a good many current social issues like racism, teen pregnancy, and crime entered the classroom through students' writing, talk about books or stories rarely focused on these political and social issues.

In Meg's classroom, it seemed that books were treated rather like stone tablets, on which the great wisdom of the world was stored, rather than occasions for reconsidering, challenging, or making an impact on that world. Perhaps because there was no tangible "product" for reading, as there was for writing, many of Meg's students preferred to write rather than to read.

Finally, although Meg and her students eventually found ways to "come together" in a kind of nexus of small social cliques, I sensed that sometimes this "harmony" was bought at a price. In their freedom to stay within these small tight circles, students could avoid the tensions that divided the classroom as a whole. As a result, seldom did Meg or her students directly address the social and political realities at the heart of these divisions. It wasn't until students' eighth-grade year—and then only seldom—that they began to venture through their reading and writing into the larger world outside their classroom walls.

Thus, while Meg and her students found ways to deal with their cultural, class, racial, and gender differences, the question of the differences themselves rarely surfaced in the official classroom discourse. In Chapter Nine, we will return to Meg's classroom and consider how these tensions and contradictions played themselves out as her students made their way toward their years beyond middle school.

CHAPTER 7

Is There an "A" Reader in This Class?: Angel and Samantha

It's interesting how Samantha and Angel have become such bookends. I can't put my finger on the reason. On the surface, they seem so different from each other; and yet they always seem linked in my mind. Today, for instance, Meg had just started what she has come to call her "Reading/Writing" Circle—an idea she seems to have adapted from her earlier "Literature Circles." She began by giving a short book talk on The Devil's Arithmetic *by Jane Yolen. A small group of students were involved in an animated discussion of what it would be like to move backward and forward in time, as the protagonist in Yolen's book does. In the midst of the discussion, I looked over at Samantha and Angel. They were sitting against the wall, heads together, sound asleep. As I looked at these two young women, I wondered when it had become impossible for me to think of one without thinking of the other. (Retrospective memo, April 3, 1991)*

I'm not sure when Angel and Samantha first became so inseparably linked in my mind. At the time I wrote this memo, they didn't look a bit like each other. Although they both were usually cooperative and engaged learners, Samantha seemed far less visible and vocal in the classroom than Angel. A pretty young girl with shoulder-length, sandy brown hair and dark eyes, Samantha was polite, congenial, on-task, often choosing to stand back a bit from the center of the action. If there was a test to be taken, Samantha would sit, diligently filling in the answers with her green "koala bear" pencil. If groups were working together, Samantha occasionally might trade leadership with another student, but rarely would take the lead herself. And when routine classroom conflicts occurred, Samantha seemed to shrink from them by looking off in the distance, almost trying to disappear from the class altogether. At other times, she behaved like a typical young adolescent, sneaking a bottle of nail polish from her purse, or leaning over another student's desk to scribble a hasty note. Most of the time, though, she seemed quiet and unobtrusive—as Meg once described her, a rather typical "good little girl."

Angel, on the other hand, was a small, perky young woman with a constantly changing hairstyle and a perpetual mouthful of gum. Like Samantha, she seemed generally well-mannered and engaged in school tasks. In the beginning of her seventh-grade year, she dressed a lot like Samantha, usually in fashionably faded polo shirts and cotton skirts or slacks with brown loafers. But, unlike Samantha, she almost always positioned herself in the center of class discussions and activities. In my early field notes, I described her as "the opposite of a 'goody two shoes.'" She often took the lead in most small-group activities. In larger class discussions, she wasn't afraid to pursue controversial topics like women's issues or gay rights, often sparking a heated discussion.

Although I probably observed Angel engaging in as much off-task behavior as other students in Meg's classroom, she rarely got in trouble for it. In fact, one day, when she and a group of friends were laughing and talking loudly together, Meg walked over and complained, "I get accused of favoritism if I let you get away with this. [Other students say to me] 'You let them do it, why don't you let me do it?'" That day I noticed that although Tessa and Angel were loudly talking, while Gary merely had been listening in, Gary was the one that Meg chose to move to another part of the room. I wondered how Angel seemed to have garnered some of what I called "eccentricity points," in terms of Meg's tolerance of her behaviors.

On another day, I witnessed a similar incident, involving Angel and Samantha. As Meg was stapling student texts to a bulletin board, Angel and Sam were sitting with their desks pulled together, giggling. Samantha was making comical faces as she appeared to be trying on earrings. Soon, the two girls drifted over to the couch, where they began laughing and talking about boys with another girl. When Meg noticed them, she came over to the couch and said, "You can't blow off the last 6 minutes of classes." Taking a notebook from Samantha, she complained, "I need a writing grade for you. So what are you working on? Is this all English? Your rough copy notebook is supposed to be all English." I sensed that the notebook was less an issue to Meg than the fact that all three students were talking about boys instead of English class. When Meg asked about her reading response notebook, Samantha explained that she had lost it. Meg warned that she would check for the notebook again on Friday. It was interesting to me that, although all three girls had been off-task, Meg chose to reprimand Samantha.

Although the friendship between Angel and Samantha was not obvious in the fall of their seventh-grade year, it grew more visible toward the end of that year. In an interview, Angel remarked that they had met several years earlier in elementary school, where the other students continued to mistake one for the other. Despite their differences in appearance, people still confused them. "It's funny," Angel observed, "because I said to her 'You're so tan!' She's mixed, that's why."

Until Angel's comment about Samantha being "mixed," I had not known that Samantha was biracial. It wasn't until 4 years after graduating from high school, in a follow-up interview, that Samantha revealed this fact. Throughout her middle school years, I never observed Samantha referring to herself as biracial or identifying more with students of one particular race or another. What was most interesting to me, however, was Angel's comment that other students continually confused the two of them, considering how different they had come to look in hairstyle and dress. In the spring of her seventh-grade year, Angel bounced into class with her head completely shaved, except for one long shock that hung stylishly into her eyes. Meg remembered:

> You know [Angel] had . . . a cute little pixie style and she kept getting it cut, and we were laughing because every 2 weeks she'd get it cut and it would be a little bit shorter, so she was working up to this thing.

In addition to her constant changes in physical appearance, Angel was undergoing other changes as well. Meg observed that perhaps much of the intensity her young girls were experiencing had to do with their discovery of boys. She remarked:

> I don't know if Samantha's been sexually active. I know Cassie has and Audrey and Tanya . . . but. . . . I mean (I thought) you know, maybe that's what we should put in the curriculum! (laughs). . . . I mean, all of a sudden everything was just description and alive and sensual and, and, and . . . (laughs)

Angel's almost manic exuberance surfaced in many of her writings. Consider, for example, this poem about music.

Voice

> A voice tweaks through the air
> vibrations fill bodies
> my mind is nourished by
>   her song
> I am lost in something
>   close to heaven.
> motion and gesture
>   come without thought
> no one knows why

> images on the screen
> cure my curiosity
> colors help my eyes
> to adjust.
> death flashes through my mind
> only once—
> but chaos and sound
> surround me.
> all around me.
> I can't escape.
> I don't want to . . .

Much of Angel's poetry exuded what Kieran Egan (1992) has called the "sense of wonder" so typical of young adolescents. Egan writes: "We can see a burgeoning sense of wonder in natural phenomena—the new realization of delight in getting drenched, in the rush of the air, in gaudy sunsets, in spring's quickening" (pp. 79–80). As she delighted in the sights and sounds of the world around her, Angel also experimented with her adolescent identity. As Egan explains, young adolescents

> imagine themselves embodying extremes of power, beauty, daring, influence, nobility, and wealth, saving the planet from wicked polluters; writing great literature; defending the weak and innocent, and so on. . . . The imagination is energetically active in all this, thinking through possibilities, probing for what fits the burgeoning self. (p. 83)

Curiously, Angel's eccentricities seemed only to enhance Meg's admiration of her as a reader and writer. In her words, "Angel's always read a lot; I know she has. And always written a lot. That's only increased with her. It's just gotten a lot bigger [over the years]." By contrast, Meg remembered Samantha in seventh grade as

> the good little girl student who . . . had no idea who she was, had learned to give a teacher what she wanted. . . . [She] read more because her friends were doing it than because she really wanted to do it. . . . [She was] quiet. Just beginning to be a little social. Very mainstream, you know . . . a nondescript kind of person . . . nothing about her that would make you remember her really.

This "nondescript" image that Meg ascribed to Samantha seems typical of a great many otherwise able adolescent girls, particularly about the time they enter middle school. As Sadker and Sadker (1994) explain:

Like the tightening of a corset, adolescence closes around . . . precocious, authoritative girls. They begin to restrict their interests, confine their talents, pull
back on their dreams. As they work on blending in with other girls, they move
toward the end of their colorful phase. (p. 77)

Unfortunately, this "blending in" can bear subtle but heavy consequences
for young adolescent girls. Sadker and Sadker go on to argue:

At the time of puberty, girls are experiencing many changes at once. They are
caught in bodies that swell and expand in puzzling ways, and when they look
ahead to options that are mysteriously shrinking, they must also deal with the
shift to middle school. It is a larger, more complicated place and, many critics
charge, harshly out of touch with the needs of adolescence. In this more chaotic and alienating school, with new rules and uncharted social norms, it is
easier to become both physically and emotionally lost. (p. 79)

According to Meg, in seventh grade, both Angel and Samantha were
"just beginning to discover [themselves]," but Angel was "moving along much
faster" than Samantha. As I observed the two girls, and later, as I saw more
of their classroom reading and writing practices, I began to realize that the
differences between them went much deeper than their hairstyles and personalities. It was Angel's ability to shift easily among multiple social roles in
the classroom—good student, avid reader, group leader, budding young
actress, social activist—that separated her from Samantha. Angel refused to
play the "good girl" game, often voicing her opposition to the structures and
restrictions of school. On the other hand, she managed her academic tasks
in a "school savvy" way, so that her teachers would have no choice but to
accept her as a good student. As the following pages will show, although
both girls were voracious readers, Angel had developed the game of school
into a fine art—one that came neither naturally nor easily to Samantha.

IS THERE AN "A" READER IN THIS CLASS?

As a high school literature teacher, I had the hardest time trying to tell
the "A" readers from the "B" or the "C" readers. It was easy to give a test
on literary techniques or textual trivia and get a range of scores, but I knew
early on that these tests had little to do with my goals for reading. I wanted
my students to read deeply and widely, of course. But before this could happen, I knew that I first had to get them to read at all. To complicate things,
I knew that it didn't matter what they did in my classroom; what really
mattered was whether they continued to read in their everyday lives. I was
haunted by the question, "Would they become lifetime readers?" And on a

more basic level, how could I possibly grade them on, or even discover whether they achieved, this long-range and rather elusive goal?

Considering the public preoccupation with "objective" evaluation during my early years as a researcher, it wasn't surprising that I spent much of my time trying to come up with some version of those "A" readers, in order to discover what teachers could do to nurture their development. I went through the 3 decades from the 1950s to the 1980s, first as student and later as teacher, entrenched in a system that called for the separation of students into the "able" and "less able." I knew instinctively that typical academic assessments like tests and quizzes failed to account for my goals as a literature teacher. But I wasn't sure what separated readers who merely "comprehended" literature from those who found it an experience to be "burned through" and "lived through," as Louise Rosenblatt (1995, p. 264) has described it.

I did notice that some readers seemed to delve deeply into the hearts and minds of literary characters, pondering over twists of plot and character motivations, while other readers seemed simply to skim the surface of what they read. I suppose because I happened to be a very social and gregarious person, always interested in what makes others "tick," I assumed that readers who could make sophisticated analyses of characters, comparing them with others in the "real" world, were those who would be more likely to read avidly and deeply.

And so, in 1988, when I first entered the world of Meg's classroom, I brought in mounds of questionnaires. I wanted to know, for instance, which students formed "complex" impressions of peers and characters, and which did not. Although I discovered many differences between Angel and Samantha, however, these differences were not related to their scores on my questionnaires; if anything, my early expectations were undermined and contradicted more often than they were confirmed. As the following pages will demonstrate, after interviewing and watching them in the classroom for a year, I decided to abandon these paper-and-pencil assessments altogether. Where these two young women were concerned, I remained in a constant process, as Wolfgang Iser (1980) would say, of "forming and overturning illusions" (p. 334) about them as readers, learners, and literate people; many of these illusions were colored by how they functioned in the complex social arena of their literature classroom.

SURVIVING THE "PERFORMANCE-BASED" CURRICULUM

As a secondary teacher, I seldom dealt with *A reader*, but instead dealt with *readers* in relation to other readers. My own experiences as a high school and college student bore this out as well. As an undergraduate in my introductory literary survey classes, I became adept at learning just enough about a text under discussion to put on a pretty convincing performance of what David Bloome (1986) calls "mock participation" and "procedural display," as contrasted with genuine learning. In truth, I rarely read a single assigned piece of literature until the night before an examination. As I sat in class, numbly unaware of the text under discussion, a bit of guilt would nip at the edges of my consciousness. But for the most part, I discovered how to listen just enough to the discussion around me that I could interject an occasional comment, without giving away the fact that I hadn't read a word of the text under critical scrutiny. On the night before each test, as I tried to cram in the hundreds of pages I had neglected to read, I'd vow to change my ways. But that never seemed to happen. I could rely on my glibness in group discussion to get me through until it was time to cram for the next test.

Later, as a high school teacher, I assumed, I suppose, that my own students would be as comfortable in group discussion as I had been. What I too often missed—because I was so busy attending to similarly glib students in whole-group discussions—was that there were students who slipped through the cracks of my "performance-based" curriculum. Like Samantha, these students might have been avid, perceptive readers, but they rarely contributed to discussion, because I had given them neither the medium nor the means to do so. Like Samantha in seventh grade, these students dwelt in the background, adrift in the great, unremarkable "mainstream" that Meg had described.

It was only after I got out from behind my own desk and began observing students who were not mine, that I realized how literary reading occurs within a whole host of social relationships, and that readers' reputations as literate people are made or broken by the skill with which they can read the "hidden curriculum" of their teachers. In the social world, readers often are nurtured and supported by other readers—parents, friends, teachers, and other important people. Unfortunately, in the classroom they are also compared with their peers on the quality of their oral and written responses. Teachers look for certain academic signs of competence; when students shy away from class discussions or writing extensively and critically about literary works, they often pay a penalty in terms of academic success. Unfortunately as well, these "shy" readers often turn out to be girls.

"DIVING OFF" AND STEPPING BACK: CRITICAL AND AESTHETIC READING

As I watched both young women in Meg's classroom, I returned again and again to that question about "A" readers. I was struck immediately by the fact that Angel and Samantha performed differently in class discussions and small groups—Angel most often taking the lead and Samantha preferring to stay in the background. Signs of these differences showed in their written work as well. I discovered that Samantha's responses to literature were highly emotional and firmly grounded in her personal experiences. For example, after the class had seen a film version of a Richard Wright story, Samantha wrote this in her journal:

Almos a man

I didn't like this story at all. Because I couldn't get into it at all. The movie was just dumb. Running away without anything but a gun is really dumb. The people around him were realy disrespectful tward him. They didn't treat him like a yong man. I just didn't like this story. (Sam)

This kind of emotionally charged, dismissive response is fairly typical in the journals of Meg's middle school students, who often found very little "middle ground" in their reactions to literature. Young adolescents either fall in love with characters, or they hate them. These love/hate relationships can change as swiftly as Angel's hairstyles. Samantha's response to Wallace Stegner's "The Colt" (1976) is similarly emotional; but this time, it leads her into a significant personal reminiscence.

The story the Colt is oh so very sad. I feel terrible for the boy he had his hopes way up there, for Socks to get better. I liked the authors discriptions of the setting. I have been in that situation before. A couple weeks ago I noticed my six year old gineua pig stopped eating. When I picked him up it felt like air. He had lost about a pound over the past week, and when you weigh three pounds that's a lot. So I tried to feed him by juicing up some parsely which he did take through a syring without a needle. He drand about an ounce, then I layed him down to sleep with a towel wrapped around him hopping he'd live longer, But in the mourning he was dead. I didn't really like the story because I could relate to it. But if I couldn't I probably would have liked it. (Sam)

Ironically, the vivid and painful memory that this story unleashed made Samantha feel unable to "relate" to it as she might have liked. Samantha's response is typical of what I have come to call "diving off" (Garrison & Hynds, 1991; Hynds, 1989). For a variety of reasons, possibly including confusion, disengagement, or painful personal memories, readers delve so deeply into personal reminiscences that they seem to lose sight of the text altogether. For an informal journal, where students were simply told to "freewrite" their responses, Samantha's entry is entirely appropriate. Contrast her journal response, however, with Angel's similarly emotional journal entry about Ray Bradbury's "All Summer in a Day" (1987).

> *This story is hard to analize because you don't really know how Margot feels after she is let out of the closet. From what I can only imagine she was feeling, she must have felt that she had missed something so special to everyone else. Since she had lived on earth, she now, probably wants to go back because she misses the sun so much. But the advantage she had over the other children is that this was the first time they remember seeing the sun, and she had seen it almost every day when she was younger. I sort of liked the story but it's so sad to think of living for 7 years without seeing the sun; it must be torture to those who have seen it before. To those who haven't, they don't know what they're missing, and may be even more sad than missing it to begin with.*

Although her response is firmly grounded in emotion, Angel seems able to use that emotional response as a springboard for speculating on the feelings and motivations of the main character. In another journal response to *Fall into Darkness*, by Christopher Pike (1991), Angel again seems to step back from her emotional response, this time using it to critically analyze her favorite author's style.

> *I haven't read very much of the book but what I have read is semi-confusing. It starts out sort of abrupt by saying that Sharon McKay was accused of murdering her best friend, Ann Rice (This is in the prologue). The catch is that Sharon is innocent but no one believes her and there was no body found. Right now Sharon is on trial and she's so scared. In fact, I'm scared also. I guess this is a good way to start a story because it gets people interested. At least, I'm interested. I got to put myself in Sharon's place, & I think that's one of the best advantages in reading. If I were in Sharon's shoes, I would be having a breakdown and be very scared as well as sad, lonely, and defenseless. What I like about Christopher Pike is that he gives the story from all the different characters' point of view so it's more of a mystery than it is.*

Like Samantha, Angel demonstrates a good deal of emotional involvement in a story. She is, however, able to analyze in some depth Margot's feelings and beliefs, as well as the larger implications of those beliefs. Moreover, in her response to Christopher Pike's book, she never loses sight of the text, often stepping back to analyze Pike's style and technique. Even in a journal, where any response is acceptable, Angel takes a critical, analytic stance that demonstrates academic competence to her teachers.

It's acceptable, and perhaps even preferable, for students to make highly personal evaluations in the private pages of a journal or in conversations with others about books. When students are passionate about their likes and dislikes, they demonstrate an emotional connection with reading. But what happens to highly emotional, personally directed students like Samantha in a test situation, where more critical competence is called for? Here, they need not only social competence in understanding the beliefs, feelings, and motivations of literary characters, but academic competence to understand the expectations of their teachers. Writing in test situations demands that readers distance themselves somewhat from their personal responses and comment on authors' techniques or fine points of meaning. This is largely due to a Piagetian assumption that students must move beyond their own egocentric perceptions, learning to decenter. From this perspective, Angel seems much more adept than Samantha at this process of critical detachment and decentering.

For example, as part of a culminating final evaluation during her students' eighth-grade year, Meg asked them to choose one of two poems and write a short response. Both Angel and Samantha chose the poem "Oranges" by Gary Soto (1990). Notice how, even in an examination situation, Samantha becomes emotionally involved in a memory, again, diving off the text into her own personal reminiscence.

> The poem "Ornanges." By Gary Soto is a magnifisint poem about first love. Kinda reminds me the time I was going to this day camp and guy I liked had sprained his knee so he couldn't go for a week. So one day I skipped camp, and met him at the university. In fact I think I'll write a poem about it. (many lines of text scratched out). Change of plans, I didn't like the poem I was writting so I'll just finish by saying first love is an experience that is precious in life to all that have loved. (Sam)

Although Angel's response is fairly vague, she does focus on a brief analysis of the author's style—arguably, a more appropriate response for a final examination than Samantha's long personal reminiscence.

> I liked this poem a lot because it was descriptive enough to guide the imagination, but not too much to make it drag along. It also had an interesting mellow texture to it. It reminded me of a swing swaying back and forth enough to make you jump before you go downwards. The author wrote about certain actions which, to me, mirrored the thoughts and feelings of the characters. (Angel)

As these excerpts of her work show, Angel demonstrates a good deal of academic savvy. She understands how texts work, often reflecting on how an author's techniques influence her responses as a reader. In a later interview, she continues to reflect in some depth about Bradbury's story.

> I don't understand why Margot when she came out, they just unlocked the door and let her out, and it just sort of ended. I think it ended a little too soon. They could have done just a paragraph more. . . . You get to the end and then all of the sudden it ends and you're like . . . that's it! . . . I felt sorry for her. . . . Because she wasn't being selfish. Usually you want the good person to win and the bad guys [to lose]. . . . But it didn't work out like that though. . . . I hate these goody goody stories where the good guys win and the bad guys lose.

Angel is able not only to respond to the book at hand, but to compare it with other books she has read. This ability to make intertextual connections will serve her well in her later academic life.

It became clear to me that Angel's ability to switch roles from typical young adolescent, to engaged reader, to literary critic, enabled her to function successfully in a classroom situation, to stand out from the crowd, and even to challenge the classroom authority with confidence and success. Unlike Samantha, Angel rarely faded into the background in class discussions. And although she was highly passionate in her response to life as well as to books, this passion was always tempered by a critical distance that proved her academic competence.

But what about the Piagetian concept of decentering? Did Samantha's responses indicate a basic egocentrism and inability to take the perspectives of others? If my questionnaires were accurate, this certainly seemed the case. Notice the difference between Angel and Samantha in their written descriptions of the character Marty in the short story "The New Kid" (Heyert, 1944). Samantha writes:

> [Marty] was afraid of (not?) fitting in. At first every one picked on him then when the new kid came he was the one they were picking on by the end of the story. He was always insucure until the fight becuase (then) the guys were on his side. (Samantha)

Angel writes:

> Marty felt almost as scared as the new kid and really extended his gloating of strength over the new kid way too much. Marty was trying to please or fit in with the other kids and in doing this he used the new

kid as an example because he knew he could win over him. Marty picks on the new kid only because he doesn't want the other kids to pick on him because w/o the new kid, he would be in the same exact position as the new kid. Deep down inside Marty would never have done anything like he did exept for peer pressure. (Angel)

Angel's response is the English teacher's dream: complex, probing, and elaborated. Like her participation in class discussions, however, Samantha's written response seems shut down and unelaborated. When I finally looked at their scores on the Role Category Questionnaires I had given them at the beginning of the year, I discovered that Angel was near the top of the "high complexity" group, while Samantha was clearly in the "low complexity" group. Did this mean, then, that Samantha was unable to *take* social perspectives, or that she was unable to *demonstrate* that she did? Something about the behaviors of the two girls and their passion for reading stopped me from leaping to that first conclusion. Although Samantha was shy, I had watched her function successfully in social relationships and become highly involved with characters in literature. As I reflected on the Role Category Questionnaire itself, I realized how close it was to traditional classroom tasks that ask students to analyze characters in writing. If students had trouble demonstrating competence on such tasks for emotional or academic reasons, their potential for taking social perspectives might go totally unnoticed. My frustration with questionnaire data reminded me of Linda Flower and John Hayes's (1980) description of studying the composing process through oral protocols as somewhat like trying to track a dolphin by catching sight of it as it leaps out of the water. I began to get a better glimpse of that dolphin as Angel and Samantha talked in interviews about their reading preferences and processes.

READING FOR SUCCESS: SOCIALIZED TO SCHOOLING

Louise Rosenblatt (1994), perhaps the most famous advocate of the reader's central position in the literary experience, has argued that certain texts "invite" more sophisticated or critical responses than others. In what she calls the literary "transaction," some texts simply lend themselves to more academically acceptable responses than do others. In my interviews with Angel and Samantha, I discovered that, while Samantha had a great deal of support for reading in her home, Angel had a particular kind of support— one that lent itself to school success.

In an interview, Angel explained that her mother used to be a librarian, who made sure that Angel always had an extensive personal collection of children's books. Each Christmas, her mother brought home library pamphlets, describing recent children's books. Angel learned about series books and various children's authors from these pamphlets. In addition, her book collection gave her the opportunity to practice the academic skills of categorizing and cataloguing. She explained:

> *Angel*: I have a lot of books. I have like 200 books. Most of them are up in the attic though. That's new books. People buy me books, my relatives, my grandmother especially. . . . The reason I don't have them all in my room is because my mom, she makes me alphabetize them. And she makes me catalogue them too.
>
> *Interviewer*: The hazards of being the daughter of a librarian!
>
> *Angel*: She says I have too many books so I have to keep track of them. She said we'll just write down the book's name, the author, and put them on index cards. She bought little index cards and index boxes for me.
>
> *Interviewer*: Well, on the bright side, I know it's probably tedious when you're doing it, but when you're looking for a book, you probably find it easily.
>
> *Angel*: I never keep up to date though.
>
> *Interviewer*: Just enough to keep mom happy?
>
> *Angel*: Yeah.

Angel's relationship with her best friend even revolves around reading. I wondered if perhaps her critical sense was developed by picking out books that her friend might like to read.

> Well my best friend and I, . . . whenever we read a book, we tell each other to go to the library to get this book. We send out postcards and write the name of the book and author and write a little blurb about it and we do that all the time. . . . Whenever I read a book that's very good I'll write down the title and a little blurb about what it's about and then I'll send it to her. . . . And if she can't find it I'll make an excuse to go and see her in Connecticut just to see her. Like she's having a graduation in June so I'm going to get all my books together and bring them to her. We can send books too because it's not that expensive.

Through all this academic modeling, as well as strong peer support for reading, Angel has become quite sophisticated in her criteria for choosing books. Just as she shaves her head and dons an earring to make a statement about her identity, she also sees book choices as a statement about her personality and tastes. In one interview, she remarked:

> I hate reading all those teenager books that they have. They're so corny, I'm sorry. They are so unrealistic, like *Sweet Valley High* [and] *The Twins*, they're really rich and they have everything and they're so popular. It's too preppy, because they have their car and they always get into fights; and I have twin brothers and it's not at all like that. . . . I like reading books that nobody's ever heard of. I never liked reading Judy Blume or Beverly Cleary because everybody was reading them. . . . I like books with disappointing endings.

For Angel, books must do more than engage her interest. Her book choices must mark her as a unique individual, who stands out from the crowd. Being "different" is a characteristic she prides herself on—whether different in physical appearance, political commitments, or reading tastes.

Although Samantha receives support for reading at home, this support does not have the same academic underpinnings as the support that Angel receives. Although she regularly reads the *New York Times* book review with her grandmother and occasionally shares books with her mother, she does not report the kind of *academic* modeling that Angel experienced, as the following interview reveals:

> *Interviewer*: Let's turn to your family for a minute. Do other members of your family like to read in general? . . .
>
> *Samantha*: Not as much [as they once did] because they're too busy. . . . My mom's too busy with studying because she's getting her BSN in nursing. My stepfather is going back to school for some degree, I don't know what.
>
> *Interviewer*: So they're reading, but they're reading more textbooks and stuff like that?
>
> *Samantha*: They're reading because they have to.
>
> *Interviewer*: Did they read before, when they weren't involved in this, can you remember?
>
> *Samantha*: My mom did. She read over the summer, like every summer she reads *Dandelion Wine* . . . and we both read *The Christmas Pageant* every Christmas.

Thus, although Samantha reported positive attitudes toward reading in her home and an abundance of books in her personal library, she did not have regular exposure to the kind of "school-like" reading behaviors that Angel did. In seventh grade, she also lacked a strong social support for reading. When I asked if her friends read, she replied, "No. Like my friend Jill, she has the same kind of books on her shelves from when she was a child. I've gotten her into reading more, but she still doesn't read as much as I do."

In contrast to Angel, Samantha seemed much less particular about her book preferences, remarking, "I like anything that I can read. I like love stories, fairy tales, murder mysteries, comedies, anything that I can read. . . . I'll stick to it and read it 'til I'm done." Thus, although Samantha becomes highly emotionally invested in books and can make a great many connections between what she reads and her real life, she is not what I would call a "critical reader." Rarely, if ever, does she step back from a text to comment on the nuances of an author's style or to make comparisons with another text. In fact, once engaged in a book, she rarely steps back at all. As it turns out, reading within the walls of school poses a great deal of difficulty for her.

"CAN DO" OR "WILL DO": READING FOR SCHOOL AND READING FOR LIFE

There's a difference between ability or competence—what James Hoetker (1970) has called "can do" behaviors—and exercising that competence, or what he calls "will do" behaviors. As a teacher, I knew that many of my students could perform admirably on tests or quizzes, but, whether from lack of desire, time, or commitment, they might never pick up a book outside the classroom. These "competent" readers may or may not consider themselves "readers" beyond their years of formal schooling. I was always frustrated at the end of the year, when my students would drift off into other teachers' classrooms, leaving me wondering if they would ever pick up a book once their days of schooling had ended. Often I questioned my curriculum and evaluation methods. If my goal was to create lifetime readers, would it follow that my "A" readers would be lifetime readers, and my "C" readers would not?

As it turns out, I had to follow Angel and Samantha around a bit and widen my lens of interpretive possibilities to uncover more about both their "can do" and their "will do" behaviors. From watching both girls and reading their written work, I naturally would have assumed that Angel would consider herself an avid reader; but I wasn't so sure about Samantha. Angel was gregarious and always seemed "at home" in the world of school, while Samantha, especially in seventh grade, tended to sit along the sidelines, always doing her work, but more withdrawn and less vocal. Yet, when I asked them both in interviews whether they considered themselves to be readers, I was surprised at the similarities in their responses. Angel's response was fairly predictable.

> *Angel*: People always associate me with carrying around a book.
> *Susan*: Is that right?
> *Angel*: And it's always a different book.
> *Susan*: You're saying that everybody associates you with not only having a book but having a different book.
> *Angel*: Most of the time.
> *Susan*: Do you get through books quite quickly?
> *Angel*: Yeah.

Samantha reported a similar enthusiasm for reading.

> *Samantha*: I love reading. I love finding out new adventures and putting myself into the situations of the setting and the story. It's neat.
> *Susan*: Do you read quite a bit?
> *Samantha*: I can read a 180-page book in 2 hours.
> *Susan*: Wow!
> *Samantha*: If I really keep on going.
> *Susan*: Wow! Are you a speed reader?
> Samantha: No.

In terms of my "pleasure reading" goal, Angel and Samantha were both exemplary readers. However, by purely cognitive measures like the Role Category Questionnaires, Samantha did not appear particularly sophisticated. In the case of these two young women, my earlier hunch about social complexity and its relationship to reading for pleasure came to a dead end.

Did this mean that Angel was able to create a rich and imaginative inner drama as she read, while Samantha was not? On the contrary. My interviews convinced me that, although both girls became imaginatively involved in reading, Angel was able to suspend this private imaginative process of "private response" to engage in various classroom tasks of "public responding"—a feat that Samantha was never able to manage successfully, especially not within the walls of school.

GETTING THROUGH: READING AT HOME AND SCHOOL

By the time I entered Meg's classroom, I was fairly comfortable with the notion that, although there are always individual differences, there are also some personal universals that can be counted on, in terms of readers' processes, preferences, and reading styles. I am much less comfortable with that notion today, as are other researchers who have moved more toward a social constructivist stance.

I came to understand that Samantha was at least two different readers: one who "got through" the routines of assigned reading in school, and another who savored, immersed herself in, and enjoyed her pleasure reading at home. This shouldn't have been surprising, since so many of Angel's and Samantha's classmates had mentioned the differences between reading for home and school in my early interviews. As I considered why so many young adolescents experienced this schizophrenia, I thought about what happens in the typical classroom reading experience.

- Longer texts are read in pieces. Often, novels are broken into short, assignable sections, which are discussed each day.
- Each truncated reading experience is almost always followed by some kind of written or oral response "in progress."
- Much weight is placed on these in-progress responses, in terms of figuring out if students have read and/or understood the texts.

In light of these common academic practices, how does Louise Rosenblatt's (1994) "aesthetic reader" fit into the typical structures of classroom reading? I got a clue as I listened to both Angel and Samantha talk about their reading processes. Angel described response processes that seem entirely compatible with the typical segmented school-sponsored reading activity.

> When I bring a book to school, a lot of the times I just read one or two pages a day. And also I read a lot of books at a time. Right now I'm reading three books. It's because [if] I get bored with one book, I can just mark my page and go on to the next book. And then if I get bored with that one, I can go to the other one. I don't get bored that way.

Samantha, on the other hand, becomes so aesthetically immersed in her reading, that any interruption or distraction can ruin the experience for her. She explained:

> *Samantha*: When I read I tend to read the whole book.
> *Susan*: As opposed to what?
> *Samantha*: Reading like chapters. How we read the book, *The Friends*, and we would just read it in class. [But] I would just read it [on my own]. I'd have the book and I would read the book.

Susan: What does it do for you when you read it in pieces in class like that?

Samantha: It doesn't make it as clear. When you read the whole book it makes it clear. It doesn't break it up.

Susan: When you're doing activities in class, how is that?

Samantha: It gets me off-track a lot and I have trouble writing things. Then I have to write [my response] first or write it last, because I can't write over a period of time.

Susan: What if you were to read the whole book and then write something?

Samantha: I could do that.

Susan: So when you read at home, how is it different?

Samantha: I pick up a book and read it until I am finished. Unless if I have to go to the bathroom or if I have to eat.

Susan: Is that why maybe reading responses get in the way for you?

Samantha: Yeah.

Samantha: I think that reading in school isn't as good. I like silent reading and on Fridays but not as much because there are interruptions, like a book falling or someone talking to you. I need silence when I read because I get into the book deeply.

So, even *within* the same reader, Is there really "A" reader? I don't think so. It is clear that Samantha is a very different reader at home and in school. Whereas Angel seems at home reading anywhere, Samantha is not comfortable reading anywhere but at home. As someone who must have silence in order to "get into the book deeply," any request to respond, even in journals, seems to close down, rather than open up, her thinking. Remembering the day Samantha told Meg she had "lost" her reading notebook, I wondered if she had really lost it, or had abandoned it because it so interfered with her concentration.

"Closet Readers": The Academic Consequences of Aesthetic Reading

Samantha and Angel forced me to look back on my own reading as an adolescent and an adult. Then and now, I read very much as Samantha does. I realize what a risky admission this is, especially for someone who teaches courses in young adult literature and tries to be a resource for teachers who are seeking out quality fiction for their students. However, there are many times when, on finishing a book, I cannot recall details of plot, the author's name, or even the names of main characters. I am busy living the life within the text and can't be bothered with what I need to take away afterward. There are many times when I will get halfway through a book before realizing that

I have already read it. That is why I was both sympathetic and amused at Samantha's journal entry.

> *The book I'm reading is called "A SEPARATE PEACE". It's a very merirable [memorable] story in terms of the character who's name I have forgotten.*

Readers like Samantha remind me that what we call "pleasure reading habits" often have little to do with academic success. I also am coming to believe that "aesthetic readers," as Louise Rosenblatt envisioned them, rarely, if ever, make an appearance in school. I have found too many of these "closet readers" like Samantha over the past decade to believe otherwise. Along these lines, Pamela Kissel (1994) studied two adult recreational readers who read up to 10 books per week. One was an English teacher; the other was a retired man who had gone through a GED program and had never gone to college. Both read primarily for plot and neither read many books that would be considered, by the standards of most high school English teachers, "good literature." Yet, each was so addicted to reading that neither could envision a life without books.

In terms of critical or academic competence, Angel would be the clear "winner" in my quest for the "A" reader. However, in terms of the propensity for pleasure reading, Samantha is an "A" reader as well. In schools, we like to believe that creating critical readers is a major goal. But does one have to be a critical reader to be a pleasure reader? I'm beginning to think not. It is probably true that being a critical reader leads to academic success, which could, in turn, support reading for pleasure. Whatever the case, it is probably not coincidental that Angel seems to take so naturally to being a critical reader, and her mother was a librarian, who engaged her daughter in academic tasks like cataloguing books on little index cards. Samantha, on the other hand, is perhaps Rosenblatt's ideal aesthetic reader. She becomes totally immersed in what she reads, selects from a vast array of genres, and is drawn to books for the way they touch her life. Regrettably, aesthetic readers like Samantha are not always successful in the "performance-centered" curriculum of many literature teachers.

Toward the end of her eighth-grade year, Samantha confided that she didn't think she was revealing her avid reading behaviors to Meg. Although she was quite certain that her friends and family members would see her as "a compulsive reader," she admitted that her passion for reading was probably lost on Meg.

> *Samantha:* [Mrs. Andrews] probably thinks I don't read a lot because I never do reading responses even though I read like 15 books a month. I try to read one every day if I can.

Susan: You're serious? About 15 books a month?

Samantha: Yes.

Susan: But you don't do responses though?

Samantha: I don't feel like I want to write about it. . . . If I really like a book, I don't want to write about it, I just want to think about it. When I don't like a book I tend to write about it. Because it's just like another book.

Ironically, Samantha couldn't have been more mistaken about Meg's opinion of her as a reader. By the time Samantha reached eighth grade, Meg was actually quite aware of Sam's abilities as a reader and writer. In fact, when I asked Meg to compare Samantha in eighth grade and seventh grade, she replied:

Meg: Last year I didn't see much of a change, but this year, she's off the scale in every area. And the stuff that she writes is—I mean— far surpasses anything I've ever written. I mean, just blows me away.

Susan: What about reading?

Meg: You know one [book] after the other . . .

Susan: Was she like that in 1989?

Meg: I think a little bit, but now I think she's reading more for her own, you know, and not so much because just her friends are doing it.

Susan: [How do you think Samantha did] on my test of peers and characters?

Meg: Last year, "Low." "Low."

Susan: This year?

Meg: "High," " High."

Susan: Because of?

Meg: Because of her development as a person. I think she was very— I saw her as kind of one-dimensional. And I think that, uhm, that wasn't necessarily true, but the part of her that was anything else was held very private and secretive. And now she's had the courage through her friends and through seeing that other kids write in journals, other kids write poetry, other kids write about death, and about religion, and about all these other things, and have questions, and it's okay.

Unlike a great many middle school teachers, over her 2 years with Samantha, Meg had many chances to know her beyond what she revealed in her classroom activities. In eighth grade, both Sam and Angel had become involved in Meg's extracurricular play writing group. As Meg met after school with the two girls, she got to know them as poets, playwrights, actors, and struggling adolescents. In the process, she sometimes was precariously drawn into their personal lives. Meg recalled the painful incident with Samantha and her friends the night of the school dance: "That whole thing when [the kids] got drunk and that whole group went to the park and . . . and just working with [Sam] in the play, I mean, . . . we have such a close relationship."

Looking back on Meg's comments, I'm struck by two things. The first is how much of our students' lives go on beyond the boundaries of our classrooms, and how little of that life becomes visible in their "official" classroom words. If she had only one year with these students, and if her knowledge of them stopped at tests, journals, and worksheets, would Meg have missed the signs of Samantha's hidden literate life? Considering Sam's shyness and the plight of a good many adolescent girls, I expect she would have. Sadker and Sadker (1994) have concluded that "unlike the smart boy who flourishes in the classroom, the smart girl is the student who is least likely to be recognized" (p. 50). Considering this finding, I wondered in how many other settings Samantha had rendered herself invisible to her teachers. The fact is that even those of us attuned to gender issues can miss students like Samantha. There are simply too many demands in the course of a busy school day to divert our attention. Maureen Barbieri (1995), a former teacher in Exeter, New Hampshire, eloquently describes this problem as she recalls the subtle gender biases in her curriculum.

> If I thought in terms of gender at all back then, my concern had been for the boys. How could I get them to love poetry? How could I find more contemporary novels to hold their attention? And what about writing? Were they doing enough reflecting? Were they stretching themselves? When I look back, I realize I expected the girls to read and write; I expected the boys to need my extra attention and encouragement. As I read some of the student journals I've saved from those years, I am filled with remorse. My girls were calling out to me from their own "underground." There were issues on their minds, turmoil in their lives, and questions in their hearts that I had been unwilling or unable to hear. (p. 7)

Sam was more fortunate than Barbieri's girls. She had 2 years to overcome her shyness and become involved in an extracurricular activity that allowed Meg to know her on a personal level. Even so, despite Meg's high regard for her as a student and literate person, Samantha still based her own self-image as a reader on her ability to do reading responses, and not on avid reading behaviors. In what Sadker and Sadker (1994) call the "looking-glass girl" phenomenon, adolescent girls like Samantha often learn to value being popular and accepted by others much more highly than academic success. As a result, they base their self-esteem on the opinions of peers, parents, and teachers, rather than their own intuitive knowledge. Unfortunately, many girls view being bright as in conflict with being popular.

Although there's a good chance that our "A" readers will become life-time readers, Samantha has taught me that you can't always tell the *readers* from the *non-readers* by their academic performance. The challenge is to not discourage readers like Samantha by taking them out of their aesthetic absorption and forcing them into a critical stance. Obviously, Samantha is attracted to personal narrative rather than critical analysis. If "critical" think-ing is important to us, we might ask ourselves how critical and analytic skills can be nurtured through encounters with narrative. Literary reading is full of occasions for asking critical questions—questions of value ("Was this character right?"); questions of social relevance ("Were her actions just?"); and questions of personal import ("What would you have done in her situa-tion?"). Students like Samantha can be turned gently toward thinking about literary techniques and intertextual connections. She can be asked to pick a book that totally absorbed her, then to explore what the author did in order to influence her in this way. In journals, rather than responding to books in process, Samantha can be asked to look over her book selections and write for a bit about what they "teach" her about herself as a reader. Or perhaps she could draw on her considerable experience as a reader by writing reviews for other students in the class. Interestingly, Samantha explained that she loved to write book reports. When I asked her why, she replied, "I like tell-ing people about a book. I just like it. Because I think you should know about [a good book]."

It isn't that Samantha is antisocial or unwilling to think critically about her reading; it's just that her reading processes and preferences aren't sup-ported by the academic constraints of the typical literature classroom. Writ-ing journal entries just to prove that she has read a book, discussing books in a large group in order to demonstrate critical competence, or responding on examinations and quizzes are acts so divorced from "real reading" that they make no sense to her. Yet, like Angel, Sam will, I am certain, continue to read throughout her lifetime. When I asked whether they would be life-time readers, their responses were practically identical. Angel remarked: "Definitely." Samantha enthusiastically remarked: "Oh, definitely. [When] I'm [on] my deathbed I'll have a book. I'll be like 'No, I have to finish this first.' If I don't, I'll probably come back haunting people. 'Let me read that book!'"

On a rather ironic note, toward the end of the study, Angel volunteered her impression of Samantha as a reader: "Samantha, she will pick up a book and not put it down until she's finished. . . . We both read the same book. I read it in 2 months, she reads it in 3 days!" When I asked Angel how that made her feel, she remarked, "Dumb."

Reading-out-of-Bounds

Beyond the boundaries of the classroom is a vast reading room with shelves upon shelves of books, comfortable furniture, and time that stretches beyond the 40-minute class period. In this haven, young readers like Samantha choose (and abandon) texts at will, read in uninterrupted silence, swap books, visit bookstores, talk about what they read with parents and peers. This kind of *reading-out-of-bounds* transports the mind beyond the limits of print. Readers become immersed in the plight of characters by "becoming" those characters and coloring in the spaces left by the author with shades of personal and social meaning. They speculate silently on the significance of stories. Here, the line between outside reading and real life stretches thinner than the vast divide between the classroom and their social worlds.

Samantha lives and reads in this world beyond. To survive as a reader, she must bypass the typical "public" approach to reading in school and nurture her avid reading habit in the comfort and security of her home. For readers like Sam, in this private reading sanctuary, there is no teacher intermediary who receives the interpretation before it has time arrange itself into a kaleidoscopic array of words, meanings, shapes, and emotions, all collectively much greater than any of the individual parts.

Readers like Samantha are Louise Rosenblatt's ideal "aesthetic reader"— immersed in the momentary act of reading and oblivious to all else. They enter into the reading process in what Deanne Bogden (1990) calls "stasis," or a "pre-critical state," marked by a "near paralysis of linguistic powers" (p. 119). Although most of us claim to recognize and value this pre-critical response, we unfortunately lack the ways to "give credit" for it in classrooms. There is little space for silence, little room for engaged absorption within the world of school. Language for demonstration is still our prime means of communication in this chaotic and public place. We fear the silences in class discussions, because they whisper to us that we must not be teaching right if students don't respond quickly and critically to our questions. But for students like Sam, the public act of *responding* eclipses the private act of *response*.

ANOTHER BRINK: FOUR YEARS LATER

In the summer of 1995, Meg and I invited both Samantha and Angel back for a conversation about what had happened to them in the 4 years since their graduation from middle school. I was surprised to learn that the two girls had drifted apart, rarely running into each other and never choosing to spend time together. What little they knew about each other was gleaned from gossip in the ever-widening circles of friends they had each joined since middle school. Although they were still both eager and avid readers, the once-similar qualities of their reading lives had drifted apart as well.

"Just the Facts, Ma'am!": Samantha

Samantha walked in the door of Meg's classroom that summer, considerably matured and carrying a large black portfolio. At a time when she should just be graduating from high school, she was in the second year of a photography program at a local community college and hoped eventually to transfer to Rochester Institute of Technology.

She had dropped out of Briarcliff High School in her junior year, belieiving that her classes were irrelevant and her principal was oppressive. She explained, "It was just so chaotic at Briarcliff. It was crazy. I did okay in my freshman year, mainly, 'cause I didn't go. I just didn't go at all." Mr. H., the new principal, had transferred to Briarcliff from another city high school that year and, in Sam's words, "he knew where everyone was supposed to be, at every single time. He even knew us, before he introduced himself to us, like he studied all the yearbooks and everything."

Fed up with her high school experience by her junior year, Samantha convinced Mr. H. to let her attend "afternoon school," which she described as a program for "bad kids." To Sam, the experience was "so stupid; it was like, can you add two and two together?" She endured the meaningless curriculum because she knew it would earn her a letter from the principal, allowing her to enroll in community college. She explained, "I did it, 'cause I knew it would be completely easy. It would be no stress to me."

When I asked Samantha to describe herself in seventh grade, she chuckled, "Oh my goodness . . . ah, I was a tag-a-long, I was kind of preppie. I wanted to be liked by everyone." Gradually, as she reached eighth grade, became involved with an informal network of peer readers, and joined Meg's play writing group, her personality began to evolve into more than a "good girl." She explained, "I wasn't so much a rebel, I just [became] more of . . . a[n] individual. . . . I started hanging out with people that weren't like part of the herd."

Then came high school. Samantha knew it wouldn't be the same as middle school, but didn't realize "how different it would be." On her first day in freshman English, she remembered:

> We started learning about commas, punctuation, and I could not believe it. I was [thinking] like, what is this crap? It just seemed so unimaginative; it didn't seem like it had a purpose to it. So what if you know how to put a semicolon in where it's supposed to be? That doesn't make you a good writer!

Largely because she had spelling problems, Samantha was placed in English 099, a noncredit remediation course. She complained, "It kind of sucks, when I've got all these good ideas, and I don't know how to spell. . . . It was a waste of time, but I had to do it." In her middle school classrooms, she explained, "there was a, kind of a free style, like a kind of lack of structure. But the kids were under control." In high school, "it was just the opposite; kids were out of control, and there was . . . massive structure."

I was, of course, most curious to see whether Samantha still considered herself an avid reader. She replied without hesitation that she still couldn't fall asleep at night without a book: "I don't find that I have as much time to read now as I would really like to, because I have so much stuff going on. . . . So, the only time I really find time to read is right before I go to bed."

With pleasure, Meg recalled the times when she would overhear Samantha and her friends in the hallways: "You girls talked about books all the time." At the same time, Meg chuckled, "you guys were the ones who wouldn't read in class." Remembering her resistance to writing in the response notebook, Sam seemed surprised that Meg knew about her passion for reading. Meg continued:

> I would overhear your conversations every day, and I would often think, if anyone else ever came in here, like a person to observe my teaching or something, one of the first comments would have been how off-task you all were. Well, I could have turned around and said, "These are my best!"

Samantha admitted her resistance to writing responses: "[Mrs. Andrews] knew we read the book. So why did we have to write a reading response?" At the same time, she remarked, wistfully, "I guess if I could get back into a situation, like Mrs. Andrews's class was, . . . it would be like heaven. I just love[d] it." Given that much freedom again, Sam admitted that she wouldn't even mind writing in her response notebook. I reminded Samantha that, at least in middle school, she seemed to respond emotionally and to read literature in an absorbing, aesthetic way. She remarked that this was true, even today: "I don't put [a] book down, unless my eyes close."

Meg remembered Samantha as a young woman of many contrasts. Together, we read the poetry in Sam's middle school writing folder. Meg gasped in admiration, as she pointed out the line "night blackness gobbles me." She laughed: Samantha "would sit here and talk about makeup and nothing, and hair and all this. And she would stop for 2 seconds . . . and come out with this! . . . It was amazing!" Sam agreed: "Most of my expression that I couldn't, like, say out loud. I did it through poetry."

As we looked further through the folder, we came upon her final examination in eighth grade. She read the response to Wallace Stegner's "The Colt," where she focused on the death of her own guinea pig. Ignoring the academic content of the piece, she flashed back on the death of her pet: "I stayed awake all night. My mom's boyfriend yelled at me when I tried to go down and see if he was okay. I was so mad!" When I asked whether a highly personal response like hers would be acceptable in a high school English examination, she responded, "I don't believe it would be." In high school, Samantha explained:

> They wanted stuff that was very technical. They . . . didn't want to know about you. They just want the facts. Just the facts, Ma'am! They didn't really care how this relates to you in a situation. They just wanted to know what everything meant in the literature.

Samantha laughed at her high school teachers' narrow expectations: "How do you know what [literature] means, unless . . . you can tie it into something about yourself . . . 'cause that's where the meaning is?"

Finally, I asked her to talk about her friendship with Angel in middle school. She remarked, "I was more likely to go along with what she said, to not cause any waves. I'm like that now. I'm very submissive; I don't like to make a lot of waves." Sam remembered how Angel "always had to be the best. . . . She is a national honor student now. And she always was into getting the grade, very into getting 100 averages." Samantha, on the other hand, sometimes strove for good grades, but most of the time didn't care. In middle school, Meg's class was her "biggest priority," along with social studies, "just 'cause I loved the teachers so much."

In schooling, as in literature and life, Samantha needed to be personally and emotionally involved in whatever she did. In addition, her shyness and her fear of not being "liked by everyone" made her panic when asked to respond on-the-spot in school. In tests or class discussions, when teachers asked her to describe a character in literature, she would "talk about the outside stuff." When given some time to think about her response, however, she would "go into everything . . . I hated being rushed doing anything." Sam's comment reminded me of Sadker and Sadker's (1994) argument that "wait time" is often essential in encouraging young girls to participate in class discussion. They observe:

> In classrooms where discussion moves rapidly and less than one second goes by between the teacher's question and a student's answer, girls may be left out.

This breakneck pace, usually set by boys, blocks the participation of shy students who need more time to think or muster their confidence. When teachers consciously extend their wait time to three to five seconds, especially where a thoughtful response is warranted, more girls—and quiet boys—are pulled into the discussion. (pp. 269–270)

For the rest of our time together that afternoon, we perused Sam's photography portfolio. Suddenly, I came upon a photograph of a young man on a skateboard and thought immediately about the skateboarding metaphor that eventually would make it into the introduction of this book. I asked Sam if I could have permission to use her photograph for the cover. As she proudly gave it to me, I thought that with what she called "2 years of college under her belt" and a GED, Samantha was in many ways more mature and self-assured than a good many young people who go through schooling in more traditional ways. How sad, I thought, that Samantha had to escape her public high school in order to get to this place.

"You People Over Here Can Be the Waitresses": Angel

In the fall of 1995, Angel was preparing to attend a prestigious northeastern college and major in women's studies. Like Samantha, Angel had left her urban high school in her junior year. However, unlike Sam, Angel transferred to Hendricks Hall, an upper middle class private school with little racial or ethnic diversity. In addition to being totally unengaged by the curriculum at Briarcliff, Angel had an ongoing conflict with the principal because, as she put it, her boyfriend was "number one on Mr. H.'s 'I hate you' list." The principal would call Angel into his office and warn her that she was intelligent and might be "sucked in" by her boyfriend. Angel was constantly put off by Mr. H.'s intrusions into students' personal lives. She remembered a student who skipped classes because he was only interested in going to the pottery room. Mr. H. eventually got the boy's house key and waited in his living room, to make sure he wasn't going home from school each day. Eventually when he couldn't even go home to eat during the day, the boy began to hitchhike around the city. When Angel began to recognize what she saw as constant chaos in the classroom, contrasted with oppressive administrative control, she convinced her mother to send her to private school.

Ironically, Angel saw the Hendricks Hall curriculum as more directly focused on social and political issues than her public school had been. Although at first Angel thought of Hendricks as a "preppie school," she eventually felt that this setting nurtured her interest in national and international politics much more than her more racially and ethnically diverse public high school had. In middle school, Angel had just started to become politically conscious, as she learned that she "didn't have to be like everybody else." While she was still in middle school, her mother criticized her generation for not caring about the world. In response to this challenge, she started volunteering for Planned Parenthood in eighth grade. Through high school, she served on their teen advisory board. As part of her work, she was sent to three family conferences at the state capital and found herself talking with legislators and congress people. At this point, Angel "realized how stupid politics was." Bitterly, she remembered a conversation with a state legislator who asked, "Do you want me to go out and buy poor people Mercedes?" Angel couldn't believe his simplistic response: "and he's talking about health care!"

Ironically, although Angel's consciousness about women's issues was piqued in middle school, she didn't realize the bias of the traditional literary canon until she took an English course at Hendricks Hall taught by a former African-American studies professor from the nearby university. Angel remembered: "I hadn't read any African-American [literature]" in high school. At Hendricks, she began to read Toni Morrison, as well as nonfiction books like *And the Band Played On* (Shilts, 1988), books about the Holocaust, and critiques of the American educational system. When I pointed out the irony that she had to leave her public high school to explore the political issues of race, class, and gender, she explained that even though she might have only two students of color in her classes at Hendricks Hall, "you hang out with them more often." By contrast, she explained, Briarcliff is segregated, "and I don't think it's by choice, from the students. I think it's sort of forced." Angel went on to explain that Briarcliff is "not prejudiced," but that students are from very different neighborhoods, and that those who are from neighborhoods "not directly outside of" Briarcliff "feel really alienated and cling to what they know best, which is the kids in their neighborhood."

At Logan, where there was no academic tracking, Angel had many African-American friends. At Briarcliff, on the other hand, academic tracking gave students "a very clear message as soon as you come in the door: 'These are the people that we are prepping to go on to be doctors and lawyers and all that, while you people over here can be the waitresses and the garbage men.'" Angel recognized that the college tracking system is even worse: "Whatever college you go to, that is a track." The heavy emphasis on tracking at Briarcliff ensured that few, if any, students of color were in her classes. Instead they were placed in lower tracks, where they were "guaranteed not to learn." Angel's boyfriend, for example, was put into the lowest track, mainly because of his reputation as a troublemaker. Today, Angel remarks sadly, "He barely graduated from high school and he's like, talking about meteorology. He knows about this stuff that I don't even know."

When I asked Angel what advice she would give to her high school teachers, her reply was unequivocal. She remembered being at Briarcliff during the aftermath of the Rodney King trial:

> I never heard anything about it in class, and I was upset. I have to say I was upset! I mean we had a walkout! The only thing [the principal] said was, "Well, it's their citizen's duty to speak up for their rights; if they want to walk out, I'm going to let them." He wasn't going to do anything about it. . . . He never said, "Let's take an hour out of the school day to have a discussion about it."

In the heat of the racial conflicts at Briarcliff, Angel thought for a time that "the school was just going to die!" Rather than ignoring students' anger, she believed that teachers and administrators should have responded to it, making it a central issue in the curriculum. She lamented:

> Parents don't teach their kids stuff like that . . . you know, writing as a release, reading as a release, and speaking as a release, and being with other students and talking with them and listening to them as a way to express yourself.

At some point, I reminded Angel of her ability to "play the game of school," and asked if this was still true in high school. She remarked:

> *Angel* (jokingly): I just always knew how to do what the teacher
> wanted me to do. . . . Like a science teacher might want you to
> write a lab [report] a certain way and you should just do that,
> 'cause that's the way to get a good grade. . . . If the teacher is
> into sappy little stuff, like Mrs. Andrews is, then you write that
> stuff. (laughs)
> *Meg*: Not, not sappy! Geez!
> *Angel*: S-A-P-P-Y! (laughs)

At some point, I asked her to talk a bit about Samantha. Although the two girls had lost touch in high school, Angel remembered that in middle school

> [Sam] could read a book in 2 days, a big fat book in 2 days, if she wanted to. She was a nonstop reader. I think she still is, actually. . . . I was always a slow reader. . . . I still am a slow reader.

I was surprised that Angel saw herself as better at math than Samantha, but not as good in reading and writing. Although she described Samantha as "brilliant," she observed, "Sam had less motivation than me. She liked to do what she liked to do, and she really didn't care about things that she didn't like to do."

Despite her admission into an ivy league college, Angel surprised me when she said, "I definitely need help with English, because I don't think English is my forte. Math and science are my forte." She described her experience in high school English as a sharp contrast with Meg's classes.

> I hated high school English, except for my AP class. . . . I hate ripping apart literature. . . . I know how to do Cornell notes. . . . I hate doing it though. . . . I think you should just read a book and if you go, "Wow, it's a good book!" You don't have to say why.

Interestingly, most of her negative self-image as a reader and writer came from not being able to "pick up on all . . . [those] rhetorical devices . . . it doesn't come naturally to me." I asked if Meg had, in a sense, disabled some of her students by not preparing them for the formalistic high school curriculum. Angel countered, "I think it is enabling. . . . In Mrs. Andrews's class, people were doing things that they liked to do, and I think that's more important than necessarily learning how to do things that people don't like to do." In addition, Angel remarked that "Mrs. Andrews . . . puts students on equal level. . . . I think Mrs. Andrews did more learning from us than we did from her. . . . [She] had a way of thinking . . . [kids] are people. Sometimes people don't think kids are people."

Angel would never have done any "creative writing," had it not been for Meg. In high school, she didn't remember doing any at all. Despite her middle school prediction that she would be a lifetime reader, Angel seldom read fiction anymore. This was somewhat ironic, considering that in seventh grade she hated nonfiction. In an interview during middle school, she had remarked:

> If I have to do a report, I have to read nonfiction, and that's kind of boring because it goes on and on and on. It's like "on this date this happened and at this date this happened." . . . It sort of just keeps repeating itself.

That summer, however, Angel had gotten a job reading documents and articles from *The Wall Street Journal* and now reads mostly newspapers. When she reads nonfiction, Angel explains, "I don't have to read a lot. I can skim through. . . . I don't have to sit there and really think about it."

Today, I am convinced that each of these two young women has found success within her own definitions of that term. I am not surprised that Samantha continues to read voraciously, despite the heavy demands and responsibilities of her college program. I am, however, surprised to learn that Angel sees herself as unsuccessful in English and has virtually abandoned reading literature for pleasure. This may, of course, change as time goes by. If I have learned anything from my time with these two young women, however, it is that our academic standards for "good reading" have little to do with whether our students will continue to read literature beyond their years of formal schooling.

More compelling, perhaps, is the indictment that both Samantha and Angel level at the rigidity and irrelevance of their public high school English curriculum. Along these lines, Peter McLaren (1991) has criticized the process of American schooling, arguing that "there exists a bifurcation between school knowledge and real-life knowledge, with the potency of real-life contrasting dramatically with the lifelessness of school knowledge" (p. 26). McLaren suggests that teachers construct "an arch of social dreaming" (p. 2)—one that allows students like Angel and Samantha to see school knowledge not as a set of "tasks to do," but as a "system for helping them understand and act upon the world" (p. 26). Following these students beyond their high school years has convinced me that a good many readers like Samantha and Angel often slip silently past the irrelevant academic structures of the typical secondary English class. If we are to engage their interest, we simply must help them to build that arch of social dreaming that McLaren describes.

CHAPTER 8

"Can 'the Gifted' Play Football?": Luis

I believe all students need the opportunity to do something basically, and I don't think [there is] that opportunity for black students. . . . They're going into these easy courses and everybody's calling them stupid and everything else. (Luis, 1995)

It is early one morning in the spring of 1991, when I arrive to find Meg's class considerably smaller. She explains that the schedule will be a bit changed that day because her students from "the gifted" program are attending a special assembly. I notice Luis Thomas standing by her desk, near where I usually sit with my tape recorder and notebook. As Meg makes her announcement, Luis casts a sidelong glance in my direction and muses sarcastically, "Hm . . . I wonder if 'the gifted' can play football." We both chuckle at this for a moment. Actually, I'm pleasantly surprised. After several months of seeing me in his classroom, Luis has finally begun to acknowledge my presence. Although not an official member of "the gifted team," Luis knows that *he can* play football. In fact, when isn't getting into trouble with the coach—which is rare—he is working out with the Briarcliff High School football team, in preparation for graduation from middle school, when he will play varsity sports.

I couldn't help thinking back that morning to the first time I met Luis, a year earlier when he was in seventh grade. Early in October 1989, I had just scurried up the stairs of Logan, wearing my best "university professor" suit and lugging an enormous pile of dittoed questionnaires. I entered Meg's room a few minutes after the bell had rung. Apparently she had just been called to the office over the intercom and saw my arrival as a good chance to take care of some business. As she whizzed past me, she said, "I'll be back in about 30 minutes. I've told them you were coming in today. Go ahead and get started without me. Bye." She was out the door before I could say a word.

For a split second, all the horror stories I'd heard from "substitute" teachers over the years flashed through my mind. Since I was a relative newcomer in Meg's classroom, I was sure I'd be treated as one. I managed to swallow this panic, however, and asked the students if they would help me by answering some questions. I explained that their participation was totally voluntary and that there were no right or wrong answers. I was just interested in how kids their age felt about reading. After getting the students into their seats and responding to a few concerns, I proceeded to hand out the questionnaires.

Some students looked at me with blank stares; others went on talking noisily to their neighbors; a few wandered out of their seats. Finally, I got them quieted down, but I was still a bit nervous. Luis didn't help matters. He shoved the questionnaire to the edge of his desk and, looking up briefly from his folded arms, he shook his head in an unmistakable "No way!" For just one millisecond, I opened my mouth to challenge him. Luckily, I realized that this was not my classroom; mine was a voluntary study; and from the looks of Luis's football player's physique, I could be in great physical danger at this very moment. I quickly withdrew from the confrontation, passing by Luis's desk and assuring him that he didn't have to participate unless he wanted to. From that moment, although Luis wasn't an "official" part of my study, he began to work his way into my consciousness and, I must admit, eventually into my heart.

COUNT LUIS

In his seventh-grade year, I began to joke that Luis was something of a vampire. Just as Count Dracula couldn't be photographed or cast a reflection in a mirror, Luis refused to be captured on the pages of my questionnaires or the cassette tapes I carried into class each day. I remember vividly one day when I was taping Meg as she conferred with students. She walked over and put my tape recorder back on my desk, apologizing, "I have to give this back to you. Luis is coming over to conference and he'll kill me if he sees this."

It took a long time before Luis would acknowledge my presence in the classroom. Although he was a key player on a football field, his usual position in the classroom was on the sidelines. Often, he would stand in the doorway, appearing to pass judgment on the class activities, before deciding whether he should leave or stay, enter the circle or stand on the margins. Occasionally, he might toss in a comment or two during a particularly lively discussion in Literature Circle, but, for the most part, he kept to himself and rarely mixed with other students. He was in eighth grade before he began occasionally to wander up to where I was sitting, cast a brief glance in my direction, and mumble an almost inaudible "Hi." Although I always suspected that there was a great deal more to Luis than meets the eye, I began to get a glimpse of his literate life in eighth grade. Toward the middle of that year, I witnessed a slow but subtle transformation, as he seemed to expand his identity beyond "football player" and "tough guy" to include "student," "writer," and "actor." This transformation became visible to me when I discovered him actually reading aloud a piece he had written during the Friday Sharing Time. As he read, I surveyed the room, noticing how he commanded the respect and rapt attention of his classmates. His writings that year consisted mostly of graphic, sometimes profane pieces about life in the city, interracial dating, and violent accounts of fights with other boys.

Although Luis had a Hispanic first and middle name (Luis Gonzales Thomas), he clearly identified himself as Black. This fact was revealed in his writing. During his eighth-grade year, Luis took a rather dramatic turn from his "tough guy" image and surprised us all by beginning to write poetry. Four years later, in an interview, he was to admit that he surprised even himself. I have only a few poems that Meg saved from his writing folder. One was this:

> I'm proud to be black
> 'Cause black is what I am
> blacks are the people I love
> and I will stand for their rights.
> I'm proud of being who I am
> and that doesn't mean sacrificing
> the brother man.
> Whites show the struggle of
> the black man by trying to hold
> us back.
> But they can't stop progress and
>   respect for the black man
> like I said, I'm proud to be
>   Black

The poems that Luis wrote were very different from the abstract and often dreamy poetry that students like Samantha and Angel wrote. His were more grounded in the concrete realities of life. Rather than inviting reflection on the world, they seemed to invite action on it. In this sense, they were perhaps more accurate reflections of the real Luis Thomas than any of the interviews or writings I might have collected, had he been an official part of my study from the start. It seemed that Luis could not become engaged in any activity—within or outside of school—that did not both reflect and *affect* the world in which he lived.

Although I was surprised that Luis was willing to take the plunge and reveal himself as a poet in Meg's classroom, I was never more astounded than I was one day, when this young man who seemed so full of anger and resentment walked up to a microphone in front of 300 students and "went public" as a writer. I had seated myself to the right of the stage as Ed Jackson, the artist in residence, greeted the students and their teachers who had gathered that morning to hear their classmates perform the pieces they had been writing all term. To my astonishment, suddenly Luis was striding up to the microphone, sturdy, strong, and smiling! He began:

> This is a short story. I'm not gonna read the whole thing, 'cause it's got cursing in it. "In the ——— up streets of New York, there's nothing but crime and poverty. Gangs fighting over turf, children doing drugs, innocent people getting killed in gang wars. But the police don't give a ———."

It was a piece about life in the streets of New York. The main character was a boy named "Tino" (although I wasn't aware of it at the time, one of Luis's close friends in Meg's class was named Tino Hernandez). Luis was right about the cursing. In my observer notes that day, I wrote the following:

> *As Luis begins to read, he is making a big deal of substituting each word of profanity with the word "blank." The kids are laughing conspiratorially as he does this. The piece moves into a description of a Latino boy named Tino, who seems to make a career of fighting Black boys. I'm not surprised by the violence. But I am struck by how much credibility Luis seems to have with the other students in the audience. They seem respectful, almost awestruck, as I am. I flash back to my first encounter with Luis, when he refused to fill out any of my questionnaires, and I think how far these students have all come. The idea of macho Luis getting attention, not from destructive acts, but from sharing his writing—from being a literate person—it leaves me speechless.*

In retrospect, I wonder if I would have been quite so astounded if a White student had made the same transformation as Luis had. The fact was that I had witnessed other African-American students take a great deal of criticism from their peers for engaging in "academic" behaviors. Such activities, in the minds of some Black students, were a sign of abandoning Black culture and giving in to the White power structure—what John Ogbu (1988) calls "acting white." Ogbu argues that

striving for academic success is a subtractive process: the individual black student following standard school practices that lead to academic success is perceived as adopting a white cultural frame of reference, as emulating white, or
as "acting white" with the inevitable outcome of losing his or her black identity, abandoning black people and black causes, and joining the enemy, namely,
white people. (p. 177)

Along these lines, Hale (1994) argues that while all African-American children are required to master two cultures (African-American and European)
in order to succeed in school, African-American males must master three
cultures, since most elementary school classrooms are taught by White
women, who "tend to be more comfortable with and knowledgeable about
the behavior of white female children and, to a lesser degree white male
children" (p. 191).

Surprisingly, Luis had risked "acting White," yet had met praise, rather
than censure, from his Black peers. I surmised that perhaps he could afford
this risk because of his success on the athletic field—a pursuit that historically has been accepted by Whites and Blacks as part of the Black experience. Along these lines, Ogbu (1988) observes that "[black] students who
do relatively well in school while still accepted by their peers are those who
are either simultaneously successful in sports or activities regarded as black
or students who have found ways to camouflage their academic efforts and
outcomes" (p. 178). While I had never witnessed Luis trying to camouflage
any of his activities to please others, I suspected that he had earned enough
credibility with his peers so that his emergence as a writer was not held against
him. Besides, considering his physical stature, I doubted that any other students would dare to taunt or criticize him.

I had genuinely liked the piece he shared in the assembly, and the very
next time I saw Luis, I made a point of telling him so. This may have precipitated the occasional "Hi" he dropped in my direction when he would drift
over to Meg's desk during class time. Luis seemed to come in from the sidelines, rarely approaching school tasks with head-on enthusiasm. Yet beneath
the reticent exterior, I could sense a yearning to be involved—to be part of a
group. This subtle yearning seemed counterbalanced by a silent anger that
often kept him at arm's distance from the adults and other students in the
room. Although I never personally witnessed Luis being violent in Meg's
classroom, this anger seemed always present, probably held at bay by some
sheer force of will. In November of his eighth-grade year, he wrote a piece,
oddly about his summer vacation, that gave me a glimpse of this angry side.
Apparently, that summer a fight had started after a boy named Peter had
been taunting Luis for several weeks. Although the composition began, "I

had a pretty good summer vacation," it quickly degenerated into a vivid description of his fight with Peter.

> *I told somebody to hold my glasses. Then that's when I gave him*
> *the worst beating he ever had. He started holding on to me so I*
> *punched him in his mouth about fifty times. then his blood splattered*
> *all over my shirt. He still wouldn't let me go so I slammed him down*
> *on the concrete by his neck. Then I stuck my fingers in his eyes and*
> *in his mouth and tried to tear his face apart. . . . Then some people got*
> *me off. So then I figured I was finished for the day. But a few days*
> *later he said he beat me. So I started looking for him the rest of*
> *the summer before school started. I never saw him. But I'm going to*
> *get him.*

Clearly, this account pushes the edges of the typical "How I Spent My Summer Vacation" piece and reveals just a bit of the pent up anger that Meg and I both sensed in this young man, who always seemed so much older than his years. Throughout middle school, Luis seemed to vacillate between a reputation for violent behavior and a desire to be successful in school. Luis may be typical of a good many young athletes, encouraged toward violence by the culture of organized sports. As Sadker and Sadker (1994) argue:

> Sports remains a focal point of school life and growing up male. . . . Aggression, repressed in the classroom, is harnessed by coaches, put to work on the athletic field, and released against the opposing team. . . . The playing field becomes a legitimate arena for fighting, hostility, and competition. (p. 210)

In Luis's case, however, I sensed an ambivalence toward the "tough guy" image he had worked so hard to perpetuate. He lingered on the edges of the classroom, yet his overall attendance was good. He gave the outward appearance of resisting many school tasks and conflicted even with his football coach, yet always managed to turn in enough homework to maintain a respectable grade point average. To me, these were signs of the yearning to be successful in something other than physical pursuits like sports and fighting. The tension between acceptance and resistance that I sensed in Luis has been aptly described by Vivian Gadsden (1995): "Although there is enormous hope within many segments of African-American communities, there may be an equal level of pessimism and cynicism about the value of literacy in the lives of African-American youth and their families; occasionally, this hope and cynicism exist in tandem" (p. 4). Throughout my observations of him, Luis constantly negotiated this precarious balancing act between resisting and pursuing academic success.

JOINING "THE GIFTED"

Eventually, during the spring of his eighth-grade year, Luis got his chance to be one of the gifted and to share his gifts with others. As the school's drama director, Meg always produced a spring play. In previous years, she'd used professional scripts like *The Diary of Anne Frank* (Goodrich & Hacket, 1956), but this year she and a group of students were collaboratively writing an original play script called *Rapid Eye Movement*. To Meg's surprise, Luis had actually decided to try out for the play writing group. I hadn't known about Luis's involvement in this group until the night of the final performance. Meg had arranged with the manager of a local downtown theatre to allow the students to perform on a professional stage, rather than the so-called Logan "cafetorium." Somewhere in the middle of the play, I caught sight of Luis as he swaggered to the front of the stage and, in his characteristic style, talked about life in the streets, hard times in the inner city, and what it meant to grow up Black in a White man's world.

As he became a more active presence in classroom as well as extracurricular activities, he seemed to open up just a bit, not only with other students, but with Meg as well. His journey toward trust was neither steady nor smooth, however. We both suspected that, although he experienced many successes in Meg's class and on the stage, he was still conflicted about his affection for and dependence on a White woman. This emotional ambivalence seemed to surface in a very painful incident involving Meg. A few weeks earlier, Meg had gone to sit in her chair and instead fell with a crash to the floor. The chair had been removed from beneath her. The fall was not only embarrassing, but acutely painful, since her tailbone was already fragile from a previous automobile accident. The worst part was that, although she had no proof, she suspected Luis of the prank, since he was physically closest to the chair right before the incident.

Although she was injured both physically and emotionally, she refused to follow up on the incident in any formal way, deciding instead to simply tell all the students how disappointed and hurt she had been. Somehow she knew that Luis was just beginning to trust her at what seemed to be a crucial juncture in his life. A referral to the office at this time, considering his other run-ins with the principal, might have meant expulsion from school and have tipped him over the edge into the violence and antisocial behavior that always seemed just a heartbeat away. As it turned out, this was a wise decision.

"PEOPLE SEEMED TO LISTEN": LITERACY AS SOCIAL ACTION

As his trust in Meg and his peers began to grow, Luis edged steadily toward a vision of himself as a literate person. For him, writing served not only to demonstrate his gift for language, but to affect changes in his social world. Toward the end of the year, Luis recalled his writing in Meg's class. In what she called her "final communications packet" (a clever substitute for the mandatory "final examination" at Logan), she had asked her students to describe the piece of writing they were most proud of and explain why they had selected that piece. Luis wrote:

> *I liked the very first time I shared because people seemed to listen to what I had to say. . . . The writing I think I expressed most was when I wrote about why I go with white girls so often I told people I go with a paticular white girl because I like her and she looks good I read it in front of a group blacks just to see what they would do. So now no one disrespects me anymore by calling me white.*

Students of color, like Luis, in predominantly White schools cannot afford to be "color blind." They are constantly, and often painfully, reminded that social differences exist, that they belong to cultures that historically have been oppressed, and that the world is seldom easy or fair. Literacy had become a way for Luis to reach out and change that world in his own small way. At one point, Meg reflected on the power of reading and writing in the lives of students like Luis.

> *[Some of my students] are outcasts, runaways, grievers, delinquents or exceptionally lonely young people who have learned somewhere along the line that if they can express their feelings in writing, or lose themselves in a good book, they can make it through any given day that would otherwise be impossible for them. Reading and writing for them is not mere entertainment, nor the development of talent; it is what keeps them going from day to day in a world that they find altogether too difficult.*

Part of Luis's identity as a Black male involved a consciousness about issues of race, poverty, crime, and substance abuse, not in an abstract sense, but as he saw these issues touching his own life and world. For this reason, although I had little data to corroborate my hunch at the time, I suspected that Luis resisted the White, ethnically homogeneous literature and worksheets that were the standard fare in the "reading" course he took as a support for Meg's class.

"READING USE TO BE NICE"

Students at Logan were given examinations four times a year. All those identified as "average" or "below average" in reading were required to take a reading course, in addition to their regular English class. Luis was enrolled in this course. Although in seventh grade he identified himself as a competent reader and writer, he saw these pursuits as peripheral to his life. His reading teacher only made matters worse. In his autobiography as a reader and writer for Meg's class, he wrote:

> I do not remember anything from a long time ago like some of the other students. But I have known how to read and write for a long time. I have always been good at it. I can not write poetry or short stories because I am not good at it. I can write fictional stories, articles, and do my schoolwork. That is about the only kind of writing I can do. I have known how to read for a long time. I can read very well. I think I learned when I was in the second grade. I do not see how I could have learned there, because that is the grade I had to repeat. I failed because I skipped for mostly the whole school year. But by the third grade, I was above level. I also knew how to spell pretty good even though I do not know where I learned. I do not like reading too much now. It seems like a waste of time and boring. I can read poetry good anywas. So I'm not going to read unless I have to. I started disliking reading in the seventh grade. The reading teacher I have is boring we don't even read out of the reading books. We do worksheets everyday. Reading use to be nice, but it isn't anymore.

I had heard similar comments about this particular reading teacher from Kianna. At the time, I wondered why, since Luis seemed pretty intellectually astute, he had been tracked into the reading course in the first place. He apparently had the intelligence to learn to read despite his chronic truancy in second grade, and actually was above level in third grade. Sadly, his story is not unlike that of other African-American students, who experience an ever-widening gap between their literacy skills and those of European-American children, beginning in early elementary school. Labov (1995) has noted:

> The overall picture is that young black children arrive at kindergarten full of enthusiasm for the educational adventure, with a strong motivation to succeed from their parent or parents. The pattern of reading and educational failure that follows is progressive and cumulative. Though it may be conditioned by early handicaps, it is largely the result of events and interactions that take place during the school years. (p. 44)

At the time, I curbed my instinct to confront this "reading teacher" with how she had successfully managed to turn students like Luis and Kianna against reading with her dittoed sheets. Here, too, I realized that African-American students, who are most likely to be tracked into remedial programs, often suffer from the mindless busywork of the "deficiency" model called remediation. Linda Darling-Hammond (1995) has argued that

> In part as a function of the limited skills of their teachers, students placed in the lowest tracks or in remedial reading programs too often sit at their desks for long periods of the day, matching the picture in column (a) to the word in column (b), filling in the blanks, and copying off the board. They work at a low cognitive level on fairly boring literacy tasks that are profoundly disconnected from the skills they need to learn. Rarely are they given the opportunity to talk about what they know, to read books, or to construct and solve problems. (p. 183)

Fortunately, through his writing, sharing, and performing in Meg's classroom, Luis had managed to salvage his identity as a literate person. He taught me that even the most hardened "noncontributing" student often is aching to become part of a classroom family. Sometimes, like Luis, these students seem to skate on the edges of literate activity, appearing uninvolved, detached, following their own private path. But then one day, their teachers discover that, all along, they were just waiting for the moment to join the action, to be at the center, and to find their own special niche in this place called school.

MEETING ON THE THRESHOLD

At least that was what I surmised at the time. Since Luis had not given his permission to be one of my "official" case study informants, I had not been able to gather much concrete data to support my hunches. But he lingered in my mind long after my data had been collected. I saw him for the last time in his middle school years on the steps of Logan. I was going to visit Meg, when he and I spotted each other. I congratulated him on the fine job he had done in the play and asked him where he was planning to go to high school. With pride, he told me that he would be going to Briarcliff High School and playing on the football team. I remember thinking that whatever lay ahead for Luis, he still seemed tenuously poised between "making it" in the world of school and career, and drifting off to less socially acceptable pursuits.

I bid goodbye to a proud and considerably matured Luis Thomas, wishing him only the best. But for the next 4 years, I could not keep his memory out of my mind. He haunted me, as so many of my students had haunted me in years past—students like Luis who drifted beyond the doors of my classroom, still poised on the edge of two very different futures. Most of the time, I never heard from these students again. They were part of a great and nearly invisible mass of young people, positioned on the edges of school. As a result, they either failed to rise to my attention, or were so visibly troubled that it took all of my energy not to look the other way and focus on more "promising" students. It was all too easy to let them stay on the margins. I wondered, even when I tried to help them, how much of an impact I could make in my few short months with them. And more disturbing, I wondered how many students like Luis I had failed to notice at all. It would be 4 years before I would again get a glimpse into his world and begin to explore some of these questions anew.

After our meeting that day, I doubted I would ever see Luis again. When I finally decided to look him up, 4 years after he had graduated from eighth grade, my efforts were rather like the "search and find" expeditions that Meg engaged in so often as she tried to lure him away from the streets and into the activities of her classroom. After learning that he was no longer in the city school system, we finally located a former foster mother, Mrs. Corcoran. To our disappointment, we learned that she hadn't seen Luis in more than 2 years. She knew he was in a nearby city called Altonville, but had no other information, since Child Protective Services does not allow foster parents to contact children formerly in their care. I thought it sad that a system created to protect and shelter children would end up separating them so abruptly and sometimes irrevocably from their past.

I called several numbers at Altonville High School before reaching the building principal, who informed me that Luis was, indeed, a senior at the school. In fact, whether for good or ill, he seemed to know Luis quite well. As I expected, the principal could not give out Luis's number or address, but agreed to hand deliver a note if Meg sent one. We mailed the note and crossed our fingers for 2 weeks. On Wednesday, as I hurried to Logan for an interview with another student, Meg announced, "Rumor has it that Luis was in the building a couple of days ago, looking for me. He mentioned some interviews we were doing." My hopes rose for just a moment, before being doused by a flood of reality. Why, after all, would a young man who had refused to fill out my questionnaires be motivated to look us up and engage in an interview? He had been "missing in action" for all these years. Why would he make the effort to contact us again? We agreed that if Luis showed up at any time that week, I would drive to the school immediately and interview him on the spot.

The next day, I walked into Meg's classroom, expecting to interview Samantha, when I was greeted by Meg. She joked: "We have double jeopardy today. Luis is upstairs talking to one of the seventh-grade classes, and he has agreed to come down for an interview once he finishes." At that moment, Meg's principal called over the intercom and asked her to come down to the office. An instant replay of my first encounter with Luis flashed through my mind. What if he spotted my tape recorder and notepad and left on the spot? But I didn't have time to entertain those fears. An hour later, as I was finishing up my conversation with Samantha, Meg leaned into the room and beamed conspiratorially: "Luis is coming."

The young gentleman in round, wire-rimmed glasses, white shirt, and flowered tie who walked through the door still bore all of the physical signs of Luis Thomas, except that his body had grown more muscular and full, and he didn't seem quite as tall as he had in the seventh grade. His head was neatly shaved, and his face curled into a gentle smile as he shook my hand and agreed not only to be tape recorded, but to sign all of my publication release forms. As he signed his name, he focused on Meg: "I've come by several times, but you were always sick or absent or something." I joked that Meg was probably just "skipping school."

Meg immediately remembered a powerful incident when Luis was in the eighth-grade play writing group. To my surprise, she had never told me about it before. Apparently, on the first day of rehearsal, the students were doing what Meg called some "touchy feely" exercises, while Luis lounged, as usual, on the outside of the group, refusing to participate. It was the students who insisted: "Luis, if you're going to be part of this group, you've got to participate with the rest of us." He reluctantly joined the circle. Taking Meg and the students by surprise, as soon as the exercise began Luis broke into a wave of tears and stormed into the hall. This was a turning point in his life. That day he "entered the circle" in more ways than one. As they stood in the hallway, Luis shared with Meg just part of the story of his difficult life. Apparently this trust was warranted. Although we had been good friends for many years and Meg had shared so much with me throughout the research project, until this moment she had never shared a word of Luis's story. She thought back to that day 4 years earlier, saying to Luis:

> You just broke down and you went out into the hall. And when
> I got out there you were just crying from the gut. And I think at
> that point, you couldn't have held it back. You know, it just
> struck something in you. And that's when you told me about
> living on the street, and [that] you didn't know where you were
> gonna live, and [that] you'd left your mother. And that's when I
> went to the guidance counselor and tried to find out, you know,
> about what was going to happen with you, and you know, [if
> we] could get some advice . . . and . . . that moved me so much,

I thought, "There's no way that I'm gonna let this kid go off and be this hurt and not have a place to feel good and safe and all that." So I kept at you to stay in the play.

Apparently, keeping Luis in the play was no easy task. Each day Meg secretly wondered if this would be the day that he would refuse to show up or walk out in an angry moment. She explained her fear that if he dropped out, it might be a final breaking point, a permanent withdrawal from school that might jeopardize the rest of his life.

I'd say, "Oh, please, just let Luis keep on doing this." Because I can remember thinking every day, one of these days he's gonna turn to me and say, "I'm not doing this anymore." And the day that you [performed] I was just amazed that you were sticking with it, especially when some of the kids in the play were just such fleas to you, you know (laughs) [you'd act like] "Get off me . . ."

Now, 4 years later, we listened as Luis filled us both in on many of the missing details of that time in his life. The story that follows was taken largely from a 90-minute interview with Luis in June 1995, as well as several pieces of writing produced after middle school that he had brought in a folder to share with us that day.

HIS "MOVING LIFE": LIVING ON THE EDGES

As Luis shaded in the missing pieces of the "connect-the-dots" picture we had formed of his fragmented life, he also revealed some of the reasons behind its outward manifestations: his underlying anger, his resistance toward authority figures and the mindless routines of schooling, but mostly why he always appeared so much older than his years. As it turned out, he had left home at the age of 13 because his mother was an alcoholic and physically abusive to him and his sister. He wrote in an essay, "One night after one of [my mother's] whippings I took off and went to a friends house. That was the beginning of my moving life." Unfortunately, according to Luis, his mother's condition had been slowly deteriorating over the years.

My mother started drinking heavier and heavier and when she drank too much she would take her frustrations out as a beating on my sister and me. For a while I dealt with the beatings. Then one night I thought I had to think about myself. I figured she was eventually going to hurt

*us. I also started to think with the grades I'm getting I can do better
than this. I believed staying with my mother would hold me back, and
as the years went by, she proved me right.*

For a time Luis lived with relatives. Despite his tenuous living situation, in
an odd mix of faith and mistrust he kept up his attendance, rarely missing
classes. He recalled: "The first thing I thought even then was I want to keep
up my grades in school 'cause I don't want to wind up homeless, which is
where I would go if I didn't get any grades."

Eventually, his aunt could no longer care for him and called Child Protective Services to report his mother for abuse and abandonment. He was
removed from the family and placed in foster care. For 2 years, he lived with
a foster parent, Mrs. Corcoran, whom he called "the closest thing to a mother
I ever had." In his words, "I had discipline with her. I would do what she
said because of how she was. She was an intelligent person. . . . Living with
her I learned respect, discipline, and overall stability, which I didn't have
before that." He stayed with Mrs. Corcoran until he graduated from Logan
and entered Briarcliff High School. What followed shortly after he entered
Briarcliff was a seemingly endless parade of foster homes and living situations that kept Luis always feeling on the margins of a safe and normal life.
Despite these odds, he refused to share his burden with most people and
maintained a strong sense of personal belief and pride. In his autobiographical essay during high school, he wrote:

> *Even though I have attended seven schools and had eight jobs, lived in
> 11 homes, I have never let anyone feel sorry for me. In fact, I haven't
> let anybody know about me because my feeling was they would feel
> sorry for me. I didn't want sympathy from anybody I just wanted
> people to treat me as a regular student and person.*

His fear that he would be treated differently as a result of his home situation
caused Luis to appear, in his words, "a little bit tougher than I really was."
This toughness was one more way to keep a safe distance from those who
had not yet earned his trust. Describing himself in retrospect, he mused:

> It was like, "If I don't know you, don't speak me, if I don't know
> you, surely don't touch me. . . ." I'd tell the teachers, "Don't
> touch me. You don't know me. . . ." I looked at everybody as not
> knowing me, and if you did, then you wouldn't touch me.

Part of the reason why he kept his peers literally at arm's length had to
do with getting blamed for the actions of other children in foster homes.

Because of his size (and presumably also his race), he found himself a prime suspect whenever anything went wrong. For example, at one point, another child in a foster home had stolen a gold necklace, and Luis was accused without evidence. He recalled the incident bitterly: "I don't even wear jewelry. Just 'cause she [his foster mother] didn't see me all night, she blame it on me. [I said to her], 'I mean I don't wear jewelry, what are you talking about?'" And so, to survive suspicion for the acts of others, he kept himself on the edges of social relationships that might have provided some comfort during this difficult time in his life.

In his first year at Briarcliff High School, Luis quickly engaged in a conflict with the football coach. However, this time his behaviors had greater consequences than had his earlier run-ins in middle school. As he explained, a series of these conflicts started him on a difficult journey from one high school and one football program to the next.

> I couldn't stand the coach there over at Briarcliff, who wound up getting fired actually, so I did the right thing. Then I went over to Cameron 'cause of Mr. Ortony. . . . He said, "So why don't you come over here?" I came over there for a year, but I was gonna get kicked outta that school 'cause of Brannon [the principal] who was riding me. This guy wrote me a letter at the beginning of the summer, right after we got outta school here and had me come in and told me he heard about my reputation. . . . I mean he wasn't gonna let me get off with a clean slate. He just wanted to tell me he knew who I was, you see, so then if I was late, he'd call me truant. Every little thing he could get me on, he would. Then I got into a fight, which I had no control over, I mean, I got hit first. I had to explain my way outta that. . . . So he gave me a formal hearing from that. So I went and uhm, had to bring a lawyer and all that, and uhm, then he quieted up and I never had any problem after that [but] I figured if I stayed there I was gonna wind up at Allen [a school for "problem" students], and I didn't want to go to that school, so I started thinking about football again, and Alabama was the place to go, so football's a big deal down there, and it was to me at the time.

Considering Luis's physical size and his penchant for violence, it is not surprising that his principal may have seen his behaviors as a sign of social deviance or pathology, and tried to take the situation firmly in hand before matters grew worse. Unfortunately, the principal's aggressive stance only ended up alienating Luis and convincing him that he had no choice but to leave. Although Luis's behaviors undoubtedly played a major part in his movement from school to school, there is some reason to suspect that other students less vocal, critical, and resistant to the practices of schooling might not have paid as dearly as did Luis. As Michelle Fine (1995) has argued, "It is often the academic critic resisting the intellectual and verbal girdles of schooling who 'drops out' or is pushed out of low-income schools. Extraordinary rates of suspensions, expulsions, and discharges experienced by African-American and Hispanic youths speak to this form of silencing" (p. 215).

Football always seemed to play a major part in Luis's many transfers from high school to high school. He went from Briarcliff to Cameron on the invitation of a football coach. And when he conflicted with the principal at Cameron, he seemed to view the football program in Alabama as an upward move toward the college career he longed for. Unfortunately, although it is sometimes advisable for students to transfer into other schools for academic reasons, it was questionable whether a transfer away from a solid family situation to pursue athletic activities would significantly improve Luis's situation. In his study of Canadian adolescents, Solomon (1992) has noted that

> transfers to higher-track schools for academic pursuits can prove emancipatory and be upwardly mobile for working-class immigrant students. School hopping for athletic reasons, on the other hand, tends to reproduce the marginal status of the black working class. (p. 97)

Thus, on the one hand, Luis's movement from school to school could be seen as a healthy form of resistance. However, considering the time and effort that athletics draws away from academic pursuits, and the inordinate pressure on African-American students to participate in sports, his reasons for moving to Alabama were misinformed at best and potentially damaging to his school success at worst.

On His Own Again

As with many African-American teenagers, Luis saw football as a way out. He was much larger than his classmates and already old beyond his years. Football, he figured, would be his ticket to college and, eventually, to an independent life. It was not for the love of the sport—the reason so many young adolescent males are drawn to athletics—but for a desire to move himself beyond an impoverished life that Luis pursued football so avidly. Solomon (1992) has observed that participation in sports serves three main functions in the life of Black students: "It helps in the formation of black culture and identity; it preserves machismo; and it is pursued as a viable channel for socioeconomic advancement" (p. 76). However, Solomon also notes that sports, a feature of Black identity formation, "marginalize rather than mobilize the working class" (p. 114). Further, he proposes that participation in sports leads to a form of social control, perhaps unwittingly exercised by schools: "Capitalizing on the black students' cultivated interest in sports, the school establishes a marriage between sport participation and allegiance to school rules" (p. 77).

For good or ill, to pursue his football career Luis left the only woman who "had been a mother" to him and went to Mobile, Alabama. In making the decision to move out of state, he finally managed to be released to his own custody. He explained, "They just told me well, 'He gotta take care of himself.' That's basically what I had to do." Unfortunately for Luis, things grew increasingly uncomfortable in Alabama. "You see, in Black families," he explained, "the color of your skin—how light you are—is really important. And my aunt started to make fun of me—calling me names all the time. I knew I couldn't stay there." In addition to having trouble with his aunt, Luis, being what he called an "intelligent Black man of fairly large stature," was a target for bigoted southern White men. He remembered:

> There were boys that put guns to my head because they had the impression that I thought I was "bad." I told the guys if they wanted to kill me, do it. Because at that time I figured they were smarter than they looked. I took a risk but I didn't retaliate because then there would have been even more violent repercussions.

As the fights with his aunt grew more frequent, he knew that he would have to move again. To earn the money for his bus ticket, Luis sold newspapers in the street. One night, after a heated argument with his aunt, he "took the first Greyhound bus" back to New York. He arrived at another aunt's house, to learn that she felt he was a "dangerous person" and would not let him stay, even temporarily. For a brief time, his worst fears came true; he was homeless.

> I slept in my aunt's car. Nobody ever knew where I was, nobody ever knew, I still never told anybody. I figured just, I'll take care of myself. As long as I got to school, as long as I didn't come to school smellin' bad or anything like that, nobody'll know, and nobody did know.

Finally, when his uncle found out about his situation, he agreed to take Luis in, but only on the condition that he begin going to church. Luis resisted this idea: "[My uncle] meant well, but . . . at that time I was not ready for religion. So he said if I wasn't ready for religion, I wasn't ready to live with him. So I told him I had to go." After a brief time in a shelter for teenage boys, Luis sought out his former seventh-grade math teacher, Mrs. Manning, who had once offered him a place to stay in Altonville if things didn't work out in Alabama. Unfortunately, she was now pregnant and could not spare the room in her house for Luis. So, in his words, "They shopped around Altonville for a place for me to live. . . . They put [out] my name, that I was looking for a place to live, like I was a foreign exchange student or something (laughter)."

This move had social and emotional consequences for Luis. Altonville is a rural community in the northeast that recently has undergone some racial and political upheavals. Until a large state prison was built in the town, there were few Black residents. Today, many of the African-American townspeople are families of convicts, while a good many of the European-American townspeople are related to prison guards and other staff. Shortly after Luis arrived, a group of White supremacists applied for and obtained a permit to hold a rally on the steps of the town hall on Yom Kippur. On the day of the rally, they were routed out by a group of protestors. In the past year, community members and a group of mostly White high school students railed against a proposal to name the high school for a famous African-American woman, whose house—a major stop on the underground railroad—stands on the outskirts of the town. When Luis first came to the school, a group of anonymous students distributed racist flyers that compared Black people to monkeys. At first, Luis did his best to stay out of the confrontations that followed, despite the viciousness of the attacks. In his words, "The first years [at Altonville] I had no problem, no ISSS, no detention. I basically stayed to myself and did those kind of things." He remembered that immediately after the flyers had been passed around, "you could go into that room, sitting there listening, and looking at all the girls crying, it was just the girls crying too, it was the Black girls crying, but uhm. I kind of kept quiet about the whole thing."

I was a bit surprised that Luis chose to endure these vicious racial attacks with such restraint. At this point in his life, however, he could not risk another confrontation with school authorities. Michelle Fine (1995) criticizes the many ways in which urban schools effectively "silence" students of color, arguing that

> students of color who voice literacies for critical consciousness are today disproportionately chastised within their schools (coded as *discipline problems*), are pushed out (coded as *dropouts*), and/or, if they are "successful," learn to bend their social critique toward individualistic explanations. At best, they learn to practice what Dubois calls "double consciousness." At worst, they forget

where they came from. The "I" drops out of their texts. Images of mobility *out of* their communities litter their work. "Rising up" and blaming "them" prevails. (p. 202)

While he struggled to restrain his opinions on political issues, he encountered a great many personal difficulties in trying to adjust to his new life circumstances. He recently had moved in with the Altonville wrestling coach and his family. Years of living on his own or in temporary foster homes had made it difficult for him to adjust to family life. He was reluctant to let anyone assume a parental or caretaking role. Luis accepted part of the responsibility for the situation: "Cause of my lack of speaking . . . I don't speak a lot, I guess I wasn't a real family guy. . . . I just never spoke with them. . . . I was an individual living with a family. Those two don't mix." Although he appreciated everything his foster family had done for him, he felt that his silence made him look "antisocial." He recalled, "The only way I figured was to say 'thank you.' That's not enough in a family and I didn't know what else to do."

Because his foster parents "wanted to be parents" and Luis "wasn't going to be nobody's son," he felt compelled to leave. He explained that moving didn't bother him: "I had done it all my life." His next foster home was with the school librarian. This time he warned her that he was "not much of a family person." However, in Luis's view, she and her husband still wanted a son, and eventually began to treat him "like a child." This time, though, he resisted his instincts to move away. "I knew I didn't have any choices so I tried to deal with it."

During his first semester at Altonville, his grades were relatively low, so his foster family forbid him to participate in the wrestling club he recently had joined. No one had ever told him he couldn't wrestle, and he was angry. Considering their desire to make him feel part of a family, this decision was probably unwise. Messner (1990) has argued that participation in organized sports can provide a sort of family, particularly for males who do not have strong family connections. Perhaps participation in athletics was serving a powerful social role for Luis, in some ways more important than the academic success his foster family wished for him. At first he threatened to move, but eventually came to a compromise. They agreed that he could continue to be in the club if he kept his average above 80. Although his new family offered to help him any way they could, he refused their help "and proved [he] didn't need it by getting an 89 average."

In his senior year, even though he had begun to take some college courses, he was still expected to keep an 80 average. "So," he reasoned, "I never spoke. I figured my grades would do the telling. My report card came out and I had a 92 average." Despite his academic success, his foster parents were disappointed that he still refused to share anything with them. Unfortunately, Luis recalled, "we started to communicate less." To complicate matters, they had loaned him the money for a car and, in order to afford the insurance, he took a job from 8:00 P.M. to 2:00 A.M. When his foster parents complained that he merely slept in their house and didn't relate to the family, Luis observed, "I don't beg, so I said 'I agree.'" For once, however, he resisted the temptation to move out of town and further disrupt his life. His girlfriend convinced him to stay and try to find his own apartment. With no offer of help from social services, he managed to find people who were willing to rent him an apartment without a security deposit. At last, Luis was truly on his own. "I figured it was time for me to live alone since I was an individual who was not in need of a family. I was turning into a man."

"You Gotta Beat Me Twice to Be the Man": Making It on His Mind

It was toward the end of his high school career when, for the first time, Luis began to seriously reconsider his lifetime goal of "making it" in the world of athletics. He realized that "Black men have always been used for their bodies," and suddenly wanted to be recognized for his intellectual abilities. It was through watching Johnny Cochran in the O.J. Simpson trials that Luis discovered a role model "who was making it on his mind" rather than his body. It had occurred to him that few White people these days were involved in professional athletics. He argued: "See how many White guys are on the bench playing basketball? How many guys are out on the court? It's just not happening. In football there's not too many white guys." This "White mind, Black body" stereotype strongly influenced his middle school career, where "people were always [saying], 'Yeah, that's a big guy.' That's all I was looked at [for]. Nobody ever said that I had a good mind, and I never thought about it until towards my senior year." Luis recognized the damaging effects of this stereotype on a national level as well.

> Like Georgetown University, I mean, uhm, this guy, John Thompson, he's a great coach but, he's complaining about NCAA standards being too high against Blacks and I have another opinion about that, but also he's getting people in with just 700s—the best basketball players in the country—into Georgetown University. This is supposed to be a tough college and they're getting in there, so you know what they're being used for—their bodies.

At the same time as he was becoming aware of racial and political issues on a national level, he found it increasingly difficult to stay uninvolved in the racial tensions at Altonville. Eventually, he got into a fight with a White football player that culminated in his injuring a teacher. At the beginning of his senior year, he was on the verge of being suspended from yet another school. In an essay, entitled "The Choice Then and Now," Luis reflected on the confrontation.

> *One day a white male student touched me, so I beat the hell out of him. But in the process some white male "teachers" were hurt. Because I was a black male who hurt some of their white brothers they had me arrested. I should of been smarter because I let the white man beat me at his own game. If I were a white guy I would of received a verbal reprimand. But since I was a "dangerous" black male they had to do whatever they could to get rid of the threat. They accomplished their goal. I lost the game this time, But as I say in wrestling, "you gotta beat me twice to be the man."*

Believing that he had to escape from yet another high school, and unwilling to give up his dream of graduation, he arranged with the principal to finish up his high school classes and to begin taking some college classes at the same time. He had remembered Mrs. Hankin's prediction in middle school that he could maintain a 90 average if it wasn't for the demands of his football schedule; early in the season, an encounter with the football coach gave him the chance to test it out. He recalled:

> I said, "Well, coach, . . . I need to get out early and miss practice one day [to take college courses], is it all right if I do it? 'Cause all he wanted us to do is just watch films. . . . And he say, "No." So I say, "Okay, you made it easy for me." So I went. I just left him and went straight to the library and I started on my sociology and English, and my grades just went up and went up.

For the first time in his long and erratic journey, Luis was making a move toward academics rather than athletics. Finally, he was engaging in a form of resistance that at least held the promise of moving him further toward his dream of a better life. Solomon (1992) has compared school transfers by Black students in his study with the "job hopping of Black school graduates in Britain." This shifting of jobs allows these young people to "prove to themselves and to one another that they are discontented with the position the schools have prescribed for them in the social structure." Likening this "school hopping" to "not settling in dead-end situations," Solomon concludes that such behavior is a sign that these students are not passive victims, but "the most critical and politically astute students" (p. 96). He argues that "by 'escaping' to other schools instead of dropping out, [Black students in his study] are affirming their desire for a better education" (p. 96). Although Luis was clearly escaping the "White mind, Black body" stereotype, even his move toward academics was not without its social and emotional consequences.

"Thinking Like White Guy": Race, Resistance, and Real-Life Literacy

Mostly on his own, Luis continued to nurture his strong interest in race and politics, reading books by and about African Americans. For example, he recently had read *The Autobiography of Malcolm X* (X & Haley, 1992) and *Makes Me Wanna Holler* by Nathan McCall (1994). At the same time, he was reading books about totalitarian regimes, such as *A Day in the Life of Ivan Denisovich* (Solzenitsyn, 1984). He began questioning the myopic view of history he had been presented within school. "We have European history, but no history of the African nations," he complained. "European history is fine, but this ain't Europe, so why study that?" Luis's observation strikes at an unfortunate reality for many students of color in American schools. As Fordham (1996) has observed:

> African-American students beyond the elementary level appear to understand the power of writing in the larger society. They seem to know—despite the draconian efforts of school officials to keep this knowledge from them—that African-Americans have been repeatedly misrepresented in the nation's major "public transcripts," their identities bludgeoned and blurred in ways that rape them of their humanity and fuel their rage as well as the rapaciousness of those who (mis)represent them in written documents. (p. 8)

Luis tried to rectify this misrepresentation in his own small way. For example, in social studies class, he was asked to impersonate a famous historical character. Since his college course didn't have many Black students, Luis observed, "you might end up hearing about people like maybe Abraham Lincoln and other people you already know about." Rejecting the usual array of White heroes, as well as more docile Black heroes, Luis chose Nat Turner, a historical figure who violently opposed the mistreatment of Black Americans and was viewed as insane by White people. Luis mused: "Everybody else that went up there had wrote down what they were gonna say. I didn't write a single thing. I just went up there and played Nat Turner and I think I scared quite a few students."

Before his high school experience, he admitted, "I didn't think of race as much, [but] as I got older . . . [I] started working more into sports and school, and reading the statistics, and seeing how there are more Black males in prison than there are in college." If racial issues had not been particularly apparent to him in middle school, they became acutely obvious in high school, where Luis observed, "they really start separating" the students on the basis of academic ability. The racial stratification of academic tracking was visible proof to him that institutional racism was alive and well in high school. It was obvious that there were few other Black faces in his higher-level classes. They stayed in the lower tracks where, according to Luis, they grew increasingly disenchanted with school. This fact has been corroborated repeatedly in studies of tracking and African-American youth. For instance, Ogbu (1995) has observed that

> Many involuntary minority students such as black students, for example, often avoid taking advanced-level science, math, and foreign language courses because they often do not see other black students in such classes. This situation has given rise, in many areas of the United States, to a misconception among many black students that advanced-level mathematics, science, and foreign language courses are too difficult for black students and should be avoided. (p. 97)

Fortunately, Luis refused to give in to the stereotypes about Black people as intellectually impoverished. He saw his White classmates as the "people I'm gonna have to compete against—these White males who are, right now, very jealous." This competition didn't seem to bother him; if anything, it motivated him to try even harder to succeed. For example, one day a White classmate asked about his grade in American history. Luis admitted, "I got a 95. I figured I worked for it." His classmate challenged, "You don't have a 95." Luis just chuckled and said, "Look for yourself." Smiling at us, he mused, "He's sittin' there with this 80."

Even though he was tracked into higher-level courses, Luis often found the academic curriculum rigid and irrelevant to his life. For example, at one point during his senior year, he was placed in "Regents" English (a class for advanced students who were trying to obtain a Regents diploma that would ensure their entrance into a state university). He quickly grew disenchanted with the curriculum, however, which was based largely on textual analysis from a New Critical perspective. In his words, "They wanted me to figure out the right answer to what a book means, and I thought, 'Who needs that?'" Such text-centered, "one-correct-answer" approaches seemed to violate his identity as a Black male and to confirm his suspicion that White teachers were out to control his thinking. Earlier, Meg had broken through some of this resistance by being one of the few teachers to allow him to use profanity in his writing. Luis viewed this as a sign of her acceptance of his Black identity. He told her:

I remember I could write whatever I wanted to write and . . . if it
had swearing in it, [you said] "Go ahead and write it." . . . That
made things a lot easier for me. . . . I guess, if you wouldn't let me
write what I wanted to think, I'd be like probably, "White people
want to control what I think," which is what I think at the high
school a lot.

Although as a high school student, Luis was willing to "play the game"
of academic success to a certain point, his comment reminds me of how pre-
sumptuous it is to ask students from marginalized groups to choose the tenuous reward of academic success over the significant social validation and
support of a peer group. Along these lines, Eli Goldblatt (1995) has argued:

> To ask students from marginalized communities to take on academic discourse
> as their own is to invite them into a world where they have no power, requir-
> ing that they check their former badges of power at the door. (p. 27)

By the time he reached high school, Luis was perhaps more willing to
"check his former badges of power at the door" in order to succeed in school.
At the same time, he was also aware of the subtle forms of racism often practiced by teachers of "advanced level" courses. Disappointed by the rigidity
of his Regents English class, he went to speak with his teacher, who informed
Luis that he did not belong in the higher-level class. Luis resisted this notion:
"I'm like [thinking] that this guy just doesn't want me in his class, he knows
I can handle [it]." Fearing that his graduation might be affected by staying
in the class, however, he dropped out and entered a "regular" English class,
where he was fortunate to discover a teacher who allowed him some choices
about using his own words, ideas, and imagination, much as Meg had done
4 years earlier. This teacher's curriculum seemed to center more on writing
than on reading and allowed Luis a great deal of latitude in choosing his own
topics and forms of expression. Luis remembered this class fondly: "All we
did was write, and he kept on giving us stuff to write and write and write. I
mean, I started to think I may have had a skill in it."

I sensed that although Luis enjoyed and appreciated being able to make
more choices in this teacher's class, he was at the point where he had enough
motivation to succeed academically, even in the face of teaching practices
he saw as essentially demeaning and racist. If the situation deteriorated, as it
did with his Regents English teacher, Luis had enough assertiveness to insist
on what he needed. By contrast, his tenuous circumstances in middle school
had rendered him much more vulnerable and in need of control, particularly
where his home language was concerned. He recalled fondly that, without
Meg, he probably would never have come to see himself as a good writer: "I

mean, [writer] just wasn't a term that was in my [vocabulary]. . . . If I wouldn't a had [her] I don't think I'd be quite as good a writer, or ever written too much."

Luis recounted another experience with a high school teacher who gave him an F– on his first paper. At first, he was going to drop the course, but eventually decided, "Okay, I just gotta think like a White guy." Instead of dropping the course, he sought a conference with the teacher, who gave Luis the impression that "basically I didn't write down what [the teacher] was thinking." In response, Luis adopted a new, and presumably more "White," strategy: "When I read something, whenever he put emphasis on it, that's what I took out [of the reading]. I never wrote a single note for that class and my grades improved." Not only did his grades improve, but Luis actually felt proud of all the writing he did for the class and what he had managed to learn, despite his teacher's rigid and, in his mind, racist philosophy.

At the same time as he resisted what he saw as White expectations, Luis took a firm stance on the importance of teaching "standard" English to all students. He was grateful, for instance, that his high school history teacher routinely and meticulously had corrected his sentence fragments. The difference in his view of these two White teachers seemed to be one of intent, rather than method. Although he learned a great deal from his English teacher, Luis felt a pressure to conform to what he saw as a White perspective. His history teacher, on the other hand, made it clear that he was correcting Luis's language as a way of nurturing his considerable potential, rather than eradicating his racial identity. Luis reasoned, "It's good to know that kind of stuff [edited English] . . . I mean like my American history [teacher] told me . . . that I would write a book one day. I was like, 'I don't know, maybe . . .'"

Interestingly, although he sought out books to fill his compelling need to know more about racial and social issues, he still had not come to see himself as a recreational or lifetime reader. He remarked that even in high school and college he was not reading "as much as [he] should be," and that other activities, especially work and studying, had gotten in the way of his reading. Now that he was in college, he reasoned, he might have more time, because he would be in a work study program. When I observed that he had begun to read some fairly sophisticated books on his own, and that he had quoted literary and historical figures like Maya Angelou in his college application essays, he remarked, "Yeah, I read the textbooks that we get from the college, 'cause you have to pay for those."

Clearly, both reading and writing had to demonstrate a concrete purpose in Luis's life, since he did not have the luxury of activities that did not directly relate to his academic and career goals. It occurred to me that concepts like "recreational" or "pleasure" reading are, in fact, privileged activities for a select group of individuals who have the leisure time and the money to nurture a reading habit. Was it any wonder that Luis, who chose West Virginia University over his first choice, Howard University, because the financial aid package was bigger, had little space in his life for pleasure reading? Rather than enjoyable intellectual pursuits, writing and reading were intricately related to his ability to succeed in school—one stepping stone toward the "better life" that Luis had been reaching toward all these years. He saw Maya Angelou as a source of material for his college application essay, rather than a source of pleasure reading. In fact, he had first heard an excerpt of one of her poems in an advertisement for the United Negro College Fund and was proud of the fact that he had been able to find the original version to use in his entrance essay. For Luis, literacy was a tool for upward mobility, rather than an end in itself. Unless teachers could connect reading, writing, and other language activities with his future goals, they would have little success with him.

"Just Chillin'": Two Sides of the Street

As I listened to Luis that day, I wondered what made him such a survivor when others in his circumstances might have given up. When I asked Luis this question, he was quick to mention several of his friends who had turned to a life on the streets. One was Tino Hernandez. Tino had been an intermittent presence in Meg's classroom, usually arriving late and staying only long enough to provoke a referral to the office. For a time during middle school, the two young men roamed the streets together, slashing tires, breaking windows, and eventually setting someone's backyard on fire. It was this last incident that brought Luis and Tino face-to-face with the law. Each was called in separately to speak with police, and each independently refused to implicate the other. Because of their code of silence, no charges were pressed. But the police officer delivered a stern lecture on life at Hillbrook detention facility for juveniles, relating a grisly story about an 11-year-old resident who had been raped there. From that moment on, Luis decided to stop his criminal behavior. "I had to get myself up and out of here. And I just couldn't go to Hillbrook," he explained.

Tino, on the other hand, continued his behavior. He had dropped out of school and was lounging on the street when Luis saw him 4 years after graduating from middle school. Over the past 4 years, Tino had gotten involved with drugs and had been kicked out of the house by his mother. Luis remarked with regret, "I wish Tino had learned from what happened when we used to do that stuff." Compared with Luis, Tino had not suffered a bad home life and, according to Luis, had "the nicest mother in the world." She would cry over Tino, but could find no way to control him.

Many of Luis's other male friends had met a similar fate. A few days before our interview, he had been driving through the streets of the city, when he saw Jamal White and Jake Flood waiting at a street light.

I was going back to Altonville and I saw 'em on the corner . . . so I turned back and I wanted to go speak to 'em see what kind of conversation I'd have with these idiots (chuckles). So, I asked Jamal, Jamal—we play—I played football with him his senior year and he played real well—his team was sorry, but he played real well. . . . I just asked him, did he graduate from high school. I guess he never expected a question like that 'cause he just said, "No." And he kind of bowed his head and didn't want to say anything else. Then I went to go speak to Jake, whose mother's a very great teacher. I mean, his brother's at Harvard University. His family's educated. And I went and asked him what he's doin'. He told me, "Just chillin'. Just chillin'." So I just said, "You just chillin'. What does that mean, Just chillin'? You [were] out here on the corner." [He said] "I ain't on no corner." [I said] "I just seen you on the corner." Then he, then he didn't say anything after that. I just said, "You just gonna keep on chillin'?" [He said] "Yeah, I just keep on, keep on chillin.'" I asked him, [if] he [was] still in school. He told me "Yeah." I said, "Well, [it's] kind of late don't you think? Should [you] be home, do some homework or something?" And he didn't say anything about that.

Tino, Jake, and Jamal weren't the only ones that Luis remembered: "Pedro—[Tino's] friend big Pedro Garcia—he's [dropped out of school] too . . . and Mateo Williams, he has a kid now." I asked Luis what happens to young men so full of promise to turn them toward a life of joblessness and delinquency. He was quick to assign some of the blame to peer influence.

Well a lot of them, they just wind up getting in a group, I see it as, well hangin' out, doing the wrong things, or they get harassed by the cops, well the first thing, in a group, you're gonna get asked questions by the cops. Then they wind up . . . doin' stuff to have reason for the cops to want to [harass them].

Beneath the surface of Luis's explanation lay a much deeper and more troubling issue: The unequal treatment of Black and White individuals by police and the frequent use of police authorities by schools in order to control Black students. Solomon (1992) has argued that the police use the school–community link to identify and monitor black youth. . . . It is this intensive monitoring of "black life" that breathes antagonism between whites and blacks, between authority and disempowered, and between dominant and marginalized cultures. (p. 100)

Rather than ameliorating problems between students and authority figures, the constant monitoring by police ends up fueling an already deep suspicion that young people of color are targets of a system that is heavily stacked against them.

As he recounted his friends who had dropped out of school or turned to a life on the streets, I wondered what happens as young adolescents approach the fine line between a life beyond the margins of social conformity and a life within its bounds. How did Luis, who, since the age of 13 and probably before that, had never been on sure footing at home, decide to make a life for himself? Janice Hale (1994) has observed that

substance abuse and premature sexual activity among young people arises because they are incarcerated in school all day and then go home to unstructured street time. These children do not have their minds engaged constructively. When one does not have one's mind on anything, the only thrill is titillating the body. Unstimulating instruction causes a disconnection from school for African American children and begins their search for physical thrill seeking. (p. 209)

Unfortunately, part of what Luis defined as success came at a considerable price—the adoption of what Fordham (1988) has called a "raceless" stance in the face of others who held power over his academic fate. "The way I figure it," he reasoned, "I don't like some White people, but for the most part, White people got things to offer Black people and we're crazy if we don't take advantage of them." Although this reasoning may have, indeed, brought him closer to his goal of going to college, I wondered at what price Luis had come to adopt such a stance.

"This Guy, He Don't Really Feel That Way": Breaking Through

After 4 years of reflection, Luis was quick to admit his habit of keeping others at arm's length by his off-putting behaviors in middle school. Once, in front of Bekka Kaplan, a Jewish student, he blurted out, "I hate Jews," and was kicked out of class. In retrospect he regretted his actions, remembering that at the time he "didn't even know what a Jew was!" The realization that his words could be damaging came to him years later, when he realized that one of his best friends was Jewish.

I just mean I figured it out myself, learned about Jews and I was being anti-Semitic, which I shouldn't have been, but I didn't know about people. I was being ignorant myself, so I've never said anything like that since and I don't think I ever will.

Unfortunately, but perhaps predictably, Luis often turned his hurtful actions toward the very people who were trying to help him. Even one of his favorite teachers, Mrs. Manning, suffered a painful encounter with Luis.

When I first met Miss Manning, I said, "I hate White people." . . . And I don't know why I said that, but I wound up apologizing to her like 3 years later, but, I shouldn't 'a said that. 'Cause she wound up takin' a interest in me anyway, even though I said that, which means that she must have said, "Well this guy, he don't really feel that way."

It seemed to me that teachers like Meg and Ms. Manning had to ignore Luis's off-putting antics in order to earn his trust and entice his potential into reality. This fact was not lost on Luis. At one point, I asked him a very direct question: "If you were a teacher, what would you do for Luis Thomas?" He replied, "[Teachers] could try speaking to me. . . . Sometimes when I first meet people I say 'off the wall' things." He continued:

Some [students] just want somebody to say somethin' to 'em. Like when I was in [Mrs. Andrews's classroom] . . . I probably called for the attention by sitting there not saying anything, just observing, when a lot of times, what [students like me] want, even though they don't say anything—and when they don't get paid attention [to] it makes 'em feel like . . . "White people don't like me or Black people don't like me" or something.

I remembered how he stood back from so many classroom activities, and asked him whether students who appear reluctant actually want to be pushed into participating. He replied, "Yeah . . . not really push but, let him know that it's there for [him], yeah. Let him know if it's there." He admitted that, although he visibly resisted most school activities, he really didn't want to be left out: "If the opportunity's there, just let him know, [he can] take it if he feel like it."

As it turns out, our earlier suspicions about Luis's ambivalence toward White female authority figures were probably accurate. I asked him if there was a moment when he remembered deciding to trust Meg, and he replied,

"Probably bein' in plays with her and around her more, I mean I think she's the only (to Meg), you were the only White person I'd been around that much back in that time, it was you and Mrs. Corcoran basically that I was around—two women."

Neither Meg nor I were prepared, however, for the confession that came next.

> *Luis* (beginning slowly): Oh, I have to apologize to you for something that I've been feeling guilty about all over the years.
> *Meg*: What?
> *Luis*: You remember once when a chair was pulled from under you and nobody didn't know who did it?
> *Meg*: Ohh . . .
> *Susan*: I remember that. Why did you do that?
> *Luis*: I don't know, I guess, to get a laugh I guess. I was kind of quiet.
> *Susan*: How'd you feel after you did it?
> *Luis*: I felt bad 'cause I didn't know about her story about her getting hurt and having a tailbone problem or whatever, I guess you had a . . .
> *Meg*: A car accident . . .
> *Luis*: A car accident, yeah.
> *Susan*: I remember the incident because Meg said she didn't know but she thought maybe it was you and it really hurt her feelings.
> *Luis*: Yeah I know, I felt bad about it.
> *Meg*: But see, I didn't pursue it because, first of all, if it was you, I didn't want to get you in trouble.
> *Luis*: Yeah they were about to kick me out of class already.
> *Meg*: Right, so I figured if it was Luis, I know that he didn't mean it. I knew that it was something that he didn't think first, you know? And if you had thought first, you wouldn't have done it, so I didn't want you to get in trouble.
> *Luis*: I didn't mean to hurt you.

Meg went on to explain to Luis:

> I just felt like you were sitting on the fence, and that at that point in your life you could have gone either way. . . . You could have gotten into some real serious trouble . . . to spite life, for all the hardship that you've been through, or you [could] have gone the way you have. And I just felt like there would have been no middle of the road for you.

Luis agreed that this might have been the case.

> Yeah. 'Cause after I graduated . . . I just basically went on with the football, but I could have—when I moved out I was like Jamal. I was rumored to be around with drugs. Avery—can't even remember his last [name], Baker, maybe, or whatever, and these guys were involved with drugs. And these guys I hung out with—I didn't really hang out with while they were doin' the drugs, but I knew who they are—and if I wanted to after I graduated, I coulda started hangin' out with them more and maybe got into that stuff, but . . .

That last qualifier hung in the air for a few minutes, as we all silently considered how close students like Luis come to tumbling over that brink between "success" and "failure" in terms of our current social and institutional power structures. Most of the time, the racism in schools is so subtle that students less astute than Luis have few ways of confronting, much less dealing with, it. As Kincheloe and Steinberg (1993) have argued:

> The most damaging form of racism is not an explicit "George Wallace in 1963" variety, but an institutional racism built into the enfolded structure of schools, corporations, professional sports, and other institutions. (p. 307)

Despite his constant experiences with racism in school, Luis remains indebted to teachers. In his words, "A lot of teachers saved me, I mean, let me do things like, Miss Manning, she let me do things . . . [even though] I probably said things that hurt her." When asked what he would tell teachers who are reading this book, he reflected:

> I believe all students need the opportunity to do something basically, and I don't think [Black students are] given that opportunity. When they first come in they're offered the general courses first. They aren't offered the Regents courses. . . . People need their minds stimulated. They're going into these easy courses and everybody's calling them stupid and everything else.

It's important, however, to point out that, despite Luis's hardships, he is loathe to describe himself as impoverished. Even today, he remarks: "I don't think I've really had a bad life; I've slept different places, but I still went to school consistently." Luis will attend West Virginia University this fall, yet I can't help feeling that he remains (perhaps not as precariously) on that same brink he balanced on 4 years earlier. Ideally, he would like to be a social studies teacher in an urban school, yet is aware of the shortage of teaching positions and prefers not just a job, but what he calls a "stable profession." I am sure that on some level, Luis is aware of the odds against him. A recent report by the U.S. Department of Education (T.M. Smith, 1995) revealed that, although Black and White students had similar educational aspirations, Black students were still less likely to attend college right after high school and were likely to take longer on average to complete college. Furthermore, the report concludes that although "employment and earnings rates raise with educational attainment for both blacks and whites . . . [these rates] are lower for blacks than for whites with the same amount of education" (p. 18).

Luis faces more challenges than these sobering statistics, however. I thought back to an article in the *New York Times* magazine I had read earlier that year about a group of African-American students who had pursued academics rather than athletics in high school and who had, with the help of their debate coach, managed to get accepted into college. Of the original group of five, only three actually made it to college, and of those three, only the student who chose a traditionally Black college had been given the mentoring and support necessary for him to proceed all the way through to graduation. And yet there was that tenacity that brought Luis to school each day, even when he was living in the backseat of his aunt's car—that gave him the courage to leave an abusive mother and to move from school to school until he found an academic situation in which he could succeed. In a speech, written for the VFW "Voice of Democracy" contest, he quotes Maya Angelou (1978, p. 41):

Just like . . . moons and [like] suns,
With [the] certainty of tides,
Just like hopes springing high,
Still I'll rise.

As I thought about all that had transpired since he stood tenuously on the edges of the classroom and considered his place in the worlds of school and life, I marveled at this young man who, not always with the certainty of tides, but always with hopes springing high, has found a way to claim his position within—and sometimes in powerful opposition to—those worlds.

CHAPTER 9

Reconstructing Constructivism

There's no end to the options of what you can do. . . . Last year . . . I would teach a full class all the time, and . . . I would see a third of the class really with me, I'd see a third of the class kind of bored, and a third of the class totally tuned out. What I'm trying to do is to have [you] . . . feel that you're involved because you've chosen to do it. (Meg, introducing Sharing Time, October 1990)

As Meg's opening statement during Sharing Time reveals, *personal choice* was the fulcrum on which most of her teaching decisions seemed to rest during the second year of the pilot program. In an interview in the spring of that year, I asked her to name one overriding theme or issue that had transformed her teaching that year. She answered without hesitation: "Choice. . . . I think that's at the root of the whole thing. What makes it work." The element of choice meant more personal power not only for Meg's students, but for Meg herself, in dealing with otherwise unmotivated students. As she explained:

There is a kid who will choose [an activity] and then maybe sit down and go to sleep. Or he'll say, "I'm going to reading," and then he'll kind of blow it off a little bit . . . but then I've got some leverage in it. I can say, "Look, you chose to do reading today and now you're sitting here and you're not reading. If this really isn't what you want to do, why don't you choose something else?"

"THEY'RE NOT 'A CLASS,' BUT INDIVIDUALS": THE POWER OF PERSONAL CHOICE

For Meg, opening up choices—especially in whether students worked independently or collaboratively—increased student responsibility and reduced the many social conflicts that had surfaced in the past during whole-class instruction. Choosing their own peer collaborators in Learning Centers and Literature Circles allowed students to operate within their own comfortable social cliques. Virtually abandoning whole-class teaching freed Meg from dealing with what she called "those personalities" who are "totally tuned out" and become belligerent in a full group. In her journal that fall, she extolled the virtues of a choice-centered curriculum.

> *Today I noticed that I never leave the classroom anymore feeling like a fool. It's never "25 against one." They're not "a class," but individuals. Any exhaustion I feel at the end of the day comes from constant one-to-one contact—listening and responding to young people whom I know very well. I love it.*

Allowing "those personalities" to absent themselves from whole-group instruction and sending them to the library or computer center certainly made Meg's classroom more outwardly peaceful. On days when the library was closed, Meg would be visibly distressed at having to deal with those "pissed off kids that can't go and finish their [writing] pieces." "They're not only in [here] as more bodies," she explained, "they're in [here] as mad bodies."

In place of whole-class reading of teacher-chosen texts, Meg substituted "Literature Circles," or small reading groups that met in the center of the room twice a week to talk informally about poetry, drama, or stories. In the process, she seemed to be changing her role from expert reader to book peddler. Twice a week, she began Literature Circle with a sort of spot commercial, aimed at luring students into reading whatever poem or story she had chosen that day. For example, one morning, she began:

> Literature Circle today is poetry. . . . I know that some people have been having problems [deciding whether to] make their poems rhyme. So if any of you are interested in writing poetry and have been writing poetry, or are about to write poetry, I think that it would be good for you to join the circle. . . . I don't want to be alone. I want to have some people with me.

When students failed to show interest in Literature Circle, she sometimes engaged in a mild form of coercion, making statements like, "I don't want to be alone," or, "Remember some of you . . . were low on your Literature Circles and this is your last opportunity to get it close to where it should be for this quarter. So let me just throw off that little hint." At first, Meg was enchanted with her new literature curriculum. She wrote in her journal:

> *Well—this was my first literature circle—what a great experience—students reading a story because they chose to—others who didn't*

choose to, listening and adding their two cents to the discussion now and then. Also—the kids asked for other stories by Toni Cade—so I will have to put some at the reading center. See—connections between reading and writing already. I can feel them taking charge.

Meg not only gave choices of whether or not to attend Literature Circle, but also in how students could respond to their independent reading. Remembering her students' resistance toward reading journals a year earlier, she remarked: "They'd do those response journals saying, 'What do I say?' I really hated those things." Out of her own frustration, Meg announced one day:

Look, there's going to be many different ways you can respond to your reading. You can keep doing the journals if you want. I'm not going to write your responses, but I'll talk to you about it. Or you can have book talks with me personally. You can write another piece of literature, a spinoff from that text in some way. You can share your book in Sharing Circle with us. And all of these [are] ways to get reading responses.

To Meg, opening up the options for reading response dramatically increased students' enthusiasm for reading. She also tried to model more options for writing. One day during Sharing Time, she announced:

[You can] illustrate your pieces with someone else's pieces. . . . [If] you've been working on poetry [you can] switch to plays; if you've been working on plays you can do a commercial; if you've been doing a commercial you can work on a novel chapter. There are things like restaurant reviews and movie reviews, debates, things like that.

Meg also began to broaden the notion of writing in English class to include writing in other areas of the curriculum. She announced one day: "Anything that you do that involves writing or reading in your other classes you can do here and it will count for work here too. . . . Reading and writing isn't just for English. It's for every other aspect of your education." I thought back a year earlier, when Meg had cornered Samantha, demanding: "So what are you working on? Is this all English? Your rough copy notebook is supposed to be all English." When I mentioned her obvious change in attitude toward doing "outside work" in English class, she said:

What I try to do is zero in on chronic kids—kids who everyday I see come in and they're not engaged. . . . So I figure that if . . .

[a kid is] tired or he's got a personal problem or something and I
see him blowing off part of the period, or [I think], this kid has got
to get his math homework and he didn't do it last night and he
really shouldn't be doing math in here. But he's not going to be
good at doing anything else until he gets that homework done. . . .
It just depends; it depends on the kids or the time. Depends on
how chronic it is. But I don't see any harm in that occasionally.

Thus, by the second year of the pilot program, Meg continued to provide many collaborative activities, but seldom on the whole-class level. In
arranging students into pairs or small groups, she aimed toward the *personal*
benefits of individual choice and peer collaboration. However, in abandoning whole-class activities and allowing students to pick their own collaborators, I wondered if she had abandoned the more elusive and tricky goal of
bringing together students who otherwise might not choose to work together.
Meg eventually dealt with this same issue, as the later part of this chapter
will reveal.

"LEARNING BY OSMOSIS"

Meg described her choice-centered, individualized curriculum as a sort
of modern day "household."

I think my classroom is kind of like the household where everybody gets along with everybody but . . . they're such a strong
family that they don't always have to be together. And that so-
and-so can be watching TV up in his room, and somebody else
could be playing Nintendo over here, and mom and dad could
be talking in the kitchen over coffee, and all this is happening at
once, but not necessarily together, but it is together. And that's
what I see. I definitely like to create that family atmosphere
because I think that these kids have a very limited place where
they can go and speak their mind and fall on their face and pick
themselves up again, and in an atmosphere where they're not
abused. And so I see it very much as a family, but as a family it
sometimes works together and sometimes it doesn't. But that's
okay.

It almost seemed as if this kind of classroom family, where students were
"not necessarily together but . . . together," reflected the lives of so many of
her students, whose families seldom congregated for whole-family activities,

and whose lives often were surrounded by an array of visual and aural stimuli. Often, Meg's students talked about the need for music or television playing as they read or wrote. On learning center days, for example, students would play a radio in one corner of the room near the sofa where they sat talking quietly or reading books of their choosing. This ability to work in the midst of what might seem like aural and visual chaos seemed to come quite naturally to many of Meg's students. As Hargreaves, Earl, and Ryan (1996) have noted, "Many young adolescents today are living postmodern lives in fractured families, culturally diverse communities and fast-paced worlds of visual imagery. Yet in the school day, these postmodern lives are trapped in modernistic institutions with bureaucratic schedules, compartmentalized knowledge and little care" (p. 55). In contrast to this segmented, bureaucratic model of schooling, Meg tried to provide a family atmosphere that allowed students to work together, but seldom forced them into a whole-class activity. Most seemed quite comfortable in this loosely structured arrangement.

Perhaps as an outcome of the "fast-paced" lives that Hargreaves and his colleagues describe, Meg's students also involved themselves in more than one activity at a time, as the lines from one Learning Center to the next seemed to blend and blur. I first noticed what I called "peripheral learning" in late January 1991, as I observed Meg and a small group of students scattered on the rug reading a short story by Maia Wojciechowska called "The First Day of the War" (1979). Suddenly, the discussion grew loud and animated as students began to make connections between this story about World War II and the Gulf War, which had just broken out a few days earlier.

Right in the middle of the discussion, Meg tried to sneak in a mini-lecture about "paradox" in writing. Angel stopped Meg dead in her tracks. Obviously irritated, she said: "You sound just like Mr. Sampson!" Picking up on her irritation, Meg asked, "But don't you feel affected by this war?" Angel replied, "What's affecting me is that I have to show everybody that I care about this war. . . . They're overrating this war. . . . A lot of my friends are protesting the war . . . I just don't believe in war." Angel continued to challenge Meg: "Why, if they teach you in school not to fight, can they have a war?"

As the conversation grew more heated, students in different Learning Centers around the room started calling out their opinions. Frank and Aaron continued to work on their own projects, but managed to interject a few comments from their desks. Samantha and Jaquille chuckled to themselves from time to time. Finally, Aaron could not contain his excitement. As the discussion continued, he silently tiptoed over to the shelf, took down an anthology, and seated himself in the circle. Later that day, I wrote in my notes:

*I'm wondering here about how modern kids, so attuned to TV, are used
to attending to several things at once . . . does this give them a way to
"do" literature, at the same time as they accomplish something else?
. . . This sort of blows apart the notion of the isolated reader, focused
only on the momentary act of reading, doesn't it? . . . Are there times
when the reading itself is peripheral to the life changes of the reader—
when text acts as a springboard to something else?*

Indeed, topics like the Gulf War, so real to all of these students, drew
them into a discussion in a way that Meg's asides about literary techniques
could not. When I asked Meg later about Angel's blatant derailing of her
"English teacher" agenda, she mused, "I should just stop because when I try
to sneak in this stuff I get shot down!" She too had noticed what she called
"learning by osmosis."

I have the kids who pull desks around the Literature Circle that
will say to me that "I'm going to listen for a while and if I like it,
I'll come down, and if I don't I'm going to keep working on my
piece." Then I have the other kids who say, "No, definitely, I
don't want to do that. I have my own stuff to do." But even
some of them will pipe up here and there. I feel like anyone
who's in that room at that time when we do a Literature Circle,
is getting something from it. Even if it's by osmosis.

I began to believe that this kind of indirect participation was more comfortable than direct learning for many young adolescents, who often do more
than one thing at a time in their lives outside of school. Learning by osmosis
allowed them to talk about literature in a way that didn't require their full
commitment. Although they weren't directly "reading" the text under discussion, they were participating in a reading process of sorts. In a memo that
year, I wrote:

*Middle school students have "energy, energy, energy." Often, what looks
like "off-task" behavior is really the classroom equivalent of "doodling."
These behaviors appear to keep the body busy while the mind engages
(or gets ready to engage) in a school task. For example: Jason ties the
blind cord into knots and twirls madly in a swivel chair just before he is
about to make a presentation in front of the class; Angel smacks her
gum; Samantha plays with a bottle of nail polish; Mark stares at his
book or his hands. It's as if academic tasks can't be directly encountered.
Even "good students" must have something to occupy their incredible
energies. They learn (often) from the sidelines, as they appear to be
doing something else and not paying attention at all.*

Agreeing that middle school students "never do one thing at a time," Meg observed that whenever she tried to maintain a quiet atmosphere where all students could concentrate, they looked at her as if to say, "Where are you living?" "There's always a buzz in my room," she mused. "I think that they'd not be able to work [without it]."

Students occasionally participated in Sharing Time by osmosis as well. One day in February 1991, Meg had been engaging her students in writing valentine letters to each other. The activity had gone over well with students in her earlier classes. During sixth-period lunch, however, a group of girls from her class got into a heated personal conflict. In class later, they asked if they could talk about the situation instead of doing her valentine activity. Although she was reluctant to abandon what had been a highly successful lesson, she announced to the rest of the class, "We're having a little conflict-resolution circle today and there's just a few people that need to sort out some things today." Meg described the scene as the six girls sat with her around the circle.

> [W]e had tears. It was very intense. You talk about peripheral [learning]. Sixth period is bananas [but] you could have heard a pin drop. . . . But the girls didn't even really mind having an audience for this. And all of a sudden there was this arena. These girls were talking about heart-wrenching, gut-wrenching, personal feelings and their relationships and their friendships and their boyfriends and "You hurt me." And "When you do this, I feel this." And we had an audience the whole sixth period. . . . And at the end they all stood up and hugged each other. And the whole entire class clapped.

This kind of indirect sharing, where students were not the "official" focus of attention, seemed a comfortable alternative to the more risky, public demonstrations during whole-class learning, Sharing Time, or Literature Circle. Curiously, this learning (and sharing) "by osmosis" seemed to mediate some of the tension between private and more public dimensions of Meg's curriculum.

REVISING THE PERFORMANCE-CENTERED CURRICULUM

In her early days with her seventh-grade students, Meg admitted: "I envisioned them acting out their pieces or really doing dramatic readings and all that kind of stuff . . . a definite public speaking performance kind of thing." She had come to realize, however, that many of her students saw performing as work—something they had to prepare for. Whereas formal talk and writing had always frightened them into a right-or-wrong mentality, the talk in Sharing Time and Literature Circles became more relaxed and casual as the year progressed. In Meg's view, her students felt: "I know that I have an opinion on just about anything because I'm 12 or 13 years old and she's going to listen to me and everybody else in the class is going to listen to me." "In life," she reasoned, "how many times are people going to stand up and read your poem?"

Meg had no doubts about the advantages of giving students personal choices in the literature they read, the topics they wrote about, and the people with whom they worked each day. There was still the imbalance between reading and writing in her curriculum, however. Personal choice alone was not enough to promote the kind of creative, free-wheeling atmosphere for reading that she had created for writing. Perhaps ironically, Meg, like so many of her students, gradually developed her identity as reader through writing. Toward the end of the year, she cast off the role of "expert" and became a "fellow writer," along with her students.

Creating a Social Space for Reading

I believe that it is very difficult for teachers to create a more holistic "process-centered" literature curriculum because reading, unlike writing, does not have an end product. Despite the now common maxims about "process versus product," in the final analysis there is still always a tangible product for students' writing. A student's response to literature, however, is always private and intangible. In school, where teachers typically choose the acceptable forms of response, students' reading processes can be derailed if they are forced to "go public" before their ideas and feelings about literature have time to build and coalesce. Unfortunately, in classrooms, students' *private responses* are always eclipsed by their acts of *public responding*. The writers in Meg's classroom saw concrete proof of their accomplishments in all of the texts that began to appear on the bulletin board and the many drafts that piled up in their writing folders. Except for short entries in their response logs, conferences with Meg, or their informal talk in Literature Circle, however, students had little concrete evidence of their growth as readers.

Meg recognized this difference between reading and writing in an interview when I asked about the difference between "real life" and "text life." She replied: "Text comes from the outside and real life comes from the inside." Convincing her students to become readers meant finding a way to make literature "connect to the inside." It wasn't surprising, then, that, even in her mini-commercials for Literature Circle, she tried to appeal to their interests as writers. On a personal level, Meg admitted that writing appealed to her in a way that reading did not:

> No matter how bad something is I wrote, I wrote it! And if I pick up a book and it's bad, well it totally doesn't affect me because it came from the outside. And I can discard it. Even if I write something that I know isn't good, I somehow still can't discard it because it's mine.

Perhaps as a result of her own relationship with books, she described reading as an instrument to writing, believing that the only way to hook students into reading literature was through their natural affinity for writing.

> I have to approach reading that way for most kids. [You say to them] "You see yourself as a writer, yes. You will be a better writer the more you read because there is an enjoyment aspect here but there's also a craft. And like anything else, playing baseball, or doing anything, the more you practice, the more you look at the ways the pros do it and all that, the better you become. The more you read, the better you write." . . . That's how I sell it most. The only way I can sell reading as itself [is] when those kids have that orgasmic moment with the book.

Suddenly one day, she flashed upon an idea for relating reading and writing in her classroom. Following Nancie Atwell, Meg often began her classes with a brief mini-lesson on some aspect of language. She complained, however, that her students were too intent on going to Literature Circle or working in groups to hear her talk about "quotation marks or something." In her journal, she pondered:

> So—what if I do two kinds of circles—Literature and Writing. I can't take away from conference days, because I don't get through all the kids as fast as I would like anyway—but I could do a writing circle every third time or something—on various aspects of writing. I like it!

Soon afterward, she created what she called "Reading/Writing Circle"—a place where she might introduce students to new books to read or help them to brainstorm ideas for writing. On the day of her first Reading/Writing Circle, she urged her students:

> So why don't you seriously think about it? I don't want you to say, "Mrs. Andrews, I don't know what to write about." I encourage people to come. We had a really good one first period and the kids made up some really nice activities. . . . You just

need a pen. Why don't you come and join us? All you have to do is sit and listen. Come on, peer pressure, peer pressure (laughs).

Although Meg was pleased with this new addition to her curriculum, I noticed that talk about reading in Literature Circles was still fairly teacher-dominated and shut down, when compared with the talk about writing that went on in her room. It was through Reading/Writing Circle that Meg finally crossed the line between "teacher" and "fellow writer." In this setting, as she began to share her own writing, she dramatically changed the power relations in her classroom and opened up the social space for reading she had been trying to create.

Literature-in-the-Making: Entering the Circle

In her journal, Meg had begun to write her own poetry in response to some of the events in her class. She also had begun to write a young adult novel, called *Before the Leaves Change*. One day, after reading a particularly provocative piece of student writing, she mused in her journal: "Gerri turned in the poem 'Pictures' today. Sometimes a student can capture something that I have been trying to write. I haven't had a chance to conference with her yet, but I plan on sharing that thought with her."

Her desire to share her own writing with students continued to grow, until one day Ed Jackson brought the novel he was writing to Literature Circle. Ed's bold move gave Meg the courage she needed. That day, she wrote in her journal:

I am an observer in my own classroom today. Ed is leading Literature Circle from his novel in progress. . . . The kids are entranced with his writing. They sit, staring at him wide-eyed (they love being read to!—another thing that I forget sometimes).

Ed Jackson's example not only made Meg more confident about joining the circle as a fellow writer, but also powerfully illustrated the kind of exploratory, invested language that surfaces when real live writers talk about literature-in-the-making. Talking to a real writer in the present tense—and giving concrete suggestions about the finished product—was a more lively and purposeful act for students than talking *about* the work of anonymous published "authors" in the literature anthology. Suddenly she saw a way to make Literature Circle more like Writing Circle. She was ecstatic and explained that her students

seemed really excited about being part of Ed's writing process. They gave excellent feedback to him—were very honest about telling him about parts he needed to explain in more detail, etc. His writing is such a wonderful mixture of description and dialogue, serious thought and comic relief. By the end of each class everyone in the room was really a part of Literature Circle.

For several days, she struggled over whether to bring her own novel into the circle. Interestingly, although Ed's positive experience in sharing his novel served as an inspiration for Meg, it also heightened her anxiety. *Before the Leaves Change* was written from what Meg saw as a White female perspective, in the genre of *Bridge to Terabithia* (Paterson, 1987) and *Tuck Everlasting* (Babbit, 1975). Meg worried that, in contrast to Ed's book, her novel would not be interesting to students of color, particularly the males. The day she finally took the plunge and brought a chapter of her novel in to share with her students, she admitted:

> *I knew that I was going in with my agenda. . . . Well, I guess I did want general feedback, but I really wanted them to enjoy it—to want to read more. I wanted boys to like it as much as girls, and Black kids to like it as much as White kids.*

Eventually, she laid her anxiety aside and put herself on the line, finally entering the circle of writers in her classroom. That morning, she wrote in her journal:

> *I woke up this morning with a very nervous feeling. I was really putting myself on the line today. I read my book in progress—*Before the Leaves Change—*in literature circle. I had the same kind of feeling that I get when I know I'm going to tell a good friend a secret. I felt like I was going to do something that would either bring us closer or farther away.*

Meg opened her first sharing session, hesitantly describing the kind of response she was looking for.

> It's a book about letting go. I really want your feedback. I want you to tell me what you think of it, and I'm going to stop now and then and anything that you think that you like or anything you think doesn't fit, it's not clear or anything, I'd like you to respond to it. You are my class; this is the first time any people your age have read this. This is a book for people your age.

To her delight, her students responded with eagerness and enthusiasm. Her doubts were replaced by "a sort of magic" as her students began to respond as fellow writers and literary critics. She wrote in her journal:

That's just what it was—magic. I began reading, hearing my words affect the classroom like a soft song—lullaby I guess—not that it put them to sleep—but it had a very calming effect. Then I heard them read. They were reading my words—making inflection just where I would have. They laughed at the "funny" parts and looked sad at the sensitive parts. My words that I have kept private for so long—were affecting these kids.

For Meg, as for so many of her students, her writing was becoming not just an occasion for *reaction*, but a form of *social action*, as she witnessed the effect of her words on her students. At the same time, Meg was suddenly in touch with the perils of personal sharing that her students must have experienced. She remarked in her journal:

This experience really made me think about how the kids put themselves on the line all the time when they share their work with the class—and how imperative it is that I establish—we establish an atmosphere that is very respectful. . . . I wonder how kids ever share their work again after someone has laughed at it or has seemed very disinterested.

A Whole New Way of Talking: Reading/Writing Connections

As Meg crossed the line, becoming a classroom author, she discovered that reading/writing connections don't involve mini-lessons on technique, as much as they involve changing her entire role as teacher. Becoming a fellow writer suddenly opened up a way to talk about reading that was as exploratory and engaged as the talk about writing in her classroom.

Earlier in the term, Meg was frustrated when her students seemed to be merely biding time in Sharing Circle until it was their turn to share. Their comments to classmates were usually cursory, and often no more elaborated than "it's good" or "it's bad." She voiced her frustration to me one afternoon as students were passing to class. A couple of days later, I lent her my copy of Peter Elbow's *Writing Without Teachers* (1975) and suggested that she try what Elbow calls "movies of your mind"—a technique where, rather than evaluating each other's writing, students simply take turns describing everything they experienced imaginatively as a piece was being shared. A few days later, Meg introduced Sharing Time with these instructions:

Rather than saying whether [someone's writing] was good or bad, if we liked it or we didn't, we would just be able to give the writer or the reader . . . the pictures in our mind, what that story made us think. In this way we can help the writer to change certain parts or to really pay attention to his audience.

This technique seemed to take everyone, including Meg, off the interpretive hook. Since all students were "experts" on their own "movies," there were no wrong responses. Later in an interview, Meg remarked on the benefits of this strategy: "The fact that different kids can see [a piece of writing] differently and it's still a spinoff of the same text is very interesting to a writer." "Movies" became a popular strategy for Meg's book sharing. For example, after a description of the main character, Joanne's, house in *Before the Leaves Change*, the following dialogue took place:

> *Meg*: So what do you see?
> *Amy*: The house you mean?
> *Fred*: I see no windows.
> *Carl*: (unintelligible) and there's a little smile on the sun.
> *Lovlee*: It makes you think of when kids draw houses. They always
>   make faces . . .
> *Rameka*: I thought it was kind of like Norman Rockwell to me. It
>   reminded me of Norman Rockwell.

She was delighted at the creativity and candor of their responses, remarking:

> Instead of saying the characters are good, or general comments, somebody started talking about "oh, my father has a farm." . . . And somebody else said, "Doesn't that make you upset that he's talking about his farm and his father when we just finished this book?" I said, "No, that's the whole point." I said, "What I want to do as a writer [is] to know that kids at any given moment, are sitting there reading what I wrote and making it connect with their own lives. And that's the power of writing." And I said that "I love it when I bring in this book and I read it and you say, 'Well I once knew a kid like this' or 'I'm into baseball.' That's when I know that you're really into it. But if all you can sit there and do is [say], 'Well, you used a symbol there,' then the conversation stops there. Then I feel like this writing doesn't have any magic."

Instead of responding monosyllabically to Meg's questions and prompts, as they often did in Literature Circle, students asked real questions as she shared her book: "Was your hair ever red?" "What are polliwogs?" "What is a girl getting frogs for anyway?" "What's Joanne's last name?" "What if the dog comes home?" "How did she find his house?" "Is that a real road?"

Rather than passive respondents to a teacher's questions, they became interested fellow writers and literary critics, making comments like: "So when is it going to be published?" "I think [the book is] clear and it's not one of those things where you have to read it twice to understand it." "I think it was really good but in this first paragraph, there were so many adjectives." "I think that you should write the first chapter just describing everything, like the house that he and her live in." The talk in these Literature Circles became more like the talk in writing conferences—exploratory, personal, and invested.

In the process, Meg was able to let down her guard and share her worst fears with students. She began one day, "I'm interested in the boys who are hearing this. . . . Sometimes I'm afraid as a woman writing this, I don't know how, I mean is this okay for a boy to think this way and feel this way?" In putting herself on the line, Meg learned new ways of talking about literature and empowered her students as fellow writers in the process.

"LOSING CONTROL TO GAIN IT": SHIFTING POWER RELATIONS

One day when I was chatting informally with Meg, I asked her why, despite what she was learning about collaborative talk in sharing her novel, she still seemed to teach published literature in typical "English teacher" ways, focusing on abstract concepts like literary terminology and technique. From my vantage point outside the circle, it seemed that the larger personal, social, and political issues surrounding the students' reading and writing were far more compelling topics of discussion than Meg's mini-lectures on literary terminology. I thought back to the heated discussion about the Gulf War the day that Angel had shut down Meg's mini-lecture, and asked Meg why she would try to slip in a remote idea like paradox in the middle of such a fruitful discussion. She remarked:

> Because of this responsibility. I feel like, "Oh my God, they're going to get [into another classroom] and the teacher's going to say, 'Now what is a paradox?' and they're going to go 'Duh.'" They're not going to be able to survive. And sometimes I feel bad about that.

I teased her a bit, arguing, "Who can talk about paradox when 20,000 people could be blown away and bomb shelters are being bombed?"—a paradox of a much more immediate sort than the literary kind. Meg feared that giving up her role as classroom expert about literary techniques might be cheating her students in some fundamental way. And yet, in joining her own Reading/Writing Circle as fellow writer, she had found a way to be the novice as well as the expert. She agreed: "That's what this whole year has been about, this whole letting go thing. Letting go to gain more." "Paradox!" I exclaimed. Meg chuckled: "Everything's a paradox!"

In giving up her role as expert reader, Meg was suddenly free to learn from her students, and she found new opportunities for meaningful, productive conversations about books. In her words, she was "losing control to gain it."

> I could read 10 books a night and not keep up with them. Occasionally I'll have a kid who will say, "Read this book," and I'll read it and we'll sit and talk about it. And those are like amazing books, because I've read it and we can really get into it. It's very difficult for me to talk with a kid about something I haven't read. But I can't read everything. Sometimes when I feel insecure about the whole reading aspect of it, I just feel like, "Oh, as the teacher I should have read this." But I can't.

I marveled at how far she had come from the days when she agonized over not having read *The Catcher in the Rye* (Salinger, 1991). In fact, late in the year, she commented on how easy this role reversal—from expert to co-learner—had become for her.

> The gifted teacher assigned *All Quiet on the Western Front*. And a lot of kids are very bright and loved to read it or didn't want to read it, but were told to read it. But there wasn't one kid who didn't like that book. And I was finding it in book talks. . . . So one day in Literature Circle I said, "All of you who are reading *All Quiet on the Western Front*, let's come talk about it." Which was a very nervy thing because I had not read it.

As it turned out, Meg admitted to her students that she hadn't read the book, but promised to read it over vacation. Since that time, although she hadn't found the time to read it, she felt neither guilty nor anxious. In letting go of her perfectionistic standards about being the classroom expert, she had come to realize the power of letting students teach *her* about books. As she shed her expert role, Meg also expanded the bounds of her reading community beyond her classroom walls. She began to phone students who had recommended books to her. They were astonished that she actually looked up their number, just to tell them how much she had enjoyed a book. Eventually, she discovered a way to harness her students' natural socializing behaviors in her reading curriculum.

> I noticed a lot of kids in the library talking about their books. So I
> thought if I give them a forum to do that in class, they might
> encourage each other. And so sometimes we'd have whole-class
> book talks where I would just pick a name out of a hat and the
> kid would just talk about the book he was reading in any way.
> And that was one thing I learned from doing the response
> journals. I didn't say, "Well, there are five ways to do this." I
> said, "You could talk about your book in any way you wanted."

In addition to her "spot commercials" for Literature Circle, Meg started
enticing her students with short book talks. One day, for instance, she tried
to sell her students on Jane Yolen's book, *The Devil's Arithmetic* (1988). She
began: "Has anyone read this book? This is about a Jewish girl, it's like
modern times, 1980, and she's going to a Passover celebration and she's not
really into it." After a brief synopsis, Meg set the hook.

> You'll have to read it to find out what happens in the end. It's
> really a short, excellent book. And even though it's about a girl,
> the stuff that she writes about, the characters in the concentra-
> tion camp, it's really . . . in fact, I was laughing the other day,
> because Brad Lawrence recommended this book to me, and I
> was kind of afraid to read something Brad recommended to me
> (laughing), but it's really good.

Perhaps most surprising to Meg was that she became more relaxed about
her own relations with books. Late in the spring semester, she remarked:

> I've done a lot more personal reading this year. The kids have
> helped me to overcome my fears of reading. I've read so many
> books this year that a kid will come up to me and say, "I'm
> finished with this book, you have to read this book." And I'll
> read the book and they're right. . . . A lot of times on sharing
> days I was bringing in my writing, my writing, my writing, and
> then I started bringing in my reading and that was great. And it
> would be, "What did you like about this?" And they'd be asking
> me questions about "Why do you think I should be reading
> this?" . . . So I've become much more of a reader this year.

Responding in-process to literature-in-the-making inspired some students
to consider publishing their own pieces. One day, as Meg was explaining
her hopes to publish her novel by the end of the year, Darrell asked, "Kids
don't get to publish, right?" Meg answered, "Oh, kids can publish; they

sure can." Darrell asked, "How would I get anything published?" As Meg explained the process of sending manuscripts out to publishers, Darrell announced, "I want to write something." Meg continued to explain that students might begin by looking in the backs of magazines, where "they'll have advertisements for sending in your story."

> I've heard all different kinds of things about getting a book published. Some people say get an agent; other people say don't get an agent. Your work should be able to stand by itself. Some people say send out the whole manuscript; some people say just send out the first few chapters. I'm going to be working a lot on this [book] this year. Hopefully, by the end of the school year it will be done. I have a lot more on the computer.

Darrell shouted, "That would be awesome," as his classmates urged Meg to continue: "Read some more." "Do they kiss any more in the story?"

Later in the year, Meg reflected on the difference between these "real-life" discussions about texts and her typical "English teacher" lectures on literary terminology: "[The students and I] get off on not being able to dissect texts. . . . See that's the whole key. If there's a key to this, that's it. . . . The more you read, the better you write."

EXTENDING THE CLASSROOM WALLS

Like many "process-centered" teachers, Meg was disappointed at first when her students saw writing as relatively meaningless, and revising as downright painful. She explained:

> I was encouraging them to keep everything that they wrote and to accumulate these folders. And they didn't like to do that. They wanted [to say], "I pass something in to you, you read it, you mark up in red and give me a grade and then I throw it in the wastebasket. . . ." The getting rid of it for them is almost like a purging kind of thing. It's like one more thing I've done, I can X that off. . . . It would drive them crazy if I said, "Keep all your rough copies of your pieces and you can work on this one and then start a new one even if this one isn't finished."

It wasn't until Meg began to broaden the audiences for students' writing to include real people in real settings, that her students began to see literacy as a purposeful way of reaching out to the larger world.

During the second year of the pilot program, the Gulf War broke out. This war touched the lives of her students deeply, as a battalion of fighter pilots a few miles from the city had been sent to Saudi Arabia. Meg decided to ask students if they would like to write letters to the soldiers. The project caught on like wildfire, as suddenly students were writing (and willingly revising) real letters to real people who might very well send back real responses. Their former dread of revision, and their view of writing as something to be "crossed off their lists," began to evaporate. Meg explained:

> For some reason the fear was gone when [they] had a real-life purpose for writing. [They said], "I want to send this letter to someone in Saudi Arabia." or "I may not have this business form right, but would you help?" If they were just doing . . . an assignment, [like] "you have this character in the book, and write a letter to so and so," they would skip that one. Even though the book would be right there to show them how to do it, they don't want to get involved with that.

Although some resistance and fear toward writing were still present, Meg reasoned that students were probably willing to put their fear aside for the end product. By contrast, she explained, "they're not always willing to put [that fear and resistance] aside for writing an essay about the symbol used in a story. What's the point?"

Meg's students looked forward to writing these letters in a way that they did not with more formal classroom activities like learning the form of a business letter or writing out answers to questions about literature. In these more contrived situations, Meg explained that students tended to wonder: "Is the letter form correct?" "What does it show about my understanding of the characters?" and "She's going to evaluate what I know about this [classroom assignment], but I don't think she's going to do this with the letter [to Saudi Arabia]."

At the same time as she tried to make literacy a form of purposeful social action, she struggled with the larger political and social issues of schooling in which she was enmeshed. How, for example, could she grade students on something as personal as a letter to someone fighting a war? As a solution, Meg decided that, rather than grading individual pieces of writing or responses in reading journals, she would conduct individual grading conferences with students. Together with each student, she averaged out all of their individual grades, then asked the student to help her narrow the final grade down to a number. She embarked on this new venture with enthusiasm, writing in her journal:

> *Grades are due. This is the first time ever that I really feel like I am giving kids the grades they deserve. . . . No one failed English this quarter—and I gave no gifts either. . . . Teachers on my team are teasing me that I am too "easy." But isn't getting all of them to be successful what it is all about? Why do teachers feel like they always have to have a certain percentage who fail—or their teaching is not good?*

Despite this more negotiable approach to grading, Meg still occasionally found it uncomfortable to assign a letter grade to the complex and elusive growth processes of her students. One day later, after she had begun her grading conferences, she wrote in her journal:

> *Today reminded me that part of teaching is having to work within a system that I don't always agree with. It's really impossible to put a number grade on the work that these kids are doing. It's kind of like being able to put a price on something that's priceless. . . . But we're part of a much bigger system that needs something that is grey—to be put in black and white terms.*

Although she had made the process more public and had given her students more input than ever before, she still felt basically powerless in the face of the overwhelming prospect of assigning grades.

This "much bigger system" that surrounded Meg's teaching loomed even larger when, at the end of the pilot project, she had to face the fact that a formal final examination was mandated for all eighth-grade students at Logan. Meg was frustrated at being ordered to revert to a simplistic, sit-down, short-answer mode of evaluation as a culmination of what had become a curriculum based largely on personal choice and purposeful literacy acts. Together, we brainstormed a substitute for the final examination, called the "Final Communications Packet." Hoping that this experience would serve as an evaluation of Meg's 2-year program, as well as an assessment of students' growth, she created a series of experiences that stretched out for several weeks. Students began by writing self-evaluations of their own reading and writing. Later, they responded in class to some short pieces of literature, wrote about the writing and reading experiences that best demonstrated their growth as language users, and created short pieces of imaginative writing. They also wrote critical essays on various classroom activities in which they had engaged over the 2-year period.

On one level, Meg believed in the validity of what she was doing by opening up student choice and creating an evaluation system compatible with her learner-centered classroom. At the same time, she worried about whether

her students would suffer as they encountered a high school curriculum so radically different from her own. In an interview near the end of her students' eighth-grade year, she admitted:

> Let me tell you, through all this, the thing that's scaring me a little bit, is that I can just hear someone's high school teachers when they get some of these kids. And I'm trying to think in my mind and evaluate in my mind objectively how ready the average student in my class is for one of those high school classes. . . . It scares me that they're going to walk into the desks and rows and read *David Copperfield* and write an essay on how symbolism is used. This is the kind of thing they're going to get, and I think . . . they're not going to be able to deal with doing that kind of thing. . . . They're not going to want to.

While she was not willing to give up her learner-centered curriculum, Meg still worried about what she called her "responsibility to talk to them and warn them" about what they would encounter in the more impersonal, content-oriented high school classroom. As her students stood on the brink of graduation, we both wondered how any teacher can protect her or his students from the larger social and political realities that surround even the "safest" of classrooms.

The Limits of the Personal: Student Choice or Divide and Conquer

Surely, Meg had accomplished a great deal during the second year of the pilot program. She had opened up the options for reading, writing, and talk; created new avenues for both individual and collaborative learning; and even nurtured a positive relationship with reading for herself and her students. From my outsider's vantage point, however, there were still some troubling social issues that lurked beneath her choice-centered, individualized curriculum. True, once groups of students could leave Meg's classroom for the library or the computer room, the social confrontations decreased and the classroom felt safer and more comfortable. I wondered, however, whether sending roughly a third of her students out of the classroom wasn't a sort of "divide-and-conquer" strategy that kept issues like racism and classism safely invisible, rather than challenging students to work through them. When I asked Meg about this, she admitted: "Sometimes my own conscience says that the reason you're doing this is because you want 100% engagement and you look around on any particular day and you have only 80%."

This bit of personal guilt, however, did not override Meg's strong belief in a more individualized curriculum. Toward the end of the second year, I wanted to bring her classes together for a discussion of how they experienced their final year in the program. To make students more comfortable in sharing their honest reactions, I suggested that Ed Jackson and I might lead the discussion while Meg absented herself. Meg suggested breaking students into small groups, rather than addressing them as a whole class. When I asked Meg why, she explained:

> They're special when they're in a small group and when they've chosen what they're going to do. And otherwise I feel like I have to do 2 days of preparing them for the social studies test. Two days of hell.

To avoid these "days of hell," Meg had made the firm decision never again to return to whole-class experiences. I wondered, however, what she had lost in the pursuit of making her classroom a more "safe space."

I came to believe that in the "politically neutral," yet politically charged, arena of American schools, experiences that force students to confront and examine social and cultural issues such as race, gender, sexual orientation, ability, or social class will not necessarily happen on their own. As long as students find their own comfortable cliques, they are not challenged to work with those they perceive as "different" from themselves. Although both teacher and students found new ways to talk about reading and writing, I wondered what other conversations were going underground in Meg's learner-centered classroom. Could it be that personal choice had become a sort of silencer for larger social and political issues that might have emerged if the classroom occasionally felt a bit less like a "safe zone"?

Goodman (1989) has challenged the notion of the democratic classroom (where all participants are assumed to start out on equal footing), and argues for what he calls a "critical democracy," based on "a moral commitment to promote the 'public good' over any individual's right to accumulate privilege and power" (p. 92). In creating such a classroom, where individuals are valued, yet intricately implicated in the issues of the larger world, teachers often must risk discord and discomfort. The "safe" and "comfortable" learner-centered classroom can, but does not necessarily, afford this kind of critical stance. As Valerie Walkerdine (1990) has observed, "The happy classroom is a place where passion is transformed into the safety of reason . . . a path to omnipotent mastery over a calculable universe" (p. 24). Goodman (1989) argues, however, that "a strong sense of community does not depend on the homogenous consensus of its members. To the contrary, democratic participation often involves social discord as residents confront ways to improve conditions in their immediate environments" (p. 92).

I began to believe that the outward sense of harmony Meg gained in allowing students to work in chosen peer groups obscured the fact that these groups often were formed along racial and gender lines. Meg noticed this too, as she agonized about students' chosen segregation and their frequent refusal to listen to students of other races during Sharing Time. Although she often urged her students to "respect others," I never witnessed her explicitly bringing up the issues of racial or gender segregation as a formal topic of discussion—that is, until one day when the topic seemed to assert itself into the formerly neutral arena of Sharing Time.

"What About You White People?": Finding the Political in the Personal

Interestingly, it was not Meg, but her students, who eventually brought the topic of their chosen segregation smack dab into the center of Sharing Circle one day. Jamal had just begun talking about *The Autobiography of Malcolm X* (X & Haley, 1992), when suddenly the conversation began to take off in a variety of directions all at once. Some students argued over whether physical violence was the answer to the world's problems; others shared their own painful experiences with racism. Most interesting was the fact that the discussion suddenly was dominated by African-American students, many of whom seldom spoke during Sharing Time. For example, Tomell sparked an animated discussion about Black friends who forget "where they came from."

> *Tomell:* I had a friend who . . . goes to [the university] now. Before he went there he was wearing Nikes. He was sporting on gear. Then I went up there and I saw him and he was hanging around White people and it changed his whole attitude. He forgot where he came from. He forgot his people.
>
> *Carl:* He probably didn't forget where he came from; maybe he just wanted to be like them. He didn't want to be different.
>
> *Harvena:* You can't let anybody else change you.
>
> *Carl:* I'm saying maybe he didn't want to feel left out. Maybe he wanted to be mixed in with the crowd.
>
> *Jackson:* I'm saying, you go get a job or something, it's like not that you got to act White, but when you get a job you have to talk professional, not talk professional but . . .

Xantippe began talking about people who got ahead in the system by "acting White."

Xantippe: My mother told me to call my sister. She works for the Blue Cross company downtown. I called her, and she was like, "Hello" [mimicking a formal tone of voice]. You know how a proper voice is like?

Meg: A telephone voice, yes.

Xantippe: I was like, "Why are you talking like that?" When she's at home, she's all rowdy and everything. She's not a quiet person. [But at work] she was like a business person.

Harvena: That's what Black people always say is when you're trying to be proper: "You're acting White."

Max: I can see changing the way you look, but then you start acting and talking different. . . .

Harvena: I think, I don't think she was acting White. Say, like if a White person was on the other line—say like I was a White person and she was a Black person, and she got on the phone with me [and said], "Hello, this is the Blue Cross company" [mimicking a more casual tone]—like how we [Black people] talk—[I would be thinking], "This is definitely a Black person."

Tiombe: Somebody called up my house for my mother, and [I could tell by her voice that she was White]. My mother was [saying] like, "Who is on the phone?" [I said], "There was a White lady on the phone." And [my mother wondered] how I knew it was a White person. . . . I could tell by her voice.

Tommell: When I went to McDonald's there was a lot of White people working there. My cousin got a job there. . . . Before we got there she was all cursing and everything. Her whole attitude changed. Now that she works there, she doesn't like to be around Black people.

Suddenly, in the midst of the conversation, Rameka asked, "What about you White people? You got anything to say?"

At that moment, Meg, who had been staying out of the discussion, broke her silence on the racial segregation in Sharing Circle. She pointed out, "I want you to notice where we're all sitting by the way." Another student picked up on the cue, "Black persons over there, White people here." Meg added, "I went to one of your dances in October. I turned to Ms. Gonzalez and said, "Is this just me or is there a White side of the dance and a Black side of the dance?"

The discussion shifted to whether Black and White students were basically different and wanted to be segregated, or whether they were basically alike. Lovlee observed how so many White students had begun to imitate Black students: "Some girls put on clothes like the Black girls. Like they put on earrings like the Black girls. Or they put gel in their hair. They make their hair stand up like the Black girls."

Suddenly, Jamal asked: "You know how Martin Luther King worked so Black people wouldn't have to sit in the back of the bus? . . . Why is it they only sit in the back of the bus now?" The room grew silent for a moment, then Meg suggested that the difference now was one of personal choice.

> The point is choice. Before there was no choice involved. When you take a person's ability to make a choice away, you're taking their dignity away. Now whether you choose the back or the middle, it's your choice. That's the important thing. We all have the freedom to make choices.

Meg's statement revealed the traditional "individual achievement ideal," perpetuated by our democratic models of schooling. The common wisdom in most American classrooms is that today individuals are able to make choices and are not held back by race, gender, or other factors over which they have no control. As her Black students spoke of their painful experiences in classrooms and on city buses, however, I wondered about the truth of this democratic ideal. In the face of hidden pervasive racism, do individuals really have the kind of choices that our democratic, student-centered versions of schooling seem to advertise? Anthea's story seemed to contradict this achievement ideology.

> *Anthea:* Have you ever been on the bus, and there's those side seats in the back? And there's the back seat. And then there's a Black kid and then there's maybe like three seats. And the whole bus will be filled but those three seats. And a White person will get on the bus and they'll look back and they'll see those Black kids and they'd rather stand up than sit back there.
>
> *Tiombe:* This lady did that to me. I'm like, "You could sit down."
>
> *Anthea:* I was sitting on the bus and I had my book bag on the seat next to me. And this lady came on the bus with her daughter. And there was the seat next to me. She told the little girl to sit down and the girl said, "I don't want to sit with that nigger girl." And [her mom] just looked at her and she started smiling and they stood up. I was like, "I'd rather you not sit by me anyway. You might bite me."

Again, Rameka urged: "What about you White people?" Still, the White students kept silent, as their Black classmates continued with poignant stories of racism and exclusion.

Andrew: We can't even catch the bus down here. The school kids. We can't even catch the bus out here. I went to get on last week and the lady was like, "Are you from Logan?" and I said "Yes." And she said, "You can't get on my bus." Then some other girl—she was White and she was from our school—and [the bus driver] didn't ask her if she was from Logan or nothing and [the girl] got on the bus. And I had to walk all the way down. It was cold that day too, I was mad.

Tommell: I hate when they do that.

Max: If [Black people] are waiting, they will not stop because I guess we're too loud or something. That's why when we get on the bus, I'm like, "Let's be quiet."

Finally, Amy, a White student, spoke. "I remember we were sitting on the bus and this Black girl walked by us, and we didn't say anything to her and she just said 'Honky.'"

Xantippe: I don't call White people honky or anything but a White person called me a nigger and that really pissed me off.

Tommell: That's why that girl might have . . . walked by Amy and said "Honky." Probably that's because she said, "If I see any White person today I'm going to tell them off."

Max: My mother does that. We were in the shopping mall and the lady, my mother was on the computers, and the lady in front of my mother, her purse had got stolen. Here we were the only Black people in there, so the lady . . . in front of my mother looked in her purse and her wallet was gone. And she looked at my mother and said, "Did you take my wallet?" My mother was pissed off that day. They checked us and everything. All that day my mother was mad. She said, "These White people better not mess with me or I'll go off on them."

Matt (to his Black classmates): That's why we as Black people set the tone, man. That's why I have to act civilized and do my work. And the way I talk is proper and you can understand it and everything. That's why saying . . . "Well, he acts White" [is wrong].

Carl: What is being a White person?

Harvena: Like "You being White." What is acting like a White person?

Max: [White people think Black people] can play basketball. They say he plays . . .

Carl: Like Rasheen. He always tells me I act too civilized. What's wrong with being civilized?

Matt: It's not that I play basketball. But I have respect. And they'll
  respect me for that. I'm good at basketball and yes, I am good at
  all these sports. But they'll be like, "He's a faggot because he's
  acting like a White person." I don't hear that. I respect people
  and if somebody asks me to do something like a grown-up, I do
  it. I'm just trying to say that we set the tone. If you go out on the
  street cussing and hollering and running around and wanting to
  fight all the time, that's what they're going to expect. Like they'll
  say, "Don't let him on my bus. Look how he is." So that's why I
  be chillin' all the time.
Carl: When we act, like on the street, acting Black and cussing.
  That's what they're going to expect from us. I'm not saying you
  all, but other White people. They expect us to act Black and they
  expect us to be rowdy. But then we show them that we not
  rowdy.
Rameka: Not all White people are like that.

How interesting that one of the few times I witnessed them dominating
the discussion, Meg's Black students seemed to be rescuing their White classmates, exempting them from the racism they described. Carl's comment, "I'm
not saying you all, but other White people," was in keeping with the "no
putdowns" policy that Meg had been trying to achieve in group sharing sessions. Kimantha's next story, however, brought home the fact that racism is
not just confined to city streets and buses, but exists in hidden and overt forms
in classrooms, often invisible to White students, but to young women like
Kimantha, a painful reality.

Kimantha: I notice that some White people [don't] call on a Black
  person in class. A Black person [has] their arm raised and
  [teachers] go right to the back of the room and call on a White
  person that doesn't have their hand raised.
Kimantha: Like my hand was up that day when . . .
Meg: But, honey, you were off to the side too.
Kimantha: Still, [the teacher] turned my way two times. He turned
  around and then he turned around again. And then he said, "The
  girl in the red." He finally got to me and I had forgot my
  question.
Tiombe: You have to have patience with that. You can't be like, if he
  ignores you, like, "God! You see me over here raising my hand?"
Kimantha: I waited until after he finished talking. Then I raised my
  hand and I had my hand raised for a long time. Then she raised
  her hand, and Ginny was sitting in the same aisle.

Tiombe: In your mind you're doing all this, "Well, she's being ignorant right now so I'm going to have to wait a little longer." The next time I'm just not going to raise my hand.

Meg tried to suggest that Kimantha politely point the situation out to her teacher.

Meg: The way you could handle that if that happened and that really bothered you, is I would ask him politely, not at that moment, but afterwards. Say, "This is what I think happened in this class today and it's really offending me." You've got your point across.

Kimantha (resisting this idea): I said that I didn't like the way you did that to me and [the teacher] said, "I didn't do that to you."

Meg: Yeah, but you plant the seed though.

Kimantha: . . . . I was being as proper as I could be and he didn't even see me raise my hand. I waited 'til after Ginny asked her questions and he asked if there were any more questions. And then I put my hand up and he finally asked me.

In our democratic models of teaching and learning we are led to believe that all students should have equal access to the conversational floor and equal opportunities for making their own personal choices. I wondered, however, how many of these starkly honest conversations would rise to the surface in the learner-centered classroom that equates "safe spaces" with a lack of discord. The fact that Black students had to prod their White classmates to enter into the discussion seemed very telling to me. Never before during Sharing Time did I witness White students urging their classmates of color to enter into a discussion. The unequal power relations of most discussions seemed to play themselves out even in this one, as Black students seemed to feel the need to be more inclusive of their classmates, who were somewhat used to dominating the floor during Sharing Time. I wondered if the White students were worried about making what might be construed as racist or insensitive responses to their Black classmates' frank disclosures. It occurred to me that creating a "safe space" does not mean discouraging confrontation, but encouraging students to confront the hidden and overt racism, classism, sexism, or homophobia that lie in the unexplored realms of students' hearts and minds. Without this kind of honest confrontation, we might ask, as bell hooks (1994) does, if all of our students feel as "safe" as we think they do.

The unwillingness to approach teaching from a standpoint that includes awareness of race, sex, and class is often rooted in the fear that classrooms will be uncontrollable, that emotions and passions will not be contained. . . . Many professors have conveyed to me their feeling that the classroom should be a "safe" place; that usually translates to mean that the professor lectures to a group of quiet students who respond only when they are called on. The experience of professors who educate for critical consciousness indicates that many students, especially students of color, may not feel at all "safe" in what appears to be a neutral setting. It is the absence of a feeling of safety that often promotes prolonged silence or lack of student engagement. (p. 39)

Amidst the politically charged climate of American education, all teachers—but especially English teachers—are expected to be politically neutral. After all, we are not trained to teach social studies and, in fact, are admonished to choose books and to provide writing topics that keep us safely distant from our students' personal, political, or religious beliefs. It's no wonder, then, that English teachers seldom choose to discuss with their students what feels like dangerous issues of racism, sexism, or classism. Part of our reticence also has to do with protecting our students, many of whom are frightened by such frank disclosures. As Pearl Rosenberg (1997) remarks:

Students may feel lost in conversations of race and racism, especially when they begin to explore what it means to be white. Many of them come to see whiteness as an empty cultural space. . . . Because of a general discomfort with the topic of difference, these admissions are not so easily made in the presence of others, and often are written in private messages to the teacher or spoken in confidence in the privacy of my office. . . . [They] often take the form of subversive or "underground" conversations that take place in the stairwells, in parking lots, or in social meetings often held outside of the department. (pp. 80–81)

Unfortunately, many of our students of color know all too well the impossibility of politely pointing out racist practices to teachers and other authority figures. I believe we do them an injustice by pretending that in this society, or in any classroom, all students have an equal forum for honest opinions; they are telling us this in subtle ways. Now, perhaps more than ever, our roles as literacy teachers involve making literacy a form of social action—one that enables all students not only to be heard in the classroom community, but to make a difference in the larger world. As Gordon Wells (1990) has urged:

To be fully literate . . . is to have the disposition to engage appropriately with texts of different types in order to empower action, feeling, and thinking in the context of purposeful social activity. (p. 14)

Similarly, John Willinsky (1990) has criticized a brand of constructivism that defines culture as an equal "forum" for the negotiation of meaning.

> I . . . worry about a certain idealism in this serene image of the cultural scene. If we are talking about "life as it is lived," then, as students already know, there are few forums where all voices are either heard or treated as equal members of the bargaining unit in this language-wide negotiation of meaning. The social construction of meaning . . . brings students to the crossroads of history and power out of which whole bodies of meaning, in gender, race, and social class, have already been forged for them. (p. 205)

As teachers, we might begin by not only encouraging but initiating those conversations about larger social and political issues that are *not happening* in our "politically neutral" classrooms.

RECONSTRUCTING LEARNER-CENTERED CONSTRUCTIVISM

Both Piagetian and Vygotskian constructivism have spawned teaching approaches that seem to be set in neutral landscapes where political and power relations—between teacher and student, and among students themselves—are rendered invisible or perhaps nonexistent. Versions of social constructivism based on apprenticeship, enculturation, or other forms of expert–novice relationships often ignore important issues, such as the resistance that disempowered learners must exert, the right of marginalized learners to refuse enculturation into a realm of "knowledge" that excludes or attempts to eradicate their culture, and the responsibilities of teachers to bring larger political concerns into the public arena of the classroom. In a sense, both portrayals of constructivism seem to rest on the notion that what counts as knowledge is a politically neutral issue.

In contrast to a "social constructivism" based on the creation of a collaborative, safe community of learners, in a "sociopolitical constructivism," or what some have called a "critical constructivism" (Kincheloe & Steinberg, 1993), notions of "community" and "voice" are viewed from the vantage point of political and social issues that surround and shape classroom interactions. Meg's blend of individual constructivism (where students sought their own "personal best") and social constructivism (where students did so with the help of Meg and their peers) was successful by nearly any standards. By the end of her students' middle school careers, she had borrowed the best of both Vygotsky and Piaget. However, by clinging to what E. Smith (1995) has called a "knowing" perspective (focused on how individuals create knowledge, apart from their political or cultural realities), she still was left with many nagging questions.

Whether she believed that personal knowledge emanated from individual or social milieux, she needed to move beyond these "personal knowledge" or psychological perspectives, in order to better understand the complex social realities of her classroom. The fact that many of her students of color perceived themselves as outcasts from so many school activities sheds light on why they may have resisted her attempts to create a "safe and accepting community," and may explain why some of them might have been reluctant to join her play writing group. Through the lens of critical constructivism, she might have better understood her own struggles as "White woman teacher" trying to reach the African-American males in her classroom. Although she agonized privately and to me about these issues, I seldom witnessed her openly sharing them with students.

It was also interesting that most of the talk about reading and writing seemed to focus on topics like adolescent sexuality, drug abuse, growing up, and other issues that cut across racial and gender lines. With the exception of the discussion about race described earlier in this chapter, I witnessed very few extended exchanges about racial or gender inequity in the time I spent in Meg's classroom, despite the fact that many of the novels and stories she provided dealt explicitly with these issues. Racial tensions played themselves out constantly in students' chosen seating arrangements and the patterns of exclusion that took place during Sharing Time and Literature Circle. However obvious these nonverbal signs might have been to Meg and to me, it is interesting that they seldom were brought to the surface of class discussion, except in the form of a few "racially neutral" remarks by Meg that students needed to respect others and to exhibit polite behaviors while others shared.

Blanket prescriptions that students should choose their own topics, teachers should step out of the way and let students develop naturally, and classrooms should be "safe spaces," did little to ameliorate the complex social tensions that populated Meg's world. What she needed was a *sociopolitical* awareness that brought the multifaceted nature of "neutral" techniques like collaborative learning, personal sharing, private writing, and public performance into clearer relief.

In Chapter Ten, I will argue that, rather than stepping out of the way, Meg needed to *step in* and point out the racial, ethnic, and gender issues that surfaced in her classroom. She needed to recognize that "making the personal public" had greater ramifications for marginalized students than it did for more mainstream students. To students like Luis, who was homeless for part of his middle school career, and Rebecca, whose family was embroiled in child abuse allegations, concepts like "personal sharing" were hardly neutral. Neither Piaget nor Vygotsky—both primarily concerned with how individual learners construct knowledge—were of much help to Meg as she negotiated the complex social and political landscape of her urban classroom.

As Willinsky (1990) has argued, "to suggest that meaning is negotiated in an open forum resounds of a golden age of democracy that doesn't wash on the streets of our conurbations, if it ever did in ancient Athens" (p. 208).

A critical constructivist view of literacy teaching would call into question why all voices are not given equal respect, and recognize that teaching and learning are always political acts. Neither privileging personal response, nor assuming a placid and "safe" classroom community, this perspective would lead us closer to the creation of multicultural, anti-bias classrooms (Ng, Staton, & Scane, 1995). It is toward these possibilities that the final chapter of this book is focused.

CHAPTER 10

Aftermath

Acting as if our classroom were a safe space in which democratic dialogue was possible and happening did not make it so. . . . We needed classroom practices that confronted the power dynamics inside and outside of our classroom that made democratic dialogue impossible. (Ellsworth, 1989, p. 313)

Over the past few decades, whether influenced by Piaget or Vygotsky, constructivist literacy education has taken a variety of shapes. Piagetian constructivism posited that individual learners are active meaning-makers, and challenged the premises of transmissionist teaching. Vygotskian constructivism suggested that, since learning is primarily social in origin, students should engage in frequent collaborative experiences, learning from and with each other as well as teachers. Neither perspective, however, has explicitly confronted the power dynamics that Elizabeth Ellsworth speaks of—those that make democratic dialogue impossible. Only recently have critical theorists begun to argue that such sociopolitical dynamics not only influence learners' meaning-making processes, but also delimit their literacy practices and define their literate identities as well.

ON THE PERSONAL, THE SOCIAL, AND THE POLITICAL

The psychological theories of both Piaget and Vygotsky have undergone significant shaping and molding in the crucible of the American literacy classroom. In Piaget's case, a heavy focus on universal developmental stages by curriculum planners and test makers sometimes led to a neglect of the social and cultural factors within which individual learners develop.

Since Vygotsky originally attempted to create a Marxist psychology, it's not surprising that he fixed the origins of learning in the social, rather than the individual. Zebroski (1989), however, argues that Americans have largely misinterpreted the ideas of Vygotsky to suit their own rather limited notions of "the individual."

One of the reasons Vygotsky has been mis-read or misunderstood in the U.S. is that often we project our own notions of self—that the self is an individual, clearly bounded, static, and independent of language—onto a body of texts that come out of a differing, if not opposing, tradition. (p. 150)

Thus, although we may disagree on where knowledge originates along the continuum from self to social, American educators have used both Piaget and Vygotsky to support a model of learning based on a rather simplistic notion of the individual learner. Whether for conservative or liberal ends, the thrust of research and teaching in America has largely revolved around this individualistic notion of learning, whether we imagine that learning to occur within social contexts or not.

Unfortunately, this highly individualistic vision of democracy has ensured that only the upper classes are emancipated, to the neglect of more marginalized groups. Corporate culture and the images of advertising have flaunted "our ability to choose from an abundance of commercial goods," while at the same time channeling human desires into "a relatively narrow range as we come to identify ourselves primarily as 'consumers'" (Goodman, 1989, p. 101). Ironically, rather than promoting individuality, this capitalist ideal actually promotes a kind of conformity to consumerism and greed. Sadly for young adolescents, it often leads to the belief that "one's failure to succeed is tacitly connected to his or her personal shortcomings and not to class, race, or gender inequities" (p. 102). Caught ourselves in the Horatio Alger myth of personal success, we often fail to understand how helpless many of our students feel for their failure to accumulate material goods.

Peter McLaren (1991) further criticizes liberal humanist portrayals of teaching, which often imply

> that self-improvement and empowerment can exist without calling the existing social order into question. Issues of class, gender, and ethnic inequality are never raised. . . . It is a pedagogy steeped in the romance of the word at the expense of the world. (pp. 31–32)

Nowhere is this American individualism felt more strongly than in schools, where, ironically, the term "individualizing instruction" is as popular in whole language classrooms today as it was in the mechanistic days of SRA kits. As a result of this strong push for individuality, successful students often resist collaborative groups because they value their own individual achievement over all else. Less successful students, on the other hand, either participate passively or withdraw altogether, believing that they have little to offer their "more able" classmates.

As Meg learned, collaborative groups, by themselves, did not necessarily build tolerance or community in her diverse classroom. Assigning specific roles and tasks might have made groups more manageable on the surface, but seemed to constrain and contradict the exploratory, engaged brand of collaboration Meg had hoped for. Early in the pilot project, she realized the contradiction in bringing the presumptions of the transmissionist classroom (i.e., direct instruction on atomistic grammar skills) into collaborative learning experiences. Although there was room for difference in how students were taught the grammar rules, there was no negotiating the assignment or the "rules" themselves. Along these lines, Jim Zebroski (1989) has argued:

> Just because we do something as a group or with others doesn't necessarily mean we are moving to a "social" notion of teaching/learning. I worry that some forms of "collaborative teaching/learning" might simply become better instruments for indoctrinating and instilling an acceptable self, a self that submits, goes along, and feels obligated to share and bare its "soul" only to discover that in doing so, the Self can be *better* monitored, policed, and ultimately controlled. (p. 154)

I would argue, though, that Meg wished to do anything but "police" her students. She was savvy to the limitations of an approach to collaborative learning based on assigned task roles and easily measurable outcomes. At the same time, Meg was not altogether clear on her goals for collaborative learning, ironically at the very time that she was expected to guide other teachers in its basic principles. In fact, had it not been for the visits of the university research team, Meg told me that she would have abandoned these collaborative learning groups altogether. The point is that techniques like journals or collaborative groups are just that—techniques. Unless we ask some hard questions about the political and philosophical stances behind them, we cannot be sure whether our goals are reachable or even valid. As O'Loughlin (1992) has argued:

> Once again the *purpose* of active learning needs to be explored: Are students being engaged in the collaborative construction of meaning so that they develop shared understanding that is framed by the unique autobiographical and cultural resources that each one of them brings to school? Or is it the case that active learning has a predetermined purpose, namely, for students to get the point of the exercise, that is, to acquire the meanings that have been predetermined for them by teachers and texts? These questions bear on issues of authority, culture, and power in the classroom: Who decides on the pedagogy and curriculum of the constructivist classroom and in whose interest? (p. 806)

THE POLITICS OF POLITICAL NEUTRALITY: WORDS LEFT UNSPOKEN

Because individual freedom is so valued in America, educators often adopt what Goodman (1989) calls a policy of moral relativism, and schools present themselves as "neutral" institutions "in which all beliefs are considered of equal value" (p. 106). However, as Carole Edelsky (1992) points out, the pretense of relinquishing political positions is, in itself, a political position.

> Many people, especially in the United States, think of politics only as dirty and "backroom stuff." As a result, we regard it as not polite to engage in controversial arguments or politics; we don't want to politicize. ... The schools, because they are public schools, supposedly do not advocate any particular position. But we ignore the fact that embedded in every textbook, every basal reader, and every classroom discussion is a political perspective. (p. 325)

Thus, our "apolitical" stance becomes a political stance. Even recent literature on radical school reform that is explicitly political falls short in terms of what Goodman (1989) calls an "insistence on personal liberty and the lack of attention given to the need for educating children in a manner that will develop their compassion, altruism, cooperation, civic responsibility, and commitment to work for the general welfare of our planet" (p. 108). He argues that often such reform literature simplistically condemns what is "bad" in American education "such as formal knowledge, skills, authority or structure," while praising what is "'good' (such as individual freedom, creativity, or decision making)" (p. 108). As an alternative to such individualistic notions of democracy, Goodman supports Dewey's idea of a "critical democracy" where "each institution, whether public or private, would be organized around values of giving its members a voice in setting and implementing its goals" (Goodman, 1989, p. 92). In contrast to the unmitigated individualism of our current capitalistic democracy, a critical democracy would involve "a moral commitment to promote the 'public good' over any individual's right to accumulate privilege and power" (p. 92).

Although Meg privately agonized over the racial and social divides in her classroom, students rarely grappled with these issues on an explicit and conscious level. My hunch is that both Meg and her students viewed discussing issues such as race, class, and gender in personal terms as somehow beyond the scope of her "politically neutral" role as an English teacher. "Response-centered" pedagogy took her off the hook, in a sense, with its passionate insistence on the primacy of students' personal or autobiographical connections with literature. Discussions of politics and culture in response-based classrooms usually are relegated to sharing information about the historical or cultural backgrounds of literary characters or the cultural heritage of authors. Current social and political issues so close to the surface of the students' lives seldom enter the official stream of talk.

Thus, neither Piagetian nor Vygotskian constructivism, as translated into the published literature, moved Meg's literature program much beyond individualized responses in logs and more public sharing of responses in small groups. To ensure the success of reading logs and Literature Circles, however, Meg needed to examine the political and power relations in her class-room that stood in the way of their full effectiveness.

In retrospect, I believe several important conversations were conspicu-ously absent during Sharing Time and Literature Circle. Here are just a few. During those first few weeks, Meg might have asked her new students what, in the culture of American schooling, made some of them wary of learning from peers and yearning for individualized worksheets and teacher directives. Later, they might have explored why some students clung together in small social groups, based on race or gender, and paid attention only when people from their own peer groups shared. This kind of caring confrontation might have occasioned a discussion of how racism and classism are seldom overt and can surface in disregard and disinterest, as well as overt physical acts. Similarly, stopping to ask why plants, comfortable cushions, and colorful posters made her room "a girl's room" on that first day of class could have provoked a deeper consciousness about gender stereotyping, as well as stu-dents' expectations about schooling.

The long tradition of teacher as knower and grade giver, the irony of chosen segregation, even among people who traditionally have been margin-alized by others, the presumption of gender roles and rigid expectations about the roles of teacher and students—these larger issues seemed to lie beneath many moments of social discord that Meg and her students experienced.

It was not enough simply to put multicultural literature "out there" or to talk about the virtues of a generalized "tolerance." Bringing some of these issues to the surface and explicitly inviting students to create an *anti-bias* classroom might have been a step in the right direction that a "personal choice" curriculum did not provide. In addition, reading and writing about the purposes and forms of schooling in society might have helped students to see why they had come to view themselves over the years as passive re-ceptacles for information, rather than active learners.

TOWARD A MULTIPLICITY OF MULTICULTURALISMS

Influenced by liberal humanistic traditions, Meg was led to believe that cultural differences could be "overcome" or "celebrated," and that people of all cultures could live together in cooperation and harmony. Unfortunately, what Deborah Appleman (personal conversation) calls this "Kumbaya" per-spective often leads to a sort of "travel brochure" portrayal of multicul-turalism that amounts to little more than sampling the varied cuisines, styles, and fashions of the world. Deborah's critique reminds me of an elementary classroom in our district that culminated a unit on Mexican culture with a trip to Taco Bell.

Meg and I learned how impossible it was to fix categories such as "race," "class," or "gender" in the complicated social, cultural, and political arena of her classroom; these terms intersected in complicated ways, none of which, in isolation, defined students' identities. Kianna, for example, was much more than an "African-American female," even though race featured in many of her poems throughout middle school. By the same token, I noticed that many students from historically "oppressed" cultures strongly resisted such labels. Luis, for example, was acutely aware of the White power privilege of others around him throughout middle and high school. Did he see himself as powerless, however? On the contrary, I believe he would say today, as he told me several months ago, that he always felt in control of his own destiny. Although constructs like race and class are socially created, I believe they are individually mediated—that there is a coping mechanism in young people like Luis that does not allow them to succumb to the roles of victim or martyr. We must go beyond essentialist definitions of culture and power, realizing that we all belong to multiple cultures that empower or diminish us, depending on the way that others—and we ourselves—construct those cultural influences.

Beyond recognizing the complex interplay of race, class, gender, and other dimensions of students' identities, we also must move beyond what McCarthy (1996) calls "cultural understanding" models of multicultural education, focused on promoting racial harmony and tolerance among students and teachers. In their weakest versions, "cultural understanding" models promote what McCarthy calls a "benign stance" toward racial inequality, using "sensitivity training" programs to ameliorate prejudice. In their strongest versions, they portray White students and teachers as "flawed protagonists" (1996, p. 27) in their relations with racial minorities. Neither version is particularly effective, and, in fact, each actually can produce negative attitudinal change in students and teachers. Such models also assume cultural universals with regard to particular ethnic or racial groups, defining "racial entities in very static or essentialist terms . . . as a settled matter of cultural and linguistic traits" (p. 38). Instead, McCarthy calls for a "critical multiculturalism" that "links the microdynamics of the school curriculum to larger issues of social relations outside the school" (p. 43). In other words, teachers of literature must do more than put multicultural materials "out there," however important that first step might be. They must make the creation of an anti-bias curriculum a central concern of their work as teachers of literature and literacy.

Such an approach means more than a change in curriculum philosophy, however. It means confronting some of those political dynamics surrounding schools that Ellsworth talks about. We might begin with this irony: In America's public schools, where racial, ethnic, linguistic, and cultural diversity is perhaps at a zenith, there is less money for culturally diverse materials than ever before. Given the limitations of her school budget and classroom library, for example, Meg could offer only a few books, stories, and poems by non-White authors in her curriculum. Although she tried to make her literature selections as diverse as possible, there was really no way she could talk in any significant terms about nonmainstream literature. Thus, although it was clear that students of color appreciated "seeing themselves in the mirror" from time to time, cultural differences couldn't really be talked about in any depth on the basis of the few pieces of literature available from non-European cultures in the typical urban school system. It wasn't fair even to attempt discussing the long and rich tradition of African-American or Latino/ Latina writings, for example, on the basis of a few books, stories, and poems that had somehow sifted down to Meg's classroom shelves through the grace of a librarian or her own ability to scavenge.

The fact that money for public education continues to diminish at a time when more and more language- and racial-minority children are entering public schools makes words like "multiculturalism" seem hypocritical, when held against the current financial crisis in American public education. Larger political issues like these impinge heavily on urban teachers like Meg, limiting and constraining their ability to create the kind of anti-bias curriculum so desperately needed in American schools. It is both an irony and a travesty that young people like Angel had to transfer from her public high school to an expensive and largely White private school, before she could take courses in African-American literature or travel to the state capitol as a political lobbyist. I would argue that such neglect is a crime against our public schools and the children in them.

REVISING RESISTANCE: POWER RELATIONS IN THE CLASSROOM AND WORLD

Critical theorists have written extensively about power relations that surround and suffuse classroom teaching. During this study, I came to understand that the power relations in Meg's classroom were not fixed, but in a constant process of transformation. It would be irresponsible to ignore the White-skin privilege and the authority of our positions as teacher and university professor that Meg and I held in that classroom. What I discovered, however, was that power, like identity, is neither stable nor easily assigned. Despite, or perhaps because of, her White/teacher privilege, Meg often *felt* very powerless—for example, in feeling set apart from her African-American male students, or in not being the "expert" reader her students expected her to be.

Just as her students' identities formed and re-formed at the intersection of their various biographical and cultural histories, Meg's identities were also fluid and multifaceted. At times she was teacher as authority; at other times, teacher as co-learner or trusted adult. Each day she moved in and out of multiple social roles: teacher, mother figure, confidante, White woman, and fellow writer, to name a few. I saw the teeter-totter of power lurch and plunge—sometimes toward teacher, and sometimes toward students—throughout the 3 years I spent in their classroom. Perhaps I should say "the illusion of power," for although Meg clearly *had* racial, class, and authoritative privilege over her students, she sometimes *felt* powerless in her inability to relate to or help some students *by virtue of* her race, gender, or position as teacher.

Learner-centered pedagogy urges teachers to see children as basically untainted by the cruelties of the world. However, in the realm of the urban classroom—or any classroom, for that matter—children, as well as adults, are often cruel and unfair to others on the basis of race, gender, or class. As McLaren (1991) asks:

> What happens when students' voices are burdened by the discourse of racism and sexism? For me, the pedagogical implications to this are very important. How do you affirm these voices while at the same time questioning and challenging the racist and sexist assumptions which inform them? (p. 21)

McLaren's argument calls into question the individualistic notions of personal voice and freedom of expression, as well as the "hands-off" role of teachers often implied in accounts of learner-centered pedagogy. I began to wonder whether the neo-Nazi or the religious fundamentalist has the right to use racial slurs or talk in demeaning ways to others, in the name of exercising his or her "authentic voice"?

I came to believe that the key is not making sure that every voice is *equally heard*, but making sure that no voices are *silenced* because of prejudice or privilege. There are times when teachers must set parameters for what kind of talk is acceptable and what is damaging to others. Exercising this authority can make teachers feel uncomfortable about what might appear as "silencing" some students so that others aren't hurt or demeaned, or paying more attention to traditionally ignored students than to those who typically claim the spotlight. Yet, sometimes we must step into uncomfortable places, so that our students aren't forced into them.

Meg placed much of the burden for the success of her curriculum on the notion of personal choice and the sanctity of students' authentic "voices." What she did not count on, however, was that the concepts of "authentic voice" and "personal choice" both assume a kind of even playing field, where all voices can be equal and all choices are equally unconstrained by larger social and political issues. In criticizing what she calls "the repressive myth of the silent other," Ellsworth (1989) asks: "How does a teacher 'make' students autonomous without directing them? . . . As an Anglo, middle-class professor, . . . I could not unproblematically 'help' a student of color to find her/his authentic voice as a student of color" (pp. 309–310).

Meg's worry that her novel would not appeal to the males or students of color in her room speaks to the basic inability of any teacher to reach completely across the cultural divides of the urban classroom. Somewhat ironically, however, I believe that teachers can use their own "other-ness" to successfully shift the power relations in their classrooms. As a White female teacher, stepping into the vulnerable position of fellow writer, Meg was able to learn from her students, who were suddenly accorded the role of "expert" on their responses to a novel written explicitly for them. In the process, Meg had to put herself on the line—for example, asking males in her class: "As a woman writing this, . . . [I wonder], is this okay for a boy to think this way and feel this way?"

Interestingly, Meg's positioning herself as novice and outsider to her students' experiences fostered a kind of exploratory talk about literature and writing that had not surfaced before in Literature Circle. These conversations about Meg's novel were a striking contrast with the earlier discussions where Meg only asked questions to which she already knew the answers. Ironically, such a shift allowed Meg and her students to reach—if only vicariously and momentarily—beyond those racial and cultural divides. For her students marginalized by race or ability, helping their struggling teacher to find her way as a writer gave them a sense of empowerment they had not experienced before in her individualistic, response-centered classroom.

THE MYTH OF THE SAFE HAVEN: COALITION OR COMMUNITY?

From the beginning, Meg had tried to make her classroom a safe space— one that "didn't look like a regular classroom." When her seventh-grade students resisted her program of collaborative learning, personal sharing, and public performance, she felt guilty at her failure to create that safe haven where all students are given an equal voice and decisions can be negotiated democratically between teachers and students. However, as Elizabeth Ellsworth argues in the beginning of this chapter, simply acting as if democratic dialogue is possible does not make it so. In light of the complex inequities that surround urban classrooms, perhaps "the democratic classroom" has become an oxymoron. As Carole Edelsky (1994) argues:

In a system where wealth buys the right to over-rule majority wishes, where wealth buys the power to make decisions that affect the life and livelihood of everybody else, you can't have a democracy. In a system where corporations are so privileged that they can write the laws as well as decide which laws they'll obey, you can't have a democracy. (p. 253)

As both Edelsky and Ellsworth suggest, it is naive for teachers to believe that they can guarantee complete safety for their marginalized students in the public forum of the class discussion. In her second year of the pilot program, Meg discovered a workable substitute for the "one happy family" model of community she first had envisioned. In her classroom family, students were allowed to work alone or to choose their own smaller "affinity groups," in which they wrote, talked, or acted collaboratively. Although these groups often seemed to form around racial or gender lines, they were, perhaps ironically, necessary to building the sort of safe community that Meg had sought. Similarly, in Ellsworth's (1989) college classroom, these small affinity groups "provided some participants with safer home bases from which they gained support, important understandings, and a language for entering the larger classroom interactions each week" (p. 317).

In Meg's classroom, it was in these smaller coalitions that students like Kianna felt comfortable and powerful enough to make their collective mark on the larger classroom scene. On the other hand, because Meg saw her role as basically apolitical, she felt uncomfortable talking openly about the racial exclusivity in students' chosen groups. Portraits of the learner-centered classroom had advertised the power of personal choice, without questioning the unspoken social dynamics behind students' choices. This does not mean that Meg should have broken up these groups or forced students into an arbitrary integration. But as Meg complained in her journal one day when her students segregated themselves on the basis of race, "I want them to choose where they sit, but what do I do when it turns out like this?" I suggest that teachers have the responsibility to at least point out racial or gender segregation, *especially* if it is the result of personal choice. Although affinity groups may be a necessary stepping stone to a cohesive classroom community, there are times when students might be nudged into collaborations with other students that they might not pursue on their own.

I thought back to the one time that I heard race being discussed in highly personal terms during Sharing Time and remembered that it was not Meg, but her Black students, who brought this politically charged topic into the open. After an extensive and heated discussion, where, for once, Meg's Black students were able to adopt the "expert," insider role, Jamal leveled his question: "You know how Martin Luther King worked so Black people wouldn't have to sit in the back of the bus? . . . Why is it they only sit in the back of the bus now?" This question sparked a discussion about the particulars of racism that none of Meg's generalized comments about "respecting others" or "being polite" could have.

In retrospect, there were many occasions where Meg might have brought in literature that would have made the topics of racism, classism, and sexism an explicit item for discussion, at the same time taking marginalized groups off the hook by not expecting them to "educate" the rest of the class about such issues. In doing so, she might have broken through the strained silence that sometimes seemed to lurk beneath the surface of her peaceable classroom. As William Ayers (1997) has argued:

> A society founded on genocide, built on the labor of African slaves, developed by Latino serfs and Asian indentured servants, made fabulously wealthy through exploitation and masterful manipulation and mystification—a society like this is a society built on race. But race is unspeakable. "We don't talk that way." I'll say. We don't talk at all. And in silence a lens of distorted images, fears, misunderstandings, and cool calculatedness slips neatly into place. (p. 131)

Between the lines of what was said *and not said* in Meg's classroom, I witnessed the insidious appeal of nonconfrontation. I am convinced that, given our penchant for political neutrality in schools, topics such as racism or classism rarely will surface on their own in a whole-class discussion. This is true of American education—indeed, the entire American social scene—in general. As teachers, I believe we silence too many conversations, in our fear of stepping out of the politically neutral perspective assigned to us by society. Perhaps, too, we worry about revealing our own hidden racism, sexism, and the other inevitable psychic debris of a society where material goods matter more than human relationships, and where competition and objective distance are valued over collaboration and connection. Along these lines, Dilg (1995) argues that "many adults in this culture often simply avoid engaging in . . . cross-cultural discussions because they can be awkward, tense, or unsatisfactory. Young people, then, lack the appropriate models for this process" (p. 21).

We need to sponsor these conversations, however discomforting they may be. It became clear to me that the literacy classroom can and must be an arena for exploring the social and political dynamics of the larger world, and that the teacher often bears the responsibility for initiating such explorations.

SHARING SPACES

Individualistic, expressionistic models of literacy make discord and disagreement seem damaging to a sense of community. However, as Goodman

(1989) points out, strong communities are not necessarily built from the "homogeneous consensus" (p. 92) of all residents. Often, in fact, as community members try to improve living conditions and ensure democratic participation for all, they must deal with many moments of tension and discord. While students got along better and seemed more "on-task" when working individually or in smaller groups, they often were not challenged to confront the divisive issues that might have surfaced, had they been expected to work for a common goal in the same space.

Workshop models of instruction, where students spend many hours alone or in small groups, may go a long way in promoting individual success and a more harmonious classroom. On the other hand, they don't challenge teacher or students out of what might be dangerously comfortable places. Carole Edelsky (1994) has argued that

> most of our current progressive theories and practices—such as reader-response theory; sociopsycholinguistic models of reading, transactional theory in reading; literacies as social practices, curriculum as inquiry, whole language practices, writing process practices; whole language as described theoretically by me, among others, and so on—can as easily support *avoiding* looking at white privilege, for example, as they support looking *at* it. (p. 254)

As a former English teacher myself, I strove to keep my classroom politically neutral. In my individualistic model of teaching and learning, I saw myself as a sort of midwife for students' literacy skills, rather than as a political analyst or social commentator. In many ways, for me, reading literature was as much an escape from the world as it was a key to understanding and questioning it.

Since I was not trained in social studies, it's no wonder I still feel reluctant to step out of my league and tackle the political, as well as the social and linguistic, dimensions of my students' lives. Today, however, in the face of growing dropout rates, drug abuse, pregnancy, and crime among America's teenagers, I ask myself how long I can afford this stance. I am left to wonder: What is the place in the constructivist classroom for making disharmony and discord explicit—for closing down the social space so that everyone must find a way not only to share it, but to enlarge and improve it as well? The answer comes back resoundingly: In a constructivist classroom, the teacher cannot sit idly by while students develop "naturally" into more socially connected and responsible persons.

TOWARD A CRITICAL CONSTRUCTIVISM

> Education, then, is linked to freedom, to the ability to see and also to alter, to understand and also to reinvent, to know and also to change the world as we

find it. Can we imagine this at the core of city schools? (Ayers & Ford, 1996a, p. 89)

Believing that such possibilities can, and must, lie at the core of urban schools, I'd like to propose what Joe Kincheloe and Shirley Steinberg (1993) have called a "critical constructivism," or a constructivist viewpoint, "grounded on an understanding of critical theory and postmodernism" (p. 299). A move toward critical constructivism would implicate teachers in ways that learner-centered philosophies did not. Goodman (1989), for example, argues that

> The notion that children do not need conscious, adult intervention regarding social values and social interaction stems from the sentimental and problematic assumption that children will (if only left alone) "naturally" become concerned with the well-being of others and world around them. . . . Children in our schools must come to understand the way in which life on this planet is interconnected and interdependent, and that in caring for others we are in fact caring for ourselves. (p. 109)

The responsibility for creating what Goodman calls a "connectionist classroom" falls squarely on the shoulders of teachers. "Young people's connectionistic perspective," Goodman argues, "cannot mature in a context in which teacher's authority and responsibility are missing" (p. 110).

Schooling based on a critical constructivism would be transformative, as well as informative. In considering the possibilities of this transformative view of literacy education, I turn to a set of questions posed by Maxine Greene (1995).

> So how do public schools, presumably dedicated to equality in the midst of pluralism, even out the playing field? How do they provide more opportunities for personal, distinctive growth? How do we as teachers, cautioned against thinking in terms of predictions and predeterminations provoke all our students to learn how to learn in a world we and they already know is neither equitable nor fair? (p. 171)

I believe we begin, not by pretending to "even out" the playing field, but by enabling all students to successfully negotiate its contours. An English classroom based on critical constructivism would assist students like Kianna and Luis in forging their beliefs about race and human dignity into the shape of poetry, and through their artistry, transforming the very world they sought to describe. Through literature and writing about the roles of women and men in society, students like Samantha, Angel, Jason, and Luis might have explored how gender expectations often keep adolescent girls silent and passive, and adolescent boys macho and competitive. Angel could have nurtured her already budding interest in politics by considering the exclusion and stereotyping in textbooks and the structures of traditional schooling. A critical constructivism would allow all of Meg's students the personal choices they required, while asking them to consider the potential for exclusion in those personal choices. Perhaps in this classroom, Jason, Samantha, Kianna, Angel, and Luis would not have coalesced into one big happy family. Instead they might have gained a valuable understanding of the potentially devaluing and deskilling effects of schooling and the hidden power relations in everything from gender roles in the media to exclusivity in the literature anthology. Such critically conscious learning surely would have empowered and enlightened them, as they embarked on their difficult journeys through high school and beyond.

It is time for literature and literacy teachers to start *stepping in the way* of bigotry, inequality, and the other residues of our individualistic, "me-first" society. We must create a space for those uncomfortable conversations that lead us to a new critical consciousness. In the process, we might help our students to understand—through literature, writing, and talk—that individual achievement is not the primary purpose of schooling, and that each of us bears a responsibility for the world that all of us will inherit. As teachers, we need to become even more active than before, helping students to see literacy not as a window on experience, but as a form of social action. This means creating classrooms where, in Willinsky's (1990) terms, students can "make their mark" as opposed to existing within "institutions given to marking them" (p. 232).

TOWARD A CRITICAL PEDAGOGY OF LITERARY READING

Carole Edelsky (1994) observes that "progressive language educators help kids become literate, but we don't necessarily make them critical." In "getting critical," Edelsky urges literacy educators to begin by

> taking what is taken for granted (like having principals for schools or like selling medicine for profit), and by taking what is seen as business as usual (such as letting a test score keep people out or letting the guys think the idea was theirs) and examining it, figuring out where it came from, what it's connected to, whose interests it serves. (p. 254)

So what would "getting critical" look like in the literature classroom? Beyond soliciting personal responses to literature and writing, Edelsky suggests considering "the positions people are put in by texts, what premises we're positioned to accept, and how we accept or resist those" (p. 255).

As teachers and researchers, we also must challenge ourselves to discover which students linger on the borders of our classroom. We must develop a critical radar for detecting when males dominate the air time and our attention, for when females are pushed into being "good girls," and males are pushed into competitive macho roles. We must oppose bigotry in all of its forms, while still caring for our students who have fallen victim to its invidious appeal. We also must recognize what so many young people today know: that the deck is stacked against them in ways that adopting a more mainstream language or developing more middle class literate behaviors cannot begin to ameliorate.

Finally, we must challenge the potential for ethnocentrism in our own teaching styles. It is a fact that increasing numbers of students of color will continue to be taught primarily by White female teachers. Unfortunately, predictions for any change in this situation are disappointing at best. Drawing on a 1990 study by the AACTE, Linda Darling-Hammond (1995) has observed:

> Between 1975 and 1988, the numbers of Hispanic and Native American candidates receiving bachelor's degrees in education dropped by 40% and the numbers of Hispanic and Native American candidates plummeted by nearly two-thirds. . . . Not only do minority teachers provide important role models for black students (along with other students), they are also much more interested in teaching in urban schools than are most newly prepared white candidates. (p. 180)

The lack of people of color in teacher education programs is disturbing in another way as well. In describing the particular needs and affinities of African-American children, Janice Hale (1994) argues:

> If it is plausible that there is an African American preaching style, then it is equally plausible that there could be an African American teaching style, which would connect with the culture of African American children, inspire them, motivate them, and capture their imagination. This statement in no way implies that only an African American could utilize such a style. Just as southern white evangelists have approximated the African American preaching style and used it in their ministries, and as white rhythm-and-blues musicians and white artists like the New Kids on the Block have utilized African American musical styles, so European American teachers can utilize African American culture when it is in the interests of their students to do so. (p. 204)

In observing Ed Jackson's charisma with so many of Meg's African-American students, it was obvious to me how true Hale's observation was. This does not mean that European-American teachers cannot be successful, however.

Like Meg, all teachers might realize the virtue of "giving up their style for a while" and reaching students from nonmainstream cultures who often feel like outsiders in the world of school.

Kianna: Missing in Action

I need to say a few words about Kianna. Although, in a sense, all of the young adults in this study are still poised tenuously on the brink of many different future paths, Kianna worries me the most. Although I have almost located her many times and sent messages through teachers and relatives, for me, at least, Kianna is still missing in action. I wonder in how many other spheres she also is relegated to the invisible margins. When I began to contact the other students in the summer of 1995, I asked Meg to call Kianna's mother to see if we could locate Kianna. Her mother assured Meg that Kianna would return our call. After several weeks had gone by, Meg called a second, and then a third, time. The last time, she had barely introduced herself when Kianna's mother hung up on her.

Perplexed, I called the high school where I knew Kianna had gone after graduating from Logan, figuring that perhaps Kianna might talk to me, since I wasn't her former teacher. I reached a friend of mine in the office, who looked up Kianna's records and told me that, although Kianna was old enough to be a graduating senior, she was listed as a tenth-grade student. My friend speculated that, like a lot of female students not "on grade level," perhaps Kianna had taken time off to have a baby. If this was true, ironically, Kianna had fulfilled the prophecy of her "Teenage Mom's" poem.

Unfortunately, I was never to know the answer. A few weeks later, I managed to locate Kianna's uncle, who taught at the high school where she was enrolled. He assured me that he would deliver a message to her, along with my home phone number. After several weeks went by with no phone call, I learned through another friend in the city school district that, at the end of her tenth-grade year, Kianna had gotten expelled from her high school and was being transferred to Allen school—a situation ironically foreshadowed by Meg's joke 5 years earlier. I have no idea whether she ever attended Allen, or whether, like so many young women in her position, she finally gave up on her high school education altogether.

Kianna's situation needs no dramatizing or embellishing on my part. I must ask myself, however, how many other young women of Kianna's age are missing in action—young girls who drop out of the system, or seek unconditional love and self-esteem in having a baby, thus cutting themselves off from a financially and emotionally secure future. What I have learned most powerfully in the years since I began this study is how hard it is to represent the complexity of Kianna's situation in the pages of a book.

Like Kianna's butterfly, made up of many colors, "You may see it—you may not."

For Meg and for me, recognizing Kianna's depth and complexity meant more than just "looking hard"; it meant looking beyond and behind the antics and the posturing, so alien to us as White European-American females, to see the young woman of great promise and potential revealed in her poetry. I do not blame Kianna for not returning my phone calls. Obviously, I was neither a confidante nor a role model for her. My fervent hope is that she has met, or will meet, someone who can be those things for her—who can teach her a healthy form of resistance—one that does not push her further toward the margins of a successful life than she already may be.

I am saddened by Sadker and Sadker's (1994) conclusion that well over half of all African-American teenage girls will become pregnant at least once. Citing a study by Constance Willard Williams (1991), Sadker and Sadker (1994) observe that the Black teenage girls in Williams's study "had never been told explicitly to become pregnant," but were, in Williams's terms, "socialized to motherhood" (p. 116). Although there are many theories about why so many Black teenage females become pregnant, Sadker and Sadker speculate that babies are seen as a source of unconditional love and a sign of maturity. Furthermore, they observe that "almost half of the teenagers chose becoming a mother as the single event that made them feel good about themselves. This role brought them, they felt, the acceptance, credibility, and status that had previously eluded them" (1994, p. 117).

A closer look at the realities of teenage pregnancy reveals an even more alarming fact. Most of these underage girls become pregnant not by other teenagers, but by adult males in their 20s. Although this fact is rarely mentioned in the political rhetoric of liberals or conservatives, the problem of *adult–teen* pregnancy has been with us for a long time. In *The Scapegoat Generation: America's War on Adolescents* (1996), Mike Males cites statistics from sources, ranging from the U.S. Census Bureau to the Department of Health and Human Services, concluding that "decades of birth, marriage, and sexual disease figures are consistent. One hundred thousand or more teenage females have given birth in the U.S. every year since at least 1915, and two-thirds to 90 percent of their partners have been men age 20 and older" (p. 63). Unfortunately, Males argues, this is not a problem of low morality or slipping standards, but an economic outcome of inordinately high rates of child poverty in the United States. Males contends that, although America still boasts the most powerful economy in the world, it also ranks highest in child poverty, accounting for "70 percent of the total number of poor children" in the world (p. 7). Underage women often are lured into relationships with older men to escape from this poverty. Males argues:

"When child poverty is reduced, much of teen pregnancy and its motivations in escape and liaison with adult partners takes care of itself" (p. 75).

Unfortunately, in contrast to boys who drop out of school, girls seldom return. Although they cite many reasons for not returning to school, having a baby is seen as the single greatest cause. Sadker and Sadker (1994) argue that, for these girls,

> the costs are very high. Nearly three-fourths of adolescent mothers who are seventeen or younger will not finish high school. Without education, they have little hope of finding jobs that will support them and their children. (p. 119)

As I think about these findings, I remember a poem that Kianna wrote in eighth grade.

People!

People—
People today
Have no place to stay
They live in the streets
Have no food to eat
Sometimes I sit and wonder
How do people go under
Is it that they're too weak
To achieve the education they need
To get a job and move on their way
To have a good life in the
Future one day?
Now they have a price to pay.
They should have gotten the education
Back in those days.

We must change the American system of secondary schooling so that students like Kianna will "have a good life in the future one day." We owe this much to Kianna and, indeed, to all of our young women.

Failing Our Students in the American High School

In her article, "Transforming Schools into Powerful Communities," Deborah Meier (1996) writes:

Children go to institutions called high schools, created for a variety of reasons a century ago, which fail to sustain their curiosity. Instead they drive young people mad. Students develop ways of adjusting, techniques for handling madness, which we then attribute to their hormones. None of us, at any stage in our life cycle, would survive well in such institutions. No other institution we know of, even the army or prison, is organized so mindlessly. In no other institution do we change supervisors and peer groups every forty-five minutes, or engage in a totally different activity every time the bell rings, without any particular sequential order. (p. 133)

In the original group of Angel, Samantha, Jason, Kianna, and Luis, I find it surprising that all but Jason managed to leave their public high schools by one means or another, concretely confirming Meier's observations about the failure of the American high school. Luis was kicked out of three schools before finally graduating in an after-school program. Samantha took the GED in her junior year, and Angel transferred to a private school. Although I could never make contact with Kianna, the last I heard, she was being sent away from her public high school to an alternative facility for what the district called "at-risk" students.

Although all of these young people gave slightly different reasons for their escape, there were some common themes. Most notable was the segmented, formalistic high school curriculum that bore little relevance to their lives. While elementary and middle schools are more "home-like," high schools follow what Hargreaves, Earl, and Ryan (1996) call a "custodial" model (p. 23). I saw evidence of this custodial approach in the way that Luis's second high school principal called him in at the beginning of school to warn that his reputation as a troublemaker had already reached the administrative office. Even an academically successful student like Angel was put off by her principal's intrusions into her personal relationship with her boyfriend. Ironically, in contrast to this "policing" by school authorities, there coexisted a kind of benign neglect among teachers that made students like Jason feel they could skip out of school at any time and not be missed.

What Jason called "an overload of busywork" is unfortunately the way a great many adolescents characterize their high school experiences. In their recent study of "school leavers," Altenbaugh, Engel, and Martin's (1995) informants reported a classroom experience "dominated by lecturing, and so-called seatwork and tests. In more instances than not, teachers were portrayed as mere dispensers of subject matter" (p. 132). Interestingly, however, 65% of their informants reported "a consistent interest, even a love of reading" (p. 100). On their own, these school leavers read books by authors from Stephen King and J. D. Salinger to Nelson Mandella and Malcolm X. In school, however, they encountered textbooks that were "sterile, dull, and biased" (p. 101). Sadly, Altenbaugh and his colleagues observed that "these school leavers never recalled encountering an English course that assigned popular novels, or a history class that relied on relevant biographies" (p. 101). They further concluded:

> Sterilized textbook knowledge . . . anesthetizes students concerning inequality and vital social issues. . . . Given this social and political context, it is no surprise that many of our narrators did indeed read, and preferred biographies about minority struggles and heroes, newspapers, and literature that focused on minorities and minority perspectives. Lack of reading skills did not appear to be as serious a problem for our interviewees as we first believed, but failure to enjoy what is read, i.e., the assigned textbooks, did contribute to their alienation from reading. (pp. 101–102)

I am reminded of Jason's observation that most of his high school teachers were simply "lazy" people, earning a paycheck and assigning busywork as a way of "lessening their job." This uncaring attitude was reflected over and over again in the study by Altenbaugh and his colleagues. They concluded that "not one informant described an adult advocate, that is, an administrator or a teacher who defended the student's interests and needs in school" (1995, p. 96). As Samantha observed about her high school experience, "this is going to sound weird, like an oxymoron, but, [in high school, the] kids were out of control, and [yet] there was . . . massive structure [in the hallways]."

On Empowering Power

I will end this book with an admission and a challenge. Part of me wants to uncritically accept the notion of getting more critical in the literacy classroom, but another part resists much that is written by postmodernists and critical pedagogists because of the off-putting language in which it is couched. Isn't it odd how the language of Critical Pedagogy sets up a linguistic version of the elitism, snobbery, and marginalization it supposedly rejects? Whether postmodernist critiques are aimed at "liberating" rural peasants, the urban proletariat, or disenfranchised students, I have a hunch that the very subjects of this liberation would not bother to read the elitist and ponderous writings that have surfaced in their name. As Goodman (1992) has argued, "Whether it is found in sociological, literary, or educational discourse, the intellectual elitism that is embedded in much of the language of criticism significantly undermines its own liberatory intentions" (p. 274). An impulse in me says, let's "get critical" in the literature classroom, but let's not get *paralyzed* into a critical stance the way the new critics did. I continue to be wary of what might go down in history as just another text-centered exercise in academic snobbery.

On Love and Power

I am also suspicious of those who treat power as though there are those who have *it* (and are, consequently, blessed) and those who don't (who are, sadly, victimized). In many writings on the topic of power and schooling, students, presumably, don't have it, while teachers do. The commonsense solution to all of this seems to be to give more of *it* over to students. The catch, as Carole Edelsky (1994) argues, is that, considering the long history of power relations in school, classrooms can never be democracies, and teachers can never divest themselves of power.

I'd argue further that, even if Meg magically were able to hand all power over to her students, this alone would not have "empowered" them. The world is altogether too full of young people who feel too much *power over* (translate: *disconnection from*) those who are supposed to guide and nurture them into adulthood. Admittedly, we need to rectify the power imbalances that have kept students unquestioning and servile. On the other hand, there were many times when students in Meg's classroom seemed in desperate need of something much more tangible and comforting than power. It was easy for Luis Thomas, for instance, to shove my questionnaires to the end of his desk and refuse to fill them out. It was much harder for him, 5 years later, to own up to a hurtful prank he had perpetrated on his favorite teacher. Kianna had no trouble shouting, "I'm gonna kill you" to Meg in class, yet resisted the vulnerability of reading her poetry aloud to a group of her classmates.

Certainly, I believe that Kianna and Luis were empowered as students and literate people when they learned to share their poetry with others. But the most compelling moments of learning I witnessed in Meg's classroom were wrought from a fine balancing of love and power. It was love, after all, that sent Luis Thomas back to Logan to find Meg and thank her for the crucial role she had played in his life. And it was love, not power, that convinced Kianna to reach beyond her brash behaviors and discover the heart and soul of a poet. Ed Jackson could shove a finger in Jaquille's chest and tell him to straighten up, because he did so out of a delicate balancing of love and power. And it was love that allowed students like Samantha and Luis to trust Meg with the intimate details of their personal lives. In describing the absence of caring in today's society, Oliner and Oliner (1995) argue that

> today's problems are both material and something more difficult to name. Sometimes described as a malaise of the soul, it includes a sense of loss of place and people, a breakdown of personal commitments, and a retreat from moral norms which define and hold communities together. The character of our contemporary society seems better captured by hostility than social glue. . . . Far

too many people feel uncared for and even more feel little responsibility to care for others. Without care, hope and a sense of investment in a society's future vanish. (p. 2)

It is this sense of caring and love that seems strikingly absent in much of the power-saturated language of Critical Pedagogy. In reading this literature, I wonder, as Robert Frost did when he dutifully rebuilt the wall between his neighbor's land and his, what I was "walling in or walling out." By making power the centerpiece (or dare I say master narrative?) of any theory of teaching and learning, don't we empower the very concepts that we have argued so passionately against? How can we weave qualities such as love, caring, and connectedness throughout our discussions of politics and power? Maxine Greene (1992) urges us to begin.

There have always been newcomers in this country; there have always been strangers. There have always been young persons in our classrooms we did not, could not see or hear. In recent years, however, invisibility has been refused on many sides. . . . We are challenged as never before to confront plurality and multiplicity. Unable to deny or obscure the facts of pluralism, we are asked to choose ourselves with respect to unimaginable diversities. . . . It seems clear that the more continuous and authentic personal encounters can be, the less likely it will be that categorizing and distancing will take place. People are less likely to be treated instrumentally, to be made "other" by those around. I want to speak of pluralism and multiculturalism with concrete engagements in mind, actual and imagined: engagements with persons, young persons and older persons, some suffering from exclusion, some from powerlessness, some from poverty, some from ignorance, some from boredom. Also, I want to speak with imagination in mind, and metaphor, and art. (p. 250)

Meg taught me that I could not look at her students or her classroom and wish that "yarn was metal or wood was paint." More than this, I discovered that I could not reduce the art of teaching or the mystery of learning in her classroom to a logical equation or a straightforward prescription. These are born in a tenuous balance of caring and critical consciousness. We must begin, as Maxine Greene urges, to personalize generalities like multiculturalism, diversity, and politics with "concrete engagements in mind," as well as "imagination . . . and metaphor, and art." We also must recognize that young people like Kianna, Angel, Samantha, Luis, and Jason are both our ultimate challenge and our dearest promise. As we all stand poised on the brink of an uncharted century, they are our investment in society's future, as we are, perhaps, their greatest hope.

AFTERWORD

Meg, 1997

I remember all of these students very clearly. When I see their writing in this book, I can close my eyes and picture what each one of them was wearing, the corner of the classroom in which we were sitting, and the season that flooded through our wall of windows as I guided them years ago. Yet, if someone had given me just a list of their names, I would not have been able to recall these kids. When I see students in the mall after 5 or 10 years have gone by, I seldom remember their names. It is awkward; they remember me, but I stand speechless, until a much taller, more mature version of some past seventh or eighth grader says, "I'm so-and-so." And then I say, "Yes, of course . . ." But show me a piece of their writing or the reading response log of a child long gone from my roster, and I often can recall the most specific details of that student's life. It's interesting how it's the writer and reader in them that lives on in my mind.

I am proud of the teaching that I did when I had these students (okay— and a little embarrassed at some things, too). But at the same time, I know that I have grown a great deal as an educator since they were in my class. Seven years ago I wrote in my teaching journal that I knew that I needed to personally engage my students, but I should not let myself become emotionally involved. Well, since then I have found that to be impossible, and it probably has become my most valuable lesson in teaching. If I want to be a partner in their writing, how can I expect them to be emotionally involved if I am not? So, since then I have asked my students to bring their entire lives into my classroom and to bare it all in their writing. Now that's a scary thought, I realize. But if I want them to see the real value in placing their thoughts into writing, in relating what they are reading to their own lives, and in becoming the type of lifelong readers and writers that we all want them to be, then I better show them that writing and reading are as real as the shooting on their block last week, what happened to their cousin last night, and what they saw from the bus window on the way to school this morning. I HAVE to listen to their stories, let them cry on my shoulder, intercede for them with parents and social workers, and let them know that I am a trusted adult who cares deeply. I have to let them read and write about the issues that are important to them as adolescents. If I close off certain topics because they make me uncomfortable, then I am closing off the very curiosity and creative energy that I can use to transform a streetwise kid into a literate being.

For any of this to work, my classroom has to be a safe place, where truth can be faced and dealt with without repercussion; no easy task for an urban teacher. I began my teaching journey in a very traditional manner, evolved into a teacher who grabbed onto each new, creative teaching technique like a life preserver, and then came to understand that it is the marriage of structure and creativity that gives the gift of safety to my kids. Without structure, there would be no safety, and without safety, there would be no growth. Many city kids have no concept of safety. All the more reason why my classroom has to be a haven, a place where what they are thinking and feeling is okay, and what they have experienced in life is not going to change the way I feel about them. Only then can we really start writing.

I salute the young people in this book. It was fascinating to have the chance to connect with them years later, and get a sense of how being in my English class contributed to the people they are today. I guess I half expected them to say, "Mrs. Andrews who?" and I was amazed that their memories were as vivid as my own. After reading this book, I will have to fight the urge to ask every previous student I greet in the mall to sit down and talk to me for a couple of hours or so, about the days when we sat in the corner of the classroom, sharing our reading and writing journeys, and watching the seasons flood in, one after the other.

Thank you, Susan Hynds, for giving me this opportunity for such intense reflection. And to the readers, I hope that you all experience, through all the successes and mistakes of your own teaching, the joy of it all.

A Closer Look at Methods and Analyses

CODING OF ROLE CATEGORY QUESTIONNAIRES

"Peer complexity" and "character complexity" were derived by counting the number of interpersonal constructs in timed, written free-response measures, or Role Category Questionnaires (Crockett, Press, Delia, & Kenny, 1974), then averaging the scores together. For example, I asked students to describe, in writing, "someone their own age whom they liked" and "someone their own age whom they disliked." To determine peer complexity, I averaged the total number of interpersonal constructs in each impression. I then read two short stories aloud to students on separate occasions: "The Fourth of July" by Robin Brancato (1985) and "The New Kid" by Murray Heyert (1944). Immediately after hearing each story read aloud, students were asked to describe in writing their impressions of the story's protagonist. Character complexity was derived by averaging the number of interpersonal constructs in each character impression.

SELECTION OF CASE STUDY INFORMANTS IN PHASE TWO

I regularly observed four of the eight focal students, Angel, Samantha, Jason, and Mark, in the same English class during the fall of phase one. The remaining four focal participants—Kianna, Cassie, Daniel, and Jessie—were observed by my assistant, who took observational field notes for each class that she visited. Although observational data were collected on all eight students, I planned to focus my in-depth case studies only on the students whom I had directly observed. However, I continued to interview all eight students (including those observed by my assistant) throughout the 4-semester period of phase two. In the first two semesters of observations, I blinded myself to focal students' peer and character complexity ratings, so as not to bias any of my early hunches. I revealed these ratings to myself at the end of the second semester, in preparation for the 1990–91 academic year, when the focal informants would begin their eighth-grade year in Meg's class.

At the start of the 1990–91 academic year, I had not counted on the fluid and changing nature of the middle school schedule. That fall, I discovered that two of my original four case study students (Jason and Mark) had changed the time of their English classes to a period during the day that conflicted with my schedule at the university. Although my observations of Jason were rather limited in the final year of the study, I continued to interview him on a regular basis. By the end of the project, I had compiled a rather rich portfolio of information on him and felt confident in including him in my group of case study informants. Three students from the original group of eight were in the same classroom this year: Kianna, Samantha, and Angel. Since I could now observe Kianna on a regular basis, and would have observational notes from my assistant during Kianna's seventh-grade year, as well as my own interview transcripts over the 2-year period, I decided to add her to my case study informants.

As explained in Chapter One, I also conducted focused observations of Luis, in hopes of eventually including his story in this study. In the summer of 1995, I finally was able to interview him retrospectively and to obtain permission to include my observational notes, some of his written work from middle school, and written materials he saved throughout his high school years. Thus, at the end of phase two, the following five members of the original group of nine focal informants became the subject of in-depth case studies: Jason, Kianna, Samantha, Angel, and Luis.

OBSERVATIONS AND INTERVIEWS IN PHASE TWO

My assistant and I kept all observational notes in double-entry journals, with direct observations in the left column and questions or observer comments in the right. We also met periodically to discuss her observations and to review her notes. Although I observed the group dynamics of each class session as a totality, I also made focused observations of each case study participant at various points during each observation period. Students were observed in a variety of settings, participating in different instructional experiences. For example, I observed them in large-group discussions, working with partners or small groups, conferring with Meg and other adults, performing in assemblies, participating in Literature Circles and Sharing Time. I not only observed them in the classroom, but occasionally followed them to the library or the auditorium, to watch them during play practice or assembly.

Throughout the process of data collection, I wrote periodic analytic memos to myself, in order to document themes and patterns in my data. As these themes and patterns began to emerge, I tested them against what I was noticing in my later observations and interviews. I also scheduled regular interviews with Meg, in which I could discuss some of the insights I was generating from my observations of her teaching, from my conversations with students, and from reading her teaching journal. After all the data were collected and all tapes transcribed, I continued to write analytic memos focused on my retrospective perceptions of the data.

By April 1990, eight of the focal informants (excluding Luis) had participated in two preliminary interviews concerning their reading interests, attitudes, and experiences, as well as a final interview in which they were asked to review approximately 40 texts that had been covered in class that year and to discuss the ways in which these texts did or did not relate to their lives.

As a culminating activity, in the spring of 1991, Ed Jackson and I conducted discussions with all students in each class, focusing on their perceptions of the 2-year experience. These class sessions were taped and transcribed. In late spring of 1991, the students spent several weeks preparing a final "communication packet" that would serve as an end-of-term evaluation, as well as an assessment of the success of Meg's 2-year program. As part of this experience, students engaged in written responses to literary texts, wrote essays about their favorite readings, created original pieces of writing, reflected about themselves as readers and writers, and critiqued various classroom activities. Packets for all focal students were duplicated and saved. At the end of the experience, all focal students were asked to participate in an interview in which they discussed their perceptions of various activities, their views of reading, and the likelihood that they would read after graduation.

In all, over the 3 years of the study, I conducted interviews with 16 focal informants (eight from phase one and eight from phase two), personally observed the case study informants from phase two in their English classes, and conducted follow-up interviews in the summer of 1995 with four of the five case study informants.

References

Allen, J. B. (1990, November). *Perspectives on literacy research*. Paper presented at the meeting of the National Council of Teachers of English Assembly for Research Annual Workshop, Atlanta.

Altenbaugh, R. J., Engel, D. E., & Martin, D. T. (1995). *Caring for kids: A critical study of urban school leavers*. London: Falmer Press.

Angelou, M. (1978). "Still I rise." In *And still I rise* (pp. 41–42). New York: Random House.

Applebee, A. N. (1992a). The background for reform. In J. A. Langer (Ed.), *Literature instruction: A focus on student response* (pp. 1–18). Urbana, IL: NCTE.

Applebee, A. N. (1992b). Stability and change in the high school canon. *English Journal, 81*(5), 27–32.

Applebee, A. N., Langer, J. A., Jenkins, L. B., Mullis, I., & Foertsch, M. A. (1990). *Learning to write in our nation's schools*. Princeton, NJ: Educational Testing Service.

Atwell, N. (1987). *In the middle: Writing, reading, and learning with adolescents*. Montclair, NJ: Boynton/Cook.

Ayers, W. C. (1997). Racing in America. In M. Fine, L. Weis, L. C. Powell, & L. M. Wong (Eds.), *Off white: Readings on race, power, and society* (pp. 129–136). New York: Routledge.

Ayers, W., & Ford, P. (1996a). Chaos and opportunity. In W. Ayers & P. Ford (Eds.), *City kids, city teachers: Reports from the front row* (pp. 81–90). New York: The New Press.

Ayers, W., & Ford, P. (1996b). Introduction: City streets, city dreams. In W. Ayers & P. Ford (Eds.), *City kids, city teachers: Reports from the front row* (pp. xix–xxii). New York: The New Press.

Babbit, N. (1975). *Tuck everlasting*. New York: Farrar, Strauss & Giroux.

Banks, J. A. (1993). The canon debate, knowledge construction, and multicultural education. *Educational Researcher, 22*(5), 4–14.

Barbieri, M. (1995). *Sounds from the heart: Learning to listen to girls*. Portsmouth, NH: Heinemann.

Barnes, D. (1975). *From communication to curriculum*. Harmondsworth, UK: Penguin.

Barnes, D., & Barnes, D. (1984). *Versions of English*. London: Heinemann.

Beach, R. (1983). Attitudes, social conventions, and response to literature. *Journal of Research and Development in Education, 16*(3), 47–54.

Bizzell, P. (1991). Power, authority, and critical pedagogy. *Journal of Basic Writing, 10*(2), 54–70.

Bloome, D. (1986). Building literacy and the classroom community. *Theory into Practice, 25*(2), 71–76.

Blume, J. (1974). *Are you there God? It's me, Margaret.* New York: Laurel Leaf Contemporary Fiction.

Bogdan, D. (1990). In and out of love with literature: Response and the aesthetics of total form. In D. Bogdan & S. Straw (Eds.), *Beyond communication: Reading comprehension and criticism* (pp. 109–137). Portsmouth, NH: Boynton/Cook.

Bogdan, R. C., & Biklen, S. K. (1992). *Qualitative research for education: An introduction to theory and methods.* Needham Heights, MA: Allyn & Bacon.

Boomer, G. (1982). *Negotiating the curriculum: A teacher–student partnership.* Sydney, Australia: Ashton Scholastic.

Bradbury, R. (1987). All summer in a day. In S. D. Schaffrath & L. Sternberg (Eds.), *McDougal, Littell: Literature, red level* (pp. 132–136). Evanston, IL: McDougal, Littell.

Brancato, R. (1985). The fourth of July. In D. Gallo (Ed.), *Sixteen: Short stories by outstanding young adult authors* (pp. 102–111). New York: Dell.

Britton, J., Burgess, T., Martin, N., McLeod, A., & Rosen, H. (1975). *The development of writing abilities (11–18).* London: Macmillan.

Brown, M. W. (1947). *Goodnight moon.* New York: Harper Collins Children's Books.

Bruffee, K. A. (1984). Peer tutoring and the "conversation of mankind". In G. Olson (Ed.), *Writing centers* (pp. 3–15). Urbana, IL: NCTE.

Bruner, J. (1960). *The process of education.* New York: Vintage Books.

Burleson, B. R., Applegate, J. L., & Neuwirth, C. M. (1981). Is cognitive complexity loquacity? A reply to Powers, Jordan, and Street. *Human Communication Research, 7*(3), 212–225.

Calkins, L. M. (1983). *Lessons from a child: On the teaching and learning of writing.* Portsmouth, NH: Heinemann.

Calkins, L. M. (1986). *The art of teaching writing.* Portsmouth, NH: Heinemann.

Chomsky, N. (1957). *Syntactic structures.* The Hague: Mouton.

Cobb, P. (1995). Continuing the conversation: A response to Smith. *Educational Researcher, 24*(7), 25–27.

Crockett, W. H. (1965). Cognitive complexity in impression formation. In B. Maher (Ed.), *Progress in experimental personality research* (Vol. 2, pp. 47–90). New York: Academic Press.

Crockett, W. H., Press, A. N., Delia, J. G., & Kenny, C. T. (1974). Structural analysis of the organization of written impressions. Unpublished manuscript, University of Kansas, Lawrence.

Culler, J. (1975). *Structuralist poetics.* Ithaca, NY: Cornell University Press.

Cummins, J. (1993). Empowering minority students: A framework for intervention. In L. Weiss & M. Fine (Eds.), *Beyond silenced voices: Class, race and gender in United States Schools* (pp. 101–117). Albany: State University of New York Press.

Cunningham, P. M. (1976–77). Teachers' correction responses to black-dialect miscues which are non-meaning changing. *Reading Research Quarterly*, *12*(4), 637–653.

Cureton, G. O. (1985). Using a black learning style. In C. K. Brooks, L. C. Scott, M. Chaplin, D. Lipscomb, W. Cook, & V. Davis (Eds.), *Tapping potential: English and language arts for the black learner* (pp. 102–108). Urbana, IL: NCTE.

Danziger, P. (1975). *The cat ate my gymsuit*. New York: Bantam Doubleday Dell Books for Young Readers.

Darling-Hammond, L. (1995). Teacher knowledge and student learning: Implications for literacy development. In V. Gadsden & D. Wagner (Eds.), *Literacy among African-American youth: Issues in learning, teaching, and schooling* (pp. 177–200). Cresskill, NJ: Hampton Press.

Dewey, J. (1900). *The school and society*. Chicago: University of Chicago Press.

Dilg, M. A. (1995). The opening of the American mind: Challenges in the cross-cultural teaching of literature. *English Journal*, *84*(3), 18–25.

Driver, R., Asoko, H., Leach, J., Mortimer, E., & Scott, P. (1994). Constructing scientific knowledge in the classroom. *Educational Researcher*, *23*(7), 5–11.

Edelsky, C. (1992). A talk with Carole Edelsky about politics and literacy. *Language Arts*, *69*(5), 324–329.

Edelsky, C. (1994). Education for democracy. *Language Arts*, *71*(4), 252–257.

Egan, K. (1992). *Imagination in teaching and learning: The middle school years*. Chicago: University of Chicago Press.

Elbow, P. (1975). *Writing without teachers*. London: Oxford University Press.

Elkind, D. (1994). *Ties that stress: The new family imbalance*. Cambridge, MA: Harvard University Press.

Ellsworth, E. (1989). Why doesn't this feel empowering? Working through the repressive myths of critical pedagogy. *Harvard Educational Review*, *59*(3), 297–324.

Enright, E. (1987). Nancy. In S. D. Schaffrath & L. Sternberg (Eds.), *McDougal, Littell: Literature, red level* (pp. 114–125). Evanston, IL: McDougal, Littell.

Evans, G. (1988). *Learning to lose: Sexism in education*. London: Women's Press.

Finders, M. (1997). *Just girls: Hidden literacies and life in junior high*. New York: Teachers College Press.

Fine, M. (1995). Silencing and literacy. In V. Gadsden & D. Wagner (Eds.), *Literacy among African-American youth: Issues in learning, teaching, and schooling* (pp. 201–222). Cresskill, NJ: Hampton Press.

Fish, S. (1976). Interpreting the variorum. *Critical Inquiry*, *2*(3), 465–485.

Flower, L., & Hayes, J. R. (1980). Identifying the organization of the writing process. In L. W. Gregg & E. R. Steinberg (Eds.), *Cognitive processes in writing* (pp. 9–10). Hillsdale, NJ: Erlbaum.

Fordham, S. (1988). Racelessness as a factor in black students' school success: Pragmatic strategy or pyrrhic victory? *Harvard Educational Review*, *58*(1), 54–84.

Fordham, S. (1993). Those loud black girls: (Black) women, silence, and gender "passing" in the academy. *Anthropology and Education Quarterly*, *24*(1), 3–32.

Fordham, S. (1996). *Blacked out: Dilemmas of race, identity, and success at Capital High*. Chicago: University of Chicago Press.

Fordham, S., & Ogbu, J. (1986). Black students' school success: Coping with the burden of "acting white". *The Urban Review, 18*(3), 176–206.

Frye, N. (1967). *Anatomy of criticism*. Princeton, NJ: Princeton University Press.

Gadsden, V. (1995). Introduction: Literacy and African-American youth: Legacy and struggle. In V. Gadsden & D. Wagner (Eds.), *Literacy among African-American youth: Issues in learning, teaching, and schooling* (pp. 1–12). Cresskill, NJ: Hampton Press.

Garrison, B., & Hynds, S. (1991). Evocation and reflection in the reading transaction: A comparison of proficient and less proficient readers. *JRB: A Journal of Literacy, 23*(3), 259–280.

George, P. S., & Oldaker, L. L. (1985–86). A national survey of middle school effectiveness. *Educational Leadership, 43*(4), 79–85.

Gilyard, K. (1991). *Voices of the self: A study of language competence*. Detroit: Wayne State University Press.

Giroux, H. A. (1983). Theories of reproduction and resistance in the new sociology of education: A critical analysis. *Harvard Educational Review, 53*(3), 257–293.

Goldblatt, E. (1995). *'Round my way: Authority and double-consciousness in three urban high school writers*. Pittsburgh: University of Pittsburgh Press.

Goodman, J. (1989). Education for critical democracy. *Journal of Education, 17*(2), 88–116.

Goodman, J. (1992). Towards a discourse of imagery: Critical curriculum theorizing. *Educational Forum, 56*(3), 269–289.

Goodrich, F., & Hacket, A. (1956). *The diary of Anne Frank, drama*. New York: Random House.

Grant, L. (1984). Black females' "place" in desegregated classrooms. *Sociology of Education, 57*(2), 98–111.

Graves, D. H. (1983). *Writing: Teachers and children at work*. Exeter, NH: Heinemann.

Greene, M. (1992). The passions of pluralism: Multiculturalism and the expanding community. *Journal of Negro Education, 61*(3), 250–261.

Greene, M. (1995). *Releasing the imagination: Essays on education, the arts, and social change*. San Francisco: Jossey-Bass.

Guy, R. (1973). *The friends*. New York: Holt, Rinehart & Winston.

Haberman, M. (1996). The pedagogy of poverty versus good teaching. In W. Ayers & P. Ford (Eds.), *City kids, city teachers: Reports from the front row* (pp. 118–130). New York: The New Press.

Hale, C. L. (1980). Cognitive complexity–simplicity as a determination of communication effectiveness. *Communication Monographs, 47*(4), 304–311.

Hale, J. E. (1994). *Unbank the fire: Visions for the education of African American children*. Baltimore, MD: Johns Hopkins University Press.

Hall, G. S. (1904). *Adolescence*. New York: Appleton.

Hargreaves, A., Earl, L., & Ryan, J. (1996). *Schooling for change: Reinventing education for early adolescents*. London: Falmer.

Harris, J. (1991). After Dartmouth: Growth and conflict in English. *College English, 53*(6), 631–646.

Hawthorne, N. (1995). *The scarlet letter.* New York: St. Martin Press.

Heath, S. B. (1985). Being literate in America: A sociohistorical perspective. In J. N. Niles & R. Lalik (Eds.), *Issues in literacy: A research perspective* (pp. 1–18). Rochester, NY: National Reading Conference.

Heyert, M. (1944). The new kid. *Harper's Magazine, 189*(1129), 21–27.

Hiebert, E. H. (Ed.). (1991). *Literacy for a diverse society: Perspectives, practices, and policies.* New York: Teachers College Press.

Hoetker, J. (1970). Limitations and advantages of behavioral objectives in the arts and humanities. In J. Maxwell & A. Tovatt (Eds.), *On writing behavioral objectives for English* (pp. 49–50). Urbana, IL: NCTE.

hooks, b. (1989). *Talking back: Thinking feminist, thinking black.* Boston: South End Press.

hooks, b. (1994). *Teaching to transgress: Education and the practice of freedom.* London: Routledge.

Hornbeck, D. (1989). *Turning point: Preparing American youth for the 21st century.* New York: Carnegie Council on Adolescent Development.

Hynds, S. (1983). *Interpersonal cognitive complexity as related to the character perceptions, literary response preferences, story comprehension, and literary attitudes of adolescent readers.* Unpublished doctoral dissertation, George Peabody College of Vanderbilt University, Nashville, TN.

Hynds, S. (1985). Interpersonal cognitive complexity and the literary response processes of adolescent readers. *Research in the Teaching of English, 19*(4), 386–402.

Hynds, S. (1989). Bringing life to literature and literature to life: Social constructs and contexts of four adolescent readers. *Research in the Teaching of English, 23*(1), 30–61.

Hynds, S. (1990). Reading as a social event: Comprehension and response in the text, classroom, and world. In D. Bogdan & S. Straw (Eds.), *Beyond communication: Reading comprehension and criticism* (pp. 237–256). Portsmouth, NH: Heinemann/Boynton/Cook.

Iser, W. (1980). Texts and readers. *Discourse Processes, 3*(4), 327–343.

Johnson, J. A. (1995). Life after death: Critical pedagogy in an urban classroom. *Harvard Educational Review, 65*(2), 213–230.

Jose, P., & Brewer, S. (1984). Development of story liking: Character development, suspense and outcome resolution. *Developmental Psychology, 20*(5), 911–924.

Kelly, G. (1955). *The psychology of personal constructs.* New York: Norton.

Kincheloe, J. L., & Steinberg, S. R. (1993). A tentative description of post-formal thinking: The critical confrontation with cognitive theory. *Harvard Educational Review, 63*(3), 296–320.

King, S. (1987). *Misery.* New York: Viking.

King, S. (1993). *Tommyknockers.* New York: NAL–Dutton.

King, S., & Straub, P. (1984). *Talisman.* New York: Viking.

Kissel, P. (1994). *The role of recreational reading in the lives of two adult readers.* Unpublished doctoral dissertation, Syracuse University, Syracuse, NY.

Kozol, J. (1967). *Death at an early age: The destruction of the hearts and minds of negro children in the Boston public schools.* Boston: Houghton Mifflin.

Labov, W. (1982). Competing value systems in the inner city schools. In P. Gilmore & A. Glatthorn (Eds.), *Children in and out of school: Ethnography and education* (pp. 149–171). Washington, DC: Center for Applied Linguistics.

Labov, W. (1995). Can reading failure be reversed: A linguistic approach to the question. In V. Gadsden & D. Wagner (Eds.), *Literacy among African-American youth: Issues in learning, teaching, and schooling* (pp. 39–68). Cresskill, NJ: Hampton Press.

Langer, J. A. (1991). Literacy and schooling: A sociocognitive perspective. In E. H. Hiebert (Ed.), *Literacy for a diverse society: Perspectives, practices, and policies* (pp. 9–28). New York: Teachers College Press.

Langer, J. A. (1992). Rethinking literature instruction. In J. A. Langer (Ed.), *Literature instruction: A focus on student response* (pp. 35–53). Urbana, IL: NCTE.

Langer, J. A., Applebee, A. N., Mullis, I. V. S., & Foertsch, M. A. (1990). *Learning to read in our nation's schools.* Princeton, NJ: Educational Testing Service.

Lipsitz, J. (1984). *Successful schools for young adolescents.* New Brunswick, NJ: Transaction.

Macrorie, K. (1970). *Uptaught.* New York: Hayden.

Males, M. A. (1996). *The scapegoat generation: America's war on adolescents.* Monroe, ME: Common Courage Press.

McCall, N. (1994). *Makes me wanna holler: A young black man in America.* New York: Random House.

McCarthy, C. (1996). Multicultural policy discourses on racial inequality in American education. In R. Ng, P. Staton, & J. Scane (Eds.), *Anti-racism, feminism, and critical approaches to education* (pp. 21–44). Westport, CT: Bergin & Garvey.

McDermott, R. (1987). Achieving school failure: An anthropological approach to literacy and social stratification. In G. Spindler (Ed.), *Education and cultural process: Anthropological approaches* (2nd ed.; pp. 173–209). Prospect Heights, IL: Waveland.

McInerney, J. (1989). *The story of my life.* New York: Random House.

McLaren, P. (1991). Critical pedagogy: Constructing an arch of social dreaming and a doorway to hope. *Journal of Education, 173*(1), 9–34.

Mehan, H. (1979). What time is it Denise? Asking known information questions in classroom discourse. *Theory into Practice, 18*(4), 285–294.

Meier, D. (1996). Transforming schools into powerful communities. In W. Ayers & P. Ford (Eds.), *City kids, city teachers: Reports from the front row* (pp. 131–136). New York: The New Press.

Messner, M. (1990). Boyhood, organized sports, and the construction of masculinities. *Journal of Contemporary Ethnography, 18*(4), 416–444.

Messner, M. A. (1992). *Power at play: Sports and the problem of masculinity.* Boston: Beacon Press.

Moffett, J. (1968). *Teaching the universe of discourse.* Boston: Houghton Mifflin.

Murray, D. M. (1985). *A writer teaches writing.* Boston: Houghton Mifflin.

Newkirk, T. (1985). The hedgehog or the fox: The dilemma of writing development. *Language Arts, 62*(6), 593–603.

Ng, R., Staton, P., & Scane, J. (Eds.). (1995). *Anti-racism, feminism, and critical approaches to education.* Westport, CT: Bergin & Garvey.

Ogbu, J. U. (1988). Class stratification, racial stratification, and schooling. In L. Weiss (Ed.), *Class, race & gender in American education* (pp. 163–182). Albany: State University of New York Press.

Ogbu, J. U. (1995). Literacy and black Americans: Comparative perspectives. In V. Gadsden & D. Wagner (Eds.), *Literacy among African-American youth: Issues in learning, teaching, and schooling* (pp. 83–100). Cresskill, NJ: Hampton Press.

Oliner, P. M., & Oliner, S. P. (1995). *Toward a caring society: Ideas into action.* Westport, CT: Praeger.

O'Loughlin, M. (1992). Rethinking science education: Beyond Piagetian constructivism toward a sociocultural model of teaching and learning. *Journal of Research in Science Teaching, 29*(8), 791–820.

Orner, M. (1992). Interrupting the calls for student voice in "liberatory" education: A feminist poststructuralist perspective. In C. Luke & J. Gore (Eds.), *Feminisms and critical pedagogy* (pp. 74–89). New York: Routledge.

Palincsar, A. S., & David, Y. M. (1991). Promoting literacy through classroom dialogue. In E. H. Hiebert (Ed.), *Literacy for a diverse society: Perspectives, practices, and policies* (pp. 122–140). New York: Teachers College Press.

Pascal, F. (1992a). *Sweet valley high.* New York: Bantam.

Pascal, F. (1992b). *Sweet valley twins.* New York: Bantam.

Paterson, K. (1987). *Bridge to Terabithia.* New York: Harper Collins Children's Books.

Phillips, D. C. (1995). The good, the bad, and the ugly: The many faces of constructivism. *Educational Researcher, 24*(7), 5–12.

Piaget, J. (1950). *The psychology of intelligence.* London: Routledge & Kegan Paul.

Piaget, J., & Inhelder, B. (1969). *The psychology of the child.* New York: Basic Books.

Pike, C. (1991). *Fall into darkness.* New York: Pocket Books.

Postman, N., & Weingartner, C. (1969). *Teaching as a subversive activity.* New York: Dell.

Probst, R. E. (1984). *Adolescent literature: Response and analysis.* Columbus, OH: Merrill.

Purves, A. C. (1972). *How porcupines make love.* Boston: Ginn/Xerox.

Purves, A. C. (1973). *Literature education in ten countries: An empirical study.* New York: Wiley.

Purves, A. C. (1986, November). *Cultural literacy and research in response to literature.* Paper presented at the meeting of the National Council of Teachers of English Assembly for Research Conference, Chicago.

Purves, A. C., Rogers, T., & Soter, A. O. (1995). *How porcupines make love III: Readers, texts, cultures in the response-based literature classroom.* New York: Longman.

Ray, H. A. (1973). *Curious George.* Boston: Houghton Mifflin.

Rehak, J. (1996). Go back and circle the verbs. In W. Ayers & P. Ford (Eds.), *City kids, city teachers: Reports from the front row* (pp. 270–285). New York: The New Press.

Remarque, E. M. (1984). *All quiet on the western front.* Manroe, WA: Barros.

Rogers, C. R. (1986). Some significant learnings. In J. Stewart (Ed.), *Bridges not walls: A book about interpersonal communication* (pp. 104–111). New York: Random House.

Rosenberg, P. M. (1997). Underground discourses: Exploring whiteness in teacher education. In M. Fine, L. Weis, L. C. Powell, & L. M. Wong (Eds.), *Off white: Readings on race, power, and society* (pp. 79–89). New York: Routledge.

Rosenblatt, L. M. (1968). *Literature as exploration.* New York: Noble & Noble.

Rosenblatt, L. M. (1994). *The reader, the text, the poem: The transactional theory of the literary work (with a new preface and epilogue).* Carbondale: Southern Illinois University Press.

Rosenblatt, L. M. (1995). *Literature as exploration* (5th ed.). New York: Modern Language Association.

Sadker, M., & Sadker, D. (1994). *Failing at fairness: How our schools cheat girls.* New York: Simon & Schuster.

Salinger, J. D. (1991). *The catcher in the rye.* Cutchouge, NY: Buccaneer Books.

Salisbury, J., & Jackson, D. (1996). *Challenging macho values: Practical ways of working with adolescent boys.* London: Falmer.

Seuss, Dr. (1957). *The cat in the hat.* New York: Random House Books for Young Readers.

Seuss, Dr. (1960). *Green eggs and ham.* New York: Random House Books for Young Readers.

Shilts, R. (1988). *And the band played on: People, politics, and the AIDS epidemic.* New York: Viking Penguin.

Sinclair, U. (1981). *The jungle.* New York: Bantam Books.

Smith, E. (1995). Where is the mind? Knowing and knowledge in Cobb's constructivist and sociocultural perspectives. *Educational Researcher, 24*(7), 23–24.

Smith, F. (1984). Reading like a writer. In J. Jensen (Ed.), *Composing and comprehending* (pp. 47–56). Urbana, IL: NCTE.

Smith, T. M. (1995). *The educational progress of black students.* Washington, DC: U.S. Department of Education Office of Educational Research and Improvement.

Smitherman, G. (1986). *Talkin and testifyin: The language of black America.* Detroit: Wayne State University Press.

Solomon, R. P. (1992). *Black resistance in high school: Forging a separatist culture.* Albany: State University of New York Press.

Solzenitsyn, A. (1984). *A day in the life of Ivan Denisovich.* New York: Bantam Books.

Soto, G. (1990). Oranges. In *Braided lives: An anthology of multicultural American writing* (pp. 134–135). Minneapolis: Minnesota Council on the Humanities.

Stegner, W. (1976). The colt. In E. Daniel, E. J. Farrell, A. H. Grommon, O. S. Niles, & R. C. Pooley (Eds.), *Counterpoint in literature* (pp. 151–160). Dallas: Scott Foresman.

Strahan, D. (1983). *Schools in the middle*. Reston, VA: National Association of Secondary School Principals.

Sudol, D., & Sudol, P. (1991). Another story: Putting Graves, Calkins, and Atwell into practice and perspective. *Language Arts, 68*(3), 292–300.

Vipond, D., & Hunt, R. A. (1984). Point driven understanding: Pragmatic and cognitive dimensions of literary reading. *Poetics, 13*(3), 261–277.

Vygotsky, L. (1962). *Thought and language*. Cambridge, MA: Harvard University Press.

Vygotsky, L. S. (1987). In R. W. Rieber & A. S. Carlton (Eds.), *The collected works of L.S. Vygotsky*. New York: Plenum Press.

Walker, A. (1995). *The color purple*. Cutchouge, NY: Buccaneer Books.

Walkerdine, V. (1990). *Schoolgirl fictions*. London: Verso.

Wells, G. (1990). Creating the conditions to encourage literate thinking. *Educational Leadership, 47*(6), 13–17.

Williams, C. W. (1991). *Black teenage mothers*. Lexington, MA: Lexington Books.

Willinsky, J. (1990). *The new literacy: Redefining reading and writing in the schools*. New York: Routledge.

Willinsky, J. (1991). *The triumph of literature/the fate of literacy: English in the secondary curriculum*. New York: Teachers College Press.

Wojciechowska, M. (1979). The first day of the war. In H. B. Haupt, L. Heston, J. Littell, & S. Solotaroff (Eds.), *Literature lives! (green level)* (pp. 301–306). Evanston, IL: McDougal, Littell.

Wolf, S. A., & Heath, S. B. (1992). *The braid of literature: Children's worlds of reading*. Cambridge, MA: Harvard University Press.

Wright, R. (1945). *Black boy, a record of childhood and youth*. New York: Harper & Brothers.

X, M., & Haley, A. (1992). *The autobiography of Malcolm X*. New York: Ballantine Books.

Yolen, J. (1988). *The devil's arithmetic*. New York: Viking Children's Books.

Zebroski, J. T. (1989). The social construction of self in the work of Lev Vygotsky. *Writing Instructor, 8*(4), 149–156.

Index

Abstract thought, 51–52
Academic tracking. *See* Tracking
Adolescence, 30–33
  onset of puberty and, 33, 53
  as social construct, 30–31
Aesthetic reading (Rosenblatt), 16, 178–
  184
African Americans. *See* Students of color
Allen, JoBeth, 141
All Quiet on the Western Front
  (Remarque), 47, 239
Altenbaugh, R. J., 274–275
And the Band Played On (Shilts), 189
Angel (focal informant), 162–192
  character complexity rating, 26
  emotional involvement in reading, 170–
  173
  follow-up interviews with, 25, 188–192
  and home versus school reading, 177–
  184
  peer complexity rating, 26
  poetry writing and, 164–165
  self-concept as reader, 191
  support for reading and, 173–175
Angelou, Maya, 217, 218, 224
Applebee, Arthur N., 23–24, 80, 89, 159
Applegate, J. L., 19
Appleman, Deborah, 260
Are You There God? It's Me, Margaret
  (Blume), 35
Asoko, H., 22
Atwell, Nancie, 7, 10, 11, 56, 134, 233
Autobiography of Malcolm X, The (Haley
  & Malcolm X), 214, 246
Ayers, William C., 77, 266, 267–268

Babbit, N., 235
Baby boom, 33
Banks, J. A., 83
Barbieri, Maureen, 182

Barnes, D., 4, 10
Barnes, D., 4
Beach, R., 17
Biklen, S. K., 24
Binge reading, 115
Bizzell, Patricia, 75
Black Boy (Wright), 82, 89
Black English, 80–81, 101
Bloome, David, 168
Blume, J., 35
Bogdan, Deanne, 184
Bogdan, R. C., 24
Boomer, G., 11
Bradbury, Ray, 87, 89, 170
Brancato, Robin, 86, 281
Brewer, S., 20
Bridge to Terabithia (Paterson), 235
Britton, J., 10
Brown, M. W., 35
Bruffee, K. A., 11
Bruner, J., 5
Building blocks perspective, 5
Burgess, T., 10
Burleson, B. R., 19

Calkins, Lucy M., 7, 10, 56
Call-response pattern, 101
Cassie (focal informant)
  character complexity rating, 26
  peer complexity rating, 26
Cat Ate My Gymsuit, The (Danziger), 154–
  155
Catcher in the Rye, The (Salinger), 127,
  239
Cat in the Hat, The (Seuss), 35
Center for Learning and Teaching
  Literature, 159
Character complexity, 20, 21, 26
Choice. *See* Student choice
Chomsky, Noam, 5

295

Class discussions, 49, 50
Classroom management
  Conference Days, 158
  "Getting Started" Center, 90
  Learning Centers, 72, 134, 225–226
  Literature Circle, 54, 79, 89–90, 95, 118, 134–135, 152, 153, 154, 156, 158–159, 194, 225–227, 232, 233, 234, 237, 238, 240, 254, 260, 264
  Reading/Writing Circle, 93, 118, 233–239
  Sharing Time, 54, 91, 94, 135–136, 138–139, 142–144, 152, 158, 195, 225–228, 231, 232, 236–237, 246, 251, 254, 260
Cliques, in middle school, 41–43, 143–144
Cobb, P., 9–10
Cochran, Johnny, 212
Collaborative learning, 11
  classroom environment and, 60–65, 257–258
  gender equity and, 107
  importance of, 52
  limits of, 8, 131, 228
  and myth of safe haven, 264–266
  politics of, 141–144
  sharing spaces in, 266–267
  writing groups in, 95–96, 105–106
Color Purple, The (Walker), 138
Comic books, 44
Compulsory schooling laws, 32–33
Conference Days, 158
Constructivism, 6–11, 225–255
  complexities and contradictions of, 6–7
  critical. *See* sociopolitical, *below*
  extending classroom walls in, 241–253
  limits of learner-centered, 7–9
  psychological, 9–10, 73–77
  social, 10–11, 73–77, 253–255
  sociopolitical, 9–11, 74–77, 152, 253–255, 267–269
Critical constructivism. *See* Sociopolitical constructivism
Critical democracy (Dewey), 245, 259
Critical Pedagogy, 269–277
Critical reading, 43, 45
Crockett, W. H., 19–20, 281
Culler, J., 17
Cultural literacy, 5–6
Cummins, Jim, 11

Cunningham, P. M., 81
Cureton, G. O., 96
Curious George (Ray), 35

Daniel (focal informant)
  character complexity rating, 26
  peer complexity rating, 26
Danse Macabre (King), 119
Danziger, P., 154–155
Darling-Hammond, Linda, 202, 270
Dartmouth Conference (1966), 5
David, Y. M., 9
Day in the Life of Ivan Denisovich, A (Solzenitsyn), 214
"Deficiency" model, 202
Delia, J. G., 20, 281
Devil's Arithmetic, The (Yolen), 240
Dewey, John, 5, 10, 259
Diary of Anne Frank, The (Goodrich & Hacket), 199
Dilg, M. A., 266
Driver, R., 22
Duncan, Lois, 81

Earl, L., 33, 128, 229, 274
Edelsky, Carole, 259, 264–265, 267, 269, 276–277
Efferent reading, 16
Egan, Kieran, 48, 114, 165
Elbow, Peter, 236
Elkind, David, 118, 139
Ellsworth, Elizabeth E., 256, 261, 264, 265
Emotional problems, 54
Engel, D. E., 274–275
Enright, Elizabeth, 87
Ethnocentrism, 270
Evaluation, alternative methods of, 9
Evans, Grace, 83

Fall Into Darkness (Pike), 170–171
Fear, and learner-centered approach, 62–63, 64, 65–66, 67, 69–72
Finders, Margaret, 43
Fine, Michelle, 149, 208, 210–211
Fish, S., 17
Flower, Linda, 173
Foertsch, M. A., 80
Ford, P., 77, 267–268
Fordham, Signithia, 83–84, 149, 214, 220

Friends, The (Guy), 42, 52–53, 87–88, 89, 107, 178–179
Frost, Robert, 277
Frye, Northrop, 5

Gadsden, Vivian, 198
Garrison, B., 169
Gender and gender roles, 43–44, 83, 106–107, 113
    "blending in" by girls, 165–166
    gender bias of teacher and, 148–152
    "looking-glass girl" phenomenon and, 182–183
    "wait time" in classroom and, 187–188
George, P. S., 3
"Getting Started" Center, 90
Gifted program, 15, 199
Gilyard, Keith, 81
Giovanni, Nikki, 139
Giroux, H. A., 83, 102, 124
Goldblatt, Eli, 216
Goodman, J., 245, 257, 258–259, 266–268, 275
Goodnight Moon (Brown), 35
Goodrich, F., 199
Grant, Linda, 148–149
Graves, Donald H., 7, 10, 56
Great Books philosophy, 160
Greene, Maxine, 13, 102–103, 268, 277
Green Eggs and Ham (Seuss), 35
Growth model, 5–6
    conflict between knowledge model and, 5–6
Guy, Rosa, 42, 52, 87–88, 89, 107

Haberman, Maxine, 62
Hacket, A., 199
Hale, C. L., 19
Hale, Janice E., 84–85, 94, 197, 220, 270
Haley, A., 214, 246
Hall, G. Stanley, 30–31
Hamilton, Virginia, 53
Hargreaves, A., 33, 128, 229, 274
Harris, J., 5–6, 160
Hawthorne, N., 127
Hayes, John R., 173
Heath, Shirley Brice, 17, 78, 86
Hesse, Hermann, 122
Heterogeneous grouping, 33
Heyert, M., 172

Hidden curriculum, 37–39, 168
Hiebert, E. H., 6
High schools
    custodial approach and, 274–275
    junior high school as mini version of, 32
    problems of, 273–275
Hoetker, J., 176
hooks, bell, 149, 251–252
Hornbeck, D., 3
Hughes, Langston, 53
Humor, 53–54
Hunt, R. A., 43, 88
Hynds, Susan, 17, 19, 20, 22, 169

Inclusive classrooms, 141
Individualism, 257
Information-driven reading, 88–89
Inhelder, B., 5
Inner drama, 18–20
Integrated language arts approach, 7
Interdisciplinary teams, 33
Iser, Wolfgang, 167

Jackson, D., 44, 104, 106–107, 113, 132
Jackson, Ed, 89, 283
Jason (focal informant), 104–132
    character complexity rating, 26
    and college application process, 129
    follow-up interviews with, 25, 120–132
    in high school, 120–132
    journal writing and, 114–115
    need for choice, 110–111, 117–120
    peer complexity rating, 26
    poetry writing and, 120, 121, 124, 129–130
    reading history of, 108–111
    self-concept as reader, 106, 110–120, 127–128, 130–132
Jenkins, L. B., 80
Jessie (focal informant)
    character complexity rating, 26
    peer complexity rating, 26
Johnson, J. A., 77
Jose, P., 20
Journal writing, 49, 50
    problems of sharing and, 67
    by teacher, 133, 135, 137, 146–151, 154, 235–236, 242–243
Jungle, The (Sinclair), 127

Junior high school
   dissatisfaction with, 32–33
   middle school versus, 3, 32–33
   as mini high school, 32
   origins of, 31–32
   Piagetian development and, 51

Kelly, George, 18, 19
Kenny, C. T., 20, 281
Kianna (focal informant), 78–103, 201–
   202, 261
   character complexity rating, 26
   characters in literature and, 85–87, 99–
      100
   and literature as performance, 87–89,
      95–103
   as missing in action, 25, 271–273
   pariah behaviors of, 84–85, 149
   peer complexity rating, 26
   play writing and, 92–93, 95
   poetry writing and, 89–95, 96–98,
      273
   reading history of, 80–82
Kinchloe, J. L., 152, 223, 253, 268
King, Rodney, 190
King, Stephen, 43, 44, 47, 113, 115, 116,
   117, 119, 122, 274
Kissel, Pamela, 180
Knowledge model
   growth model versus, 5–6
   transmission approach in, 4–5, 6, 7, 8,
      57, 160
Kozol, J., 5

Labov, W., 96, 201
Langer, Judith A., 19, 80, 159
Leach, J., 22
Learner-centered approach, 56–77, 263.
      See also Constructivism
   balance between reading and writing in,
      152–156
   challenging, 73–77
   classroom environment and, 60–65
   extending classroom walls in, 241–
      253
   fear and, 62–63, 64, 65–66, 67, 69–
      72
   limitations of, 7–9, 145
   middle schools and, 33

multicultural issues and, 75–77
   performance-based curriculum and, 65–
      66, 167–168, 180, 231–238
   reconstructing, 253–255
   student choice and, 8, 66, 70–73, 76
   student resistance to, 56–70
Learning Centers, 72, 134, 225–226
Learning disabilities, 38–39, 54
Lesson plans, 68–70
Lipsitz, J., 3
Literacy autobiographies, 35
Literary Interest Questionnaire, 20
Literate behaviors (Heath), 17–18
Literature as Exploration (Rosenblatt), 16,
   73
Literature Circle, 54, 79, 89–90, 95, 118,
   134–135, 152, 153, 154, 156, 158–
   159, 194, 225–227, 232, 233, 234,
   237, 238, 240, 254, 260, 264
Logan Middle School, 14–16, 33–35
"Looking-glass girl" phenomenon, 182–
   183
Luis (focal informant), 193–224
   "acting white" and, 196–197, 220
   character complexity rating, 26
   follow-up interviews with, 25, 202–224
   in gifted program, 199
   in high school, 202–224
   home life of, 205–211
   initial involvement in study, 25
   and literacy as social action, 200–202
   peer complexity rating, 26
   play writing, 199
   poetry writing, 195–196
   as survivor, 218–220
   tracking and, 199, 201–202, 215

Macrorie, K., 5
Makes Me Wanna Holler (McCall), 214
Malcolm X, 214, 246, 274
Males, Mike A., 272
Mandela, Nelson, 274
Mark (focal informant)
   character complexity rating, 26
   peer complexity rating, 26
Martin, D. T., 274–275
Martin, N., 10
McCall, Nathan, 214
McCarthy, C., 83, 149, 261

McDermott, R., 84–85
McInerney, Jay, 158
McLaren, Peter, 192, 257, 263
McLeod, A., 10
Mehan, H., 152
Meier, Deborah, 273–274
Messner, M. A., 44, 113, 121–122, 211
Methodology, 14–27
  coding of Role Category Questionnaires, 281
  evolution of study and, 16–20
  focal informants and, 21–22, 24–27, 281–283
  follow-up interviews, 25–26, 281–283
  phase one, 15, 20–22, 27
  phase two, 22–25, 27, 281–283
  setting of study, 14–16, 33–35
Middle school
  abstract thinking and, 51–52
  cliques in, 41–43, 143–144
  concept of, 3
  gender roles in, 43–44
  junior high school versus, 3, 32–33
  key aspects of, 33
  negotiating between maturity and childhood in, 29–30
Miller, Arthur, 130
Miller, Henry, 122
Miller, James, 5
Misery (King), 116
Mock participation, 168
Moffett, James, 5
Morrison, Toni, 189
Mortimer, E., 22
Mullis, I., 80
Multiculturalism, 11, 33, 260–262. *See also* Racial issues; Students of color
  cultural understanding models of, 261
  learner-centered approach and, 75–77
  literature and, 260
Murray, Donald M., 56

National Literature Project, 159–160
National Middle School Association, 32–33
National Writing Project, 23, 158, 159–160
Natural literacy, 9

NCTE Research Foundation, 24
Neuwirth, C. M., 19
New Criticism, 16, 73, 128, 160, 215
Newkirk, Tom, 10
New Literacy, 6–11, 69
Ng, R., 255

Ogbu, John U., 83, 196–197, 215
Oldaker, L. L., 3
Oliner, P. M., 276–277
Oliner, S. P., 276–277
O'Loughlin, M., 258
Orner, Mimi, 75

Palincsar, A. S., 9
Papers, writing, 50
Parental neglect and abuse, 54
Pariah behaviors, 84–85
Pascal, F., 42
Paterson, K., 235
Pedagogy of poverty, 62
Peer complexity, 20, 21, 26
Performance-based curriculum, 65–66, 167–168, 180, 231–238
Peripheral learning, 228–231
Personal interpretation, 18–20
Philips, D. C., 10, 74
Piaget, Jean, 5, 10, 11, 51, 73, 74, 131, 253, 254, 256, 257
Pike, Christopher, 170
Pirsig, Robert, 122, 130
Pleasure reading, 40–41, 42, 177–184
Point-driven reading, 88–89
Political neutrality, 258–260
Postman, N., 73
Power relations, in classroom, 238–241, 262–264, 275–277
Pregnancy, teenage, 272–273
Press, A. N., 20, 281
Private response, 50, 232
Probst, R. E., 10, 16, 75
Procedural display, 168
Process-centered teaching, 6, 10
Psychological constructivism, 9–10, 73–77
Puberty, earlier onset of, 33, 53
Public response, 50, 232
Purves, A. C., 10, 17, 20, 75

Questions, in School Reading, 46, 47

Racial issues. *See also* Multiculturalism; Students of color
 bias in literature and curriculum, 189–190
 racial identity of teacher and, 146–152
 racial segregation, 246–253
 racism in schools, 223, 246–253
Ray, H. A., 35
Reading
 as action, 43–45, 200–202, 236
 aesthetic, 16, 178–184
 binge, 115
 critical, 43, 45
 efferent, 16
 as hard work, 45–46
 hidden curriculum and, 37–39, 168
 as information-driven, 88–89
 pleasure, 40–41, 42, 177–184
 as point-driven, 88–89
 reasons for, 39–41
 School Reading, 46–50
 as story-driven, 88–89
 strategies for, 47
 student history of, 35–37, 42
Reading groups, 36–37
Reading Interest and Background Questionnaire, 20
Reading-out-of-bounds, 184
Reading/Writing Circle, 93, 118, 233–239
Rehak, J., 136
Remarque, E. M., 47
Resistance
 to learner-centered approach, 56–70
 pariah behaviors and, 84–85
 theories of, 102–103
 unproductive forms of, 124
Resource rooms, 38–39
Response-centered perspective, 6, 7, 10, 19–20, 75, 160, 259
Responses to reading
 class discussions, 49, 50
 journals, 49, 50. *See also* Journal writing
 papers, 50
 public versus private, 50, 232
 story creation, 49, 50
Rogers, Carl R., 55
Rogers, T., 75
Role Category Questionnaire, 19–20, 21, 173, 177, 281
Rosen, H., 10

Rosenberg, Pearl M., 252
Rosenblatt, Louise M., 16, 18, 67, 73, 167, 173, 178, 180, 184
Ross, Diana, 53
Ryan, J., 33, 128, 229, 274

Sadker, D., 94, 107, 120, 127, 131–132, 149, 151, 165–166, 182, 187–188, 198, 272, 273
Sadker, M., 94, 107, 120, 127, 131–132, 149, 151, 165–166, 182, 187–188, 198, 272, 273
Salinger, J. D., 127, 239, 274
Salisbury, J., 44, 104, 106–107, 113, 132
Samantha (focal informant), 162–192
 character complexity rating, 26
 emotional involvement in reading, 169, 172
 follow-up interviews with, 25, 164, 185–188
 and home versus school reading, 177–184
 journal writing and, 169–170
 peer complexity rating, 26
 self-concept as reader, 176–177
 support for reading and, 175–176
Scane, J., 255
Scapegoat Generation, The (Males), 272
Scarlet Letter, The (Hawthorne), 127
School Reading, 46–50
 questions and, 46, 47
 responses to, 48–50
 testing in, 48
Scott, P., 22
Seuss, Dr., 35
Sharing Time, 54, 91, 94, 135–136, 138–139, 142–144, 152, 158, 195, 225–228, 231, 232, 236–237, 246, 251, 254, 260
Shilts, R., 189
Simpson, O. J., 212
Sinclair, U., 127
Skills-based approach, 5
Smith, E., 22, 253
Smith, F., 44–45
Smith, T. M., 224
Smitherman, Geneva, 101
Social action, literacy as, 43–45, 200–202, 236
Social aspects of learning, 17–18

Social cognition, 19–20
Social complexity, 21
Social constructivism, 10–11, 73–77, 253–255
Sociopolitical constructivism, 9–11, 74–77, 152, 253–255, 267–269
Solomon, R. P., 208–209, 213, 219–220
Solzenitsyn, A., 214
Soter, A. O., 75
Soto, Gary, 39, 98, 171
Speed reading, 47
Squire, James, 5
Stand, The (King), 116
Staton, P., 255
Stegner, Wallace, 99, 169, 187
Steinberg, Shirley R., 152, 223, 253, 268
Stories
  creation of, 49, 50
  personal, 11
  story-driven reading and, 88–89
Story of My Life, The (McInerney), 158
Strahan, D., 3
Straub, P., 47
Structural-affect story rating scale, 20
Student choice
  evaluation system and, 243–244
  importance of, 110–111, 117–120, 225–228, 232
  and learner-centered approach, 8, 66, 70–73, 76
Students of color, 52–53. See also Kianna (focal informant); Luis (focal informant); Multiculturalism; Racial issues; Samantha (focal informant)
  "acting white" and, 196–197
  and bias in literature and curriculum, 189–190
  Black English and, 80–81, 101
  "raceless" stance of, 220
  racial identity of teacher and, 146–152
  racial segregation, 246–253
  "silencing," 210–211
  teacher education programs and, 270–271
Sudol, D., 7
Sudol, P., 7
Sweet Valley High (Pascal), 42
Sweet Valley Twins (Pascal), 42

Talisman (King & Straub), 47
Teachers and teaching. *See also* Classroom management
  balance between reading and writing and, 152–159
  constructivist approach, 6–11
  cultural literacy and, 5–6
  difficulties of student lives and, 136–144
  eighth-grade year in study, 133–161
  gender issues and, 148–152
  growth model and, 5–6
  journal writing, 133, 135, 137, 146–151, 154, 235–236, 242–243
  "learning by osmosis" and, 228–231
  politics of collaboration and, 141–144
  power relations in classroom and, 238–241, 262–264, 275–277
  racial issues and, 144–152
  seventh-grade year in study, 56–77
  transmission approach, 4–5, 6, 7, 8, 160
Teaching as a Subversive Activity (Postman & Weingartner), 73
Testing, in School Reading, 48
Thinking aloud, 19, 21, 45
Thoreau, Henry David, 127
Tommyknockers (King), 115, 116
Tracking, 31–32, 189, 199, 201–202, 215
Transmission approach, 4–5, 6, 7, 8, 57, 160
Triumph of Literature/The Fate of Literacy, The (Willinsky), 16
Trust, 62–63, 64, 65–66, 67, 69–72
Tuck Forever (Babbit), 235
Turner, Nat, 214

Unbank the Fire (Hale), 84

Vipond, D., 43, 88
Voice, 75, 83, 263–264
Vygotsky, Lev, 5, 10–11, 74, 253, 254, 256–257

"Wait time" in classroom, 187–188
Walden (Thoreau), 127
Walker, Alice, 138
Walkerdine, Valerie, 245
Weingartner, C., 73
Wells, Gordon, 252
Whole-group discussion, 168
Whole language approach, 6, 7

Wilde, Oscar, 122, 130
Williams, Constance Willard, 149, 272
Willinsky, John, 6, 16–17, 69, 74, 253–255, 269
Winfrey, Oprah, 53
Wojiechowska, Maria, 229
Wolf, S. A., 78, 86

Workshop model (Sudol & Sudol), 7
Wright, Richard, 82, 89, 169
Writing Without Teachers (Elbow), 236

Yolen, Jane, 240

Zebroski, J. T., 256–257, 258

About the Author

Susan Hynds is Professor and Director of English Education in the Reading and Language Arts Center at Syracuse University. She is a graduate of the University of Illinois at Urbana and Vanderbilt University. She has served or is currently serving on the Editorial Board of Research in the Teaching of English and the Executive Committees of the National Conference on Research in Language and Literacy and the Conference on English Education. A co-founder of the Special Interest Group in Literature for the American Educational Research Association, she has also served as chair of the National Council of Teachers of English Assembly for Research.

Before beginning her university career, she was a teacher of English, speech, and drama of the middle school and high school levels for nine years. For more than a decade since that time, she has studied the literacy development of adolescents and young adults in a variety of settings. She is interested in how teenagers come to see themselves as literate in their lives within and outside of school. Her books include *Perspectives on Talk and Learning* (1990, with Donald Rubin), *Developing Discourse Practices in Adolescence and Adulthood* (1990, with Richard Beach), and *Making Connections: Language and Learning in the Classroom* (1994).